SONNET

SONNET

The Very Rich and Varied World of the Italian Sonnet

RINALDINA RUSSELL

Copyright © 2017 Rinaldina Russell.

All rights reserved. No part of this book may be used or reproduced by any means, graphic, electronic, or mechanical, including photocopying, recording, taping or by any information storage retrieval system without the written permission of the author except in the case of brief quotations embodied in critical articles and reviews.

Archway Publishing books may be ordered through booksellers or by contacting:

Archway Publishing
1663 Liberty Drive
Bloomington, IN 47403
www.archwaypublishing.com
1 (888) 242-5904

Because of the dynamic nature of the Internet, any web addresses or links contained in this book may have changed since publication and may no longer be valid. The views expressed in this work are solely those of the author and do not necessarily reflect the views of the publisher, and the publisher hereby disclaims any responsibility for them.

Any people depicted in stock imagery provided by Thinkstock are models, and such images are being used for illustrative purposes only.
Certain stock imagery © Thinkstock.

Biblia sacra iuxta vulgata versionem, adiuvantibus B. Fischer [and others] recensuit et brevi apparatu critico instruxit Robert Weber. Stutgard: Deutsche Babelgesellschaft, c. 2007.

ISBN: 978-1-4808-4579-4 (sc)
ISBN: 978-1-4808-4580-0 (e)

Library of Congress Control Number: 2017904909

Print information available on the last page.

Archway Publishing rev. date: 10/21/2017

Contents

Preface
vii

Introduction
xi

1 From Imperial Court to Democratic Commune
1

2 Time of Transition and Unrest
71

3 From Democratic Commune to Princely Court
135

4 Invasions, Reversals, and Reformations
203

5 Humankind, the Universe, and Death
265

Sections, Authors and Sonnets
347

Bibliography
355

Studies
359

Notes
365

Preface

My interest in the Italian sonnet derives from years of teaching Italian literature and from the lectures I gave on the sonnet to general audiences. While the class discussions brought out the perfection of the form and its flexibility as a teaching tool, the nonacademic lectures showed how the Italian sonnet in particular, because of its wide range of subjects and its diversity of authorship, could appeal to a great variety of people. When teaching and public lectures were over, I decided to place what I know at the disposal of anyone who might be interested. I have therefore assembled this collection of three hundred sonnets in the original and in translation, with accompanying introductions, notes on the texts, and commentaries, for the pleasure of the culturally curious, lovers of the form, and students of literature.

Because of their concise organization of meaning, sonnets in general allow quick glimpses into the lives of individuals and their surroundings. They can reveal what people loved, hated, idealized, and found ridiculous or grotesque. Italian sonnets exhibit a remarkably wide range of content and form. In Italy, sonnet writing was not the purview of a selected group of talents who took up a literary fashion imported from abroad, as was the case in other countries. In the span of time I cover in this volume, from the sonnet's appearance in the first half of the thirteenth century through the Renaissance and on to the baroque age, writing sonnets was an activity people at all levels of society and of all intellectual and literary backgrounds practiced. In addition, because the peninsula was subdivided in many states politically and culturally at variance from one another, the sonnet reflected considerable regional differences as well. In that period, furthermore, many were the political, social, and cultural changes. Italians experienced the secular sway of imperial supremacy and the control of church theocracy; they lived in democratic forms of government and in princely domains, in conditions of political independence and under the authority of foreign powers. Their outlook on life went from one based on a theological perception of the cosmos, with humankind at the center, to another that threatened all sense of human supremacy and security. There were also changes in the way sonneteers distributed their messages in the space of the sonnet. They varied its rhyming scheme and altered its metrical arrangement.

I chose the poems included in this volume with the intent of offering as wide a range of content, background, style, and function as possible. Of each author, I selected the sonnets that would highlight his or her distinctive personality and literary innovations. While any poem, or group of poems, is different from the others, each is an integral part of the assembled whole. I give my own rendition of all of them. Some sonnets, being the favorites of textbooks, have already found more than one translator; many other lesser-known sonnets appear in translation here for the first time.

My selection, therefore, originates on one hand from a more comprehensive view of the uses and functions of the form than is generally found in selective anthologies and, on the other hand, from a desire to avoid repetitions and redundant examples of literary influence. Above all, my aim was to allow readers to approach each sonnet from the poet's perspective rather than exclusively from the critical viewpoint intentionally or unavoidably implied in modern textbooks.

I have organized the volume in five parts chronologically progressive, each devised with these orders of consideration in mind: historical and social background, cultural change, new literary fashions, and prescriptions and eccentricities peculiar to the genre—all factors that determine the content and form of any literary construct.

Within each of the five parts, I've grouped the poems into thematic sections. Their titles might indicate a theme, a particular setting, or the poetic production of specific professional men or social milieus. They might reveal an interesting individual frame of mind or a change in collective thought and behavior. The sections have titles, such as "At the Imperial Court," "A New Morality of Love," "In a Satirical Vein," "A Confessed Sensualist," and "In the Realm of the Divine," which provide readers with the possibility of browsing freely among them and selecting the type of verse best suited to their taste and mood of the moment. I also conceived and organized the sections to allow readers to approach each section separately and in the order they wish. Everywhere are cross-references connecting similar themes, stylistic devices, and the sonnets of the same author. One can therefore read the book straight through or jump from section to section in any direction desired.

Medieval and Renaissance poets expressed their ideas clearly along a solid line of reasoning that progressed through well-reasoned, logical transitions. Accordingly, in the translations of all sonnets, I have endeavored above all to convey the meaning and the structure of thought of the original as faithfully as possible. The sound effects, verbal gymnastics, colloquialism, and music of versification, inescapably tied as they are to the original language, tend to elude the translator.

The rhyme scheme of the sonnet creates a constant rhythm: it separates octave from sestet and often distinguishes quatrain from quatrain and tercet from tercet. The line of reasoning, however, does not always respect the rhythm of the meter. Although supported by it, the reasoning flows freely above the metrical scheme, just as in music, the rhythm of the harmony supports the melody of a song. My translations, leaving sound and metrical effects by the side, aim primarily at reproducing the rhythm of thought and the argumentative sweep that gives each sonnet its character.

When a translation close to the text became cumbersome, or when the Italian phrasing was too complex, I altered the order of words and lines, always preserving the meaningful unit of the original structure. If an Italian word carried multiple connotations, I often used two words in place of one. I did not hesitate now and then to shorten a period or lengthen the text in order to remove some obscurities. When it seemed reasonable, I substituted the original topical expression with one familiar to the English reader. Occasionally, in order to offer a clearer and more logical sequence of meaning, I modified punctuation that previous editors introduced in the original text. Considering that words and phrases change meaning through time, I kept to the principle that a translation seeking to remain faithful to the meaning and intention of the author cannot be a word-by-word translation; it must be an interpretation of the text.

When the effect of a sonnet rested on vocabulary of abuse and sexual allusions, I did not give a sanitized version; rather, I tried to give what I hope is a plausible English rendering of the intended effect. All the translations of Latin and Italian texts other than the sonnets under consideration are also mine, unless otherwise indicated.

Overall, my intention has been to historicize the sonnets in multiple directions—historically, sociologically, and literarily—in order to approach as much as possible the meaning as intended by the authors and understood by contemporaries. The introductions to the sections are a running presentation of the sonneteers and their cultural and historical backgrounds. The notes to the texts aim to clarify the meanings of words, expressions, and direct or implied references. The commentaries, not always kept apart from the notes, intend to point out the strategy of construction and give an idea of what the translation does not convey: the rhythmic and verbal effects of the Italian text and the sharpness of its sallies and topical allusions. They might also unravel a difficult passage by giving a paraphrase of it. I invite readers—whether they have some knowledge of Italian or none—to flip to the sonnet, or the translation, and back to the notes. I have provided additional information of various kinds in the endnotes. I hope that altogether, introductions, commentaries, and notes will allow new readers to approach the subject with growing interest and old readers of Italian sonnets to go over them again with fresh awareness.

A book of this character is never the work of a single author. In each presentation, I expressed my opinions and followed my taste, but I also drew abundantly, as it is the custom, on the work of historians and literary specialists who have dealt with the same subject throughout the centuries. I acknowledge my indebtedness and gratitude toward them. In some of my commentaries, I closely followed—and declared of doing so—some previous interpretations that, in themselves, seemed stimulating additions to the text. At other times, I gave a confutation of elucidations offered by others. I have indicated an authorial attribution whenever I was able to attribute a difficult and distinctive interpretation, to the best of my knowledge, to a single commentator-critic. In the case of an elucidation of a sonnet or specific passage long shared by the community of scholars or considered obvious by anyone with a knowledge of classical texts, I supplied no specific bibliographical reference.

At the end of the volume, I have provided a bibliography of first and secondary works for the benefit of those who want to further compare opinions and presentations. As I've aimed the book at a wide audience, and because I like to keep the page clear, I eliminated footnotes, and all along, I gave page numbers for quotations and briefly mentioned texts and authors, always referring to the publications listed in the bibliography.

And finally, I wish to express my thanks for the professional services provided by the staff of Archway Publishing.

Introduction

In "Immagine del Sonetto," Giovanni Getto provokingly wrote that the history of the Italian sonnet implies the entire history of Italian literature—to which one might add the history of Italian life and culture in general. Even so, history as such, literary or otherwise, is not within the scope of this book. All information I offer here has the sole purpose of elucidating the texts and informing the reader about the personal and societal contexts that gave life and lasting relevance to the poems. Furthermore, this volume restricts the choice of verse to the period when the sonnet form maintained a relevant position in the literary canon, expressing the thoughts and feelings of the intellectuals, literarily ambitious, and politically committed, as well as the people engaged in the ordinary tasks and experiences of life.

1. The sonnet, a fourteen-hendecasyllable lyric form divided into octave and sestet,[1] made its first appearance in the poetry of Giacomo da Lentini, a lawyer active in Sicily in the first half of the thirteenth century. Lentini was one of the many men who wrote poetry and who worked, in various capacities, for the court of Palermo or served as part of the entourage of Frederick II, king of Sicily and southern Italy. The frame of mind of these poets—referred to as "the Sicilians" regardless of their geographical origin—was different from that of the European troubadours who preceded them. The training they received at the universities of Bologna and Salerno made them skilled in deductive reasoning and the technique of disputation. Reflexively, their lyrics tended to theorize on the nature of love and impose on their emotional experience a pseudoscientific superstructure.

By the middle of the century, the poets of the northern regions of the country were imitating all the forms of Sicilian poetry. Transposed into a freer, less controlled society, the sonnet opened to a wider range of subjects, from personal emotions to political concerns. As emperor of the Holy Roman Empire, a title he inherited from his father, the German emperor Henry VI, Frederick faced both the hostility of the popes and the rebelliousness of the northern communes, which were jurisdictionally his subjects. Furthermore, within each city, opposing factions competed for economic and political power. In the heat of the external and internal hostilities, in every town and region, the sonnet became the expression of fierce ideological engagement; it gauged the odds of impending battle, and it reflected the exaltation of the victor, the anger of the vanquished, and the pain of those caught in the destruction of war and the misery of exile.

In the communes, the representation of love was also strikingly different. From the cognitive curiosity and syllogistic reasoning of the Sicilians, the northerners proceeded to write poems that, in comparison, appear realistically circumstanced. Their sonnets are erotically charged and engaged in down-to-earth discussion of emotional and sexual needs; they express, in turn, tenderness and aggressiveness, passionate engagement or cynical detachment, and adoration or disrespect.

The sonneteers were many, and among them was Compiuta Donzella, the first female poet we have certain knowledge of in Italian literature. She was, as some sonnets reported here demonstrate, the object of incredulous astonishment on the part of her male peers. Among male poets, rivalry and skepticism toward all innovations were no less pronounced. Much criticized were the stilnovo poets, who carved for themselves a space of intellectual superiority by claiming a correct knowledge of love and the creation of a style appropriate to its description. They brought about changes in the organization and metrical scheme of the sonnet as well. Most remarkable in this group were Guido Cavalcanti, who investigated the hazards of passion and the limits of human self-control, and Dante, who used love as a metaphor of self-empowerment and spiritual elevation.

The Sicilian sonneteers and their Tuscan imitators had spelled out their subject matter in linear, logical order and with a succession of rhymes that favored a smooth linearity of thought: the alternating rhyme (*rima alternata*) ABABABAB was constant in the octave, while the schemes CDCDCD and CDECDE prevailed in the sestet. The philosophical and ontological inquiries of the stilnovists, on the other hand, required a greater syntactical articulation and more flexible rhyme arrangement. Therefore, they used a new rhythmic plan in their sonnets: two quatrains of crossed rhymes (*rima incrociata*) in the octave, ABBA ABBA, and a variety of interlaced rhymes, such as CDC CDC, CDC DCD, or CDE EDE, in the sestet. These arrangements allowed a more faceted and articulated progression of thought.

Against the self-aggrandizing stance of the stilnovo poets rose the derisive humor of the satirical sonneteers. Besides trying to dismantle the contemplative fancies and stylistic pretensions of the highbrow poets, the sonnets of Cecco Angiolieri and Rustico Filippi made fun of their friends and denigrated their competitors. Rustico's sonnets, many about or addressed to women and men easily identifiable, could be especially vituperative and shocking, but they are representationally always effective.

2. Before entering Italy to oust the late emperor's son, Manfred, from the southern lands and from Sicily, Charles of Anjou promised considerable economic privileges to his Italian Guelf supporters. After his victory at Benevento in 1266, the Tuscan enterprises were able to extend their trades in Italy and in Europe, and a long period of prosperity began for most of the peninsula. Among the authors of sonnets who enjoyed the advantages of money was Folgòre da San Gimignano. His sonnets of the months are a paean to the variety of entertainments and games that a good position in society and compatible friends made possible. Cenne della Chitarra, who did not dispose of an adequate supply of funds, took up Folgòre's would-be aristocratic gatherings and sports in contrary fashion.

The sonnet continued to be a mirror reflecting individual and communal concerns, but its historical and political background had changed. After a few failed attempts on the part of newly elected emperors to reestablish their authority, in Italy, the empire entered a long period of decline. In 1305, under the pressure of the French king, the seat of the church moved to Avignon. The power void left the Italian states free to concentrate their hostility on one another, and correspondingly, the factional turmoil within each state went on more fiercely than ever. Society too had changed, giving new opportunities to some and nostalgic distress to others. At home or in exile, poets exchanged sonnets revealing circumstances and moods that were bitterly resentful, ironically jocular, scolding, or injurious. Poets who had made a name for themselves in the past died. Among them were Dante and Emmanuel Romano, two men who suffered a destiny of persecution and exile. Around the two poets, who might or might not have met, I have gathered a number of sonnets that are memorials of friends and acquaintances.

Far from the hub of political power, some sonneteers described the lives they lived in towns and in the country. Their medium- and low-style sonnets mirrored the social ambiance of the neighborhoods and the lives of professional people, merchants, and members of the smaller guilds. Giovanni Boccaccio, the future author of *The Decameron*, was in training in a Neapolitan bank. In his spare time, he created delightful pictures of girls frolicking up and down nearby beaches. In the Tuscan countryside lived Pieraccio Tedaldi, a minor public official who was guardian of the castle of Montopoli. He rhapsodized in verse about his condition and possibilities. The bell ringer of Florence, Antonio Pucci, described his small pleasures and his discontents with practical forbearance. These poets made frequent use of dialogue and local dialect. They also brought about a permutation in the metrical scheme of the sonnet, arriving, with the *sonetto caudato*, at a considerable alteration of the form.

The changes in the sonnet form usually occurred in medium- and low-style sonnets, especially in the satirical category. They came about either by inserting extra lines within the body of the sonnet or adding a tail at the end. This volume includes one example of the first type of deviation, Lapo Gianni's "Amor, eo chero mia donna in domino" in section 1.5. Of the tailed or caudate sonnet, there are far more examples. The tail—or *cauda* in Latin—may consist of two rhyming hendecasyllables, their rhyme being different from any of the preceding lines, or of three lines of verse: one *settenario* (seven-syllable line), rhyming with the last line of the sonnet proper, and two new rhyming hendecasyllables. We find caudate sonnets of the first type among those of Cecco Nuccoli, Antonio Beccari, Francesco Vannozzo, and Giovanni Dondi. Those of the second type appear frequently in the poetry of Antonio Pucci in the fourteenth century, Burchiello in the fifteenth century, and Francesco Berni in the sixteenth century. The three-line cauda is sometimes repeated more than once in an interlaced manner: eFF, fGG, gHH. This volume includes three-tailed sonnets by Burchiello and by Pulci; one four-tailed sonnet by Pasquino; and one six-tailed sonnet by Berni. By that time, the caudate sonnet had become the accepted form of all the realistic, comic, burlesque, and satirical poets, all excoriating literary and political protesters.

Whatever its form, the tail is usually independent of the preceding fourteen lines, and it can be extrapolated without damage, constituting—in the poetry of Pucci, Burchiello, and Berni, for instance—a stronger conclusion, sententious finish, warning, or witty retort. Less frequently, the tail is syntactically and meaningfully part of the sonnet proper, whose argument flows smoothly into it, as into an extension needed to provide a more articulated conclusion.

The high-style sonnet, consciously constructed as such, continued its canonical history in the town of Perugia. A gaggle of local lawyers enjoyed the offerings of town and country, and in elegant sonnets, they waxed lyrical on the ventures and misadventures of their homosexual affairs.

Among the political expatriates, a master of the sonnet emerged. A child of exiles and a spiritual exile by destiny and choice, Petrarch discarded the bureaucratic career that his father had pursued and recommended; took minor orders; and, with the comfortable sinecure provided by that position, dedicated himself to poetry and the study of classical literature. For Dante, Beatrice had been the symbol of a transcendent reality. For Petrarch, Laura represented his desires, ambitions, temptations, and regrets. The fluctuating lines of Petrarch's contradictory attitudes and moods converged on her image. She was the pivot on which turned all worldly attractions, his meditations on the transience of life, and his desire for literary glory. Bembo and his followers canonized his type of sonnet in the sixteenth century, and it became known in England as "the Italian sonnet."

3. By the middle of the fourteenth century, the fortunes of literati without great talent and powerful connections had become precarious. Antonio Beccari and Francesco Vannozzo—one was a political exile, and the other had migrated for economic reasons—looked for work and patronage at the courts of northern lords. Giovanni Dondi dall'Orologio, on the other hand, a scientist able to provide princes

and society with something useful and desirable, fared much better. While the rhetorically ambitious sonnet triumphed in high literary spheres, far from the erudite circles and the noble palaces, less ambitious sonneteers expressed the wisdom and desires of ordinary people. Their sonnets have few intellectual pretensions and displays of stylistic devices; they make use of dialogue and frequently of dialect. The names of the authors are sometimes unknown.

Meanwhile, the democratic communes of central Italy proved incapable of sustaining the military effort necessary to face aggressive neighbors and secure peace and prosperity for their own citizens. Gradually, several republican states became hereditary principalities or were absorbed by bigger political entities. By the end of the century, five main regional states remained in the Italian peninsula: the duchy of Milan; the oligarchical republic of Venice; Florence, nominally still a democratic republic; the papal territories; and the kingdom of Naples.

When the territorial expansion of Milan encroached upon the sphere of influence of Florence, the sonnet became a weapon of political propaganda. Coluccio Salutati, the Florentine secretary of state, inveighed vehemently against Giangaleazzo Visconti, the lord of Milan. In a sonnet, he called him a viper (the serpent was the Visconti's family emblem), a cruel tyrant about to swallow Florence and the whole of Italy through cunning and deceit. Poets invoked classical democratic values to oppose the growing Medici ascendancy.

Sonneteers were emerging from the class of engineers, artists, and architects, men like Brunelleschi, Ghiberti, and Cellini. These trained professional people had little patience with the pretensions of academic intellectuals and spaced-out philosophers. They viewed the writing of poetry as a technique, like painting and engineering. Their sonnets had few intellectual pretensions and displays of rhetorical figures; their sonnets expressed what they thought about their professions and the obstacles they faced. In the busy crowd of little shop owners, an interesting personality appeared: that of a barber, Burchiello. A man of original popular talent, with his rhymes, he fascinated his fellow citizens, and he, in turn, found the men in power fascinating. For them, he campaigned in verse against the growing Medici preeminence, and when the opposition won, he left the city.

Once in power, however, the Medici became active promoters of the cultural life of all classes, humanistic studies, and popular literature. The best-known member the family, Lorenzo de' Medici, called the Magnificent, demonstrated a considerable literary talent in a variety of genres and, with his sonnets, revived the interest in the lyric tradition.

The promotion of culture had long been a custom in the seigniorial courts of the north. For the Visconti and the Sforza of Milan, the Este of Ferrara, and the Gonzaga of Mantua, the sponsorship of literati and artists was a means of exercising prestige and power and having fun as well. While humanistic interests dominated the universities and academies, lyric poetry, especially the sonnet, became a vehicle of intense personal expression and the means to entertain a public of enthusiasts. In the fifteenth century, several members of ruling families engaged in literary activities: Leonello d'Este, Gaspare Visconti, and Niccolò da Correggio penned refined and delicate sonnets. Count Matteo Maria Boiardo—who, for the entertainment of the court, wrote a chivalric epic, the *Orlando Immanorato*—outshined all sonneteers as the best lyric poet of the century. To represent the sonnet production in the Naples of the Aragon kings, I have selected Giannantonio Petrucci and Benedetto Gareth, who were both courtiers but had tragic, divergent destinies. Sonnets penned by northern commoners follow: those of Gian Francesco Suardi, mayor of Massa de' Lombardi; Giorgio Sommariva, a lawyer; and Antonio Cammelli, a man of sundry occupations.

4. In the last decades of the fifteenth century, the sonneteers who enjoyed the most enthusiastic accolades were Antonio Tebaldeo and Serafino Aquilano. Their poems stood out for the use of extravagant metaphors, witty conceits, and epigrammatic arrangement of content. Their ability to surprise and amuse made them the rage of many courts where literature had become part of a well-regulated program of entertainments. The epigrammatic type of sonnet retained its popularity throughout the following century, in competition with the model upheld by Bembo, and was afterward taken over by the metaphysical sonneteers of the late Renaissance and the baroque age.

At the end of the century, the Italian world entered a long period of political, social, and cultural change. The balance of power between the Italian states that Lorenzo de' Medici had helped to maintain shattered after his death in 1492. Quarrelling among themselves, the Italian princes invited foreign intervention for reinforcement and protection. Big armies, well trained and equipped with modern weaponry, poured into the peninsula, where they either found no opposition or easily overcame the resistance of the states that tried to oppose them. France and Spain, the main contenders for European supremacy, began to fight their wars on the much-coveted Italian territory. The invasions, protracted wars, and reversals of regime continued for decades, reverberating in the sonnets of Visconti, Pistoia, Machiavelli, Guiduccioni, and Alamanni. Their poems revealed the errors of diplomacy and horrors of war, the military and political weaknesses of the leaders, and the consequences suffered by the general population.

In Rome, in compliance with a long local tradition, various types of writing, among them many sonnets, were hung on public statues for everyone to read. Unabashedly, they derided the habits and initiatives of the authorities, the pope, and the members of the Roman curia. Such criticism and freedom of expression were the reverse side of the political influence and cultural prestige that the Church of Rome still exercised in Italy and abroad.

The architect and magician of the new clerical culture was Pietro Bembo. A man endowed with a great literary intuition and multifarious potentials, Bembo launched into a program of writing and editing that brought about the greatest production of sonnets ever seen. In *Asolani*, a dialogue influenced by contemporary Neoplatonic theories, he showed how human love, given a spiritual direction, could sidestep the perennial conflict between religious aspirations and human emotional needs. With a new edition of Petrarch's *Canzoniere*; his *Prose della volgar lingua*, a treatise on literary language and style; and two editions of his own poetry, he gave examples of how to turn Petrarch's poetic model into a literary model that also functioned as a behavioral code of conduct for the refined and the highminded. Furthermore, the great number of pocket-size anthologies of lyric verse produced by Italian publishers, especially those in Venice, contributed to turning the reading and writing of sonnets into a popular fashion and making Italian poetry known and imitated in other countries.

Many outstanding personalities wrote sonnets. In abstract and unadorned progression of thought, Vittoria Colonna turned the celebration of her dead husband into an exalted search for transcendence. In his sonnets, Michelangelo platonically contemplated the beauty of nature that he extracted from marble as the soul's outer reflection of the absolute beauty of God. There were other outstanding sonneteers. Galeazzo di Tarsia described the unrestrainable force of love in restless sonnets, in rare and vigorous analogies. Gaspara Stampa turned traditional poetic imagery into the affirmation of a life intensely lived and willingly burned at the altar of love.

Stampa was one of the many women who had literary productions published. When Bembo, at the beginning of the century, wedded the occasions and iconic imagery of Petrarch's love story to the soul's Platonic journey to the divinity and fashioned from it a social code acceptable in high social and religious milieus, women realized that a way to an honorable presence in society and to literary authorship was open to them. Out of the avalanche of women's sonnets that came out of the Italian presses in the sixteenth century, I have arranged together—besides those of Vittoria Colonna and Gaspara Stampa, who are treated separately—a few poems by Veronica Gàmbara, Tullia d'Aragona, Barbara Torelli, Isabella di Morra, and Chiara Matraini.

5. The sixteenth century was also the great season of satire. Poets employed biting humor and raw criticism to demystify the high standards of entire classes of people and condemn men in power, whether warriors, political leaders, or members of the high clergy. While the satire of Francesco Berni, secretary to a cardinal, was gentle and more subtly humorous, disenfranchised men, such as Pietro Aretino and Niccolò Franco, gave vent to transgressive, vituperative moods in sonnets intended to shock and insult. Present here are also some examples of the humor that poets and artists exercised, more or less aggressively, at the expense of other poets and artists.

While in earlier times, popular and high-style poetry would occasionally and experimentally intermingle, from the second half of the fifteenth century on, when the distance between those near the source of power and those far from it widened, there tended to be a wider gap between high and low culture and between the literary and popular brands of literature. At that time, the dialect sonnet developed its own independent identity. Poets such as Gian Francesco Suardi, Giorgio Sommariva, and, much later, Paolo Foglietta consciously chose the local idiom as a form of expression alternative to the high literary fashion. Such assertion of regional pride acquired a political tinge in the works of Giulio Cesare Cortese, whose Neapolitan verse described the conditions of men and women of the urban lower classes.

In the high-style category, Giovanni della Casa's verse showed a propensity to evade into a world of classical fantasy and maintain an intense, dramatic questioning line that expressively disrupted the organization of thought within the strophic structure of the sonnet. The languid, brooding moods of Torquato Tasso created images and musical effects that continue to transport the reader into a world of fantasy and dream.

As a defense from private and public upheavals, many took refuge in religion. The sixteenth century saw society go through the permissive Catholicism of the Renaissance, the fervor of the would-be reformers, and the moral and theological controls of the Counter-Reformation. In her sonnets, Vittoria Colonna traced a path from a yearning for religious renewal to dangerous sorties into heresy. Giordano Bruno invited his readers to enter a transcending dimension and look, through the magic of metaphor, at the universe for what it is: infinity without a center, a limitless conglomeration of widely differentiated worlds. In his sonnets as well as his prose, Tommaso Campanella expounded a political philosophy meant to bring about the reorganization and moral rejuvenation of humankind.

The wars and social changes that came in their wake, as well as the ongoing geographic discoveries, had a major impact on the mood of the population and on literature. To Giambattista Marino, the world appeared as a kaleidoscopic projection of images, a world of immensurable possibilities to be captured through the senses. His experimental technique aimed at a mesmerizing sensual suggestiveness and great opulence of descriptions. For him and the many avant-garde poets who followed his example, the extended metaphor and the conceit became the means to capture nature and describe what escaped ordinary sensory experience. In their hands, the sonnet became a display of stylistic acrobatics and a mirror for all unusual subjects, for anything that would surprise, tease, shock, and delight.

Complementary to such enthusiasm for experience were a pervading sense of insecurity and the constant thought of impending death. Ongoing geographic discoveries had shown that the earth contained unsuspected faraway lands inhabited by strange human beings. Cosmology no longer justified the hierarchical order of society. Scientific revelations had suddenly removed humankind from the center of the universe and left it hanging in a space that had no apparent limits. Such shifts in the perception of the earth and order of life originated sonnets that expressed a disquieting feeling of existential insecurity. Material objects, such as fountains, water plays, gardens, labyrinths, fireworks, telescopes, and clocks of all kinds, appeared on the poetic scene as symbols and reminders of a world that destroyed and recreated itself relentlessly. An enhanced figurative language of poetry endeavored to extend the limits of expression; it strived to get at what escaped the human capacity of perception, to capture the transcendent and the metaphysical. These are the features of the baroque style, a fashion that prevailed in European literature from the end of the Renaissance to the beginning of the modern age.

The span of time this volume covers saw the people inhabiting the Italian peninsula go from political independence to subjection to foreign powers, from affluence to relative poverty, and from artistic and literary European hegemony to a relatively marginal cultural importance. It shows a well-definable change of mental outlook from the inquisitive secularism of the Sicilian court to the apprehensively repressive mentality of the Counter-Reformation. At the end of the seventeenth century, except for a few successful episodes of revival, the history of the sonnet as the preeminent lyric genre was over. In the canonical literary hierarchy, the epic heroic poem had supplanted lyric poetry; later, fictional prose would dominate the literary canon. The sonnet would continue a marginal life. In the verse of the high-style practitioners, it would occasionally appear as an antiquarian exercise. Under the pen of literarily less ambitious versifiers, it would be the means—until relatively recent times—to mark the happy occasions of life, to celebrate family, friends, and local events.[2] The sonnet continues to have a successful, although peripheral, existence in some dialects.

1

From Imperial Court to Democratic Commune

1.1 Philosophizing at the Imperial Court

Scholars attribute the invention of the sonnet to Giacomo da Lentini, a lawyer by profession and an outstanding poet among many literati who flourished around the court of Palermo in the first half of the thirteenth century. Legal documents spanning the years from 1233 to 1240 refer to Lentini as "Jacopo from Lentini, notary to the Lord, the Emperor" (*Jacobus de Lentino domini imperatoris notarius*).[3] The lord and emperor in question was Frederick II Hohenstaufen (1194–1250), who had inherited the kingdom of Sicily and southern Italy from his Sicilian Norman mother, Costanza d'Altavilla, and ancestral lands, with the title of emperor of the Holy Roman Empire, from his German father, Henry VI.[4]

Here is one of the first sonnets ever written and the best known of those Lentini penned:

> Io m'aggio posto in core a Dio servire,
> com'io potesse gire in paradiso,
> al santo loco, ch'aggio audito dire,
> u' si mantien sollazzo, gioco e riso.   4
> Sanza mia donna non vi voria gire,
> quella c'ha blonda testa e claro viso,
> ché sanza lei non poteria gaudere,
> estando da la mia donna diviso.   8
> Ma no lo dico a tale intendimento,
> perch'io peccato ci volesse fare;
> se non veder lo suo bel portamento
> e lo bel viso e 'l morbido sguardare: 12
> ché lo mi teria 'n gran consolamento,
> veggendo la mia donna in ghiora stare.

> I have set my heart on serving God,
> so that one day I might go to paradise,
> the holy place where, I heard them say,
> are perpetual solace, mirth, and play.   4
> Without my woman, I am loath to go,

the one with radiant face and golden hair,
because, without her, I could not rejoice,
should I perchance be away from her.   8
But I do not say this with any intent
or a desire to indulge in sin with her,
but in order to gaze at her fine bearing,
at her beguiling looks and graceful glances: 12
for it would be to me a boundless solace
to look at my woman in heaven's glory.

In the octave, Lentini daringly declares the speaker's determination to go to heaven in the company of a woman and then deferentially justifies that determination in the sestet. The speaker advances his argument couplet by couplet, showing a linear development of ideas and correspondence with an alternating rhyme scheme: ABABABAB CDCDCD. The sonnet closes with an image of paradise that connects the end to the beginning. Critics argued about its meaning. Some considered it a serious and sacrilegious challenge to religion; others saw in it an attempt to reconcile courtly love with love for God. The concluding hyperbolic protestation of love already had and would continue to have a remarkably long life. "Without you I would not want to be in heaven," Ovid wrote in *Amores*, 2, 16. Many centuries later, in Mascagni's *Cavalleria rusticana*, Turiddu thinks of Lola and sings: "Oh Lola … if I die for you and go to paradise, I will not go in, if I cannot see your beautiful face" (*O Lola … se per te mojo e vado in paradiso, non c'entro se no vedo il tuo bel viso*).

Love begins when one person looks at another with pleasure and then thinks about it insistently until a passion develops in his or her heart: *"Amor est passio quaedam innata procedes ex visione,"* declared André le Chapelain in *De Amore*, a book from the 1180s that became an authority on matters of love. Lentini meditates on the physics of that phenomenon in this sonnet:

Or come pote sì gran donna entrare
per gli occhi mei, che sì piccioli sone?
E nel mio core come pote stare,
che 'nentr'esso la porto laonque i' vone?   4
Lo loco laonde entra già non pare,
ond'io gran meraviglia me ne done;
ma voglio lei a lumera asomigliare,
e gli occhi mei al vetro ove si pone.   8
Lo foco inchiuso poi passa di fore
lo suo lostrore, sanza far rottura:
così per gli occhi mi pass'a lo core,
no la persona, ma la sua figura.   12
Rinovellare mi voglio d'amore,
poi porto insegna di tal crïatura.

Now, how can so big a woman enter
through my eyes, which are so small?
How can she afterward remain in my heart

for me to carry her wherever I go? 4
The way she comes in no one can see,
and at that I myself greatly wonder;
so I want to compare her to the light
and liken my eyes to the glass it enters. 8
The flame, which is within, lets its brightness
come through without breaking the glass,
so she—her image, I mean, not her person—
is able to reach my heart through my eyes. 12
I shall consecrate myself to love anew,
for in me is the imprint of so great a creature.

The apparent paradox in Chapelain's theoretical question—how can something as big as a woman go through something as small as the lover's eyes and take up residence in his heart?—finds a tongue-in-cheek resolution, it seems to me, through a logical development of thought. The first eight lines posit the paradox and promise a solution; the sestet resolves the paradox by way of a natural analogy. The sonnet concludes with a firm determination: the poet will devote himself to love, for he holds in his heart the image of an exceptional woman.

Lo basilisco a lo speclo lucent
traggi a morire cum risbaldimento;
lo cesne canta plu gioiosoamente
quand'è plu presso a lo so finimento; 4
lo paon turba, istando plu gaudente,
cum'a soi pedi fa riguardamento;
l'augel fenise s'arde veramente,
per ritornare in novo nascimento. 8
'N tali nature eo sentom' abenuto
chi allegro vado e miro a le belleze,
'nforzo lo canto presso a lo finire,
estando gaio torno dismaruto, 12
ardendo in foco inovo in allegreze:
per vui, plu gente, a cui spero redire.

The basilisk is drawn to the dazzling
mirror, and there it dies in contentment;
the swan sings by far more joyously
as he comes closer and closer to death; 4
the peacock agitates, but with pleasure,
when he glances down at his feet;
the phoenix burns down completely
in order to go back to life again. 8

I feel I have turned into these creatures:
I too run blissfully to look at her beauty,
I too increase my singing near my ending,
while I feel happy, I too become distressed,
and while burning in fire, joyfully I am born again: 12
because to you, most lovely, I'll hopefully return.

In line 1, the basilisk is a mythical lizard-like reptile with fatal breath and burning eyes. In line 3, *cesne*, or *cigno*, means "swan." In line 4, *finimento* means "end" or "death." Regarding line 6, peacocks were thought to go wild when they looked at their feet (White 149.10–13). With regard to line 10, most editors write *vado a moro*, which would be Sicilian for *vado a morire* (I go to die). I chose instead the version given by the *Vaticano Barberino Latino 3953* (one of four codices containing the sonnet) because it gives a good correspondence between the two terms of comparison: when they look, both the peacock and the lover suffer and feel pleasure. Cumulatively repetitive in the first part, the sonnet reaches a symmetrical structure in the sestet by reasserting the lover's condition in ways that correspond to the behavior of the animals mentioned before—the basilisk, swan, peacock, and phoenix.

The following is another example of what Hugo Friedrich (1.33) called figurative logic—that is, a logical progression of thought upheld and reinforced by similes and metaphors, as we have seen above.

A l'aire claro ho vista ploggia dare,
ed a lo scuro rendere clarore;
e foco arzente ghiaccia diventare,
e fredda neve rendere calore;   4
e dolze cose molto amareare,
e de l'amare rendere dolzore;
e dui guerreri in fina pace stare,
e 'ntra dui amici nascereci errore.   8
Ed ho vista d'Amor cosa più forte:
ch'era feruto, e sanòmi ferendo;
lo foco donde ardea stutò con foco.
La vita che mi dè fue la mia morte;   12
lo foco che mi stinse, ora ne 'ncendo:
ché sì mi trasse Amor, non trovo loco.

I saw the rain fall in clear weather
in a darkish day a lightning bolt strike,
I saw a blazing fire change into ice,
I saw the gelid snow generate heat,   4
sweet things become very bitter,
and bitter ones give a pleasure sweet.
I saw two enemies live in perfect peace
and acrimony arise between friends.   8
But I saw Love doing stranger things:
for I was stricken, and he cured me by striking,

the flame that burned me, he put out with fire;
the life he gave me has become my death,   12
the fire that stifled me now makes me glow:
for Love drives me so that I find no respite.

Regarding line 3, people believed that lightning bolts brought down hail. With regard to line 4, the theory was that water reduced to a low temperature formed crystal. The crystal then, as lens, could burn the object on which it reflected the sunlight. Per lines 5–6, sweet drink might taste bitter to a sick person, while to another, something bitter might seem sweet—that is, the lover might find pleasure in suffering. In line 10, *sanòmi ferendo* tells us that love cured the man's wounds by wounding the woman with his arrow and making her fall in love. Regarding line 12, her return of love has increased his passion, thus increasing his suffering. The topsy-turvy world of analogical paradoxes is locked into place by an arabesque of correspondences and stylistic devices. *Claro* and *clarore* of lines 1 and 2 tie with the phrases *rendere clarore*, *rendere calore*, and *rendere dolzore* of lines 2, 4, and 6. *Dolze cose* and *amareare* of line 5 refer, in reverse, to *de l'amare* and *dolzore* of line 6, while *feruto* and *ferendo* of line 10 refer to *lo foco* and *con foco* in line 11.

In "Sì alta amanza ha preso lo me' core," love is as obstinate and overpowering as the wind that bends trees and as the rain when it breaks up a diamond. Again, Lentini used natural phenomena in lieu of scholastic demonstrations.

Sì alta amanza ha preso lo me' core,
ch'i' mi disfido de lo compimento,
che 'n aguila gruera ho messo amore.
Ben este orgoglio, ma no fallimento,   4
ch'amor l'encalza e spera, aulente frore:
ch'albor altera incrina dolce vento,
e lo diamante rompe a tutte l'ore
de lacrime lo molle scendimento.   8
Donqua, madonna, se lacrime e pianto
del diamante frange la dureze,
la vosta alteze—porria isbassare
lo meo penare—amoroso, ch'è tanto,   12
umilïare—la vostra dureze,
foco d'amor in vui, donna, allumare.

My heart is caught in so high a loving
that I am despairing of its consummation,
for to a crane-catching eagle my love has turned.
That is boldness, not an error on my part,   4
for love compels me to hope, fragrant flower:
because a mild wind may bend a lofty tree
and a gentle and persistent rain of tears
time and again a diamond may break.   8
So, my lady, if tears and weeping can

> shatter the hardness of the diamond,
> my persistent loving, which is so steady,
> might bring down your haughty pride,   12
> soothe and diminish your harshness,
> and ignite in you, woman, the flame of love.

The octave states the proposition and confirms it: the lover has fallen in love with a proud, unreachable woman, a woman who is as unreachable as a high-flying crane-catching eagle (*aguila gruera*). *Donqua* (therefore), in line 9, is the pivot (the *volta*) that directs the poet's syllogistic reasoning toward the conclusion: if a gentle wind can lower a powerful tree and if drops of water can shatter an unbreakable diamond, the quiet persistence of his love will be able to overcome the woman's haughty indifference (*umiliare la vostra dureze*).

The intellectual interests and natural investigations pursued at Frederick's court revealed a protoscientific and secular frame of mind. The functionaries of the realm who, encouraged by the emperor, wrote love poetry as a diversion from their bureaucratic duties showed a propensity to turn the experience of love into a scientific investigation.[5] When addressing a woman, their plea for reciprocation tended to theorize—to become a lecture on the nature of passion and the behavior of lovers in general. Their penchant for debating the question—a practice common in the universities they had attended—is better exemplified in the Sicilian *tenzone*.[6]

A tenzone is a debate between two or more poets. The following tenzone on the nature of love consists of three sonnets. Its tone, in my opinion, is good humored, if not openly jocular. Jacopo Mostacci proposes the thesis to debate, Pier della Vigna states the counterthesis, and Jacopo da Lentini offers the solution. The poems have the same rhyme scheme—ABABABAB CDE CDE—and in all three, the sestet repeats a rhyme of the octave: *-ire*, *-ente*, and *-ore*, respectively. They are also tied to one another thusly: Pier della Vigna takes up the rhyme *-ire* from Mostacci, and Lentini repeats the *-ore* rhyme used by Mostacci and the *-ente* rhyme used by Piero.

Jacopo Mostacci, court falconer and supervisor of the emperor's favorite game, opens the debate.[7] There is a question (*dubio*) to resolve (*determinare*). The question, of course, is ironic: many say that love is a substance, something that, by scholastic definition, exists in itself and can therefore be perceived by the human eye; others say that it is only a temporary quality, that of being in love. He ends by saying, essentially, "I have never seen love, so you explain what it is."

> Sollicitando un poco meo savere
> e con lui mi vogliendo dilettare,
> un dubio che mi misi ad avere
> a voi lo mando per determinare.   4
> Ogn'omo dice ch'amor ha potere
> e li coraggi distringe ad amare,
> ma eo no li lo voglio consentire,
> però ch'amore no parse ni pare.   8
> Ben prova l'om una amorositate,

la quale par che nasca di piacere,
e zo vol dire che sia amore.
Eo no li saccio altra qualitate, 12
ma zo che è, da voi lo voglio audire:
però ven faccio sentenziatore.

Stimulated by an interest to know,
and wishing to have a little fun with it,
I am sending to you, to be resolved,
a question that popped into my mind. 4
Everybody says that love has the power
to compel men's hearts to fall in love,
but I do not go along with this opinion,
for no one ever saw love and never will. 8
Man no doubt tends to become enamored,
induced, it seems, by a feeling of pleasure:
such propensity people insist in calling love.
I myself know of no other quality of it, 12
but what it is I wish to hear it from you.
So I ask you to be the judge of the question.

With regard to line 3, the rhyme *avere* stands for the original Sicilian rhyme *avire* and, for this reason, is called Sicilian rhyme. This substitution, and many others like it, occurred when northern scribes copied the Sicilian manuscripts—now lost—and adapted the Sicilian language to their idiom.[8] Per line 8, if our eyes cannot see love, it cannot be an independent entity. The scholastic distinction is between substance and accident. Substance is the essence—what a thing is in itself and what can be perceived by the eye—and accident is whatever temporary quality the thing may take on, which in it iself, independently of the thing, cannot be perceived. In lines 9–10, the octave has advanced the question. The first tercet presents the possible objection: people fall in and out of love; therefore, such disposition—the temporary *amorositate*—is accidental to their nature, not an integral part of it. In the last tercet, the falconer concludes, "Then how can love be a substance in itself?" To his query, Pier della Vigna offers a first answer.

Pier della Vigna (ca. 1185–1249), born in humble circumstances at Capua, had studied jurisprudence at the University of Bologna and was by this time an eminent jurist. The emperor made him his chief secretary (*logotheta*), prothonotary, and, subsequently, *judex magnae curiae*, chancellor, and governor of Apulia. Piero was probably the court officer who drew up the constitutional and legislative code of the imperial government, known as the Melfi Constitutions.[9]

Però ch'amore no si pò vedere
e non si tratta corporalemente,
manti ne son di sì folle sapere
che credono ch'amor sïa nïente. 4
Ma po' ch'amore si face sentire
dentro dal cor signoreggiar la gente,

molto maggiore presio deve avere
che se 'l vedessen visibilemente.   8
Per la vertute de la calamita
como lo ferro attira no si vede,
ma sì lo tira signorevolmente;
e questa cosa a credere mi 'nvita   12
ch'amore sia; e dami grande fede
che tuttor sia creduto fra la gente.

Since love no one can ever see
and no one can feel by touching,
many are of such foolish opinion
as to believe that it does not exist.   4
But since love makes people feel
that it controls them in their hearts,
more consideration they should give it
than if they did see it with their eyes.   8
By what strength the magnet
pulls the iron to itself we cannot see;
nonetheless, it does so overpoweringly,
and this leads me to believe that love   12
is a substance, and I am fully persuaded
that people will always think of it as such.

If love is endowed with the invisible and supernatural power that it obviously exercises over people, it cannot be but a substance, maintains Pier della Vigna—that is, it cannot be but a god. My translation of *ch'amore sia* as "love is substance" retains both the general sense of the tenzone and the meaning of "to be," which, in a medieval philosophical context, meant "to be a substance." Della Vigna does not propose a theory, according to Contini 88: he advances a dialectic rhetorical fiction, albeit one syllogistically declined. To repeat: love reigns over the hearts of men; therefore, it is—or, in scholastic terminology, it is a substance. Piero's rather colorless sonnet receives some vivacity from the comparison with the magnet in the first tercet and from the celebration of love in the closing lines.

Famous is the solution of the question offered by Giacomo da Lentini.

Amor è uno desio che ven da core
per abondanza di gran piacimento;
e gli occhi in prima generan l'amore
e lo core li da nutricamento.   4
Ben è alcuna fiata om amatore
senza vedere so 'namoramento,
ma quell'amor che stringe con furore
da la vista de li occhi ha nascimento.   8
Ché li occhi rapresentan a lo core
d'onni cosa che vede, bono e rio,

com'è formata naturalemente;
e lo cor, che di zo è concepitore,
imagina, e li piace quel desio: 12
e quest'amore regna fra la gente.

Love is a yearning rising from the heart
from an overflow of concentrated pleasure;
first, the eyes generate the longing, and then
the heart provides it with nourishment.   4
A man, at times, may per chance fall in love
without seeing the object of his longing,
but the love that turns into a throbbing passion
has its beginning in a person's sight.   8
This is because the eyes send to the heart
the image of everything they see, good or evil,
the way all things are shaped in nature;
and the heart, if pleasured in conceiving   12
that image, holds it and longs for it in the mind:
This is the kind of love that rules humankind.

Per lines 3–4, if the sight of a person produces pleasure in one's heart, the mind keeps the memory of that pleasurable sight alive, and one falls in love. According to medieval physiology, the heart, center of blood circulation, was the seat of life, and in it resided the faculties of perception, subjective feeling, memory, and thought. In line 5, the reference is to the *amor de lonh* (love from afar) sung by Provençal poet Jauffè Rudel. The legend was that Rudel, who participated in the Crusade of 1147, had fallen in love with Melisende, daughter of the king of Tripoli, without seeing her. Per line 12, the heart, as the seat of the mental faculty, contemplates that image and takes possession of it. In lines 12–13, *Lo cor, che di zo è concepitore, imagina* tells us that the heart takes in the image and begins to think obsessively about it.

Lentini's love is the *immoderata cogitatio* described by André le Chapelain in *De Amore* 4, 7: *Amor est passio quaedam innata procedes ex visione et immoderata cogitatione formae alterius sexus* (love is a passion that originates from seeing and from thinking excessively about a person of the opposite sex), and *ex sola cogitatione, quam concepit animus ex eo, quod vidit, passio illa procedit* (passion originates only from the thought that the mind conceives after what it has seen).

In discussing the question, Lentini takes a completely different tack from that of the other two debaters. Mostacci had raised the question (*dubio*) "Should love be considered an entity in itself?" Lentini first agrees with Mostacci in part: yes, love originates in pleasure. Then, addressing Pier della Vigna, he defines it as a natural feeling, not a deity, and explains why people personify love as a god. People call it master, or *signore*, because when nourished in the heart, love reigns (*regna*) or dominates (*signoreggia*) over the entire person. Mostacci opened the tenzone as the master of the game, just as a falconer opens the chase. The actual debate takes place between Della Vigna's feudal mythologizing idea of love—lovers must respect and obey love as a god—and Lentini's resolution of the question with the up-to-date scientific explanation given by André le Chapelain. Lentini's view is naturalistic and excludes the romanticized love of Jaufrè Rudel. We may add that from a theoretical point of view, his interpretation was potentially hazardous to hold. Its implications would lead to heretical development in Guido Cavalcanti and radical religious resolutions in Dante.

1.2 Church and Empire

As we move from the imperial court to the democratic communes of northern Italy, we find that the thematic range of the sonnet broadens to include a great variety of subjects and styles. Political concerns are forcefully present in the poetry of northern Italy, while they are strikingly absent, for good reasons, in the poetry of the Sicilian courtiers.

As emperor of the Holy Roman Empire, Frederick sought to extend his control over the north of the peninsula, a part of Italy that was theoretically subject to the jurisdiction of the empire but where many communes had become politically and militarily independent. The pope, hostile to imperial authority and claiming superior power over the empire, was quick to back the rebellious city-states. The countrywide parties of Ghibellines and Guelfs were thus born: Guelfs were the city governments dominated by the new bourgeoisie, which had financial ties with the church and supported its political plans. Ghibellines were the towns and factions that identified with the old feudal order and now claimed allegiance to the Hohenstaufen.[10]

Frederic died in 1250. His heir in Italy was Manfred, a natural son. In Germany, his legitimate successor as emperor became Conrad IV. In Italy, Manfred reorganized the Ghibelline party, and with the help of his Tuscan allies, in 1260, he routed the Florentine Guelfs at the battle of Montaperti. Fearful of the new situation, the popes—Urban IV and Clement IV, both French—invited Charles of Anjou, count of Provence and brother of the king of France, to lead an expedition against Manfred. Manfred was killed at the Battle of Benevento in 1266. Frederick's only successor was Conrad, the fifteen-year-old son of Conrad IV, who had died at the age of twenty-six, two years after his nomination. Young Conrad, or Corradino, as the Italians called him because of his young age, entered Italy at the head of a small army and was defeated at Tagliacozzo in 1268. Captured and taken to Naples by Charles, he was decapitated shortly afterward.

Two Florentines, Orlanduccio Orafo and Palamidesse di Bellindote—the first was a Guelf, and the second was a Ghibelline—exchanged sonnets dealing with the political and military events that occurred over a span of eight years, from Manfred's victory at Montaperti in 1260 to the defeat of the imperial army at Tagliacozzo in 1268. About Orlanduccio, we know only that he was a goldsmith and favored the cause of the church. Of Palamidesse, son of Bellindote del Perfetto, one of the signers of the peace agreed in 1254 between the cities of Pistoia, Prato, and Lucca, we know that he fought at the Battle of Montaperti as gonfalonier for the crossbowmen of the Porta del Duomo district. Orlanduccio addressed the following sonnet to Palamidesse in 1267, when the news reached Italy that Corradino had been elected king of Sicily and was preparing to cross the Alps.

> Oi tu, che se' errante cavaliero,
> de l'arme fero—e de la mente saggio,
> cavalca piano, e dicerotti il vero
> di ciò ch'io spero—e la certezza ind' aggio:

4

un nuovo re vedrai a lo scacchiero
col buon guerrer—che tant' ha vasallaggio;
ciascun per sé vorrà essere impero,
ma lo penzer—non sarà di paraggio.   8
Ed averà intra lor fera battaglia;
e fia sen' faglia—tal, che molta gente
sarà dolente—chi chi n'abbia gioia;
e manti buon distrier' coverti a maglia   12
in quella taglia—saran per neiente:
qual fia perdente—alor conven che moia.

You there, who are a knight-errant,
wise of mind and very fierce in battle,
ride slowly, and I shall tell you the truth
about what I want and surely will occur: 4
a new king you shall see in the battlefield
against the good fighter with many vassals;
each of them will want to dominate,
but this idea the other will not share.   8
Between them there will be a brutal fight,
and, no doubt, whoever is to rejoice,
many people will have to grieve.
Countless good mail-shielded knights   12
will be for nothing in this fight:
whoever is the loser, he will have to die.

Orlanduccio sarcastically describes his correspondent as a knight-errant because Palamidesse, or Palomides, is the name of a knight of the Round Table, as we read on the Winchester Round Table and in Thomas Malory's *Morte d'Arthur*. The families of the prosperous bourgeoisie, whatever their political affiliation, identified with the ideal of knighthood and chivalry and styled themselves as a warrior aristocracy. The new king (*un nuovo re*) of line 5 is Corradino, who, after Manfred's death, had been nominated king of Sicily. *Scacchiero* is both the chessboard and, in military jargon, the fighting field. The *buon guerrer* of line 6 is Charles d'Anjou. In lines 9, 10, and 14, the defeated ones will be the Ghibellines, the supporters of the imperial party. The vision of their impending defeat receives a martial tone from the *rimalmezzo* in the even lines of each quatrain (*fero*, *spero*, *guerrer*, and *penzer*) and in the second and third line of each tercet (*faglia*, *dolente*, *taglia*, and *perdente*). Palamidesse's answer to Orlanduccio has the same arrogant address, defiance, and number of *rimalmezzo* as his correspondent's sonnet.

Poi il nome c'hai ti fa il coraggio altero,
pur è mestero—c'aspetti stormo maggio;
e però sper' c'un nuovo re stranero
al batastero—vegna a gran barnaggio.   4
Or legga un'altra faccia del saltero;
se senno ha 'ntero—non farà tal viaggio:

> de la battaglia col campion San Pero
> om di su' ostero—n'ha levato saggio. 8
> Ma s'egli avien ca pur al campo saglia,
> mai di travaglia—non sarà perdente,
> se Dio consente—a vincer la Mongioia:
> ché Carlo crede ca sua spada i vaglia, 12
> e c'a Dio caglia—sì che sia vincente,
> e di presente—conquider chi 'l 'noia.

> Although the name makes you boldly proud,
> still you must expect a major battle;
> and I surely hope that the new foreign king
> will step onto the field with a fearless army. 4
> He better read a new page of the Psalms:
> if sound of mind, he won't make this journey,
> for a man of his house has had already a taste
> of fighting against Saint Peter's champion. 8
> But should he still come up to this fray,
> he will not be lacking in misfortunes,
> if God allows the Montjoie to prevail:
> for Charles is sure that his sword won't fail, 12
> that God will want him to be the winner,
> and swiftly defeat those who molest him.

It is only his name that makes Orlanduccio proud, implies Palamidesse. Orlanduccio is diminutive of Orlando, the Italian name for Roland, the famed hero of the *Chanson de Roland*. In line 3, *nuovo re stranero* is Corradino. In line 4, *batastero* is a transliteration from the French meaning "battle" (Contini 1, 474). In line 7, Charles of Anjou is called the champion of Saint Peter because the pope backed him. Regarding line 8, this is reference to Manfred, who was killed by the Guelfs at the Battle of Benevento. With regard to line 11, the oriflamme, the Anjou escutcheon featured on the standard of St. Denis, was called Montjoie.

Rustico Filippi's political bile displays no chivalric stance. The dislike he kindled for the Guelfs of his town is laced with biting sarcasm.

> A voi che ve ne andaste per paura:
> sicuramente potete tornare;
> da che ci è dirizzata la ventura,
> ormai potete guerra inconinzare. 4
> E' piú non vi bisogna stare a dura,
> da che non è chi vi scomunicare:
> ma ben lo vi tenete 'n isciagura
> che non avete piú cagion che dare. 8

Ma so bene, se Carlo fosse morto,
che voi ci trovereste ancor cagione:
però del papa non ho gran conforto.
Ma i' non voglio con voi stare a tenzone,   12
ca' lungo temp' è ch'io ne fui acorto
che 'l ghibellino aveste per garzone.

You who run away in terror
may presently return in total safety;
now that Fortune has turned against us,
you may start exacting your revenge.   4
You need no longer to be on the defensive,
for there is no one now to excommunicate:
still, you do consider it a great misfortune
having no cause to inveigh on us again.   8
Even if Charles were dead, you would
surely find a new pretext for striking,
for in the pope I have no confidence.
Still, with you I want no arguments,   12
for too long I have been fully aware
you take us Ghibellines to be your slaves.

In line 1, Filippi's contemptuous reference is to the Guelfs of Florence, who were forced to leave the city after they were defeated at the Battle of Montaperti in 1260. Per line 3, now that fortune has turned against the Ghibellines, the Guelfs may reenter the city without fear, the poet continues. In line 5, *stare alla dura* (to be on the defensive) implies that the Florentine Guelfs had done little fighting at Montaperti. In line 6, the poet says, "You have no one now to defend you by excommunicating the enemy." Rustico's is a denunciation of both the policy of the pope, who had used the excommunication as a political weapon, and the cowardice of the Florentine Guelfs, who profited from their allies' victory and took revenge on their defeated fellow citizens. In lines 7–8, *dare* means "to give a good beating." Even now that the Ghibellines have been defeated—by those who did the actual fighting—the Florentine Guelfs are sorry that the pope will no longer excommunicate their opponents. In lines 9–10, the poet says, in essence, "Even if Charles had died at Benevento instead of Manfred, you would like to go on fighting—with papal excommunications!"

D'una diversa cosa ch'è aparita
consiglio ch' abbian guardia i fiorentini;
e qual è quei che vuol campar la vita
si mandi al veglio per suoi assessini;   4
ché ci ha una lonza sì fiera e ardita
che, se Carlo sapesse i suoi confini
e de la sua prodezza avesse udita,
tosto n'andrebbe sopra i Saracini.   8

Ma chi è questa lonza or lo sacciate:
Paniccia egli è. Che fate, o a Fiorenza,
ch'oste non istanziate o cavalcate?
Ché s'e' seguisce inanzi sua valenza   12
com'egli ha fatto a dietro, sì gli date
sicuramente in guardia la Proenza.

Against a strange thing that has appeared
I warn the Florentines to be on guard;
and anyone wishing to spare his life
should send for the Old Man's assassins,   4
because here is so ferocious and bold a tiger
that if Charles heard of its amazing daring
and its thereabouts, he surely would launch
a campaign against the Saracens directly.   8
Now I shall tell you who this tiger is: it is
Paniccia! What are you all doing there in Florence?
Aren't you getting ready and starting to march?
For if in the days to come he will perform   12
so distinctly as he has performed in the past,
you'll make him right away governor of Provence.

Rustico's disdain focuses here on a specific member of the Guelf party, a laughable braggart. His sarcasm is rationed in maliciously controlled portions. Who the braggart might be, he does not say immediately. He says that something has appeared, a *diversa cosa*—a strange thing. To defend themselves against this unusual apparition, the Florentines should take preventive measures and send for the Old Man of the Mountain. The Old Man of the Mountain was Sheikh-el-Gebel, a legendary chieftain supposed to be living on a mountain peak in Persia, now Iran. He supposedly was the man Marco Polo talked about in his book of travels. The Old Man's followers, possibly of an Ishmaelite sect, called aššašins because they made used of hašiš, were reputed to be loyal to their leader to the point of committing suicide when asked. In line 5, the suspenseful indefiniteness of the strange thing changes into an animallike object, perhaps a ferocious animal. *Lonza*—replaced by a tiger in my translation—means "leopard." At the time, the Florentine government kept a leopard in a cage close to the city hall for the admiration of its citizens. Regarding line 6, it was Charles's ambitious plan to organize a crusade against the Muslims. Alternatively, the sentence could mean "Charles would rather fight the Saracens than come face-to-face with such a frightening creature." In line 10, we finally learn what the strange apparition that has kept us in suspense really is. It turns out to be a historical character: Paniccia Frescobaldi, an expatriate Guelf who, after the defeat of the Ghibellines at Montaperti, returned to Florence and boasted about his military exploits—without having been in any battle. With regard to line 14, Provence was the primary domain of the Anjou family and the seat of their power. If Paniccia performed as valiantly in the future as he had in the past, Charles of Anjou would surely make him governor of Provence—where there were no dangers and no enemies to fight. For Rustico Filippi, see also section 1.7.

Guido Guinizzelli was a lawyer of Bologna professionally active until 1274, the year the Guelfs seized power and Guido, who was affiliated with the Ghibelline faction of the Lambertazzi, was forced into exile. Most critics consider the following sonnet, which describes the anguish the poet suffered away from his city, a love poem. Luciano Rossi (58) has advanced the idea that it may be a *congedo*—that is, a composition about exile. I find his interpretation convincing.

> Sì sono angostioso e pien di doglia
> e di molti sospiri e di rancura,
> che non posso saver quel che mi voglia
> e qual poss' esser mai la mia ventura.   4
> Disnaturato son come la foglia
> quand' è caduta de la sua verdura,
> e tanto più che m'è secca la scoglia
> e la radice de la sua natura: 8
> sì ch'eo non credo mai poter gioire,
> né convertir—la mia disconfortanza
> in allegranza—di nessun conforto;
> soletto come tortula voi' gire,   12
> solo partir—mia vita in disperanza,
> per arroganza—di così gran torto.

> I am so distressed, so deep in sighing,
> so full of pain and of such bitterness
> that I no longer know what I would wish
> and what my destiny will turn out to be.   4
> Estranged I am from my very nature,
> just like a leaf pulled away from its tree;
> and totally so, since my bark has dried
> and so has the very root of my being: 8
> I do not believe I shall be glad again,
> whether I'll be able to turn my desolation
> into the joy of any comfort whatsoever;
> lonely as a turtledove I want to wander   12
> and live out my life in desperation,
> due to the conceit of this great offense.

Regarding line 11, in medieval bestiaries and religious writings, the turtledove appears as the symbol of loneliness and defenselessness. For Guinizzelli's more famous sonnets, see the next section.

1.3 Bourgeois Moralities of Love

In the bourgeois culture of the communes, love sonnets lost the abstract character they had in Sicilian poetry and took on the mark of real life. Poets now described love as an intensely personal experience, satisfying or demeaning but always disquieting. It could also be idealistic and express the self-ennobling ambitions of the new middleclass man.

The love that Guittone d'Arezzo (1235–94) wrote about in his early sonnets comes through as an intense desire for sexual possession froth with joy and frustration. His verse, loaded with rhetorical figures, struggles to accommodate an intricate rhetorical rhythm and disentangle an elliptical line of reasoning.

Ben saccio de vertà che 'l meo trovare
val poco, e ha ragion de men valere,
poi ch'eo non posso in quel loco intrare,
ch'adorna l'om de gioia e de savere;   4
e non departo d'a la porta stare
pregando che, per Deo, mi deggia aprere:
allora alcuna voce audir me pare
dicendome ch'eo sia di bon sofrere.   8
Ed eo soffert'ho tanto lungiamente
che devisa' de me tutto piacere
e tutto ciò ched era in me valente:
per ch'eo rechiamo e chero lo savere   12
di ciascun om ch'è prode e canoscente
a l'aiuto del meo grande spiacere.

I know well that my verse is of little value
and has reason to be of less account,
for I cannot enter the place that confers
on a man the joy and knowledge of love;   4
but I do not give up, I stand at the door,
and beseech her, for God's sake, to open;
then I believe I hear a voice that tells me
I must persist and suffer uncomplainingly.   8
I have suffered for so long that all capacity
for happiness has been taken away from me,
together with all that was vital in my being:
so I go on begging and keep appealing to the   12
wisdom of all the gallant and knowing people,
for them to come and help me in my distress.

In lines 1–2, the lover's plea is predicated on the courtly notion that only a reciprocated love (in other words, a love conquest) bestows value on a man and his poetry. In line 3, *quel loco*, meaning "that place," refers to the court of love, a euphemism for the woman's bedroom. In line 4, *gioia* refers to the pleasure of lovemaking. In line 9, *soffert'ho* means "I suffered." This intense longing for the woman's love is the suffering that the courtly lover must prove to be able to endure. A forceful, continuous line of reasoning flows through the sonnet. It begins with a statement of self-denigration, emphasized by the initial run-on line *il mio trovar / val poco* (my verse / is of scant value). Midway is a mention of carnal knowledge, euphemistically described as *quel loco … ch'adorna l'om de gioia e de savere* (the place that confers joyful knowledge on a man). The vigorous organizational structure conveys the lover's resolve: after each assertion—*Ben saccio* (I know well), *e non departo* (but I do not desist), *Ed eo soffert' ho* (and I suffered)—there follows a dependent clause explaining it, introduced by *poi ch'eo non posso* (since I cannot), *allora* (then), and *per cheo* (because I). The plea for love receives further weight from the repetition of attributions and verbs: *de gioia e de savere* (of joy and wisdom) in line 4, *rechiamo e chero* (I call on and appeal) in line 12, and *prode e canoscente* (gallant and knowing) in line 13. A long clause ends the poem with a promise of future action. The forceful reasoning and repetitive distinguishing between statement and explanation give the sonnet great power of conviction.

Selfish calculations and offensive considerations, moralizes Guittone, often motivate a suitor. In "Sì como ciascun omo," he recognizes that as a lover, he too has behaved with duplicity.

Sì como ciascun omo, enfingitore
e ora maggiormente assai ch'amante
so stato ver' di lei, di bieltà fiore;
e tanto giunto eo so dietro e davante   4
con prego e con mercé e con clamore,
facendo di perfetto amor sembiante,
che me promise loco en su' dolzore
adesso che lei fusse benistante.   8
Eo, pensando la mia gran malvagia,
e la gran fede in lei dolce e pietosa,
sì piansi di pietà, per fede mia,
e fermai me di lei non prender cosa   12
alcuna mai, senza mertarla pria,
avendo forte e ben l'alma amorosa.

Like all men, I too have been a deceiver,
and now much more than any other lover,
toward her, that great flower of beauty;
so often I came up before her and after,   4
pitiably and loudly begging her to love me,
and with such pretention of perfect affection
that she promised a taste of her sweet loving,
as soon as it would be possible for her.   8
But I, considering my great duplicity
and the trust that is in her, so sweet and kind,
I wept out of pity so that, upon my honor,
I have resolved never to take anything   12
from her without deserving it before
and to love her unwaveringly and deeply.

In line 4, *giuto* means "gone," from *gire*, meaning "to go." The sonnet is organized into two units of meaning. The octave describes what his behavior has been like so far; the sestet explains the resolve to behave reliably in the future and concludes with a promise to love the woman deeply and steadfastly.

Poi non vi piace che v'ami, ameraggio
voi dunque a forza? Non piaccia unque a Deo.
Mal aggia chi tien donna in tale usaggio
d'amarla, poiché sa dir che l'è reo.   4
Così li fa parer d'usar oltraggio,
e da cogliere orgoglio è segno reo.
Ma eo vo' che mi prendiate a grand'agio,
e diciate, ben vegna amico meo.   8
E fior vantaggio in ciò poi non farone
che vostro pro so ch'è maggio che meo;
e maggio uom, che donna, è a ragione.
E tutto che 'l principio fosse reo,   12
simiglieria la vostra condizione
se ciascun far volesse siccom'eo.

Since you do not want me to love you, should I
take you by force? God may never allow it!
Woe to those who make such use of a woman
as to love her when she says it displeases her.   4
Men think this allows them to behave offensively,
but to be proud of it is a sign of brutishness.
I instead wish you to take me at your pleasure,
and say, "Come. You are welcome, my friend."   8
Of this, I shall take no advantage whatsoever,
for your well-being matters more than mine,
for man, as to reason, is superior to woman.
And even if such opinion were wrong,   12
your condition would be comparable [to men's],
if all were willing to behave the way I do.

Regarding line 6, in old Italian, *e* (and) often has the meaning of *ma* (but). The coherence of this sonnet, which is often dismissed as irretrievably obscure, rests on one's interpretation of the sestet, and that, in turn, hinges on the meaning given to *a ragione* in line 11. One must remember that in contemporary debates on the relative responsibility of Adam and Eve for the fall of humankind, Adam was always considered more responsible than Eve because of his greater reasoning power. Similarly, in the canzone "Ahi lasso! che li boni e li malvagi," Guittone clearly stated that God holds man guiltier than woman "because he is master and capable of wiser judgment" (*quanto e' piu sire, e maggiormente ha saggia opinione*). Hence, my reading of lines 9–11 is that the lover's thoughtful consideration for the woman's well-being is due to her being weaker than any man, mentally and otherwise. In lines 12–13, where the suppression of connectives makes the meaning difficult but not impossible to grasp, the lover goes on to say that however one might interpret that theory, women's condition could be comparable to those of men (*simiglieria la vostra condizione*) if everyone behaved toward them with consideration.

S'eo tale fosse ch'io potesse stare,
senza riprender me, riprenditore,
credo farebbi alcun om amendare
certo, al mio parer, d'un laido errore: 4
che, quando vuol la sua donna laudare,
le dice ched è bella come fiore,
e ch'è di gemma over di stella pare
e che 'n viso di grana ave colore.   8
Or tal è pregio per donna avanzare
ched a ragione maggio è d'ogni cosa
che l'omo pote vedere o toccare?
Ché natura né far pote né osa   12
fattura alcuna né maggior né pare,
for che d'alquanto l'om maggior si cosa.

Were I one who could reproach others
without first reproaching myself,
I would certainly make every man rectify
what, in my opinion, is an ugly mistake: 4
when he wants to compliment a woman,
the man tells her she is as lovely as a flower,
that she is a gem, that she looks like a star,
or that her lips have the color of carmine.   8
Now, is it a tribute to praise a woman
by saying that she is really superior
to anything a man can see or touch?
For, in fact, nature cannot and dares not   12
create a creature equal or superior
whom a man will not believe himself above.

In line 8, *grana* means "berry," hence carmine, the color of a ripe berry. In line 10, *a ragione* means "really" or "in truth." In line 13, *fattura* means "creature." In line 14, *si cosa* means "he considers himself." Guittone's consideration of the moral implications of courtship continues. Accordingly, my translation of lines 9–11 gives a reading that differs from the one given by other interpreters. They read as follows: "is it a merit to exalt this way a woman who for good reason is superior to anything that man can see or touch?" Guittone's rebuke, in that case, is understood to be addressed to the poets—more specifically, to Guinizzelli, it is believed—who used natural comparisons in their praise of women. Guittone is implying that praising them in this manner is inadequate to womanly value. My reading takes instead into consideration the fact that Guittone believed in the superiority of women no more than any of his contemporaries, and his reservations were of moral character rather than being addressed to his peers' use of poetic analogies. In other words, he is scolding men for praising women falsely. His reprimand concerns men's habit of flattering women and paying them extravagant compliment—most poets did so—when in fact, they do not have such high opinion of them. Lines 12–14 confirm this interpretation: such compliments are the more insincere and deplorable as a man invariably considers himself superior to any woman, regardless of how precious she might be or how perfect Mother Nature might have made her.

Guittone d'Arezzo, author of about 250 sonnets, was born to an influential family of Arezzo, Tuscany. He was a Guelf and strongly committed to the political life of his town. In 1265, after what today would be called a midlife crisis, he gave up love poetry, abandoned both family and political commitments, and joined the Milites Beatae Virginis Mariae—Knights of the Blessed Virgin Mary—a lay Franciscan order dedicated to establishing peace among political factions, aiding the poor, and defending women and children.

Chiaro Davanzati was the son of a Florentine cotton merchant. In 1260, he fought at Montaperti, and in 1294, he became *capitano del popolo* of the Orsanmichele district.[11] He died around 1304, leaving 122 sonnets. His style tends to be light, easy, and rich in similes. The following two poems are the conclusion of a fictitious but palpably realistic exchange between a man and a woman. The social context is middle class, and the way of conceiving love can be described as open-minded, if not amoral.

> Madonna, or provedete ad una cosa,
> ché lungiamente l'aggio udito dire:
> che buono amor non fu ned esser osa
> s'unque già mai da lui nacque partire;   4
> onde, se voi di me foste amorosa
> ed io di voi, e presine desire,
> greve pena con morte dolorosa
> volete a quella gioia convenire?   8
> Ch'al primo ch'altra donna disposasse,
> richiesine primier vostra lecenza;
> dissi che 'l vostro cor, bella, pensasse:
> mostraste che non vi fosse a spiagenza;   12
> parve perciò lo mio s'asicurasse:
> però, s'io pecco, fue vostra fallenza.

> My lady, just consider one thing:
> for a long time I have heard people say
> true love never was and never could be,
> if it allows a separation to occur;   4
> so if you were in love with me
> and I with you and took my pleasure,

do you now wish serious hurt and a bitter
ending to be inflicted on a joy so great? 8
When I promised myself to another woman,
I did first ask for your permission; I told you,
my beauty, to consider it carefully in your heart;
you gave me the impression of not minding, 12
and it seemed right to me to feel reassured:
so if I do something wrong, it is your fault.

Regarding line 6, in this context, *desire* means "pleasure." In line 9, *disponsando* indicates that the man was not yet married. What had taken place between him and another woman was the formal promise of marriage, the so-called *disponsatio*—that is, the signing of the contract between the parties with the disposition of the dowry. In line 13, *lo mio* stands for *lo mio cor*, opposed to *'l vostro cor* in line 11. Here again, the octave constitutes a well-reasoned and compact unity of meaning. The lover advances a request for not ending the affair and gives the most obvious reason: If they can still find pleasure in each other, why not meet again? Changing register, the sestet refutes the reason that might have induced the woman to withdraw her favors. Here is how she replies.

Io non dico, messer, che voi pechiate
per vostra donna amare e riverire,
né v'amonisco che da me partiate
lo vostro amor, ma solo lo disdire 4
del frutto, che più aver non lo pensate,
perch'io fallar più voglia a lo mio sire
né voi a vostra donna lëaltate:
ma buono amor cortes'è da gradire. 8
E tanto v'ho d'amarvi intendimento
che d'altro non mi piace essere amata
se non dal vostro dolze piacimento;
e poria esser ch'alcuna fiata 12
il vostro amore avria congiungimento
secondo nostra amanza ricelata.

I am not saying, sir, that you are wrong
in loving and respecting your woman;
nor am I advising you to forsake your love
for me, but rather that you give up the idea 4
of its fruit and not think about it anymore;
for I no longer wish to be unfaithful to my
husband and you to be disloyal to your wife.
Yet a good courtly love is always welcome. 8
And I feel such propensity to loving you
that I would like to be loved by no one
other but by the sweet, pleasurable you;

and it might happen sometimes that 12
your love will again reach full gratification,
with the secrecy that is due to our relation.

The gallant and oblique exchange between man and woman of courtly tradition has become a down-to-earth discussion between adulterous lovers. At first, the woman proposes a platonic relationship, but then she adds an important proviso. Her "good courtly love" (*buono amor cortese*) turns out to be simple sexual pleasure. So having reviewed the past and the present situation, the lovers consider together the possibility of future pleasurable trysts.

Most anthologies single out Chiaro Davanzati among the Tuscan followers of the Sicilian school as a master of colorful comparisons. Here is an example.

Come il castor, quando egli è cacciato,
veggendo che non pote più scampare,
lascia di quello che gli è più 'ncarnato,
e tutto il fa per più in vita regnare; 4
lo cacciator, presente l'ha trovato,
immantenente lascia lo cacciare:
così facc'io, che sono inamorato,
che lascio ogn' altra cosa per amare. 8
Ma l'amor, po' ch'io ubrio ogn'altre cose,
no lascia me, ma tienmi disïoso
de l' avenente dolze donna mia,
che mi porge le gioie dilettose; 12
e son castoro fatto argomentoso,
ca, per campar, diletto segnoria.

The beaver, while he is being hunted,
when he realizes he can no longer escape,
drops what in him is deeply implanted,
—he does all this in order not to die— 4
and the hunter, as soon as he finds it,
brings the chase to a halt at once.
I do the same: being in love, for the sake
of love, I allow all else to fall by the side. 8
But even when I forget all else, Love
does not let me be; he keeps alive in me
the longing for that sweet, beguiling woman
who holds me in thoughts of great delight: 12
so I have become a very industrious beaver,
who feigns to like tyranny in order to stay alive.

In line 3, *quello che gli è piu incarnato* are the testicles. In medieval pharmacology, the testicles of the beaver, which exude a powerful odor and can provide a kind of aromatherapy, were considered an efficacious remedy against hysterical fits. According to *Phisiologus*, a medieval treatise on animal life both real and imagined, the beaver, when chased, bites off his testicles and throws them toward the hunter in order to stop him from chasing any further. In reality, the beaver's testicles, being internal, cannot be bitten off, and the *castoreum*, the unguent extracted from them, which is used to make perfume, is found in a different gland. In line 5, *presente* means "as soon as." In line 13, *argomentoso* means "industrious" or "zealous." The description of the beaver's behavior reflects the quaint medieval view of animal life but can also be seen, according to critics with a political-social frame of mind, as the interpretation given by a member of a bourgeois society who detects in the beaver the capacity of cutting one's losses efficiently and unhesitatingly.

Il Fiore (The Flower) is a sequence of 232 sonnets written in Tuscany in the 1280s. It is the irreverent adaptation of a French best seller, *Le Roman de la Rose*, which is the story of the lengthy pursuit of a woman's love, written by Guillaume de Lorris and Jean de Leun.[12] The attribution of the Italian work remains highly controversial. The author, who called himself Sir Durante, was unquestionably a versifier of high spirits who unashamedly parodied the French text and, divesting the lover's pursuit of the symbolic and doctrinaire superstructure it had in *Roman*, revealed the real subject of the tale. In the following sonnet, Sir Durante's no-nonsense advice replaces a lengthy passage of the French text (lines 7708–94), in which Friend tells the lover how to come free of the woman's defenders—Danger, Shame, and Fear—and deal with Fair Welcome, symbol of her final condescension.

E quando tu sarai co' lei soletto,
prendila tra le braccia e fa al sicuro,
mostrando allor se tu se' forte e duro,
e 'mmamtenente le metti il gambetto.   4
Né no' la respittar già per su' detto:
s'ella chiede merzé, cheggiala al muro.
Tu le dirai; "Madonna, i' m'assicuro
a questo far, ch'Amor m'ha sì distretto   8
di vo', ched i' non posso aver soggiorno;
per che convien che vo' aggiate merzede
di me, che tanto vi son ito intorno;
ché siate certa ched i' v'amo a fede,   12
né d'amar voi già mai non mi ritorno,
ché per voi il me' cor salvar si crede.

And when you are all alone with her,
take her into your arms, do not hesitate;
and to show you are strong and determined,
quickly put your leg between her thighs.   4
Do not deign to listen to what she is saying:
if she asks for mercy, let her ask the wall.
You'll say to her: "Lady, I am quite determined
to do this, for my desire for you is driving me 8

quite mad. I no longer have a moment of respite.
You must therefore show some consideration
for me, for I have been after you far too long,
and you may be certain that I truly love you 12
and that I'll never desist from loving you,
for my heart believes that only you can save it."

Regarding line 4, Giuliani gives this reading of the line in 1, 337. In line 9, *soggiorno* means "peace." The next poem is the final sonnet of *Il Fiore*, which describes the hard-fought possession of the flower.

Per più volte falli' a lui ficcare
perciò che 'n nulla guisa vi capea;
e la scarsella ch'al bordon pendea,
tuttor di sotto la facea urtare, 4
credendo il bordon meglio far entrare;
ma già nessuna cosa mi valea.
Ma a la fine i' pur tanto scotea,
ched i' pur lo facea oltre passare. 8
Sì ch'io allora il fior tutto sfogliai,
e la semenza ch' i' avea portata,
quand'ebbi arato, sì la seminai.
La semenza del fior v'era cascata; 12
amendue insieme sì le mescolai,
che molta di buon'erba n'è po' nata.

Several times I failed to thrust it in,
for there was no way it would go inside;
while the purse hanging from the staff
continued to hit her repeatedly below 4
in the hope of making the rod to enter:
but nothing that I did was of any use.
In the end, I gave it such a shove that
I managed to make it go right through. 8
Then the flower I completely deflowered
and, having plowed the ground, the seeds
that I carried with me I did throw in.
When the flower's seeds also descended, 12
I mixed them both so well together
that a lot of good grass grew out of it.

In line 3, *bordon* and *scarsella* are the staff and the satchel carried by pilgrims. Regarding lines 12–13, according to medieval biology, the embryo came into being when the male and female seeds were mixed. In Dante's *Purgatorio* 25, the Roman poet Statius explains how the male and female "blood," the first active and the other passive, intermingled in order to create a new being (*ivi s'accoglie l'uno e l'altro insieme, l'uno disposto a patire, l'altro a fare*, 46–47). Sir Durante's unashamed description of coition corresponds to *Roman*'s allegory of protracted siege, attack, and entry into a place of worship, all embellished by a cascade of great many secondary images (lines 21,533–615 of *Roman*).

Guido Guinizzelli, lawyer and jurist of renown, enjoyed a prestigious position in the city of Bologna until 1274, when the Guelfs seized power and he was forced into exile with other members of the Ghibelline faction. For his sonnet of exile, see 1.2. He exhibited a vast range of styles, and some of them are strikingly innovative. The following is a sonnet in the analytical mode of the old school of Tuscany.

Ch'eo cor avesse mi potea laudare
avante che di voi foss' amoroso,
ed or è fatto, per tropp'adastare
di voi e di me, fero ed argoglioso;   4
ché subitore me fa isvariare
di ghiaccio in foco e d'ardente geloso;
tanto m'angoscia 'l prefondo pensare
che sembro vivo e morte v'ho nascoso.   8
Nascosa morte porto in mia possanza
e tale nimistate aggio col core,
che sempre di battaglia me menaccia;
e chi ne vòl aver ferma certanza,   12
riguardimi, se sa legger d'amore,
ch'i porto morte scritta ne la faccia.

Once I could boast I had a heart,
before I fell in love with you, but now,
the insistent squabbling between you
and me has made it fiercely despondent,   4
and drives me to change suddenly
from ice to fire, from hot to cold;
so intense and so painful is my anguish
that I look alive, but I am secretly dying.   8
A hidden death I carry within my being,
and there is rancor smoldering in my heart
that continually threatens to undo me.
Whoever wishes to ascertain it may   12
gaze at me, if he can read the signs of love,
for I carry death imprinted on my face.

In line 2, *adastare* is a Sicilian term indicating anxious insistence (Contini 2, 471). In line 8, *morto v'ho nascoso* means "I hide death under the appearance of life." In line 9, *possanza* means "potentiality," or what is within one's essence.

"Chi vedesse a Lucia un var capuzzo" is a sonnet in a light, popular style.

Chi vedesse a Lucia un var capuzzo
in cò tenere, e como li sta gente,
e' non è om di qui 'n terra d'Abruzzo
che non ne 'namorasse coralmente.   4
Par, sì lorina, figliola d'un tuzzo
de la Magna o de Franza veramente,
e non se sbatte cò de serpe mozzo
come fa lo meo core spessamente.   8
Ah, prender lei a forza, ultra su' grato,
e bagiarli la bocca e 'l bel visaggio
e li occhi suoi, ch'èn due fiamme de foco!
Ma pentomi, però che m'ho pensato   12
ch'esto fatto poria portar dannaggio,
ch'altrui despiaceria forse non poco.

Whoever has seen Lucia with a little fur hat
on her head and how winsome she looks,
no man from here to the land of Abruzzo
would fail to fall deeply in love with her.   4
Dressed up like that, she looks like the daughter
of some nob from Germany or France,
and no heart of a cut-up snake would keep
beating as furiously as now does my heart.   8
Ah! To take her by force, against her will,
and kiss her mouth and her lovely face,
and those eyes, a pair of blazing flames!
But I regret what I said, after considering   12
this could have an unpleasant consequence,
for it may displease someone not so slightly.

In line 1, *var*, or *vaio*, refers to "fur," specifically that of the gray Siberian squirrel. In line 2, *co'* is northern Italian for *capo*, meaning "head" (Marti 90). Regarding line 3, in the popular imagination, Abruzzo, a mountainous region in central Italy, stood for a strange, faraway place. In line 6, *tuzzo* intends to indicate a noble of lower rank from the other side of the Alps. Line 8 notes that when a country snake is cut in half, its two separate sections keep flopping furiously on the ground.

At a certain point in his poetic activity, Guinizzelli made a break with the old Tuscan manner and adopted a poetics and style that, in Dante's estimation, made him the precursor of the stilnovo avant-garde.[13] Here is Guinizzelli's new description of the woman.

Io voglio del ver la mia donna laudare
ed asembrarli la rosa e lo giglio:
più che stella dïana splende e pare,

e ciò ch'è lassù bello a lei somiglio. 4
Verde river' a lei rasembro e l'âre,
tutti color di fior', giano e vermiglio,
oro ed azzurro e ricche gioi per dare:
medesmo Amor per lei rafina meglio. 8
Passa per via adorna, e sì gentile
ch'abassa orgoglio a cui dona salute,
e fa 'l de nostra fé se non la crede;
e no' le pò apressare om che sia vile; 12
ancor ve dirò c'ha maggior vertute:
null' om pò mal pensar fin che la vede.

I wish to praise my woman truthfully
and compare her to the rose and to the lily.
She looks more dazzling than the morning star,
so I liken her to everything shining up above. 4
She is a verdant meadow, she is the balmy air,
a flower of any color, the yellow, the crimson,
the gold, the azure, and a precious gift of jewels:
thanks to her, Love itself becomes perfection. 8
When she walks by, she is so comely and gracious
that she humbles the pride of those she greets,
and turns them to our faith, if they don't believe;
no person that is unfeeling can approach her; 12
further, I tell you, she has an even greater power:
looking at her, no one can think offensive thoughts.

In line 1, *del ver* means "appropriately," as the woman deserves to be praised. In line 3, the star is called *diana*—from the Latin *dies*, meaning "day"—because it appears before dawn. In line 4, *somiglio* means "I find similar." In line 5, *rivera* is a Provençal word meaning "riverbank" or "meadow." In courtly theory, the feeling of love makes man gentler and kinder, but this woman, hyperbolically, makes Love himself grow more refined. In line 8, *per lei* means "through her." In line 10, *salute*, meaning "greeting," has the connotation of "good health for the soul," which implies the power to bring man's moral refinement to completion. In line 11, *fa 'l de nostra fé se non la crede* is usually interpreted as "she turns him into a Christian, if he is of another faith." Here, I believe, there is no specofic reference to Christianity but, rather, a cliché hyperbole indicating religion—to use the word *Christianity* would be automatic for a Christian—and stressing the fact that the woman can perform extraordinary things, for a conversion was thought to occur by intervention of God, hence a miracle. Other interpreters maintain *nostra fé* to be the faith of those who are initiated to love.

The poetic charge of the sonnet is mostly in the octave—that is, in the vision of the woman suffused in light and color. The acclaim, now of moral character, continues in the sestet; multiple comparisons are presented in juxtaposition to one another, and the praise gravitates through a hyperbolic variation: she has the power to destroy ill will, her greeting can perform a great miracle, and she can turn those who gaze at her into better human beings.

One cannot read Guinizzelli's praises of the woman without remembering how he defined nobility and what function he attributed to womanhood in his song "Al cor gentil rempaira sempre amore" (Love always takes refuge in the noble heart). In this doctrinal poem, the worthiness of a man, his nobility, rather than being defined in terms of lineage and social standing, is gauged in terms of intellectual and moral excellence. The woman makes the man fall in love and turns his potential for nobility into actuality. There are many images that illustrate the coexistence of love and nobility; they grow increasingly more comprehensive and luminous from stanza to stanza until they culminate in a parallel between the woman, who, present in man's heart, triggers the process of his improvement, and God, who, present in the minds of the celestial intelligences, wills them to move the heavenly spheres. These are the concepts that Dante would make his own a generation later, recognizing in the lawyer of Bologna his father and the father of other new-style poets who used sweet and graceful rhymes of love.[14]

Poets were a contentious lot. They frequently engaged in lively controversy about what the content and style of poetry should be. Given Guinizzelli's doctrinaire manner and high-flown ideology, it is not surprising that his new rhymes encountered the disapproval of some of his peers.

Bonagiunta Orbicciani, a poet of the old school, took Guinizzelli to task for forsaking the traditional style of poetry in favor of one influenced by doctrines emanating from the academic circles of Bologna.

Voi, ch'avete mutata la mainera
de li plagenti ditti de l'amore
de la forma dell'esser là dov'era,
per avanzare ogn'altro trovatore,					4
avete fatto como la lumera
ch'a le scure partite dà splendore,
ma non quine ove luce l'alta spera,
la quale avanza e passa di chiarore.					8
Così passate voi di sottigliansa,
e non si può trovar chi ben ispogna,
cotant'è iscura vostra parlatura.
Ed è tenuta gran dissimiglianza,					12
ancor che 'l senno vegna da Bologna,
traier canson per forza di scrittura.

You who have changed the manner
of our pleasant rhymes of love
by altering the style they had before,
in order to outshine all other troubadours,				4
you have behaved like a lighting torch
that brightens the corners that are dark,
but cannot shine near the highest sphere,
the one that in splendor exceeds all by far.				8
This way, you are foremost in subtlety,
and no one is found who can explain you,
so incomprehensible is the way you talk.

> Besides, it is held to be real rude audacity,
> even if your knowledge comes out of Bologna,
> to force poetry out of a scholar's writing.

In line 6, *partite*, or *parti*, refers to the places where there is no light of knowledge and it is easy to satisfy the ignorant. In line 7, *alta sfera* refers to the sun. It is supposedly a reference to Guittone, who was the leader of the Tuscan school and whom Orbicciani followed. Guinizzelli, notwithstanding his ambitious attempts—says Bonagiunta—cannot shine in the field where Guittone dominates. Regarding line 13, Bologna, a university town, was the center of philosophical and rhetorical studies, among others. Guinizzelli was prompt in replying.

> Omo ch'è saggio non corre leggero,
> ma a passo grada sì com' vol misura:
> quand'ha pensato, riten su pensero
> infin a tanto che 'l ver l'assigura.
> Foll'è chi crede sol veder lo vero
> e non pensar che altri i pogna cura:
> non se dev'omo tener troppo altero,
> ma de' guardar so stato e sua natura.
> Volan ausel' per air di straine guise
> ed han diversi loro operamenti,
> né tutti d'un volar né d'un ardire.
> Deo natura e il mondo in grado mise,
> e fè despari senni e intendimenti:
> perzò ciò ch'omo pensa non dé dire.

> A man who is wise does not run too fast;
> he proceeds gradually as restraint requires:
> he first considers, then he holds his thought
> until he has become certain of its validity.
> A fool believes to be the only one to see
> the truth, not thinking others may care for it:
> no man should think too highly of himself,
> but rather ponder his status and his nature.
> Birds of strange feathers fly in the air,
> showing different ways to go about it:
> not all of them may fly and dare the same.
> God gave a gradient order to the world of nature,
> creating diversity of intentions and capacities:
> so not all can say what others may be thinking.

In line 1, *saggio* stands for "poet." Dante uses the word in this sense both in *La Vita Nuova* 20, 3 and in *Inferno* 1, 89. In line 9, *straine* means "varied," or different from the usual way or from one another. Guinizzelli's answer to his colleague's criticism seems at first diplomatically indirect. But his rebuke turns out to be uncompromising: Bonagiunta is not able to deal with the ideas expressed by Guido's new poetry, because they require a subtlety of mind that he does not possess.

About Orbicciani, we know only that he was a citizen of Lucca and died at the end of the century. He occupies, however, an interesting nook in the history of Italian literature, because he appears in Dante's *Purgatorio* (24, 49–63), inquiring about *dolce stilnovo*, the new poetic vanguard of which he, in that episode, implicitly takes Dante to be the major representative.

In the sonnets of this section, men evaluate, moralize, or bargain about love. Women remain indefinite and faraway presences whose sole function is to bring forth men's experience and definition of love. It seems fitting, therefore, to close the section with a sonnet whose voice is female. We do not know who really penned the poem, woman or man, but the point of view is that of a woman. She is heartbroken, for her man has abandoned her for someone else. Her story of betrayal is emotionally convincing, mediated as it is by the image of the falcon that has deserted her, flying away to the more promising garden of another woman.

Tapina ahimè, ch'amava uno sparvero:
amaval tanto ch'io me ne morìa;
a lo richiamo ben m'era manero,
e dunque troppo pascer nol dovìa.   4
Or è montato e salito sì altero,
assai più alto che far nol solìa,
ed è assiso dentro a uno verzero:
un'altra donna lo tene in balia.   8
Isparvero mio, ch'io t'avea nodrito,
sonaglio d'oro ti facea portare
perché dell'uccellar fosse più ardito:
or se' salito sì come lo mare,   12
ed ha' rotti li geti e se' fuggito,
quando eri fermo nel tuo uccellare.

Alas, poor me! I so loved a falcon,
I loved him so dearly I thought I died for it.
He yielded keenly to every wish of mine,
and never did I have to feed him much.   4
Now he has soared so high and proud,
higher than he had ever flown before.
He is perched inside a luscious garden,
another woman is holding him in thrall.   8
O my dear falcon, I fed you so well;
a bell of gold I gave you to wear,
so you would be bolder in your hunting:
now you've risen higher than the tiding sea;   12

you broke your jesses and flew away,
when you seemed so firm in your pursuing.

In line 1, *sparvero* refers to any bird of prey trained for hunting. In line 3, *manero* means "domesticated," or obedient to the falconer's command. In line 5, *salito sì altero* means "soared so high." This is perhaps an allusion to the rival woman's wealth or higher social condition. In line 9, *nodrito* means "nourished," or, metaphorically, "trained for love." In line 13, the *geti*, or jesses, are the short straps of leather that bind the bird's feet to its perch. The metaphor of the domesticated falcon was common in literary and art iconography. The close bond that develops between trained falcon and falconer seemed appropriate to represent the emotional and physical pull that a man might feel toward a woman. However, while in most symbolic imagery the man is the falconer and the woman the falcon trained to obey his wishes, in this sonnet, written in a female voice, the man is represented by the bird, which, subdued and trained by one woman, has flown away and now willingly submits to the desires of another.

1.4 An Accomplished Young Woman

Compiuta Donzella is the first Italian female poet of whom we have certain information. She lived in Florence between 1250 and 1280. Of her poetic production—which, in her time, must have been of sufficient quantity and quality to make her famous—only three sonnets are now extant. They are preserved in Vatican 3793, which is the most prestigious manuscript of early Italian verse.

> A la stagion che 'l mondo foglia e fiora
> acresce gioia a tutti fin' amanti:
> vanno insieme a li giardini alora
> che gli auscelletti fanno dolzi canti; 4
> la franca gente tutta s'inamora,
> e di servir ciascun tragges' inanti,
> ed ogni damigella in gioia dimora:
> a me, n'abondan marrimenti e pianti. 8
> Ca lo mio padre m'ha messa 'n errore,
> e tenemi sovente in forte doglia;
> donar mi vole a mia forza segnore,
> ed io di ciò non ho disio né voglia, 12
> e 'n gran tormento vivo a tutte l'ore:
> però non mi ralegra fior né foglia.

> In the season that adorns the world in leaves
> and flowers, a great joy surges in all fine lovers;
> together they go about strolling in gardens,
> where little birds sing melodious songs; 4
> all courteous people become enamored,

   men come forth to serve the god of love
   and every maiden basks in happiness:
   for me, there are only tears and sorrow.   8
   This is because father has done me wrong
   and often gives cause for me to despair:
   he wants to marry me against my will.
   Of that, I have neither ambition nor desire,   12
   and I spend every moment in great distress:
   thus, I derive no joy from either leaf or flower.

In line 5, *franca* means "courteous" or "of gracious disposition," hence disposed to love. In line 8, *marrimenti* means "all sorts of sadness." The image of young men and women strolling in pairs in city gardens lends freshness to the traditional topic of spring and return of love. Compiuta's father forcing her to marry against her will adds a tangible circumstance to the worn-out topos of the young girl's lament. The feeling of resignation that pervades the sonnet goes on in opposition to the joyful scene of the opening. At the end, she repeats the springtime motif, and the sonnet reaches a symmetrical completion.

   Lasciar vorria lo mondo e Dio servire
   e dipartirmi d'ogne vanitate,
   però che veggio crescere e salire
   mattezza e villania e falsitate,   4
   ed ancor senno e cortesia morire
   e lo fin pregio e tutta la bontate:
   ond'io marito non vorria né sire,
   né stare al mondo, per mia volontate.   8
   Membrandomi ch'ogn' om di mal s'adorna,
   di ciaschedun son forte disdegnosa,
   e verso Dio la mia persona torna.
   Lo padre mio mi fa stare pensosa,   12
   ca di servire a Cristo mi distorna:
   non saccio a cui mi vol dar per isposa.

   I wish to leave this world and serve God
   and tear myself away from every vanity,
   for I see an ever increasing growth
   in madness, in falsehood, and in villainy.   4
   And I see wisdom and courtesy perish,
   together with all fine values and virtues:
   so I would want neither lord nor husband,
   nor would I live in this world, of my free will.   8

Considering all men indulge in evil,
I have become disdainful of them all,
and toward God I turn all my thoughts.
But my father causes me great distress,   12
for he prevents me from serving Christ:
to whom he wants to marry me, I do not know.

Donzella bemoans the state of the world: she sees meanness of spirit and corruption prevail all around her, but she also has personal reasons to despair. She wants to enter a convent, but her father will not allow it. These few well-distributed topical touches turn the traditional woman's lament into an appeal of poignant authenticity.

"Esser donzella di trovare dotta," a sonnet that Mastro Torrigiano addressed to Compiuta, reveals the incredulous surprise men felt in hearing of a female poet.

Esser donzella di trovare dotta
sì gran meraviglia par a 'ntendre,
ca, se Ginevra fosse od Isaotta,
ver' lor di lei se ne poria contendre;   4
ed eo fo a questa maraviglia motta,
ché ne voria da voi certezza aprendre:
ca, s'egli è ver caval sonar la rota,
ben si poria la natura riprendre.   8
Ma, se difender voglio la natura,
dirò che siate divina Sibilla
venuta per aver del mondo cura.
Ed eo ne tegno di meglior la villa,   12
e credo ch'èci meglior aventura,
che ci è aparita sì gran meravilla.

A woman skilled in writing poetry
is such an astonishing thing to hear
that if Guinevere or Isotta were here,
to them indeed she could be compared.   4
I mention this as one great wonder
because I wish to be assured by you:
for, indeed, if a horse played the rota,
one could reasonably question nature.   8
But if I were to take the side of nature,
then I should say you are the divine Sybil
who has come to take care of our world.
And I believe the city has grown richer   12
and a rare venture has befallen it,
with the presence of so great a wonder.

With regard to lines 1–4, in a sonnet not included in this volume, beginning "S'una donzella di trovar s'ingegna," Torrigiano wrote, "If a woman endeavors to write poetry and strives to excel in any profound knowledge ... one is understandably astonished, for wise men believe women to be simpletons, as no intelligence is found in them by nature." Regarding line 7, the rota was a stringed instrument similar to the zither. Comparing Donzella's talents to those of a horse playing a musical instrument adds an unintended amusing touch to what is already a rather ambiguous compliment.

Another poet, not identified with certainty but presumed to be Chiaro Davanzati, was also in disbelief when he heard of Compiuta's talents. He addressed the upcoming poem to her in order—he says—to ascertain whether her fame was deserved.

Gentil donzella somma ed insegnata,
poi c'aggio inteso di voi tant'orranza,
che non credo che Morgana la fata
né la Donna del Lago né Costanza   4
né fosse alcuna come voi presciata,
e di trovare avete nominanza,
(ond'eo mi faccio un poco di mirata
c'avete di saver tant'abbondanza),   8
però, se non sdegnate lo meo dire,
vorria venire a voi, poi non sia saggio,
a ciò che 'n tutto mi poria chiarire
di ciò ch'eo dotto ne lo mio coraggio;   12
e so che molto mi poria 'nantire
aver contìa del vostro segnoraggio.

Genteel, highly accomplished maiden,
as I heard so much of your reputation
that, undoubtedly, neither Morgan La Fe,
the Lady of the Lake, nor indeed Constance,   4
nor any other woman was praised as much,
and as you have the fame of being a poet
(so much that I feel not a little astonished
at the great abundance of your knowledge),   8
therefore, if you do not mind my saying it,
I wish to turn to you, though it may be brazen,
and thus reassure myself of your abilities,
of which I still have doubts in my heart,   12
for I know I could draw great profit
from knowing about your very excellence.

In line 1, *insegnata* means "courteous" or "well brought up." Regarding line 3, in the Breton cycle of stories, Morgana, king Arthur's sister, is often mentioned as a paradigm of beauty. Regarding line 4, *La Donna del Lago*, the Lady of the Lake, was Lancelot's teacher. Costanza is probably Costanza d'Altavilla, the Norman Sicilian princess, mother of Emperor Frederick II. In line 6, *trovare* means "to write poetry," from the Provençal *troubar*. In line 10, "venire a voi" literally means "to come to you," or to take the initiative of addressing this sonnet to her. In line 14, *aver contia* has the connotation of verifying the situation and acquiring certain knowledge. Here is Donzella's reply.

Ornato di gran pregio e di valenza
e risplendente di loda adornata,
forte mi pregio più, poi v'è in plagenza
d'avermi in vostro core rimembrata   4
ed invitate a mia poca possenza
per acontarvi, s'eo sono insegnata,
come voi dite c'aggio gran sapienza;
ma certo non ne son tanto amantata.   8
Amantata non son como vorria
di gran vertute né di piacimento;
ma, qual ch'i' sia, aggio buono volere
di servire con buona cortesia   12
a ciascun ch'ama sanza fallimento:
ché d'Amor sono e vogliolo ubidire.

O man of great value and great repute,
made resplendent by the highest fame,
I value myself more, since you consent
to keep a memory of me in your heart,   4
and since you invite my scarce ability
to give you knowledge of the capacities
and the expertise you declare I possess:
but I am certain I am not so endowed.   8
I am not endowed with as much ability
and pleasing worth as I would like;
but however it may be, I am full willing
to be of service and behave with courtesy   12
toward those who love with no deceit:
for I belong to Love and him I wish to obey.

In line 2, *risplendente* (resplendent) could be a take on the name Chiaro, which means "shining." In line 5, *a mia poca possenza* means "as far as I am able." Regarding 6, according to Contini and others after him, *acontarvi* comes from the Provençal *acointar* and means "to become your friend." I take *acontarvi* to refer back to Chiaro's *aver contia del vostro segnoraggio* in line 14 of his poem. In other words, Donzella's correspondent asked "to have knowledge" (*aver contia*) of her poetic abilities, and now she says, "I am willing to let you have knowledge [*acontarvi*] of my capacities."

Donzella carries on her correspondence with Chiaro and other fellow poets in a courtly fashion. *Fin pregio* (courtly virtue), *valenza* (worthiness), *cortesia* (courtliness), *villania* (villainy), and *fin'amanti* (courtly lovers) are all terms borrowed from the aristocratic setting of the court, and so are *piacimento* (grace, or something that pleases) and *fallimento* (without failure or deceit). When she mentions being of service to Love, she simply means to behave courteously and, therefore, to satisfy Chiaro's request of a response.

> Perch'ogni gioia ch'è rara è graziosa,
> mi son tardato, Compiuta Donzella,
> d'avere scritto a la vostra risposta,
> la qual faceste a me fresca e novella.   4
> E ben si testimonia, per la loda
> che di me usaste, che voi siete quella
> in cui altezza e gran valor riposa:
> cotal albor mostr'alto sua fior bella.   8
> Sua fiore bella e d'amare lo frutto
> mostra 'n altezza, com'è d'alto stato;
> però in gioia abbo vostro detto tutto,
> e pregovi che mi sia perdonato,   12
> s'io mi 'nvitai là ove sono al postutto,
> ch'io non son degno d'esser presentato.

> Since a pleasure is greater when rare,
> I have delayed, Compiuta Donzella,
> to write an answer to the unique
> and charming reply you sent me.   4
> The praise you bestowed on me
> clearly proves you are the very one
> in whom ability and high value rest:
> such worthy tree shows a beautiful flower.   8
> It shows a fine flower and a fruit of love
> of such merit as it befits its high standing;
> so with joy I receive every word of yours
> and pray you to forgive me for inviting   12
> myself there—where I remain—for I am not
> worthy to be brought to your presence.

In lines 1–4, Chiaro's excuse for his delayed answer sounds rather clumsy. In line 13, *là ove sono al postutto* (there, where I remain) expresses the courtly concept that the lover's or admirer's heart remains with the person he loves or admires. In line 13–14, Chiaro says, "I would not deserve to be introduced to you by anyone, let alone to take the initiative of starting a correspondence, as I have done."

While her fellow poets were hesitatingly appreciative of her, Guittone d'Arezzo was decisive in his praise of Donzella. He wrote (quoted by Monaci, 170),

> My dear gentle woman, the omnipotent God has so marvelously placed the utmost of every good in you that you seem to be more a creature of heaven than one of this earth, in fame and in fact, and in all your being… I believe it pleased Him to place you amongst us in order to make us marvel, for you to be the mirror into which every good and worthy woman and

noble man, abhorring vice and following virtue, can look into, and then take you as a model; for you are the delight, the desire, and the satisfaction of all the people who see and hear you.

1.5 An Elite of Men and Women

The boost given to the commercial and financial enterprises of the Guelfs by the debacle of the Ghibelline party made the lives and prospects of the Tuscan middle classes comfortable and optimistic. The sonneteers featured in this section were a group of friends, all members of the affluent society of the day, who shared a feeling of intellectual and moral superiority, an exclusive and special view of their being in the world, how to love, and how to write appropriately about it. Literary historians refer to them as poets of *dolce stilnovo* (sweet new style)—in abbreviated form, *stilnovo*—adopting the designation used for them by Bonagiunta Orbicciani, now a soul purging his sins in *Purgatorio* 24, 57. When Dante refers to them again in *Purgatorio* 26, 112–14, he speaks of their style that is "new" because it is expressive of the true nature of love and "sweet" because it makes an appropriate use of musically suggestive sounds and a smooth and soothing syntax.

The upcoming poem by young Lapo Gianni—Lapo di Gianni Ricevuti of Florence, who, in time, became a prominent notary-lawyer—is a *sonetto rinterzato*. It gives an idea of the view of the world that animated some young members of this Florentine group.

Amor, eo chero mia donna in domino,
l'Arno balsamo fino,
le mura di Firenze inargentate
le rughe di cristallo lastricate,   4
fortezze alt' e merlate,
mio fedel fosse ciaschedun latino;
il mondo in pace, securo 'l camino,
no mi noccia vicino,   8
e l'aria temperata verno e state;
e mille donne e donzelle adornate
sempre d'amor pregiate
meco cantasser la sera e 'l matino;   12
e giardin fruttüosi di gran giro,
con grande uccellagione,
pien di condotti d'acqua e cacciagione;
bel mi trovasse come fu Absalone,   16
Sansone pareggiasse e Salamone;
servaggi di barone
sonar vïole, chitarre e canzone;
poscia dover entrar nel cielo empiro: 20
giovane, sana, alegra e secura
fosse mia vita fin che 'l mondo dura.

Love, I would like my mistress in my sway,
the Arno made of a fragrant balm,
the walls of Florence covered with silver,
the streets paved with crystal,   4
the forts crenellated and high,
all Italians beholden to me,
the world at peace, traveling safe,
no neighbor unfriendly,   8
the weather mild in winter and summer,
and a thousand pretty women and girls,
made alluring by feelings of love,
sing with me from evening to morning;   12
and spacious orchards full of fruit,
with birds in great abundance,
with many streams and lots of fowl;
and me to be as handsome as Absalom,   16
as strong as Samson, as wise as Solomon,
and musicians, good enough for barons,
to be playing viols, guitars, and songs,
and after to be able to enter paradise,   20
but first to live fit, happy, secure, and young,
for as long as this world will be able to last.

Lapo's wide-ranging daydreaming required a much longer version of the sonnet form, a version called the double-tailed sonnet, or *sonetto rinterzato* (reinforced sonnet): AaBBbA, AaBBbA, CdDD, DdDC, EE. The sonnet is *double* because two seven-syllable lines, *a* and *b*, are inserted in each quatrain, and one seven-syllable line, *d*, is added after the first and fourth lines of the sestet; it is *tailed* because it ends with an addition of two rhyming hendecasyllables: EE. In line 1, *chero* is the verb that sustains the colorful progression of all things desired. A sense of loving contentment imbues Lapo's fantastic imaginings. The faraway quality of his imagination is a good match for the dreamy atmosphere of many stilnovo poems. Regarding line 2, the Arno is the river crossing Florence. In line 7, *camino*, meaning "road," stands for travel. The road from one city to the next was open to highway robbers. In line 13, *di gran giro* indicates an ample garden in which strollers can wander at ease. Regarding line 16, Absalom, third son of David, is described as a beautiful youth. Regarding line 17, Samson was known for his strength, and Solomon was known for his wisdom. All three biblical characters appear as symbols of their respective qualities in many contemporary texts, such as Brunetto Latini's *Tesoretto*, Boccaccio's *Amorosa visione*, and Petrarch's *Trionfi*. Regarding line 20, according to medieval cosmology, nine concentric heavens surrounded the earth, and these were encircled by the empyrean, which was the undetermined and infinite space where God, the angels, and the blessed souls resided.

Expressive of the interconnection that existed among the young stilnovo poets is "Dante, un Sospiro messagger del core," a sonnet about Lapo's love for Lagia, which Guido sent to Dante around 1284. Guido Cavalcanti (ca. 1258–1300) was the senior member of the group and already a well-known poet. He belonged to an old aristocratic family, and at the time, he was a member of the city's general council. Dante became his devoted admirer, sent him some poems for him to judge, and considered him his closest friend for years to come.

>Dante, un Sospiro messagger del core
>subitamete m'assalì dormendo,
>ed io mi disvegliai allor, temendo
>ched e' non fosse in compagnia d'Amore.   4
>Poi mi girai e vidi 'l servitore
>di monna Lagia che venìa dicendo:
>"Aiutami, pietà!" sì che piangendo
>i' presi di merzé tanto valore,   8
>ch'i' giunsi Amore ch'affilava i dardi.
>Allor l'adomandai del su' tormento;
>ed elli mi rispose in questa guisa:
>"Dì al servente che la donna è prisa,   12
>e tengola per far su' piacimento;
>e se no 'l crede, di' ch'a li occhi guardi."

>Dante, a Sigh, messenger of Love,
>assailed me suddenly in my sleep
>and I woke up, being very afraid
>that he might be in Love's company.   4
>Then I turned around and saw the lover
>of Lady Lagia, who was running and saying,
>"For pity's sake, help me!" So I too began
>to weep and, full of much concern for him,   8
>I joined Love, who was sharpening his darts.
>I asked him to tell me about Lapo's anguish,
>and he replied to me in this fashion:
>"Tell that lover that his woman is caught;   12
>I am holding her so she'll do his pleasure:
>if he doubts it, tell him to look into her eyes."

Love's message is simple: Lapo can be certain of Lagia's love for him. Guido has turned it into a sequence of interconnected actions. The personification of Sigh takes center stage, and mingling with Love and with real people—that is, with Lapo and his friend—it activates a chain of events and premonitions. Lapo is running forward, crying for help. The dreamer weeps and, running after Love, who is nearby sharpening his darts, inquires of his friend's destiny. Love's reply introduces other actions: he has caught her (she is in love, that is), and she will do what Lapo wants. Also present is the prospect that Lapo might not believe the good news, so another action is foreseen: Lapo will have to look into Lagia's eyes.

The penchant for personifying psychological faculties and staging their activities dramatically in a dreamlike atmosphere and the habit of addressing one person—here Cavalcanti addresses Dante—and talk about a third one—in this case about Lapo—are the features typical of stilnovo poetry. Onesto da Bologna, another member of the old school, would refer to these features with derision, as seen in the next section.

Characteristic of the stilnovists was a sense of constituting an elite of poets endowed with great sensibility, moral refinement, and delicacy of manners—qualities that created a sense of exceptionality and both friendly interconnection and separateness from others, as this sonnet, which Dante sent to Guido, demonstrates.

> Guido, i' vorrei che tu e Lapo ed io
> fossimo presi per incantamento
> e messi in un vasel ch'ad ogni vento
> per mare andasse al voler vostro e mio,   4
> sì che fortuna od altro tempo rio
> non ci potesse dare impedimento,
> anzi, vivendo sempre in un talento,
> di stare insieme crescesse 'l disio.   8
> E monna Vanna e monna Lagia poi
> con quella ch'è sul numer de le trenta
> con noi ponesse il buono incantatore:
> e quivi ragionar sempre d'amore,   12
> e ciascuna di lor fosse contenta,
> sì come i' credo che saremmo noi.

> Guido, I wish that you, Lapo, and I
> were taken up by a magic spell and placed
> in a vessel that with any wind would
> navigate the sea to your wish and mine;   4
> that no storms, no contrary weather
> could be of obstacle to us; but rather,
> our being in great harmony together
> would enhance the desire to live as one.   8
> I also wish the good wizard would place
> with us Lady Vanna and Lady Lagia,
> and the one found at the number thirty,
> and that we always talked about love,   12
> and each of them were so contented
> as I believe you and I surely would be.

Regarding line 9, Giovanna was the woman Cavalcanti loved, and Lagia was Lapo Gianni's beloved. Regarding line 10, in *La Vita Nuova* VI, Dante mentions a poem, now lost, in which he had celebrated the most beautiful women of Florence. On that list, Beatrice was the thirtieth woman named. Rather than simply confiding a wish to embark on a fantastic journey and escape reality, the poem expresses a need to belong—a desire for the special friendship that is possible only among similarly endowed men and women and that can be better enjoyed in undisturbed surroundings, without annoying intrusions. Guido's answer was not encouraging.

> S'io fosse quelli che d'amor fu degno,
> del qual non trovo sol che rimembranza,
> e la donna tenesse altra sembianza,
> assai mi piaceria siffatto legno.   4
> E tu, che se' de l'amoroso regno
> la' onde di merzé nasce speranza,
> riguarda se 'l mi' Spirito ha pesanza:
> ch'un prest'arcier di lui ha fatto segno   8
> e tragge l'arco, che li tese Amore,
> sì lietamente, che la sua persona
> par che di gioco porti signoria.
> Or odi meraviglia ch'el disia: 12
> lo Spirto fedito li perdona,
> vedendo che li strugge il suo valore.

> Were I the man that I was, worthy of love,
> of whom I find only a faint remembrance,
> and were my woman otherwise inclined,
> then I would like your vessel very much.   4
> You who belong in the amorous kingdom
> where there is a hope of reciprocation,
> consider how disconsolate my Spirit remains:
> an adroit archer has made it her target   8
> and with so much buoyant precision
> she bends the bow, given to her by Love,
> that she looks like the master of the game.
> Now hear the startling thing that Love requires: 12
> that my wounded Spirit ought to forgive her,
> though seeing she is destroying all his powers.

In line 8, the archer is the woman, whom Love has supplied with a dangerous weapon: the arrow of love. In line 10, *lietamente* means "happily" or "assuredly," hence with assured precision. In line 11, *gioco* is usually translated as "joy," the pleasure of love. I translate it as "game" to indicate the variable moods of love, over which the woman now has total command (*porti signoria*). Again, Guido stages the lover's anguished condition in a quick succession of dramatic actions: Love has supplied the woman with a lethal weapon, she has become a dangerous archer, and now she dominates the game of love. Finally, Love orders the man to forgive his destroyer, and the sonnet closes with the traditional paradox that love draws pleasure from the very anguish it causes. For other poems by Guido and by Dante, see 1.6, 2.2, 2.3, and 2.5.

Another member of the group was Cino dei Sigibuldi da Pistoia (1270–ca. 1336).[15] The setting of

"Come non è con voi a questa festa" suggests the evanescent landscape typical of many stilnovo sonnets, where luminous maidens move on the background of other delicate, ethereal women. The occasion is festive; the state of the speaker is one of expectant trepidation.

    Come non è con voi a questa festa,
    donne gentili, lo bel viso adorno?
    perché non fu staman da voi richiesta
    che venisse a anorare questo giorno?   4
    Vedete che ogn'om si mette 'n chesta
    per veder lei girandosi d'intorno,
    e guardano quale ave adorna vesta,
    po' miran me che sospirar no storno.   8
    Oggi aspettava veder la mia gioia
    istar tra voi, e veder lo cor meo
    che a lei come a sua vita s'appoia.
    Eo vi prego, donne, sol per Deo,   12
    se non volete ch'io di ciò mi moia,
    fate sì che stasera la vegg'eo.

    Why is not at this festival with you—
    o gentle women—that fine face of hers?
    Why did you not entreat her to come
    and bestow great honor on this day?   4
    Look how people begin to look around,
    how they turn to catch sight of her
    and see the festive dress all wear;
    then they glance at me, as I go on sighing.   8
    Today I expected to find my joy
    among you and feel how strongly
    my heart clings to her, as to its life.
    I beg you women, in God's name,   12
    if you do not wish for me to die,
    let me set my eyes on her tonight!

Cino's lyrics stand out among those of his friends for the variety of content and for his occasional aggressive way of handling the love theme. A good illustration of it is the following sonnet.

    Se conceduto mi fosse da Giove,
    io non potrei vestir quella figura
    che questa bella donna fredda e dura
    mutar facesse de l'usate prove.   4
    Aduque 'l pianto che dagli occhi piove,
    e 'l continuo sospiro e la rancura,
    con la pietà de la mia vita oscura,

nïent'è da mirar se lei non move. 8
Ma s'i' potesse far come quel dio,
'sta donna muterei in bella faggia,
e vi farei un'ellera d'intorno;
ed un ch'i' taccio, per simil desio, 12
muterei in uccel ched onni giorno
canterebbe sull'ellera selvaggia.

Even if Jupiter made it possible for me,
I could not turn into a man capable
to make this cold and obdurate woman
desist from her customary behavior. 4
Then, if the tears raining from my eyes,
my relentless sighing, my suffering,
and some pity for my dejected life
do not move her, it is no surprise. 8
But if I could do what that god once did,
I would turn this woman into a fine beech tree,
and a big ivy I would grow all over it;
by the same wish, I would change into a bird
one whom I don't mention, who, perching 12
on that savage ivy each day, would surely sing.

The reference in line 1 and line 9 is to Jupiter and to the disguises he used in order to enter the bedrooms of the women he wanted to possess. Regarding line 10, the Italian word for a beech tree is *faggio*, a masculine noun, but Cino has purposely given it a feminine ending (*faggia*). Regarding lines 9–10, Philemon and Baucis were an old couple who welcomed Jupiter into their home when he traveled through Phrygia in disguise. At the end of their life, they expressed their wish not to be separated by death, and the god, in gratitude for their hospitality, changed them into a pair of trees. In line 14, *Selvaggia*, rhyming with *faggia* above, is the name of the woman Cino loved: Selvaggia dei Vergiolesi. For other poems by Cino, see 1.6, 2.2, and 2.5.

Cino became, in time, a well-known jurist and the author of a treatise on Roman law and other commentaries on jurisprudence. He also taught at the universities of Siena, Perugia, Naples, and perhaps Florence.

1.6 Philosophy of Love

Two great intellectual and poetic personalities stand out in the stilnovo group of poets: Guido Cavalcanti (ca. 1255–1300) and Dante Alighieri (1265–1321). In love's philosophical spectrum, their positions are at the opposite ends. Cavalcanti described love as a phenomenon limited to the sensitive part of human nature, therefore entirely determined by the physics of the body, and always disturbing.

Dante turned his experience of love into a progression toward the rational knowledge of a condition that transcends human nature and reaches a degree of heavenly beatitude.

Guido Cavalcanti underscored the anguishing and elusive character of love even in his praise of the woman, as in the following sonnet.

Chi e' questa che vien ch'ogn'om la mira,
che fa tremar di chiaritate l'âre
e mena seco Amor, sì che parlare
null' omo pote, ma ciascun sospira?   4
O Deo, che sembra quando li occhi gira,
dichal' Amor, ch' i' nol savria contare,
cotanto d'umiltà donna mi pare
ch'ogn'altra ver di lei i' la chiam' ira.   8
Non si poria contar la sua piagenza,
ch'a le' s'inchin' ogni gentil vertute
e la beltate per sua dea la mostra.
Non fu sì alta già la mente nostra   12
e non si pose 'n noi tanta salute,
che propriamente n'avian canoscenza.

Who is this one coming that everyone
looks at her, who makes the light tremble
in the air and brings the god of Love with her,
so no man can speak, but only sigh?   4
O God, what is she like when she glances!
Let Love say it, for I am unable to describe it;
she appears to be a woman of such gentleness
that all others, next to her, I would call disdain.   8
What her loveliness is like no one can say,
for every genteel virtue bows to her,
and Beauty parades her as her goddess.
Our mind never rose to such a height   12
and never possessed so strong a power
as to acquire of her a proper knowledge.

In line 2, the light that the woman gives forth makes the air tremble. It is an optic effect due to the intensity of the light she emanates. In line 3, she brings Love with her—that is, she makes people fall in love. In line 7, the word *umiltà* contains the aggregate meaning of "genteel," "considerate," and "unassuming," or, simply, "gracious." Per lines 7–8, she is so gentle that in comparison, any other woman seems insufferably haughty and arrogant. Regarding line 13, in this context, *salute* means to be able to achieve a perfect understanding. Therefore, to comprehend this woman's essence requires a knowledge that is beyond the capacity of the human mind. Per line 14, her perfection is inexpressible because its in excess of man's ability to conceive and express it.

The scheme of crossed rhymes in the quatrains and the interlaced rhymes in the sestet allow

Guido's considerations a greater syntactical articulation and a more flexible rhythm. The opening question, rich in biblical suggestions—"Who is this woman that advances almost like the rising dawn, as beautiful as the moon, as extraordinary as the sun?"(*Quae est ista, quae progreditur quasi aurora consurgens, pulchra ut luna, electa ut sol?*) (Song of Songs 6:9)—is a shudder of surprise, almost of apprehension. The suspense that the opening creates continues in the second quatrain with "O God! What is she like" (*O Deo, che sembra*). Emotion blocks his faculty of speech, so for a description of her, the lover turns to Love. The first tercet describes the effect of the woman's apparition: "her loveliness cannot be described … all virtues bow before her … beauty recognizes her perfection." The recitation of the impressions she produces comes to a close with the momentous revelation that "the human mind does not have sufficient power to attain a proper knowledge of her."

For Guido, the lover's failure to articulate the praise of the woman was no simple poetic hyperbole. He explains the origin and nature of love in the doctrinal song "A woman entreats me" (*Donna me prega*). Love is a phenomenon occurring in the sensitive part of the mind that activates the faculties of perception, imagination, cogitation, and memory and where the faculties of reasoning are absent.[16] Love, therefore, is subject to instinctual drives unmonitored and independent of judgment. And because love takes place in the part of the mind where there is cogitation but where no intellectual processes take place, man cannot understand the essence of the woman and her effects on him.

Voi che per li occhi mi passaste 'l core
e destaste la mente che dormia,
guardate a l'angosciosa vita mia,
che sospirando la distrugge Amore.   4
E' ven tagliando di sì gran valore
che' deboletti spiriti van via;
riman figura sol en segnoria
e voce alquanta che parla dolore.   8
Questa vertù d'Amor che m'ha disfatto
da' vostri occhi gentil presta si mosse:
un dardo mi gittò dentro dal fianco.
Sì giunse ritto 'l colpo al primo tratto,   12
che l'anima tremando si riscosse
veggendo morto 'l cor nel lato manco.

You who, breaching the eyes, entered my Heart
and stirred the Mind who was there sleeping,
please look at this anguished life of mine,
which Love is destroying in a storm of sighs.   4
He goes on slashing with such might
that my enfeebled Spirits turn to flight;
only a Figure of me remains in place,
with a feeble Voice crying out in anguish.   8
The power of Love, which has undone me,

from your gentle eyes has swiftly come
and into my flank has hurled his dart.
So well-aimed was the shot at his first try   12
that the Soul trembled and stood upright,
seeing the Heart lie dead on the left side.

Per line 5, Love slashed his way forward like a warrior advancing among the enemies, cutting and throwing them to the ground. Per line 7, only his *figura*, the outward appearance of the lover, remained. In line 9, *virtù* means "power." In line 8, *voce alquanta* means "a thread of voice."

The Sicilians wrote about love in dry, dogmatic fashion. Guittone did it in a moralistic, argumentative way. Cavalcanti personified and activated feelings and perceptions and projected them into a drama of interlocking events. In this sonnet, the initial exhortation opens the view into an undefined and timeless enclosure: it is Aristotle and Galen's abode of man's vital faculties; it is the soul, the inner stage of the heart.[17] The woman enters with a forceful irruption, and dismay pervades the scene. Man's faculties and emotions are activated: Mind is stirred out of sleep; Life is being destroyed; the Spirits are ready to run away; Voice cries out in pain; Love slashes through, bringing about the progressive fragmentation of the self; and Heart lies down inanimate, shot through on one side. Only the lover's outward appearance remains. The power of the woman has overrun the man's psychic identity, changing love into a pathology, an uncontrollable and fateful experience.

The contrast between outward appearance and inner condition is again described in this sonnet:

Tu m'hai sì piena di dolor la mente,
che l'anima si briga di partire,
e li sospir' che manda 'l cor dolente
mostrano agli occhi che non può soffrire.   4
Amor, che lo tuo grande valor sente,
dice: «E' mi duol che ti convien morire
per questa fiera donna, che nïente
par che piatate di te voglia udire».   8
I' vo come colui ch'è fuor di vita,
che pare, a chi lo sguarda, ch'omo sia
fatto di rame o di pietra o di legno,
che si conduca sol per maestria   12
e porti ne lo core una ferita
che sia, com' egli è morto, aperto segno.

You so filled my Mind with anguish
that the Soul is getting ready to depart
and the Sighs, sent out by the grieving Heart,
outwardly show it may no longer bear it.   4
Love, who can feel your great power,
says, "It pains me that you must die
on account of this forbidding woman,
who will not hear of any pity for you."   8

I move about like one who is out of life,
one who looks, to those who see him, like
a man made of copper, or stone, or wood,
one that walks by a mechanical device,   12
one who carries in his heart a wound
that of his being dead is a clear sign.

In line 5, *tu* (you) is the woman. *Valor* is the power she exercises over him. In line 6, *convien* means "it is necessary" or "you must," which conveys the sense of an inescapable situation. In line 7, the word *fiero* implies excessive pride, tinged with cruelty and violence. In line 12, *maestria* is human artfulness; it also designates any artificial or mechanical device.

The abrupt initial address opens a hallucinatory drama. The *I* is again fragmented into a plethora of personifications: Mind, Soul, Sighs, and Heart, all caught in a frantic action activated by the woman's presence. The height of the drama is at the center of the sonnet, in the second quatrain. Here, Love announces the death sentence, and the enjambment joining lines 7 and 8 stresses its tragic effect. In the sestet, the lover, paralyzed by emotion, becomes an automaton. Now he moves like a statue made of copper, stone, or wood, an inanimate object that moves thanks to a clever mechanism hidden inside. In *Nichomachean Ethics*, Aristotle maintained that man's essence and happiness lie in the full exercise of his rationality and that when man has no control over his being, he no longer can be called a man. In "Donna me prega" 39–41, Cavalcanti succinctly wrote, "When by chance man is parted from his good—that is, from the full exercise of reason—which makes him perfect, he cannot be said to have life, for he has no firm mastery over himself" (*quando da buon perfetto tort'è / per sorte, non si può dire ch'aggia vita, / ché stabilita non ha signoria*).

There was a fanciful side to Cavalcanti's character, and it is this whimsical element that makes the following sonnet a favorite.

Noi siam le triste penne isbigottite,
le cesoiuzze e 'l coltellin dolente,
ch'avemo scritto dolorosamente
quelle parole ch' vo' avete udite.   4
Or vi diciam perché noi siam partite,
e siam venute a voi qui di presente:
la man che ci movea dice che sente
cose dubbiose nel core apparite;   8
le quali hanno destrutto sì costui
ed hannol posto sì presso a la morte,
ch'altro non n'è rimaso che sospiri.
Or vi preghiam quanto possiam più forte   12
che non sdegniate di tenerci noi,
tanto ch'un poco di pieta vi miri.

We are the sad, bewildered little quills,
the tiny scissors, the grieving, tiny knife
who in great misery have inscribed

the words you have just received.	4
Now we shall tell you why we left	
and why we came here so hurriedly:	
the hand that moved us says it feels	
fearful things appearing in his heart,	8
which have caused such devastation	
and brought the man so close to death	
that nothing of him remains but sighs.	
Now we pray you, as strongly as we can,	12
not to refuse to keep us in your presence,	
until some little pity might dawn on you.	

In line 1, Guido's personifications are the goose quills, the scissors used to cut them with, and the knife used to sharpen them. They are sad, dismayed, and grieving. They have left the lover's desk, and now, in the woman' presence, charged with whimsical self-pitying irony, they plead on his behalf. In line 4, the words that the woman has heard are the verse the poet wrote with those instruments. In line 8, *cose dubbiose* means "something frightening." *Cesoiuzze* (little scissors) and *coltellin* (tiny knife) are affectionate, prettifying diminutives of *cesoie* and *coltello*.

In the upcoming sonnet, repetition of the word *spirito* and its cognate *spiritello* generate Guido's self-mockery.[18]

Pegli occhi fere un spirito sottile,	
che fa 'n la mente spirito destare,	
dal qual si move spirito d'amare,	
ch'ogn'altro spiritello fa gentile.	4
Sentir non pò di lu' spirito vile,	
di cotanta vertù spirito appare;	
quest'è lo spiritel che fa tremare,	
lo spiritel che fa la donna umile.	8
E poi da questo spirto si move	
un altro dolce spirito soave,	
che siegue un spiritello di mercede;	
lo qual spiritel spiriti piove,	12
ché di ciascuno spirit' ha la chiave,	
per forza d'uno spirito che 'l vede.	

A subtle spirit slashes through the eyes	
and wakes another spirit in the mind;	
a spirit of love is hence aroused,	
which makes all little spirits very kind.	4
No spirit that is vile may ever feel it,	
such mighty power it appears to have;	
this is the tiny spirit that makes one tremble,	
the tiny spirit that makes the woman humble.	8

And then from this spirit another
sweet, soothing spirit starts to move,
following a tiny spirit of compassion;
from this spirit many spirits are raining, 12
because it holds the key of all the spirits,
thanks to the power of the spirit who sees.

The sonnet is a paean to love, and fittingly, the poet repeats the word *spirit* in exaltation throughout. The spirit of line 1 is the glance—the spirit that sees the woman and gives rise to the process of falling in love. In line 2, we have desire, the feeling that her sight generates. The spirit of love appears in line 3 and again in lines 6–9 and 12–13. The spirits of contentment, compassion or reciprocation, and other nonspecified feelings are mentioned in lines 10, 11, and 13. The last tercet summarizes and concludes that this is the spirit of love that generates many other feelings, thanks the power of the spirit that sees—the spirit of line 1—which has the key to all the spirits that come after.

Spirit was a technical term of medical physiology, indicating the reception and perception of sense stimulations and the interaction between body and mind. Spirits were thought to circulate throughout the human organism in the bloodstream and preside over the processes of the sensory organs and memory, imagination, and cogitation. In Cavalcanti's poetry, therefore, the vital *spiriti* and *spiritelli* are the nerve impulses that bring about physiological, emotional, and cognitive processes.

The repetition of the word *spiritello* made the sonnet of the *spiritelli* diffult to understand both for modern readers and for Guido's contemporaries. "Bagfuls of spirits" (*sporte piene di spiriti*), chided Onesto da Bologna, scornful of the abstruse, newfangled style of the stilnovo poetry.

Onesto da Bologna, or Onesto di Bonacosa di Pietro degli Onesti, by profession a moneylender, was born in Bologna between 1233 and 1242 and dead by 1303. He sent the sonnet that comes up next to Cino da Pistoia sometime in the 1280s. At the time, Cino was in Bologna, studying law under the direction of Francesco d'Accursio, a renowned jurist.

"Mente" ed "umìle" e più di mille sporte
piene di spirti e 'l vostro andar sognando,
ne fan cosiderar che d'altra sorte
non si pò trar ragion de vo' rimando. 4
Non so chi 'l ve fa fare, o vita o morte,
ché per lo vostro andar filosofando
avete stanco qualunqu'è 'l più forte,
ch'ode vostro bel dire imaginando. 8
Ancor pare a ciascun molto grave
vostro parlare in terzo con altrui,
e 'n quarto ragionando con vo' stessi.
Ver' quel de l'omo, ogne pondo è soave: 12
cangiar donque manera fa per vui;
se non ch'eo potrò dir: "Ben sete dessi!"

"Mind," "humble," and more than a thousand
bagfulls of "spirits," and your habitual dreaming,

have fully persuaded us that there is no way	
to get any sense out of your way of rhyming.	4
I do not know what makes you do it, life or death:	
because, with your ceaseless philosophizing,	
you have worn out any man however tough,	
if forced to listen to your eccentric gibberish.	8
Furthermore, intolerable remains to everyone	
your addressing one person about a third,	
and talking among yourselves about a fourth.	
But any bother is light compared to you people!	12
To change your ways is therefore a must;	
if you won't, all I can say is "you are too much!"	

Regarding line 5, the stilnovo poets seemed to be always harping about life and death. In line 8, *imaginando* refers to the dreams and visions frequently described in their poetry. In the first quatrain, Onesto criticizes the use of such stilnovo words as *mente*, *umile*, and *spiriti*, as well as the tendency to evoke dreams or visions. In the second quatrain, he addresses the stilnovists' philosophical elucubrations and, in particular, Cavalcanti's habit of addressing one person and talking about another. An example of this kind of address is in "Dante, un Sospir messagger del core" in 1.5. Regarding line 11, the Stilnovo poets actually never addressed a fourth person. *In quarto* is an additional crack at the expense of the new style, as Marti suggests. In line 12, Onesto says, "But nothing is as boring as you poets are in person!"

Cino's reply follows.

Amor che vien per le più dolci porte,	
sì chiuso che nol vede omo passando,	
riposa ne la mente e là tien corte,	
come vuol, de la vita giudicando.	4
Molte pene a lo cor per lui son porte,	
fa tormentar li spiriti affannando,	
e l'anima non osa dicer "tort'è,"	
ch'ha paura di lui soggetta stando.	8
Questo così distringe Amor, che l'have	
in segnoria; però ne contiam nui	
ch'elli sente alta doglia e colpi spessi;	
e senza essempro di fera o di nave,	12
parliam sovente, non sappiendo a cui,	
a guisa di dolenti a morir messi.	

The Love that enters by the sweetest doors	
—so intimately that no passerby can see it—	
rests in the mind, and holding court in there,	
at his will gives out his verdicts about life.	4
Big torments Love inflicts on the heart,	

great anguish and distress on the spirits;
and the soul dares not say, "It is not fair,"
so frightened it is, and so utterly downcast. 8
This is the way Love pressures the heart
into his power: of the heart we tell the story,
the pains it suffers and the frequent blows;
without any similes of animals or of vessels 12
we mostly speak, without knowing to whom,
in the guise of people in pain, destined to die.

In line 2, *sì chiuso* means "so secret." Cino emphasizes the intimate nature of love and the overpowering force that devastates the lover's soul. In line 3, *riposa nella mente* refers to the fact that love is born in the mind and from there dominates the entire person, administering justice (*tien corte*), emitting verdicts of life and death for the lovers. In line 9, *Questo* refers to the lover's heart. The grammatical subject is *Amor*. Regarding line 12, the new poets do not resort to comparisons such as those used by the Sicilian and old Tuscan schools. In line 13, as Mario Marti explains (1969, 755), Cino answers Onesto's accusation of elitism, of addressing only a few select people, by saying that on the contrary, the stilnovists intend to have universal appeal, for they address no one in particular (without knowing to whom, *non sappiendo a cui*). Their seemingly strange manner is required by the real nature of love and by a wish to describe it suitably.

Immanuel Romano (1265–1328) was a poet from the Jewish community of Rome. He was also known as Immanuel of Solomon. Cavalcanti's concept of tyrannical love seems to me to have found an effective, pragmatic description in this upcoming sonnet of his.

Amor non lesse mai l'Avemaria;
amor non tenne mai legge né fede;
amor è un cor che non ode né vede,
e non sa mai che misura si sia. 4
Amor è una pura signoria,
che sol si ferma in voler ciò che chiede;
Amor fa com pianeto, che provvede
e sempre retra sé per ogni via. 8
Amor non lassò mai, per paternostri,
né per incanti, suo gentil orgoglio;
né per tema digiunt'è, per ch'i' giostri.
Amor fa quello di che più mi doglio : 12
ché non s'attene a cosa ch'io li mostri,
ma sempre mi sa dir: "Pur così voglio."

Love has never read any Hail Mary;
Love never respected religion or law;

love is a heart that neither hears nor sees,
and always ignores what measure may be. 4
Love is a simple and pure tyranny,
resolute in exacting what it demands,
like a planet that exerts its influence
and, afterward, removes itself entirely. 8
Love never gave in, neither for any paternoster
nor for enchantments—that's his privilege!—
nor can I frighten him into surrender, as hard as I try!
Love does something I most dislike: 12
he is unimpressed by anything I show,
and persists in saying, "I still want it so!"

Regarding line 1, the *Avemaria*, or Hail Mary, is the prayer to the Virgin Mary. The implication is that passion has no respect for religious feelings. In line 7, the mention of a planet's influence on humans could be a memory of lines 15–20 of "Donna me prega," in which Cavalcanti describes love as the effect of the malign influence of the planet Mars. A reminder of Guido's seems also to be Romano's use of a rhetorical figure of repetition, the anaphora: *amor* is repeated at the beginning of the first three lines and then at the beginning of each stanza. For more sonnets by and about Romano, see 2.3 and 2.5.

Dante told the story of his love for Beatrice in *La Vita Nuova*. This booklet in verse and prose, written in 1295, celebrates the changes that love produced in him and how love made his life new, meaning unprecedented and extraordinary, as the title indicates. Dante's epiphany occurred at the moment he realized that only a disinterested love based on reason and independent of changing circumstances can lead to spiritual and emotional well-being. Eschewing all forms of debilitating passion, he therefore decided to write for Beatrice only verse of praise and, abjuring his imitation of Cavalcanti's poetry, resolved to do so in a style—as he explains to Bonagiunta in canto 24 of *Purgatorio*—that is melodious, soothing, and, therefore, appropriate to the nature of real love.

The following sonnet of *La Vita Nuova* epitomizes the praise of Beatrice, the bearer of Dante's well-being.

Tanto gentile e tanto onesta pare
la donna mia quand'ella altrui saluta,
ch'ogne lingua deven tremando muta,
e li occhi no l'ardiscon di guardare. 4
Ella si va, sentendosi laudare,
benignamente d'umiltà vestuta;
e par che sia una cosa venuta
da cielo in terra a miracol mostrare. 8
Mostrasi sì piacente a chi la mira,
che dà per li occhi una dolcezza al core,
che 'ntender no la può chi no la prova:

e par che de la sua labbia si mova
un spirito soave pien d'amore,
che va dicendo a l'anima: "Sospira!"   12

So gentle and so becoming my lady
appears when she gives out her greeting,
that all tongues tremble and fail to speak,
and no one dares to rest an eye on her.   4
Hearing herself be praised, she walks on,
enfolded in benign and gracious modesty;
she appears as something that from heaven
has descended to earth to show a miracle.   8
She looks so lovely to those who see her
and, through the eyes, gives their hearts a joy
that cannot be imagined, if not known before;
and from her lips there seems to move   12
a spirit that soothes, one so filled with love,
that to the soul goes on repeating, "Sigh!"

The word *gentile*, used in line 1, contains a range of meanings. In courtly circles, *gentile* meant "noble," in the sense of aristocratic lineage. In the urban culture of the commune, it indicated those qualities of civility and refinement that supposedly always accompanied an elevated social position. In the poetics of the stilnovo—as Contini's linguistic exegesis of the sonnet, which I follow here, specifies—the term is a key word connoting gentleness, modesty, and nobility of mind. It can also mean the innate state of moral and mental refinement that only a superior kind of love may inspire. *Onesta* has almost the same meaning as *gentile*, but with a connotation of external comeliness, dignified demeanor, and elegance of manners. In line 3, *donna*, which I translate as "lady" and not as "woman," retains the original Latin meaning of "mistress [of the household]," in this case "mistress of the man's heart." Line 6 literally means "benignly dressed with humility." It indicates, in other words, the effect that being *gentile* and *onesta* has on Beatrice's demeanor. Regarding line 7, Beatrice is a heavenly vision. *Pare* of line 7 does not have the meaning of "she seems" but, rather, of "she appears," or "she manifests herself," with an accent on the idea of apparition. In line 8, *da cielo in terra* (from heaven to earth) adds a religious connotation to the whole experience: Beatrice's apparition suggests a divine presence. In line 13, *labbia* is a synecdoche indicating the whole physiognomy, the lineaments of the face. In line 14, *va dicendo* is "saying with insistence." In this atmosphere of love, a spirit moves from the figure of Beatrice and invites the onlookers to sigh.

The sonnet moves slowly with a balanced pace. The linear syntax creates a tone of gentle tranquility. Beatrice appears at the center, in the second quatrain. Her apparition unfolds under our eyes and slides by in slow motion. According to Contini, Dante is not interested in describing that vision; rather, he seeks to describe the impression Beatrice makes on the people around her. The sestet gives the reason for it: Beatrice is a creature from heaven; she is ineffable, and in her presence, all the onlookers can do is sigh.

Beatrice died in 1290. In "Un dì si venne a me Malinconia," we find an animated, multiaction scene infused with the foreboding of the beloved's death.

Un dì si venne a me Malinconia
e disse: "Io voglio un poco stare teco;"
e parve a me ch'ella menasse seco
Dolore e Ira per sua compagnia. 4
E io le dissi: "Partiti, va via;"
ed ella mi rispose come un greco:
e ragionando a grande agio meco,
guardai e vidi Amore, che venia 8
vestito di novo d'un drappo nero,
e nel suo capo portava un cappello;
e certo lacrimava pur di vero.
Ed io li dissi: "Che hai, cattivello?" 12
Ed el rispose: "Io ho guai e pensero,
ché nostra donna mor, dolce fratello."

One day Melancholy came to me
and said, "I want to stay with you awhile,"
and it seemed to me that in her
company also arrived Anger and Grief. 4
To her I said, "Leave, go, go away!"
and she answered to me like a Greek.
As she lingered and was talking to me,
I looked up and saw that Love was coming: 8
I saw he was wearing a black new cloak
and a dark mourning cap on his head,
and indeed he was weeping abundantly.
I said to him, "Poor fellow, what is wrong?" 12
And he replied, "I am fretful and distressed,
for, sweet brother, our woman is near death."

In line 1, Melancholy is the choleric melancholy of medieval medicine. Regarding line 6, *come un Greco* (like a Greek) was a proverbial expression that meant "with discourteous haughtiness." Per lines 9–10, Love's mantel is new—that is, different—because it is in mourning black. The hat too is a sign of bereavement. The sonnet describes an animated, multiaction happening as arbitrary and disturbing as any Cavalcantian dream—but not a tragic one. The tone is familiarly discursive and lacks the sacramental significance that the poet considered appropriate to the story of Beatrice. Significantly, the sonnet was not among the poems he chose to include in the narrative of *La Vita Nuova*. In that work, Beatrice's death takes on a feeling of a communal misfortune, almost of a supernatural happening.

Deh peregrini che pensosi andate,
forse di cose che non v'è presente,
venite voi da sì lontana gente,
com' a la vista voi ne dimostrate, 4

che non piangete quando voi passate
per lo suo mezzo la città dolente,
come quelle persone che nëente
par che 'ntendesser la sua gravitate? 8
Se voi restaste per volerlo audire,
certo lo cor de' sospiri mi dice
che lagrimando m'uscireste pui.
Ell' ha perduta la sua bëatrice; 12
e le parole ch' om di lei pò dire
hanno vertù di far piangere altrui.

O pilgrims, who walk by deeply thinking
perhaps of things that are not here,
are you coming from lands so far away
—as it seems by looking at you— 4
that do you not weep, while you travel
through the center of this desolate city,
like people who seem to understand
nothing of what causes its great distress? 8
If you cared to stop awhile and listen,
—my sighing heart tells me—afterward you
would certainly depart from here in tears.
The city has just lost its Beatrice, 12
and the words one could say about her
have the power to make all people weep.

In line 6, *per lo suo mezzo* means "through the center of town," or along the street where stood the houses of Beatrice's family, the Portinari. In line 8, the word *intendere*, meaning "to know" or "to understand," indicates an act of the intellect that is nearer to the mystical intuition than to the common faculty of reasoning. It was the time before Easter. Christianity was mourning the death of Christ, and as Dante explains in the prose section (*La Vita Nuova* XL, 7.1), pilgrims were passing through Florence to go to Rome to see the Veronica. The Veil of Veronica, it is believed, is the cloth with which a woman by that name wiped the face of Christ as he walked toward Calvary.

The Italian text has the slow movement and desolate tone of Jeremiah's lamentations. Its sacramental sources suggest a parallel between the death of Beatrice and the passion of Christ. One source is Luke 24:18–19: "Are you the only pilgrim in Jerusalem who does not know what has happened here these days?" (*Tu solus peregrinus es in Jerusalem, et non cognovisti quae facta sunt in illa his diebus*), Cleopas asks Christ after the resurrection. Other sources are Lamentations 1:1, which says, "How solitary is the city" (*Quomodo sedet sola civitas*), and Lamentations 1:12, which says, "All of you who pass by, pay attention and see if there is any grief as strong as mine" (*O vos omnes, qui transitis per viam adtendite et videte si est dolor sicut dolor meus*). The city of Florence is immersed in an atmosphere of tragic hallucination. The streets are deserted but for the pilgrims passing through. Beatrice's death is not simply the cause of a personal grief; it has become a public loss. She was a heavenly creature, and the heavens have reclaimed her. The poem closes with a final hyperbole: even the words that people utter in reference to her death can make people weep.

Oltre la spera che più larga gira
passa 'l sospiro ch'esce dal mio core;
intelligenza nova, che l'Amore
piangendo mette in lui, pur su lo tira.   4
Quand' elli è giunto là dove disira,
vede una donna, che riceve onore,
e luce sì, che per lo suo splendore
lo peregrino spirito la mira.   8
Vedela tal, che quando 'l mi ridice,
io no lo intendo, sì parla sottile
al cor dolente, che lo fa parlare.
So io che parla di quella gentile,   12
però che spesso ricorda Beatrice,
sì ch'io lo 'ntendo ben, donne mie care.

Beyond the widest circling sphere
goes a Sigh that issues from my heart;
a new intelligence, which Love, weeping,
has instilled in him, pulls it up and up.   4
When he has arrived where he desires,
he sees a woman receiving so great an honor
and so dazzling appearing, that the pilgrim
Spirit gapes at her, through her splendor.   8
He sees her to be such that when he tells me,
I do not comprehend, so subtly he speaks
to my grieving heart, which urges him to say.
But I know he speaks of that noble one,   12
because to me he often mentions Beatrice;
this I understand well, my beloved women.

Regarding *la spera che più larga gira* in line 1, in medieval cosmology, the "widest sphere" is the uppermost and outermost sphere of the nine spheres that surround the earth. Beyond them is the empyrean, the space enveloping the whole world, as it was then known. In the empyrean are God, the blessed souls, and the saints. The poetic charge of the sonnet is in this opening, in that glimpse into infinity, in the visionary movement that goes beyond the ninth heaven and ascends into the empyrean, moving toward God. In line 2, Sigh (*sospiro*), here personified, is a metonymy for deep thought. In lines 3–4, Love is weeping for Beatrice's death, in sympathy with Dante. The "new intelligence" (*intelligenza nova*) connotes a capacity of intuition that is out of the ordinary. The poet posits a difference between reason and understanding, the latter being nearer to mystical intuition than to the human rational faculty. In line 7, *e luce sì* means "it shines so." In *The Divine Comedy*, the heavenly souls appear as lights; they are not delineated as figures. In line 8, *lo peregrino spirito* means "the pilgrim Spirit"—that is, the Sigh of line 2. In line 9, *sottile* means "subtle" or "difficult to understand." In line 12, the subject of *parla* (speaks) is Sigh, the pilgrim spirit.

In the commentary to the poem, Dante explains that being unable to penetrate the essence (*qualitate*) of the woman, he could not fully understand what she really was (to penetrate *là ove lo pensero mi trae, cioè, a la sua mirabile qualitate*), but he was able to intuit her presence. Cecco Angiolieri did not see, or pretended not to see, this distinction when—in the upcoming poem—he mockingly reproached Dante for contradicting himself.

This is the last sonnet of *La Vita Nuova*. In the prose commentary, Dante announces that he will not write again about Beatrice until he is able to say of her what has never been said about any woman before. In *The Divine Comedy*, Beatrice would appear as the angelic intelligence who intercedes for his salvation and meets him in paradise. At the completion of his journey and his poem, Dante would have a vision of the universe, God, and the Trinity. Everything is revealed to him in a flash of light that does not last, but the effect will remain forever (*Paradiso* 33, 141–44). Thus, Guinizzelli's simile of the woman-angel presiding over man's progress toward a true nobility of the heart became, for Dante, an ontological discovery of universal religious validity.

Was the following sonnet by Cecco Angiolieri a prankish tease, or was Cecco seriously quibbling at the apparently contradictory claim that Dante had made in the poem above?

Dante Allaghier, Cecco, i' tu' serv'amico,
si raccomand' a te com' a segnore:
e sì ti prego per lo dio d'Amore
il qual è stat' un tu' signor antico,   4
che mi perdoni s'i' spiacer ti dico,
ché mi dà sicurtà 'l tu' gentil cuore:
quel ch'i' vo' dire è di questo tenore,
ch'al tu' sonetto in parte contradico.   8
Ch'al meo parer nell'una muta dice
che non intendi su' sottil parlare,
di que' che vide la tua Beatrice;
e poi hai detto a le tue donne care   12
che tu lo 'ntendi; e dunque contradice
a sé medesmo questo tu' trovare.

Dante Alighier, Cecco, your servant friend,
recommends himself to you as to a lord:
I pray you, in name of that god of Love
that has been your master for so long,   4
forgive me if I say something untoward,
for your noble heart reassures me on it.

> What I mean to say is of this tenor:
> to a part of your sonnet I must object.   8
> In my opinion, in one tercet, it says
> you do not understand the subtle speech
> of him who has seen your Beatrice;
> then you say, to your beloved women,   12
> that you understand it well; therefore
> this sonnet of yours contradicts itself.

Cecco ostensibly takes Dante to task for saying in line 10, "I do not comprehend, so subtly he speaks" (*io non lo intendo, sì parla sottile*), and then for saying in line 14 that after all, he understands it well (*io lo 'ntendo ben*). In the prose commentary of *La Vita Nuova*, Dante gave a meticulous explanation of the apparent contradiction.[19] We know that Dante wrote the prose sections of *La Vita Nuova* when some poems were already in circulation. Cecco, therefore, if he read the sonnet without the prose explanation, might have made his objections in all seriousness—so most critics contend. Whatever the case, the sonnet begins with a mock submission to Dante's superiority. A tease is also detectable in the dubious plea he makes in the name of the god of Love, zeal scarcely credible in the scoffing Cecco. The reference is to the story Dante told in *La Vita Nuova* of having fallen in love with Beatrice when he was nine years old (see the sonnet "Io sono stato con Amore insieme" in 2.2). Cecco's teasing continues to the end, to "your beloved ladies" (*le tue donne care*) in line 12, which repeats Dante's "my beloved women" (*donne mie care*), and is also a reminder of the many pleas the Stilnovo poets advanced to their friends and women. Cecco's cheeky mimicry and quibbling on Dante's logic have a clear demystifying effect on Dante's exacting metaphysics of love and on the quasimystical affectations of many of his friends.

1.7 In a Satirical Vein

Scholars refer to the poems of this section alternatively as realistic, jocose, or satirical. Rather than realistic, their descriptions are hyperbolic, parodic, and, at times, fiercely grotesque. They cannot collectively be called jocose, because they are often bitterly sarcastic and intentionally destructive. Their common and most prevalent trait is satire. In most cases, they satirized people in good humor, making fun of common values and conformist attitudes.

Above all, they eschewed courtly manners. They replaced the pursuit of moral perfection that inspired many high-style poets with an avowed dedication to vice. They substituted the philosophical considerations about love with unabashed descriptions of sex, at times in their coarsest manifestations. With their reports of wayward behavior and with the occasional use of lewd terms, they intended to amuse and provoke in disregard of moral customs and in defiance of the authorities.

The best known among the thirteenth-century satirical poets is Cecco Angiolieri. Angiolieri was born in Siena around 1260 to an old and God-fearing family of small bankers.[20] He fought in the Arezzo War of 1288, and one year later, he was at Campaldino when the Guelfs defeated the Ghibellines.

Here is a parodic counterimage of the courtly woman.

La mia malinconia è tanta e tale,
ch'i' non discredo che, s'egli 'l sapesse
un che mi fosse nemico mortale,
che di me di pietade non piangesse.   4
Quella, per cu' m'aven, poco ne cale,
che mi potrebbe, sed ella volesse,
guarir 'n un punto di tutto 'l mie male,
sed ella pur: "I' t'odio" mi dicesse.   8
Ma quest' è la risposta c'ho da lei:
ched ella non mi vol né mal né bene,
e ched i' vad' a far li fatti miei,
ch'ella non cura s'i' ho gioi' o pene   12
men ch'una paglia che le va tra' piei.
Mal grado n'abbi Amor, ch'a le' mi diène.

My melancholy is so deep and such
that I have no doubts that even a mortal
enemy of mine, if he knew about it,
would weep out of pity for me.   4
The woman that causes it cares not
one bit; the one who in a single moment
could cure me, if she wished, of all my ills,
if she would simply say, "I hate you."   8
But this is the answer I get from her:
that she neither hates me nor loves me;
that I ought to go about my business,
for she cares for my happiness or distress   12
less than for a straw lying between her feet.
Cursed be Love, who has given me to her!

Regarding line 1, medieval science defined *melancholy* as the dark mood brought about by the frustration of desire. The whole sonnet—more openly, the first quatrain—makes fun of concepts typical of courtly love: the personification of love, the lover's pitiful condition, the sympathy of the onlooker, the curing power of the beloved, and Love's arbitrary decision over the man's destiny. The woman makes her appearance in the second quatrain, ideally and stylistically reversing the traditional image of the beloved. In contrast to the silent, gentle demeanor of the stilnovo lady,[21] Cecco's woman is aggressively and contemptuously outspoken. She cares not a fig about him and tells him to bugger off. The dynamic of the sonnet is all in the contrast between the ideal and the real situation, between the courtly veneer and the down-to-earth relationship of Cecco and his mistress. Even the final curse is the opposite of the courtly declaration of total submission to Love.

"Becchin' amor!" "Che vuo', falso tradito?"
"Che mi perdoni." "Tu non ne se' degno!"
"Merzé, per Deo!" "Tu vien' molto gecchito."

"E verrò sempre." "Che saràmi pegno?"   4
"La buona fe'." "Tu ne sei mal fornito."
"No inver di te." "Non calmar, ch'i' ne vegno."
"In che fallai?" "Tu sa' ch'i' l'abbo udito."
"Dimmel' amor." "Và, che ti veng' un segno!"   8
"Vuo' pur ch'i' muoia?" "Anzi, mi par mill'anni."
"Tu non dì bene." "Tu m'insegnerai."
"Ed i' morrò." "Omè, che' tu m'inganni!"
"Die te 'l perdoni." "E ché, non te ne vai?"   12
"Or potess'io!" "Tegnoti per li panni?"
"Tu tieni 'l cuore." "E terrò co' tuo' guai."

"Becchina, my love!" "What you want, devious traitor?"
"To be forgiven." "You don't deserve it."
"Have pity, by God!" "Aren't you ever so humble!"
"I shall always be!" "What will be the guarantee?"   4
"My good faith." "Of it, you are badly provided."
"Not toward you." "You don't fool me, I have proof."
"What did I do wrong?" "You know what I heard!"
"Tell me, love." "Go away, may the plague get you!"   8
"Are you sure you want me dead?" "I can't wait."
"These are not nice things to say!" "Then you'll teach me."
"Then I will die." "Too bad, you are only fooling me!"
"May God forgive you!" "Well? Aren't you going?"   12
"I wish I could!" "Am I holding you by the coat?"
"You hold my heart!" "I shall keep it and torment it."

The galloping rhythm of the sonnet is due to the swiftly paced dialogue between the poet-lover and Becchina, as the two modify their stance in response to the reaction each provokes in the other. Becchina, diminutive of Domenica, was the daughter of a leather worker named Benci (Contini 2, 373). In line 8, *che ti veng' un segno* may mean either "may you get a disease that leaves a sign" or "may you get a disfiguration as a sign that God has marked you out." The picture Cecco gives of himself as the suffering lover is not to be taken too seriously if he wrote the sonnet that follows.

I' sono innamorato, ma non tanto
che non men passi ben leggeramente;
di ciò mi lodo e tegnomi valente,
ch'a l'Amor non son dato tutto quanto.   4
E' basta ben se per lui gioco e canto
e amo e serveria chi gli è servente:
ogni soperchio val quanto niente,
e ciò non regna in me, ben mi dò vanto.   8
Però non pensi donna che sia nata
che l'ami ligio com'e i' veggio molti,

sia quanto voglia bella e delicata,
ché troppo amare fa gli omini stolti; 12
però non vo' tener cotal usata,
che cangia 'l cor e divisa gli volti.

I am in love, but not so much as not
to be able to adjust to it comfortably;
with that I am pleased, for it is commendable
not having surrendered to Love entirely. 4
It is all right for me to play and sing for love,
and I will love anyone who in turn will love me,
but all exaggeration isn't worth a farthing:
that is not for me, and I pride myself for it. 8
Therefore, no woman in the world should think
that I might love as meekly as I see many do,
no matter how fine and delicate she may be,
because too much loving turns men into dunces: 12
so I will not follow a custom that disfigures
a man's features and turns around his heart.

Tre cose solamente m'ènno in grado,
le quali posso non ben ben fornire:
cioè la donna, la taverna e 'l dado;
queste mi fanno il cuor lieto sentire. 4
Ma sì me le convene usar di rado
ché la mie borsa mi mett' al mentire;
e quando mi sovien, tutto mi sbrado,
ch'i perdo per moneta 'l mie desire. 8
E dico: "Dato li sia d'una lancia!"
ciò a mi padre, che mi tien sì magro,
che tornere' senza logro di Francia.
Ché fora a torli un dinaro più agro 12
la man di Pasqua che si dà la mancia,
che far pigliar la gru ad un bozzagro.

Three are the only things that please me,
but in these likings I am not able to indulge:
they are women, the tavern, and the dice;
these are the things that gladden my heart. 4
Such pleasures are for me forcibly rare,
for the pocketbook gives me the lie;
for lack of money, I lose what I desire,

and thinking of it, I fall into black despair.   8
I say, "May he be pierced through with a lance!"
That is my father, who keeps me so squeaky thin
that with no loss of weight I could walk from France.
It is harder to snatch a penny from his hand   12
on Easter Sunday, when people give out tips,
than forcing a small kestrel to bring down a crane.

In line 11, I read *senza logro* (from *logorare*, meaning "to wear out") as "with no loss of weight," which is consistent with *mi tien sì magro* (he keeps me so thin) of the previous line. On the other hand, since *logro* is also the lure that the falconer displays in order to make the hawk fly down onto his arm, the line could mean—as Marti reads—that Cecco is so thin that like a hungry hawk, he would fly down for a morsel without a *logro*—that is, without any enticement.

The leitmotif of wine, women, and dice reminds us of the *clerici vagantes*, the medieval university students, and that wandering goliard of all goliards, the Archipoet's profligate persona who sings in the *Carmina Burana*, "Estuans intrinsecus ira vehementi."[22] Cecco's irreverent bravados are generally considered more a literary stance than a real indication of character. Even so, he must have chosen the models that would best express his general attitude or his moods of the moment. In Pazzaglia's view, the character of the sonnet and its use of slang—*ben ben* and *mett' al mentire*—suggest a story told in a tavern to a group of friends by someone who, to force laughter out of his listeners, makes fun of himself by exaggerating a great deal.

Per sì gran somma ho 'mpegnato le risa,
ched io non so vedere come possa
prendere modo di far la rescossa:
per piu l'ho 'n pegno che non monta Pisa.   4
Ed è sì forte la mia mente asisa,
che prima me lasserei franger l'ossa,
che ad un sol ghigno eo facesse la mossa,
tanto sono da' spiriti 'n recisa.   8
L'altrier un giorno sì me parve en sogno
un atto fare che rider volesse:
svegliaimi; certo ancora me 'n vergogno.
E dico fra me stesso "Dio volesse   12
ch'i' fusse 'n quello stato ch'i' mi pogno,
ch'uccidere faria chiunca ridesse!"

For such a high figure I pawned my laughter
that I do not see how I will ever be able to find
a way to redeem it: for I pawned it for a greater
sum of money than the entire worth of Pisa.   4
My mind is so strongly set on this decision

that I would let someone crush my bones, rather
than make the mere suggestion of a grimace,
so far removed I am from any cheery mood.   8
In a dream, the other night, I thought I was
almost on the point of wanting to crack a smile.
I woke up and, even now, I feel ashamed of it.
Besides I say to myself, "Should I, God willing,   12
become as powerful as I would like to be,
I would order to execute anyone who laughs!"

Cecco has renounced all happiness—he has taken his merriment to the pawnshop—and his resolution not to be happy is so unshakeable that he would rather receive a good thrashing than feel even the slightest temptation to laugh. He dreamed that he was on the point of making the slightest grimace of a smile, when the overpowering guilt woke him up abruptly. A wishful thought closes the sonnet: were he to gain absolute power, he would have all those who laugh put to death.

S'i' fosse fuoco, arderei 'l mondo;
s' i' fosse vento, lo tempesterei;
s'i' fosse acqua, i' l'annegherei;
s'i' fosse Dio, mandereil' in profondo.   4
S'i' fosse papa, sare' allor giocondo,
ché tutt' i cristiani imbrigherei;
s'i' fosse 'mperator, sa' che farei?   8
a tutti mozzarei lo capo a tondo.
S'i fosse morte, andarei da mio padre;
s'i' fosse vita, fuggirei da lui:
similmente farìa da mi' madre.   12
S'i' fosse Cecco, com'i' sono e fui,
torrei le donne giovani e leggiadre,
e vecchie e laide lasserei altrui.

If I were fire, I would burn the world,
if I were wind, I would blow it away;
if I were water, I would let it drown;
if I were God, I would dash it into hell.   4
Were I the pope, I would then be glad,
for all the Christians I would distress;
were I emperor, guess what I would do:
I would chop their heads all around!   8
If I were Death, I would go to my father;
If I were Life, I would run away from him;
the same I would do with my mother.

If I were Cecco, as indeed I was and am, 12
I would take the young and pretty women,
the old and ugly I would leave to others.

The subject matter appears right away so obviously deviant that the neat organization of content passes almost unnoticed. In the first quatrain, Cecco fancies exercising natural and divine powers; in the second, he slides from the supernatural to the politically mundane. In the first tercet, superhuman powers, those of life and death, are at his command, and in the closing one, he is again on personal territory. The rhythm slows down correspondingly, gradually revealing his threats to be a rambunctious bluff, and the sonnet ends in a cheeky joke.

Li bon parenti, dica chi dir vole,
a chi ne pò aver, sono i fiorini:
quei son fratei carnali e ver cugini,
e padre e madre, figliuoli e figliuole. 4
Quei son parenti che nessun sen dole,
bei vestimenti, cavalli e ronzini;
per cui t'inchinan franceschi e latini,
baroni, cavalier, dottor de scole. 8
Quei te fanno star chiaro e pien d'ardire,
e venir fatti tutti i tuoi talenti,
che se pòn far nel mondo over seguire.
Però non dica l'omo: "E' ho parenti," 12
ché s'e' non ha denari, e' pò ben dire:
"E' nacqui come fungo a tuoni e venti!"

The good relatives, say what you will,
are the florins—if you can have them:
they are blood brothers and true cousins,
father and mother, sons and daughters. 4
They are the relatives no one regrets,
they are fine clothes, race and pack horses;
to them Italians and French will bow, so will
barons, knights, and doctors of philosophy. 8
They'll make you famous, proud, and daring;
They will make real all your potentialities,
whatever you wish to pursue and procure.
So nobody ought to say, "I do have relatives!" 12
if he has no money, he may well say, "I was born
exposed to wind and thunder, like a mushroom!"

The rebelliousness and the blaspheme of the goliards might have inspired Cecco's verse; nonetheless, the tenor of his life makes us suspect that what he wrote was largely autobiographical. Documents refer to an unruly life and to reprimands for questionable military behavior, participation in brawls, and the dissipation of inherited patrimony. When Cecco died around 1312, his sons renounced their inheritance because it was overburdened by debts. Whatever his personal circumstances, Cecco's sonnets and those of poets of similar bent offer a plausible impression of the times in which they lived and, implicitly, of society's conventions and basic values.

Rustico Filippi, or Rustico di Filippo (ca. 1235–ca. 1300), was born into a Florentine family of the merchant class. He was, as we saw in 1.2, a fierce Ghibelline. His satire—fifty-eight sonnets of his are extant—have a clear antecedent in the Roman satirical tradition. The outrageous verse he wrote about women and well-known citizens of Florence, usually of the Guelf party, is unquestionably in the manner of the Roman *vituperium*, but its mischievous irony and power of topical description transcend all possible models.

> Quando Dio messer Messerino fece,
> ben si credette far gran maraviglia,
> ch'uccello e bestia ed uom ne sodisfece,
> ch'a ciascheduna natura s'apiglia: 4
> ché nel gozzo anigrottol contrafece,
> e ne le ren giraffa m'asomiglia,
> ed uom sembia, secondo che si dice,
> ne la piagente sua cera vermiglia.   8
> Ancor risembra corbo nel cantare,
> ed è diritta bestia nel savere,
> ed uomo è sumigliato al vestimento.
> Quando Dio il fece, poco avea che fare, 12
> ma volle dimostrare lo suo potere:
> sì strana cosa fare ebbe in talento.

> The day God created Sir Messerino,
> he knew he was performing a miracle;
> at one blow he pleased man, bird, and beast,
> for the man takes after the nature of each.   4
> In the goiter, he imitates a duckling;
> around the waist, he looks like a giraffe;
> and in his purple cheery face, if we believe
> what they say, he looks almost like a man.   8
> When he sings, he sounds like a crow;
> as to his mind, he is an authentic beast;
> and in the way he dresses, he's almost human.

When he made him, God had little else to do 12
and it pleased him to show his power: such fancy
took him to produce a creature as weird as this!

With regard to 1, Messerino has been identified with an Albizzo dei Caponsacchi who died in 1279. A Latin document refers to him as *dominus Messerinus*. *Gran meraviglia* (great marvel) in line 2 and *piagente cera* (pleasant complexion) in line 8, used here derisorily, are common terms in the courtly praise of women. Messerino had apparently an ugly reddish face. In line 10, *savere* indicates the man's intellectual powers and overall judgment. Per line 11, Messerino is a marvel—a monstrosity, in fact—created by the Almighty when, in order to fight off boredom, he brought to life a creature that combined the features of more than one species.

Oi dolce mio marito Aldobrandino,
rimanda ormai il farso suo a Piletto,
ch'egli è tanto cortese fante e fino,
che creder non dei ciò che te n'è detto. 4
E non star tra la gente a capo chino,
che non sei bozza, e fòtine disdetto;
ma, sì come amorevole vicino,
con noi venne a dormir nel nostro letto. 8
Rimanda il farso ormai, più no il tenere,
ché mai non ci verrà oltre tua voglia,
poi che n'ha conosciuto il tuo volere.
Nel nosro letto già mai non si spoglia. 12
Tu non dovéi gridare, anzi tacere:
ch' a me non fece cosa ond'io mi doglia.

O Aldobrandin, sweet husband of mine,
do return his doublet to young Piletto,
for he is such an obliging and charming lad,
and you must not believe what it was said. 4
Do not stand head-down in the crowd,
for you are not a cuckold, for this I vouch;
all to the contrary, it was as a loving
neighbor that he came to sleep on our couch. 8
Send back his doublet now, do not keep it,
for he shan't come again against your will,
after he has learned what you desire.
He will not disrobe again in our bed; 12
do not be cross, instead be quiet,
for he did nothing to me that I disliked.

Regarding line 1, the husband in question was Aldobrandino di Bellincione, a well-known member of the Guelf party. The *farsetto* mentioned in line 2 was an underwear garment men would not ordinarily take off in someone else's home. The wife's speech is mellifluous and mendacious. The appellative *dolce* for her husband and the adjectives used for Piletto—he is such a polite and courteous boy!—are ferociously mocking, used as they are together with terms typical of low-style satire, such as *bozza* (cuckold), *fòtine disdetto* (I deny it) in line 4, and *voglia* (wish) in line 10. The woman's impudence erupts at the end, when she urges her husband not to get angry because Piletto did nothing about which she would complain. (Muscetta-Ponchiroli 1956)

The two sonnets that now follow are examples of Rustico's famous vitriolic attacks on individual people. His descriptions, which in one case intend to hurt and in the other to entertain, are not to be confused with pornography, whose only objective is to arouse sexual excitement, and are not to become a delimiting factor in the appreciation of the poet's talent for representing people and situations in a palpably realistic manner. About some pornographic sonnets, see note 84.

Da che guerra m'avete incominciata,
paleserò del vostro puttineccio,
de la foia, che tanto v'è montata
che no s'attuteria per pal di leccio.   4
Non vi racorda, donna, a la fiata
che noi stemmo a San Sebio a tal gineccio?
E se per moglie v'avesse sposata,
non dubbiate ch'egli era un bel farneccio!   8
Ché foste putta il die che voi nasceste:
ed io ne levai saggio ne la stalla,
ché 'l culo in terra tosto percoteste.
E sed io fosse stato una farfalla,   12
maraviglia saria, sì mi scoteste:
voi spingate col cul, quando altri balla.

As you have begun to wage a war against me,
I shall make public all your whoring,
your ravenous lust, which has grown so strong,
that the trunk of an oak would not quench it.   4
Don't you remember, woman, that time
when we messed about at San Sebio?
Had I taken you as my wife, it would
have been a bitchy trick, have no doubt!   8
You have been a whore since your birth;
I had a proof of it in that stable, where you
plumped your ass on the ground so fast.
Had I been a butterfly, it would have been   12
a sight, so much you shook me; so heartily you
push up your ass, when the other is dancing!

Regarding line 6, critics say that San Sebio probably stands for Sant' Eusebio and might indicate the day of the meeting, as in "the day of Sant' Eusebio," or the place where the meeting occurred, such as San Sebio, in the Rectory of Montaione in Valdelsa. Marti refers the word *gineccio* to the Latin *gynaeceum*, indicating the woman's apartment in a Greek house—by extension, a brothel. But the word, in my opinion, is not to be taken literally. In line 8, *farneccio* comes from the Latin *fornicium*, which was the fine imposed on men guilty of sexual violence. The depiction of the woman sounds vindictively autobiographical rather than simply inspired by the old and rich literature against women. In their misogynistic diatribe, men always emphasized women's incontrollable lust, but here, Rustico's attack takes on a rather personal tinge. The unbecoming details of a past encounter are redeemed in the end by the image of the man, who finds himself caught up in an unescapable movement, bounced about surrealistically above the woman like a butterfly frantically flapping its wings.

Quando ser Pepo vede alcuna potta,
egli anitrisce sì come destriere,
e non sta queto: innanzi salta e trotta
e canzisce che par pur un somiere.   4
E com' baiardo ad ella si raggrotta
e ponvi il ceffo molto volontiere,
ed ancor de la lingua già non dotta
e spesse volte mordele il cimiere.   8
Chi vedesse ser Pepo incavallare
ed anitrir, quando sua donna vede,
che si morde le labbra e vuol razzare!
Quello che di poi par, non si ricrede: 12
quando v'ha 'l ceffo sì la fa sciacquare,
sì le stringe la groppa ch'ella pede.

When Sir Pepo sees a woman's cunt,
he begins to frisk and neigh like a horse
and cannot stay calm; he jumps, he trots,
and gets a hard-on as big as a donkey's.   4
Then, like a bay horse, down he squats
and he puts his snout to it so very eagerly,
and has no qualms working with his tongue,
and bites the little crest repeatedly.   8
You should see Sir Pepo turn into a horse
and neigh, when he sees his woman! He bites
his lips, and stallion-like wants to procreate!
What happens next you will not believe!   12
With his snout there, he swashes her about
and grips her rump so as to make her fart!

In line 8, *cimiere* means "clitoris." In line 9, *incavallare* is a verb that refers to making the movements of a horse in heat. In line 11, my translation of *razzare* as "procreate" derives from the zoological term of *razzatore*—from *razza*, meaning "race"—which indicates a stallion selected for reproduction. Some of the texts I checked equate *razzare* with "pawing the ground" (in excited expectation of what is to come next, I suppose). Per line 12, whoever has seen Pepo in such position will not be surprised to hear what happens next.

The sonnet unabashedly ridicules the virility of Sir Pepo dei Rinaldeschi, a Florentine city councillor, who was a Guelf, of course. The description of his lovemaking is outrageous and pitiless, but it has none of the vindictiveness of the previous poem; rather, it shows a wish to amuse and be amused. The aesthetic and recreational factor of the sonnet prevails on its indiscretions, in my opinion, for the metamorphosis performed by the city councillor and the effect of his exertions are spectacularly successful.

El Muscia sì fa dicere e bandire,
qual donna non avesse buon marito,
ch'aggia picciol dificio da servire,
che vad' a lui, cad e' n'è ben fornito.   4
Ed ancor questo fa nel bando dire,
ch'è sedici once, sanza il rimonito;
e dice ben, se non la fa pedire
a ogni tratto, ch'e' vuol perder lo 'nvito.   8
Ma se se ateranno al mio consiglio,
inanzi il proveranno ver' di mezzo,
que' c'ha la schiena bianca e 'l co' vermiglio;
e poi, quando verrà colà 'l da sezzo,   12
darannovi con ambo man di piglio,
ch'a ben ripalleggiarlo egli è un vezzo.

Muscia has publicly announced
that any woman having no good a husband
and too small an edifice to serve,
ought to go to him, for he's well provided.   4
Furthermore, in his ban, he has stated
that it measures, without fringe, sixteen inches.
He has also specified he is ready to lose his bet,
should he fail at each blow to make her fart.   8
Were women willing to follow my advice,
they would first try it toward the middle
—the thing with white back and reddish head—
then, when what is at its end arrives,   12
they should handle it with both their hands,
because, in managing it well, it's a real delight.

We have no certain identification of so exceptionally endowed a man, whom Rustico exalts and ridicules at the same time. In line 3, *dificio*, meaning "edifice," refers to the male member. Per line 6, it measures sixteen inches, or about forty centimeters, without counting the testicles. Apparently, the reaction in line 7 was considered a sign of great pleasure. With regard to lines 9, 10, and 13, the subject of *aterranno*, *proveranno*, and *darannovi* is *women*.

2

Time of Transition and Unrest

2.1 In Celebration of the Good Life

In 1263, Pope Urban IV invited Charles of Anjou to come to Italy and oust Manfred, Frederick II's natural son and heir to his Italian domains. In exchange for their financial and military support, Charles promised Florence and her Tuscan allies considerable economic privileges. After his victory in 1266, the Florentine merchants and bankers were able to extend their trade to Naples; to Provence, which was Anjou territory; and farther into northern France and the Flanders. In the first half of the fourteenth century, Florence was, with Genoa, Milan, Venice, and Paris, one of the most populous cities in Europe, and it was perhaps the richest.

Giacomo di Michele (ca. 1275–1330), called Folgòre by his contemporaries, was among the men who could enjoy the many privileges that wealth provided. He was a citizen of San Gimignano, a town of many towers some kilometers from Florence. In those days, San Gimignano had far more turrets than can be seen today, each the property of a family prominent in the affairs of the community. Folgòre served in the army and in diplomatic missions, and in view of his services, the commune made him a knight. For his political poetry, see 2.3.

The five poems shown here are part of a garland—fourteen sonnets all together, including a dedication and a conclusion—in which, in the manner of the Provençal *plazer*,[23] the poet feigns to offer his friends a different pleasurable pastime for each month of the year. He proposes hunting and fishing parties, cavalcades, tournaments, leisurely banquets, and outdoor and indoor games. Men's clubs, called *brigate*, organized these activities.[24] Their members belonged to the *popolo grasso*, the "well-oiled people." In political life, such class vehemently opposed the aristocracy, but it vied with the old families in lifestyle and oftentimes in wastefulness. In his dedicatory sonnet to Niccolò di Nigi, a politician and public officer of San Gimignano, Folgòre describes the club members as "more courteous and valiant than Lancelot; men who, if necessary, would be ready to joust lance in hand as they do in Camelot" (*prodi e cortesi più che Lancillotto; se bisognasse, con le lance in mano fariano torneamenti a Camelotto*).

Few poets have evoked the comforts and pleasures that money can buy with as much vivacity and graceful gusto. The magnificence of the images, the colorful inventions, and the joyous abandonment to pleasure were, in fact, what won Giacomo di Michele the nickname of Folgòre (Splendor).

    I' doto voi, nel mese di gennaio,
    corte con fochi di salette accese

camer' e letta d'ogni bello arnese,
lenzuol' di seta e copertoi di vaio, 4
tregèa, confetti e mescere arazzaio,
vestiti di doagio e di rascese:
e 'n questo modo star a le difese,
muova scirocco, garbino e rovaio. 8
Uscir di fòr alcuna volta il giorno,
gittando della neve bella e bianca
alle donzelle che staran da torno;
e quando fosse la compagna stanca, 12
a questa corte facciasi ritorno:
e sì riposi la brigata franca.

In the month of January, I shall give you
a hall heated with roaring smokeless fires,
bedrooms supplied with fine furnishings,
with sheets of soft silk and coverlets of fur, 4
with comfits, sweetmeats, fortified wines,
and with clothes from Douai and Arras:
this way we shall be very well protected,
may it blow *scirocco*, *garbino*, and *rovaio*. 8
Then to go out sometime in the day
to throw balls of good white snow
at the maidens who are standing by;
and, when the company is well worn out, 12
to come back indoors to this very hall,
so the genteel company may repose.

In line 1, *voi*, meaning "you," refers to the friends to whom Folgòre proposes the convivial house gathering. Wild winds blow menacingly outside, but inside, the company is warm and well protected. In line 2, *salette* are a kind of marsh plants that, when dried, were used to produce a robust and smokeless flame. In line 4, *vaio* is a type of squirrel whose skin was used to make bed covers. In line 5, *tregèa* refers to fruit confections. *Confetti* refers to sweet pastries, not the Italian confetti of today, which are a sort of candy. With a number of editors, I choose to read *arazzaio* as "fortified wine." Alternatively, if we read *a razzaio* as "a cold place," the translation would be "cooled wine." In line 6, *doagio* and *rascese* are types of cloth made at Douai and Arras, respectively. The specificity of the objects enhances the effect of comfort and luxury. In line 8, *scirocco* is a southeast wind that blows from the Sahara. *Garbino* is a southwest wind, now more frequently called *libeccio*. *Rovaio* is better known as *tramontana*, a northern wind. Regarding line 14, *franca* has the composite meaning of "free, spirited, and genteel."

E di febbrai' vi dono bella caccia
di cervi, di cavrioli e di cinghiari,

corte gonnelle e grossi calzari,
e compagnia che ve deletti e piaccia;   4
can da guinzagli e segugi da traccia,
e le borse fornite di danari,
ad onta degli scarsi e degli avari,
o di chi 'n questo vi dà briga e 'mpaccia.   8
E la sera tornar co' vostri fanti
carcati de la molta selvaggina;
avendo gioia ed allegrezza e canti;
trar del vino e fumar la cucina,   12
e fin al primo sonno star razzanti:
e poi posare 'nfin' a la matina.

In February, I'll give you some fine hunting
of deer, of roebucks, and wild boars,
short coats and high hunting boots,
a company that pleases and delights you,   4
dogs held by the leash or running in pursuit,
and wallets well supplied with money,
to spite the miserly and the hoarders,
the troublemakers and the thwarters.   8
In the evening, we shall go back home,
the servants laden with abundant game,
brimming with happiness, jollity, and song.
Then we'll draw wine, set the kitchen aflame,   12
all tipsy we shall stay until the early hours
and after we'll slumber until the latest morn.

In the octave, the hunters and their dogs are ready for the chase, all depicted in vivid detail, with appropriate clothing and accoutrements. The joyous listing climaxes in lines 7–8, with some down-to-earth words against creditors and disciplinarians "who thwart your pleasures and make trouble" (*chi vi dà briga e impaccia*). In the sestet, time has progressed: hunters and their servants are now slowly returning home. More pleasures are relished in the evening, when the exertion of the day gives way to gratifying libations, the rambunctious joviality of a banquet, and then a night of contented rest.

Di marzo sì vi do una peschiera
d'anguille, trote, lamprede e salmoni,
di dèntici, dalfini e storïoni,
d'ogni altro pesce in tutta la Riviera,   4
con pescatori e navicelle a schiera
e barche, saettie e galeoni,
le qual ve portino a tutte stagioni

SONNET • 73

a qual porto vi piace alla primèra: 8
che sia formito di molti palazzi,
d'ogn'altra cosa che vi sie mestèro,
e gente v'abbia di tutti sollazzi.
Chiesa non v'abbia mai né monastero: 12
lassate predicar i preti pazzi,
che hanno troppe bugie e poco vero.

In March, I shall give you a fishing pond
full of eels, trouts, lampreys, and salmons,
of brims, of dolphins, and of sturgeons,
with other kind of fish swimming through; 4
let there also be anglers, an array of boats,
of dinghies, schooners, and of galleons,
which with no delay, in any weather, might take
you to whatever harbors you may want to go. 8
And may our destination abound in palaces,
In all the things that one could ever need,
and in people amenable to any pleasure.
Let neither church nor priory there be, 12
let crazy priests deliver their sermons:
their fibs are many, and trifling is their truth.

Per line 1, stream and saltwater fish swim together in Folgòre's fishpond. In line 3, the *dentice*, or bream, is a saltwater fish with delicious meat, resembling somewhat the perch but with protruding teeth and a delineated spine. With *in tutta la riviera* of line 4, the description of the pond, which somehow extends to the river, is colorful in its variety of fish but not realistic. The quatrain in lines 5–8 conjures a flotilla of diversely identified boats. The *saettie* are fast-sailing, slender schooners once used in the Mediterranean by the military. They are also called lateeners because they made use of a triangular sail called a lateen. With the boats ready to cast off for a mysterious destination, the last line of the octave marks the shift to a new tonality. The sestet opens wide the view on an enthralling harbor, well-appointed palaces, and people eager for pleasure. The excursion ends abruptly with the mention of the castigating clergy, and in the closing, the company is back to reality.

Di maggio sì vi do molti cavagli
e tutti quanti siano affrenatori,
portanti tutti, dritti corridori,
pettorali, testiere con sonagli; 4
bandiere e coverte a molti 'ntagli
e di zendadi e di tutti li colori;
le targhe a modo degli armeggiatori,
viuole, rose, fior ch'ogn'om abbagli; 8

e rompere e fiaccar bigordi e lance,
e piover da fenestre e da balconi
in giú ghirlande, ed in su melarance;
e pulzellette e giovani garzoni 12
baciarsi nella bocca e nelle guance:
d'amor e di goder vi si ragioni.

In May, I shall give you many horses,
all responding quickly to the rein,
all good amblers, all upright trotters;
with breast frills, headgear, and tingling bells, 4
banners and caparisons with rich inlays
embroidered with silks of many colors;
and long shields in the jolly style of jousters,
violets, roses, and flowers to dazzle everyone. 8
Oh! to break and shatter spears and lances!
To watch from windows and from balconies
oranges soaring and garlands descending,
many young men and lovely maidens 12
kissing on the cheeks and in the mouth,
with much talking of pleasuring and love.

May was the great month for jousts and tournaments. In line 4, *pettorali* refers to the leather trappings that go over the horse's breast. *Testiere* refers to headgear. In line 5, *coverte*, or caparisons, are ornamental horse coverings. In line 6, *zendadi* refers to very fine silks. In line 9, *bigordi* refers to poles, or fake spears, used in the factitious fights carried out in jousts. The scene comes to life with a great movement of men, horses, and jousters and with details in the decorations of the armor, trappings, and coverings. The description of the tournament reaches line 9. In line 10, the great motion of the race changes into one of a serene festivity: women throw flowers and garlands down on the men on parade, and the men fling oranges up to the women leaning from windows and balconies. It is the May Day festival, the Calendimaggio; in a display of colors, perfumes, violets, and roses, young men and women ogle one another and exchange gifts, kisses, and promises of love.

Di giugno dovvi una montagnetta
coverta di bellissimi arboscelli,
con trenta ville e dodici castelli,
che sian intorno ad una cittadetta, 4
ch'abbia nel mezzo una sua fontanetta;
e faccia mille rami e fiumicelli,
ferendo per giardin e praticelli
e rinfrescando la minuta erbetta. 8
Aranci e cedri, dàttili e lumie
e tutte l'altre frutte savorose
empergolate siano su per le vie;

e le genti vi sian tutte amorose,   12
e faccianvisi tante cortesie,
ch' a tutto 'l mondo siano grazïose.

In June, I'll give you a little mountain
covered by some lovely little trees,
with thirty villas as well as twelve castles
that go all around a pretty little town,   4
which has in the middle a little fountain
flowing into a thousand rivulets and brooks,
which go through little lawns and gardens
to refresh there the small tender grass.   8
Oranges and citrons, dates and limes,
and all other kinds of savory fruit
may dangle in the streets from bowers,
and the people may be so amorous   12
and pay each other so many gallantries
as to be amiable to the whole wide world.

The many diminutives—little mountain (*montagnetta*), little town (*cittadetta*), small fountain (*fontanetta*), tiny grass (*erbetta*)—all in strong position at the end of the line, turn the landscape into a miniature. The minutely landscaped topography comes to life almost by an act of poetic magic in the octave: a little dreamy town sits on a tiny green hill; the green countryside is scattered with tiny farms (the Roman villas), towers, gardens, brooks, and bowers of fruit. In the sestet, the description turns to people. Their presence is indeterminate but vividly felt; their courteous and amorous behavior reflects the beauty of the land of which they are an integral part.

About Cenne della Chitarra, we know only what the codex containing his rhymes tells us: he was a jongleur from Arezzo, and he died before 1336. The sonnets that this man of scant financial resources wrote in the forms of the *enueg*[25] is possibly a near description of the living conditions of the poor, drawn in juxtaposition to the comfortable life of Forgòre's bourgeois class.

Io vi doto, nel mese di gennaio,
corti con fumo al modo montanese,
letta qual'ha nel mare il genovese,
acqua e vento che non cali maio,   4
povertà di fanciulle a colmo staio,
da bere aceto forte galavrese
e stare come ribaldo in arnese,
con panni rotti, senza alcun denaio.   8
E ancor vi do così fatto soggiorno:
con una vecchia nera, vizza e ranca,

catun gittando de la neve a torno,
appresso voi seder in una banca, 12
e resmirando quel so viso adorno;
così reposi la brigata manca.

In the month of January, I shall give you
rooms full of smoke, as in mountain lodges,
beds like those of the Genoese at sea,
huge downpours and unrelenting winds, 4
and scarcities of women by the ton,
strong vinegar from Calabria to drink,
and being done up to look like tramps,
in raggedy style and with no money to spend. 8
Afterward, I shall have you settled thus:
as snowballs are thrown by others all around,
a woman that is old, filthy, wrinkled, and lame
shall be sitting on a bench very close to you 12
and you mesmerized by her alluring face:
so may repose the ill-provided group.

In line 3, *Genovese* comes from Genova, a sea-faring city whose men, when onboard, slept in uncomfortable cots. In line 4, *a colmo staio* means, literally, "by the bushel." In line 6, *galavrese* refers to being from Calabria. In line 13, *resmirando*, or *riguardando*, refers to looking at something intently. In line 7, a *ribaldo* is a man without good qualifications, generally living by his wits and al fresco.

Di giugno siate in tale campagnetta,
che ve sieno corbi ed argironcelli;
le chiane intorno senza caravelli:
entro nel mezzo v'abbia una isoletta, 4
de la qual esca sì forte venetta,
che mille parte faccia e ramicelli
d'aqua di solfo, e cotai gorgoncelli,
sì ch'ella adacqui ben tal contradetta. 8
Sorbi e pruni acerbi siano lìe,
nespole crude e cornie savorose;
le rughe sian fangose e strette vie;
le genti vi sian nere e gavinose. 12
e faccianvisi tante villanie,
che a Dio ed al mondo sïano noiose.

In June, I wish you to be in such little land
where there'll be flying gulls and ravens,
and around it a marshland and not a vessel;
in the middle of which will be an islet, 4

> from which a strong little spring will run
> into a thousand little veins and puddles
> of sulfurous water, with bogs and puddles,
> so abundantly as to water this small little land.   8
> Sorb-apples and prunes will also be there,
> with sour medlar trees and bitter berries;
> muddy will be the roads, narrow the streets;
> the people shall be filthy and scrofulous,   12
> and the behavior of all so discourteous,
> as to be to God and the world distasteful.

In line 2, *argironcelli*, or *garzette*, are egrets, which, for Cenne, apparently were not a thing of beauty. To render his idea, therefore, I have replaced egrets with ravens, far less attractive birds. In line 3, *chiane* are marshes. *Caravelli* refers to boats. In line 5, *venetta* refers to a little vein of water. In line 7, *gorgoncelli* are bogs. In line 10, *cornie*, or *ciorniole*, are berries. In this sonnet, as in the previous one, every detail stands in parallel line and in opposition to what Fòlgore described in his.

2.2 Friends and Enemies

The following sonnets are part of a tenzone in which Dante and Forese Donati engaged between 1293 and 1296.[26] Far from the intellectual stance of the Sicilian tenzone (1.1) and the gallant correspondence between Compiuta Donzella and her admirers (1.4), the Dante-Forese tenzone is an aggressive exchange of sonnets larded with insults and monetary and sexual double entendres. How serious their anger was and what might have been its cause remain a matter of speculation. Their animosity might have been due to differences in lifestyle or divergent political convictions. In those years, Florence was experiencing a difficult stretch of social turbulence. The Guelfs had split into two factions: the Whites, who objected to the interference of Rome into Florentine affairs, and the Blacks, who had strong financial ties with the church and were ready to sacrifice the independence of the commune to their personal interest.[27] Forese was the brother of Corso Donati, the Black leader. Dante belonged to the party of the Whites and was resolutely opposed to the political intrusion of the pontiff.

> Ben ti faranno il nodo Salamone,
> Bicci novello, e' petti de le starne,
> ma peggio fia la lonza del castrone,
> ché 'l cuoio farà vendetta de la carne;   4
> tal che starai più presso a San Simone,
> se tu non ti procacci de l'andarne:
> e 'ntendi che 'l fuggire el mal boccone
> sarebbe oramai tardi a ricomprarne.   8
> Ma ben m'è detto che tu sai un'arte,
> che, s'egli è vero, tu ti puoi rifare,

però ch'ell'è di molto gran guadagno;
e fa sì, a tempo, che tema di carte
non hai, che ti bisogni scioperare;
ma ben ne colse male a fi' di Stagno!

The breasts of partridges will tie you up
good, with a Salomon knot, Bicci boy!
But the loin of mutton will fix you better,
for its skin will revenge the meat you eat
and you will get closer to San Simone,
unless you manage to run away from it:
be aware that abstaining from the bad morsel
could be too late now to redeem your debts!
They tell me you are expert in a certain art
which, if true, could make you solvent again,
for it happens to be exceedingly profitable.
Therefore, see that, in the future, fearful obligatory
papers may no longer put you out of work:
for no good came from it to Stagno's sons!

With regard to line 1, the Salomon knot was supposedly inextricable. In line 2, *novello* means "young," either as an expression of contempt or because Forese's grandfather too was nicknamed Bicci. Regarding line 3, the list of public debtors was written on a parchment of lamb or on mutton skin. With regard to line 5, the house of the Donati and the Burella prison were located in a district named after the Church of Saint Simone. The sonnet maintains that if Forese does not stop incurring debt, he will soon get nearer to prison than he already is, in the house where he lives. Per line 12, Forese's *arte* is the art of stealing. *Arti* was also the name of the guilds of industry and trade. In line 13, *scioperare* is a verb meaning to be out of work or to go on strike. Forese will be out of work—that is, he will no longer be able to guzzle gourmet food, which is the habit that forced him to borrow money. In line 14, *ne* refers to Bicci's foresaid habit of steeling. Stagno's sons had been condemned to death for theft.

Chi udisse tossir la malfatata
moglie di Bicci vocato Forese,
potrebbe dir ch'ell'ha forse vernata
ove si fa 'l cristallo, in quel paese.
Di mezzo agosto la truove infreddata:
or sappi che de' far d'ogni altro mese!
E non le val perché dorma calzata,
merzé del copertoio c'ha cortonese …
La tosse, 'l freddo e l'altra mala voglia
non l'addovien per umor ch'abbia vecchi,
ma per difetto ch'ella sente al nido.

> Piange la madre, c'ha più d'una doglia, 12
> dicendo: "Lassa, che per fichi secchi
> messa l'avre' 'n casa del conte Guido."

> Whoever heard Bicci's hapless woman
> cough—the wife of the man called Forese—
> would say she has been spending the winter
> in the land where rock crystals are made. 4
> You will find her shivering in mid-August;
> imagine how cold she must be in other months!
> Sleeping with her stockings on won't help her,
> because of the coverlet, which is far too short … 8
> Cough, cold, and other indispositions
> are not due to her humors growing old,
> but to something missing in her nest.
> Her mother weeps for more than one woe 12
> and says, "Alas, for a few dried figs I could have
> married her into Count Guido's household."

Per line 4, Nella, Forese's wife, is spending the winters in a cold climate, infers Dante. According to Aristotle's *Physics*, ice turns into rock crystal at a very low temperature. In line 8, the words *copertoio*, or *coverlet*, and *cortonese* (from Cortona, a name containing the word *corto*, meaning "short") turn the geographical detail into a rude insinuation that Forese's organ is too short to satisfy his wife's sexual needs. The innuendo extends to line 11, where *nido* (nest) is a metaphor for vagina. Regarding line 6, sexual intercourse was considered necessary for a woman to keep her humors (*umor*) flowing. With regard to line 14, the Guidi were a rich and noble family of Cosentino, a mountainous region in the upper valley of the Arno River.

Here is Forese's retort:

> L'altra notte mi venne una gran tosse,
> perché i' non avea che tener a dosso;
> ma incontamente che fu dì, fui mosso
> per gir a guadagnar ove che fosse. 4
> Udite la fortuna ove m'addosse:
> ch'i' credetti trovar perle in un bosso
> e be' fiorin coniati d'oro rosso;
> ed i' trovai Alaghier tra le fosse, 8
> legato a nodo ch'i' non saccio 'l nome,
> se fu di Salamone o d'altro saggio.
> Allora mi segna' verso 'l levante:
> e que' mi disse: "Per amor di Dante, 12
> scio'mi." Ed i' non potti veder come:
> tornai a dietro, e compie' mi' vïaggio.

The other night I had a big fit of coughing,
for I did not have a single blanket to wear;
so as day broke, I wandered outside
to make a little money, may that be anywhere.   4
Now hear what Luck brought down on me:
I did expect to find in a ditch some pearls
or some florins of flaming gold, when, instead,
among the graves, I found Alighiero tied up   8
in a knot, whose name I do not know,
perhaps Solomon's or of another know-it-all.
So I turned to the east and made the holy sign;
and he said to me "For the love of Dante,   12
untie me!" but I did not see how I could:
so I turned around and ended my jaunt.

Regarding line 8, Alighiero, Dante's father, had died in 1283. From him, the family had taken the name of Alighieri. Per line 11, Forese presumes Alighiero to be a damned soul, so he turns toward Jerusalem and makes the sign of the cross. At first, Forese replies to Dante's insinuations by joking about himself: he does not have a warm bedcover and suffers fits of coughing, just as his wife does, and at night, he goes out on thieving expeditions. Soon, however, he brings up an indirect reference to Alighiero's supposed misappropriation of money, and his jocular banter turns into a denigrating counterattack. Documents going back to 1246 and 1257 attest that Dante's father had been a moneylender. The church did not condone the sin of usury until the usurer returned the funds he had appropriated. Forese's reproach, therefore, might refer to Dante's failure to repay the money supposedly exacted by Alighiero in his business dealings. Accusations aside, Forese's sonnet is effective in evoking a restless night, a thieving errand gone wrong, and his fright at the sight of a ghost springing out of a nearby grave. Paolo Orvieto suggests that Forese's nocturnal outing and his coming across Alighiero among the tombs of a cemetery are a parody of *Inferno*, which Dante presumably began writing at this time, while he was still living in Florence.

To make amends for the abusive tenzone, in *The Divine Comedy*, Dante staged a scene of repentance. Traveling through that realm of penitence—that is, purgatory—Dante the pilgrim comes across Forese—dead by this time—and, in a scene of reconciliation, recollects with regret the hostile exchange he had with him: "If you remember what I was to you and what you were to me, the memory is too much to bear." Furthermore, regretting his disrespect for Nella, Forese's wife, in the same purgatorial scene, Dante has her husband lovingly collect her as "my little widow, whom I loved so much, as dear and beloved of God as she is outstanding in her good works" (*Purgatorio* 23, 115–17 and 85–90).

The feuding between the nobles, who held the most important public offices, and the bourgeois class, who demanded a bigger share in the city government, culminated in the Ordinances of Justice (*Ordinamenti di giustizia*), which Giano della Bella introduced in 1293. These regulations prevented the nobles from running for office, and Guido Cavalcanti, who was a member of the old aristocracy, was banned from public life. Dante, on the other hand, who was of a family of small means and did not qualify as noble, enrolled in one of the guilds representing the bourgeoisie and was allowed to enter the political arena.[28] Having reoriented both philosophical convictions and political position, Dante began to befriend individuals whom the reserved Cavalcanti shunned.

Guido Cavalcanti sent Dante "I' vegno 'l giorno a te 'nfinite volte" sometimes in the mid-1290s.

I' vegno 'l giorno a te 'nfinite volte
e trovoti pensar troppo vilmente;
molto mi dol della gentil tua mente
e d'assai tue vertù che ti son tolte.   4
Solevanti spiacer persone molte;
tuttor fuggivi l'annoiosa gente;
di me parlavi sì coralemente
che tutte le tue rime avie ricolte.   8
Or non ardisco, per la vil tua vita,
far mostramento che tu' dir mi piaccia,
né 'n guisa vegno a te, che tu mi veggi.
Se 'l presente sonetto spesso leggi,   12
lo spirito noioso che ti caccia
si partirà da l'anima invilita.

I come to you countless times a day
and find you sunk in such debasing thoughts
that I deeply grieve for your noble mind
and for all your virtues that now are gone.   4
Once many people did displease you,
you always avoided the annoying crowd,
and of me you spoke with such affection
that I was moved to collect all your rhymes.   8
Thanks to your awful life, now I do not
dare to show I like your writing, nor I come
to you in any way that you can see me.
If you read the present sonnet often,   12
that annoying spirit that now haunts you
will take leave from your dejected mind.

In line 2, *pensar ... vilmente* is to think basely. These words could indicate a period of discouragement for Dante, such as might have been caused by Beatrice's death, or they might refer to the frequentation of people whom Guido considered unworthy. In line 7, *coralemente* means "feelingly." Here again is the sense of privileged separateness, the shared belief of belonging to an elite of intellect and taste, such as the feeling that had united the members of the stilnovo group (see 1.5). Per line 11, the poet says, "I do not come to you in person, so you can see me, but in thought," as implied by the first line.

Significant political events were to separate the two friends even further. In 1300, when Dante was occupying the high position of *priore*, the government made a bipartisan attempt to reduce the climate of violence in the city and banished several members of both White and Black factions. Guido

Cavalcanti was among those exiled. At Sarzana, in the swampy countryside of Maremma, he caught malaria. His banishment was revoked because of his illness, but Guido died in Florence soon after. For other sonnets by Cavalcanti, see 1.5 and 1.6.

The next sonnets take us to the first decade of the new century. Cavalcanti is dead. Dante and Cino da Pistoia are in exile.

The Sigibuldi family, to which Cino belonged, traditionally sided with the Black faction. In 1302, when the Whites of Pistoia seized power, Cino left the city. Dante had left Florence in 1301. Pope Boniface VIII, angered by the sanctions inflicted on some Florentine banks that had dealings with the Vatican, sent Charles of Valois to negotiate a compromise between the two factions. Instead of trying to restore peace, Charles backed the Blacks when they moved to take hold of the government. Dante, who was away on a diplomatic mission, was accused of misusing public funds in absentia, sentenced to a fine, and banished from public life for two years. Having refused to return to Florence to answer the charges, he had his sentence commuted to one of perpetual exile and, later, death.

In the early years of their exile, Dante and Cino exchanged letters and poems. In one sonnet, Cino confessed that he felt strongly attracted to a woman he had just met. Should he yield to this new passion? Is it possible for anyone to go from love to love? Is resistance to sexual attraction possible? Dante's reply follows here. The answer is surprising, considering Dante's avowed conviction of the rational foundation of love and man's responsibility to control his passions.

Io sono stato con Amore insieme
da la circulazion del sol mia nona,
e so com'egli affrena e come sprona,
e come sotto lui si ride e geme. 4
Chi ragione o virtù contra gli sprieme,
fa come que' che 'n la tempesta sona,
credendo far colà dove si tona
esser le guerre de' vapori sceme. 8
Però nel cerchio de la sua palestra
liber arbitrio già mai non fu franco,
sì che consiglio invan vi si balestra.
Ben può con nuovi spron punger lo fianco, 12
e qual che sia 'l piacer ch'ora n'addestra,
seguitar si convien, se l'altro è stanco.

I have been subject to Love since the time
of my ninth revolution of the sun and I know
how he refrains and how he goads people on,
and how one laughs and groans under his sway. 4
Whoever opposes reason or virtue to him
acts like a man who makes noises in a storm,
expecting to abate the battle of the clouds

all the way up there, where the thunders roll.	8
Within the circle of Love's battleground,	
no man has ever been able to act freely;	
in there, therefore, reason will battle in vain.	
Love can indeed prick our flank with new spurs	12
and wherever the present craving is leading us,	
we must follow, when the old desire is spent.	

Dante expresses the unyielding strength of instinctual passion and the futility of resisting with images drawn from astronomy, meteorology, and equestrianism and other sports and by the use of harsh-sounding words, such as *sprona*, *sprieme*, *sceme*, *palestra*, *balestra*, and *addestra*, all placed for emphasis in rhyming positions. Regarding line 2, as he wrote in *La Vita Nuova*, Dante fell in love with Beatrice at nine years of age. With regard to lines 6–8, the belief was that thunder was generated by the collision of damp clouds with dry winds. There was a story about some people who made a big racket during a storm in the hope of silencing the thunder at its source, up in the sky. In modern Italian, *palestra*, used in line 8, means "fighting ring" or "gym." In line 11, *balestra*, from *balestrare*, is "to fight with a crossbow," "to fight back," or "to resist." Carnal passion is an inclination of the senses that neither reason nor moral discipline (*consiglio*) can subdue. Per line 12, love can indeed excite one's desire with new urges. In line 13, *piacer* is both beauty and the pleasure and desire that beauty generates.

The sonnet "Io mi credea del tutto esser partito" is about Cino's propensity for philandering. Wishing to distance himself from his friend's inclination, Dante now rejects any interest in further theorizing about love. By this time, he had turned his mind and passion to loftier problems: the consideration of the human condition and the moral evaluation of man's choices and behavior, matters that would be the foundation of *The Divine Comedy*.[29]

Io mi credea del tutto esser partito	
da queste nostre rime, messer Cino,	
ché si conviene omai altro cammino	
a la mia nave più lungi dal lito:	4
ma perch' i' ho di voi più volte udito	
che pigliar vi lasciate a ogni uncino,	
piacemi di prestare un pocolino	
a questa penna lo stancato dito.	8
Chi s'innamora sì come voi fate,	
or qua or là, e sé lega e dissolve,	
mostra ch'Amor leggermente il saetti.	
Però, se leggier cor così vi volve,	12
priego che con vertù il correggiate,	
sì che s'accordi i fatti a' dolci detti.	

I thought I had definitely left behind	
these rhymes of ours, Messer Cino,	
for now my ship must steer a course	
much further out from the usual shore;	4

but as I have often heard that you let
yourself be caught by every snare,
to my weary hand I shall gladly lend
such pen as this a little while longer. 8
Those who, like you, fall in love here and there,
binding themselves to someone, then letting go,
show that Love has hit them very lightly.
So if your fickle heart is spinning you around, 12
I beg you, restrain it with your resolve, and may
your actions befit the gentleness of your rhymes.

In line 2, the phrase *queste nostre rime* refers to the poetry that Cino, Dante, and the other members of the stilnovo circle used to write about love. In line 4, the ship heading for higher seas symbolizes Dante's new choice of subject matter. Indeed, at this time, other thoughts occupied his mind, both philosophical and practical in nature. He had progressed to a different order of studies and weightier concerns. Having joined other exiles in an attempt to displace the Florentine Blacks from power, he had made common cause with the recently exiled Whites and the long-exiled Ghibellines. However, when, in 1304, the Whites were defeated at La Lastra, Dante was forced to set aside for a while his dream of seeing Florence again.

Cino replied to Dante's austere advice with a witty jest.

Poi ch'i' fu', Dante, dal mio natal sito
fatto per greve essilio pellegrino
e lontanato dal piacer più fino
che mai formasse il Piacer infinito, 4
io son piangendo per lo mondo gito
sdegnato del morir come meschino;
e s'ho trovato a lui simil vicino
dett'ho che questi m'ha lo cor ferito. 8
Né da le prime braccia dispietate,
onde 'l fermato disperar m'assolve,
son mosso perch'aiuto non aspetti;
ch'un piacer sempre me lega ed involve, 12
il qual conven che a simil di biltate
in molte donne sparte mi diletti.

Since a grievous exile, Dante, has made me
an unhappy pilgrim far from my homeland,
separating me from the highest pleasure
that the Infinite Pleasure ever did create, 4
I have being going around the world in tears,
angry that I should come to such dismal end;
and when I found a beauty similar to hers,
I said it was the only one that pierced my heart. 8

But from those first pitiless arms I never strayed,
when no help I expected from her, even though
the hopelessness of it would have excused me:
one love still holds me always and keeps me bound,   12
forcing me to take delight only in the beauty that is
hers, which spread out in many women can be found.

In line 4, *Piacer infinito* refers to God. In line 7, *a lui* refers to the *piacer* of line 3—that is, to Cino's woman. In line 8, *questi* is the new *piacer*. In line 10, *il fermato disperar* refers to Cino's hopeless despair for not being reciprocated by Selvaggia. For other sonnets by Cino, see 1.5 and 1.6.

2.3 Politics and War

In 1310, at Aix-la-Chapelle, the German princes elected Henry VII of Luxemburg emperor of the Holy Roman Empire, and the pope recognized him as king of the Romans. The event revived Dante's unabated desire to return to Florence and made him dream about the restoration of imperial authority and peace in the country. As soon as Henry crossed the Alps to receive the imperial crown in Rome, the pope switched his allegiance to Philip the Fair of France, and the Florentine commune soon followed. Not long after, while fighting against Florence, Henry caught malaria and died.

The sonnet "Se vedi gli occhi miei di pianger vaghi" reflects Dante's bitter disillusion.

Se vedi gli occhi miei di pianger vaghi
per novella pietà che 'l cor mi strugge,
per lei ti priego che da te non fugge,
Signor, che tu di tal piacere i svaghi;   4
con la tua dritta man, cioè, che paghi
chi la giustizia uccide e poi rifugge
al gran tiranno, del cui tosco sugge
ch'elli ha già sparto e vuol che 'l mondo allaghi;   8
e messo ha di paura tanto gelo
nel cor de' tuo' fedei che ciascun tace.
Ma tu, foco d'amor, lume del cielo,
questa vertù che nuda e fredda giace,   12
levala su vestita del tuo velo,
ché sanza lei non è in terra pace.

If you see my eyes in a mood for weeping,
because of a new sorrow gnawing at my heart,
I beg you, Lord, for the sake of her who never
strays from you, restrain them from their desire;   4
with your righteous hand do punish him

who murders Justice and then escapes to the
great tyrant and sucks up the poison he has
started to spread, wishing to flood the world;   8
he has put such a chill of fear in the hearts
of your faithful that each one of them is silent.
But you, fire of love, light of heaven,
raise and dress in your veil this Virtue   12
that lies down naked and cold, because,
without her, there is no peace on earth.

In line 2, the new sorrow (*novella pietà*) is Dante's sorrow about the French and papal hostility toward Henry VII. At the announcement of the emperor's arrival, Dante had written him a letter of encouragement, and when the Florentine Black party organized an army to oppose his entrance to the city, he wrote to the Florentine priors, condemning their hostility and prophesizing disaster. In line 3, *lei* is Justice, mentioned in line 6. Per lines 6–7, the killer of Justice is Pope Clement V. The trampled figure of Justice and Clement V, the man "who murders justice," dominate the sonnet. The tyrant who protects Clement is Philip of France. Clement was the former Bertrand de Got, archbishop of Bordeaux, elected pope by the French cardinals, who dominated the conclave.[30] In line 12, *questa vertù* meaning "this virtue," is again Justice.[31]

The decline of the empire and the crisis of the church, whose seat, under French pressure, was moved to Avignon in 1305, left the Italian states to their own devices, free to turn their hostility against one another. After the ousting of the Ghibelline faction, Florence gained considerable ascendency in the region and for a while seemed secure in her gained position. Ghibelline Pisa, however, having found a protector in a daring soldier of fortune by the name of Uguccione della Faggiuola, reported two spectacular victories over the Florentines: the first in 1315 at Montecatini and the second in 1325 at Altopascio.

For Folgòre of San Gimignano, the defeat of the Guelfs was the defeat of God. In the upcoming sonnet, he accuses the Almighty of having allowed the disaster out of indifference for human affairs.

E non ti lodo, Dio, e non ti adoro
e non ti prego, e non ti rengrazio,
e non ti servo: ch'eo ne so' più sazio,
che l'anime di stare 'n purgatorio: 4
per che tu hai mess' i guelfi a tal martoro,
ch' i ghibellini ne fan beffe e strazio;
e se Uguccion ti comandasse il dazio,
tu 'l pagaresti senza perentoro.   8
Ed hanti certo sì ben conosciuto,
tolto t'han San Martin ed Altopasso
e San Michel e 'l tesor c'hai perduto;
e hai quel popol marcio così grasso,   12

    che per soperbia cherranti 'l tributo:
e tu hai fatto 'l cor che par d'un sasso.

    I do not praise you, God, I do not worship you;
I do not pray to you, and I do not thank you;
and I do not serve you, for I am sicker of it
than are of waiting the souls in purgatory.   4
You put the Guelfs through such suffering
since the Ghibellines tear them apart and jeer;
and, if Uguccion ordered to levy a toll on you,
you would pay it without any grumbling.   8
They have figured you out so very well
that they robbed you of San Martin, Altopascio,
San Michel, and of the treasure that was lost.
You let the rotten scoundrels grow so strong   12
that, out of conceit, they will ask for a tribute,
because you have turned your heart into a rock.

Regarding line 8, the *perentoro* was the term within which a debt had to be repaid. Both the old Italian word *perentoro* and the English *peremptory* derive from *peremptum*, past participle of the Latin verb *perimere*, meaning "to destroy"—that is to say, to deal with the enemy peremptorily (as it was done with Carthage!). Regarding lines 10–11, with the help of Castruccio Castracani, Uguccione defeated the army of Lucca; sacked the city; and took possession of the Guelf strongholds of San Martino, San Michele, and Altopasso. During the sack of the city on June 14, 1314, the Ghibellines purloined the treasure kept in the church of San Frediano. In line 12, *tu hai grasso* means "you have favored." For other sonnets by Folgòre, see 2.1.

Pietro dei Faitinelli (ca. 1290–1349) was born in a prominent family of Lucca, which, in political life, sided with the rich aristocracy against the popular party. When, in 1314, Uguccione took possession of the city, Pietro moved to Florence. He penned his sonnet "Voi gite molto arditi a far la mostra" the following year, when the Florentines, too slow in moving against the advancing army, were defeated by Uguccione at the Battle of Montecatini. Faitinelli's political passion lashes sarcastically about, whipping mordant descriptions of the Florentine warlike spirit.

    Voi gite molto arditi a far la mostra
con elmi e con cimiere inargentate
e par che lo leon prender vogliate
per Firenze entro, quando fate giostra.   4
E per magnificar la terra vostra,
che non n' è oggi delle più onorate,
a guisa di conigli vi intanate
e 'l viso, ove si dee, non si dimostra.   8

Lassate far la guerra a' perugini
e voi v'intramettete della lana
e di goder e raunar fiorini.
Voi solevate soggiogar Toscana,   12
or non valete in arme tre fiorini,
se non a ben ferir per la quintana.

You do show an amazing courage
in wearing headgears and silver crests, and look
daringly resolute to conquer the lion, within
the walls of Florence, when you play the joust.   4
And to exalt the glory of your town—
currently, not one of the most respected—
you hide just like rabbits inside their burrows
and do not show your faces where you should.   8
You let the people of Perugia do the fighting,
while you keep busy with your wools,
with your carousing, and in making money.
Upon a time, you dominated Tuscany;   12
today, as soldiers, you aren't worth three florins,
except for scoring hits at the Quintana.

Regarding line 3, the lion, called Marzocco, is the symbol of Florence. In line 4, *per Firenze entro* means "inside Florence." The Florentines show a lot of courage when they are inside the walls, far from the battlefield. In line 5, *terra* means "land," which here stands for "city." Regarding line 9, Perugia and some cities of the Marche had sent contingents to fight against Pisa. Regarding line 10, wool exports were the major source of revenue for the Florentines. The florin mentioned in line 13 was the Florentine currency. It was coined in 1232 and had a wide European circulation. The Quintana mentioned in line 14 was a jousting game in which the equestrians hit the wooden figure of a Saracen brandishing a mace and rotating on its axis. The word *quintana* was also a euphemism for sexual activity, the reference here being to the courageous sexual exploits of the Florentines.

The expatriates produced by the factional feuds of the communes felt a keen nostalgia for their hometowns, and that feeling often turned them into a dangerous external force. Homesickness eventually freed the exiled Faitinelli of all animosity.

S'i veggio en Lucca bella mio ritorno,
che fi' quando la pera fie ben mézza,
in nullo core uman tanta allegrezza
già mai non fu quant'io avrò quel giorno.   4
Le mura andrò leccando d'ogn'intorno
e gli uomini, piangendo d'allegrezza;
odio, rancore, guerra ed ogni empiezza
porrò giú contra quei che mi cacciorno.   8
Qui me' voglio 'l bretto castagniccio,

    anzi ch'altrove pan di gran calvello;
    anzi ch'altrove piume, qui il graticcio.
    Ch' I'ho provato sì amaro morsello,   12
    e provo e proverò, stando esiticcio,
    che bianco e ghibellin vo' per fratello.

If I see myself again in gracious Lucca
—that shall be when the pear is ripe!—
in human heart there never was happiness
as boundless as I will feel that very day.   4
The city walls I will be licking all around,
and the people besides, crying out of joy:
hatred, rancor, hostility, and all nastiness
I shall forsake to those who threw me out.   8
I shall enjoy more simple country bread
in Lucca, than cakes elsewhere, more a bed
of wicker there, than one of feathers anywhere.
I have tasted such bitter morsels in my exile,   12
I tasted and shall still taste, that now I could
welcome as brothers Ghibellines and Whites.

Per line 2, Faitinelli will be able to go back to Lucca, he thinks, when the metaphorical pear has matured—that is, when the Ghibelline party has disappeared. In line 7, *empiezza*, which I translate as "nastiness," implies vindictive action. In line 9, *castagniccio* is a type of bread made with chestnut flour, not so valued at the time. In line 10, bread *di gran calvello* is bread made with refined flour. In line 11, *graticcio* refers to a bed of crisscrossed wicker. In line 13, *esiticcio* means "exiled." Besides the half-pathetic and half-amusing image of Pietro licking the town walls, what makes the poet's nostalgia compelling are the foods, the objects, and the use of local terms (*aspera, castagniccio, calvello, graticcio, morsello*), all evoking sensations experienced at home, whose enjoyment he now vividly remembers. Faitinelli was able to go back to Lucca in 1331 and lived there the rest of his life, practicing law.

Immanuel Romano (1265–1329) was born in Rome as the son of Rabbi Šelomoh Zifronì. For a while, he was secretary-treasurer of the Roman Jewish community; later, he became secretary and tutor in well-to-do Jewish families of Fabriano, Ancona, Gubbio, and other towns of the Marche region. He might have been also a guest at the court of Cangrande della Scala in Verona, and there, he might have come across Dante. Romano wrote Italian verse as Manoello and Hebrew poetry as Immanuel ben Solomon.[32] In the following sonnet, he boasts, in characteristic satirical fashion, of belonging to all parties and to no party, a weathercock always flapping in the direction of prevailing winds.

    Io stesso non mi conosco, ogn'om oda,
        che l'esser proprio si è ghibellino:
        in Roma so' Colones' ed Ursino,

 e piacemi se l'uno e l'altro ha loda.   4
Ed in Toscana parte guelfa goda;
in Romagna so' ciò ch'è Zappettino;
mal giudeo sono io, non saracino;
ve' li cristiani non drizzo la proda.   8
Ma d'ogni legge so' ben desiroso
alcuna parte voler osservare:
de' cristiani lo bever e 'l mangiare,
e del bon Moisès poco digiunare,   12
e la lussuria di Macòn prezioso,
ché non ten fé de la cintura in gioso.

 I do not know what I am, you all listen,
for my real temperament is that of a Ghibelline,
in Rome I am both for Colonna and for Orsini,
and I am pleased when one or the other is praised.   4
May the Guelf faction prevail in Tuscany!
In Romagna, I know well who Zappettino is.
I am a wicked Jew, but surely not a Saracen,
neither do I steer my boat toward Christianity.   8
Of each Law, however, I am wholly inclined
to observe a certain section of regulations:
of the Christians, the eating and the drinking,
of the good Moses, hardly doing any fasting,   12
and of precious Mahomet, the lovemaking,
which, from the belt down, respects no faith.

 Regarding line 3, the Colonna and the Orsini were, and still are, two prominent Roman families. They had vied for power for centuries. In Immanuel's time, the Colonna were Ghibellines, and the Orsini were Guelfs. Regarding line 5, the Guelf party was dominant in Tuscany. Regarding line 6, Zappettino degli Ubertini di Valdarno, captain of the Ghibelline army, had defeated the Guelfs of Bologna in 1299. At the time, he was holding power over the whole region of Romagna. The sonnet must have been a great success with Romano's audience, for he penned another in much the same frame of mind, in which, however, in looking out for himself, he sounds even more ecumenical.

 Se San Pietro e San Paul da l'una parte,
Mosès ed Aaròn da l'altra stesse,
Macòn e Trivican, ciascun volesse
ch'io mi rendesse a volontà né a parte;   4
ciascun di lor me ne pregasse in sparte,
duro mi pare ch'io gli ne credesse,
se non da dir a chi me' mi piacesse:
"Viva chi vince, ch'io so' di sua parte!"   8
Guelfo né Ghibellin, Nero né Bianco,

a chi piace il color, quel se ne porte:
che ferirò da coda e starò franco.
E mio compar Tradimento stia forte: 12
ch'i' di voltar mai non mi trovo manco,
aitar ciascun che vince infin a morte.

If Saint Peter and Saint Paul, on one side,
Moses and Aaron, on the other, and also
Muhammad and Tarmagant asked me to convert
to their faith of free will and not only in part,   4
if each one begged me person-to-person,
I do believe I would determinedly resist,
except I would tell the one I liked best
"Hurrah for the victor! I am on your side!"   8
I am neither Guelf nor Ghibelline, neither Black
nor White, who likes a color he may wear it.
I'll fight in the rearguard and will save my life.
Turncoats, my good friend, can be sure   12
that I will never fail in changing sides,
to the death I shall fight for those who win!

Regarding line 3, in chivalric and Carolingian poems, the couples Peter and Paul, Moses and Aaron, and Macon and Trevican stood as representatives of the Christian, Jewish, and Islamic faith, respectively. I translated *Trivican* as *Termagant* because this was the name of a supposed Muslim deity introduced into English literature as an effect of the Crusades. Regarding line 9, Immanuel's position is radically ecumenical: in principle, he refuses all religions and political parties; however, in both religion and politics, he is always amenable to agree with those who are winning. For other sonnets by and about Immanuel, see 1.6 and 2.5.

Bonuccio Salimbeni was born in Siena in a wealthy merchant family known for its passionate participation in political life. He died in the 1330s. His sonnet "Quando si può, si dee" makes a plea for fighting wars that cannot be avoided.

Quando si può, si dee, sanza disnore
di sé o di sua parte o di sua terra,
a dritto e a torto fuggir l'altrui guerra,
perché fa servo de' servi il signore.   4
Ma quando 'l senno non vince l'errore,
talora è senno errar contro chi erra,
ché chi pur fugge e pur le porte serra
raccende più lo sfrenato furore.   8
Il troppo sofferir cresce baldanza

alla disordinata voluntate,
e dà matera a 'ngiurar buon' usanza.
Sì che talvolta egli è necessitate   12
volgere il viso contro l'arroganza
e secondo i danar render derrate.

When possible, without dishonor to oneself,
to one's party, or to one's country, one must avoid,
right or wrong, to fight other people's wars,
for that turns a lord into the servant of servants.   4
But when good sense does not prevail on error,
it is wise at times to fight those in the wrong,
because, by dodging and closing one's doors,
one allows an unchecked turmoil to stir up more.   8
Continuous misery increases the boldness
of men with unchecked proclivities, and offers
excuses for injuring men of good propensities.
Therefore, at times, it becomes a necessity   12
to face up to arrogance and render a profit
proportionate to the sum that was invested.

In accordance with the laws of civil communality and reciprocal respect, one should avoid wars as much as possible, maintains Salimbeni, because war may take down those who enjoy a status of control to a condition of subjection. However, when coming to terms with an adversary is impossible, then one must fight and repay him by the same coin (pay him the return due to the investment he has made).

Franco Sacchetti (1340–79) was a Florentine merchant living and working in the town of Ragusa, now Dubrovnik, at the time a Venetian domain. While holding a series of political and administrative positions in Tuscany and Romagna, he authored a book of verse, some commentaries on the Gospels, and the *Trecento Novelle*, a collection of short stories that made him famous.

Là dove è pace, il ben sempre germoglia;
matrimoni con feste e balli e canti;
ridon le ville e le donne e gli amanti;
ogni mente s'adorma in vaga voglia.   4
Là dove è guerra, non par che ben coglia;
van tapinando vergini con pianti;
morti, arsioni di case e luoghi santi,
presi innocenti con tormenti e doglia.   8
Colui che 'ngrassa su questi lamenti
non goderà già mai di tal ablati,
aspetti pure il cavator de' denti;

ch' e' mal che seguon, da lui principiati,   12
cento per un, gli fian pene dolenti,
e spesso fa il mondo tal mercati.

Wherever is peace, well-being always flowers,
and so do weddings, festivities, dances, and songs;
the countryside smiles, so do women and lovers,
the people's minds entertain their best desires.   4
Wherever is war, no good seems to hold:
young women live wretchedly and cry,
deaths, burnings of homes and of holy places,
innocent people captured, tortured and hurt.   8
Those who grow rich by these misfortunes
will never derive joy from their robberies;
they may be sure their Chastiser will come,
for the evils that follow, which they have begun,   12
will yield a hundred percent in dire penalties:
because the world often makes such transactions.

In line 3, *ville* refers to country estates, villages, and the countryside in general. In line 11, *il cavator de' denti*, translated here as "chastiser," literally means "man who pulls out teeth." In those days, having a tooth pulled by a so-called dentist must have been an experience few looked forward to. This poem is one of twelve sonnets that Sacchetti sent to Manfredi Astore, lord of Faenza.

The upcoming "Fiamma dal ciel su le tue treccie piova" is the first sonnet Petrarch wrote castigating the vices of the papal court of Avignon. It was probably penned toward the end of the pontificate of Clement VI—that is, before 1352. Clement—to the world, Pierre Roger—was the former archbishop of Rouen. He was known for keeping an elegant court, spending extravagantly, favoring his relatives, and being unquestioningly pro-French.

Fiamma dal ciel su le tue trecce piova,
malvagia, che dal fiume et da le ghiande
per l'altrui impoverir se' ricca et grande;
poi che di mal oprar tanto ti giova;   4
nido di tradimenti, in cui si cova
quanto mal per lo mondo oggi si spande,
de vin serva, di lecti et di vivande,
in cui Luxuria fa l'ultima prova.   8
Per le camere tue fanciulle et vecchi
vanno trescando, et Belzebub in mezzo
co' mantici et col foco et co li specchi.
Già non fustú nutrita in piume al rezzo,   12
ma nuda al vento, et scalza fra gli stecchi:
or vivi sì ch'a Dio ne venga il lezzo.

A flame from heaven may rain on your hair,
o evil one, you, who from water and from acorns
have grown big and rich by making others poor;
for you greatly profit from your vicious conduct;   4
you are a nest of treason, in which breeds the evil
that today is spreading throughout the world;
you are addicted to wine, to food, and to sex;
lewdness in you exerts its utmost power.   8
In your rooms, old men and young women
copulate, and in their midst is Beelzebub
with bellows, with mirrors, and with fire.
You were not reared in leisure and in feathers,   12
naked in the wind you went barefoot over thorns:
now you live so that your stench rises to God.

In line 1, *fiamma*, meaning "flame," is a reference is to the rain of fire that destroyed the towns of Sodom and Gomorrah. *Trecce*: tresses, hairs, metonymy for the great whore of Revelation 14:8 (cf. *Inferno* 19, 106–11, and *Purgatorio* 32, 149–50). In line 2, *dal fiume et da le ghiande* (from the river and from acorns) is understood to mean the humility and poverty of the early Christians, from which the papacy had grown rich and dominant. In the fourteenth century, the religious authorities were strongly opposing all movements advocating the refusal of property. One of them was the order of those Franciscans who decided to follow the strict rule of St. Francis. In line 4, *giova* is to be taken in the Latin sense of "to like." In line 10, *trescare* is dancing the *tresca*, a rather energetic country dance. Euphemistically, it indicates sexual intercourse. In line 11, the metaphorical bellows blow on the fire of lasciviousness, and the mirrors multiply its images. In line 12, *al rezzo* literally means "in the shade"—that is, in comfort. Regarding line 14, I read this line as a plain statement. Others read it as an optative sentence meaning "may the stench of your sins reach the heavens," in the assumption that God would then send down an appropriate punishment. Other sonnets by Petrarch are in section 2.8.

Braccio Bracci addressed "Deh non guastare il popolo Cristiano," which is a caudate sonnet, to Pope Gregory XI during the Florentine War of Eight Saints. The saints in question were the eight members of the Committee on War. They were called saints in contempt of the pope. When, in 1370, Gregory XI, petitioned by St. Catherine of Siena and St. Brigitte of Sweden, decided to go back to Rome, it became necessary to restore papal authority in the domains of the church. Relations with Florence had taken a turn for the worse when Pierre de Noellet, papal legate in Romagna, failed to send Florence the wheat meant to supplement a poor harvest. In turn, the Florentines refused Noellet the money he needed to pay his mercenary army. In 1375, the pope excommunicated Florence, he forbade its priesthood to perform religious ceremonies, and his troops invaded the Florentine countryside. In defiance of the interdict, the Committee of Eight, who had been chosen from Ghibelline ranks, organized a League of Allies and proceeded to promote a religious rebellion: they expropriated all church property, nullified every religious regulation, and, especially, encouraged the confraternities and practices that the pope had just condemned.[33]

Deh non guastare il popolo cristiano,
vicar di Dio, nè voler tal balìa:
la mitra e 'l pastoral tuo arme sia
e lassa altrui tener la spada in mano.   4
El Vangel di Dio leggesti invano,
che pace predicò per ogni via,
e tu fai guerra e mettici in resia,
e 'l corpo e spirto tuo si vede insano.   8
Questo giardin che guasti fu di Pietro,
che ci mostrò la via di nostra fede,
ch'anco riluce più che nessun vetro.
Certo la mente tua qui poco vede,   12
poi ch'è occupata di nuvolo tetro
che di fare alcun ben non ti concede.
Però, come Naaman, fa che ti lavi
acciò che di tal lebbra sì ti sgravi.

Pray, do not destroy the Christian people,
Vicar of God, refrain from so great a power!
May miter and crosier be your weapons
and leave all swords in the hands of others!   4
You read the gospel of God to no profit:
He prayed everywhere for peace, while
you wage war and change us into heretics:
you seem insane in body and in spirit!   8
Once the garden you devastate was Peter's;
the one who showed us the way of our faith,
which still shines far brighter than any mirror.
No doubt, your mind can see so little   12
because a murky cloud has obscured it,
allowing you to perform no good action.
So, like Naaman, do cleanse yourself,
get free of the leprosy that is infesting you.

In line 2, *balìa* is "power," with reference to the temporal power of the church. In line 3, the miter and crosier are symbols of spiritual power and ecclesiastical authority. In line 7, *mettici in resia* means "you make heretics out of us, and excommunicate us." In linen 11, Peter's garden is the community of the faithful. Peter, says the poet, was worthier than this pope, and he refers to the papacy—not to this pope—as a *vetro* (glass)—that is to say, a mirror that reflects the will of God. Regarding line 15, the Aramaean king, Naaman, was cured of leprosy after dipping seven times in the waters of the Jordan River (2 Kings 4:5–14).

The chancellor of Florence was Coluccio Salutati, a champion of the humanistic ideals of republicanism. During the conflict, he sent a red flag with *Libertas* written on it to all members of the League of Allies as a symbol of the struggle they were fighting together against foreign tyrants. The tyrants were the French pope and his foreign mercenary army. The papal soldiers were led by John Hawkwood, an English condottiere whom the Italians called Giovanni Acuto. Both sides conducted the war mostly by covert action. Florence started their campaign by instigating rebellion in papal territories, while the church authorities kept busy damaging Florentine interest everywhere in Europe. The conflict ended when Pope Gregory died. Urban VI, now residing in Rome, negotiated the peace in 1378. Urban lifted the interdict upon a payment of two hundred thousand florins. To the Florentines, who earlier in the conflict had arrived at a nonaggression pact with Hawkwood at the sound of 130,000 florins, the whole war cost two and a half million florins.

2.4 Society Changes

Il Fiore contains sonnets that forcefully reflect the political climate of the city-states. The struggle between the emerging middle classes and the old landed gentry, whose ancestors had been forced by impelling financial realities to set up residence in the nearby city, continued unabated throughout the thirteenth century. For *Il Fiore*, see 1.3.

> Vedete che danari hanno usorieri,
> siniscalchi e provosti e piatitori,
> che tutti quanti son gran rubatori,
> e sì son argogliosi molto e fieri.   4
> Ancor borghesi sopra i cavalieri
> son oggi tutti quanti, venditori
> di lor derrate e atterminatori,
> sì ch'ogne gentil uom farà panieri,   8
> e conviene che vendan casa o terra
> infin che i borghesi sian pagati,
> ché giorno e notte gli tegnono in serra.
> Ma io, che porto panni devisati,   12
> fo creder lor che ciascheun si erra,
> e 'nganno ingannatori e ingannati.

> See how much money the bankers make,
> and all sorts of magistrates and lawyers,
> all of them such high-style robbers,
> and so very proud and so arrogant.   4
> Indeed nowadays all the burghers
> have risen far above the knights,
> by offering their wares on short-term credit
> they'll turn the aristocrats into paupers;   8
> for these must sell their homes and lands
> in order to reimburse the city dwellers

who go on harassing them day and night.
But I, who wear a different cloak, make   12
them both believe they are in the wrong:
this way, I mislead misleaders and misled.

Regarding line 1, the bankers are called usurers. In line 2, *siniscalchi* and *provosti* were different kinds of city officials. *Piatitori*, from *piata* (brief), are the solicitors. In line 5, *borghesi*, or burghers, are city dwellers, as opposed to the old landed gentry. In 7, the *atterminatori*, from *termine* (term), were the businessmen who sold merchandise on fixed-term credit. In line 12, the character speaking is False Seeming, who in *Il Fiore*—and in *Le Roman de la Rose*, of which *Il Fiore* is an Italian adaptation—lectures and gives the lover advice on how to conquer the flower. He is a friar and therefore wears "a different cloak."

In *Le Roman de la Rose*, False Seeming makes only a brief mention of the "people" and the "folks of small means." The corresponding Italian character is more class conscious and fully aware of changing economy and politics: the old noble families, owners of country estates and short of cash, the author of *Il Fiore* specifies, are reduced to borrowing from city bankers at high interest rates and eventually lose both property and political influence.

By the first decades of the fourteenth century, power was solidly in the hands of the affluent bourgeoisie, who were economically and politically organized through the major guilds, or *arti maggiori*. These guilds represented the bankers, woolen cloth manufacturers, furriers, Calimala merchants (who carried on a much diversified trade), jurists and notaries, doctors and apothecaries, and spice dealers.[34] The minor guilds, or *arti minori*, represented artisans and shopkeepers. At the bottom of the social scale were the *popolo minuto* (small people)—that is, the less prosperous artisans and the salaried workers. In Florence, as everywhere else, there were those who deplored the enterprising spirit of some fellow citizens. Being comfortable with the old order and fearing all social changes, they were in no mood to appreciate the novel ways and progress brought about by the people with upward mobility.

Among the complainers was Pieraccio Tedaldi. Of him, we know little: he was in the army fighting for Florence, and in 1325, the Pisans took him prisoner at the Battle of Montecatini. For other sonnets by this poet, see 2.6.

Il mondo vile è oggi a tal condotto
che senno non ci vale o gentilezza,
se e' non v'è misticata la ricchezza
la qual condisce e 'nsala ogni buon cotto.   4
E chi ci vive per l'altrui ridotto
non è stimato e ciascuno lo sprezza
e ad ognuno ne vien una schifezza
con uno sdegno, e non gli è fatto motto.   8
Però rechisi ognun la mano al petto
ed in tal modo cerchi provvedere
ch'egli abbia de' danar: quest'è l'effetto.
E poi che gli ha, gli sappia mantenere,   12
se e' non vuole che poi gli sia detto
—Io non ti posso patir di vedere!—

This vile world is reduced to such a state
that wisdom and kindness are not worth a zilch,
unless mixed with them somehow is money,
which seasons and flavors all worthy collations.   4
If his livelihood depends on someone else,
a man won't be respected, he is despised by all;
people are bound to grow for him revulsion
and anger; nobody will utter to him one word.   8
Therefore, let us place a hand on our hearts
and let us set our minds on making money,
because these are indeed the simple facts.
So when we have it, we must be able   12
to keep it, if we do not want to be told,
"I cannot even stand looking at you!"

The reference in line 5 is to salaried people, those who work for someone else. In line 11, *effetto* refers to the result, or the truth of the matter.

In the following sonnet, Bindo Bonichi takes a resigned view of people's ambitions and discontents.

El calzolai' fa 'l suo figliol barbiere,
così 'l barbier fa 'l figliuol calzolaio;
el mercatante fa 'l figliuol notaio,
così 'l notaio fa 'l figliuol drappiere.   4
Mal contento è ciascun di suo mestiere,
ch'a ciascun guadagnar par col cucchiaio,
l'altro gli par li faccia con lo staio:
non ha l'uom sempre tutto quel che chiere.   8
Null'uom nel mondo si può contentare:
chi star può fermo nel luogo fallace
ovver sicuro in tempestoso mare?
Assai fa l'uom se ben porta in pace   12
l'avversità che li convien passare
mentre che sta in quest'ardente fornace.

The cobbler wants his son to be a barber,
the barber wants his son to be a cobbler;
the merchant wants him to be a lawyer,
and the lawyer wants him to be a clothier.   4
Everyone is discontent with his occupation,
thinking he is earning money with a spoon
while others gather riches by the bushel:

no man can have everything he wants. 8
In this world no one is satisfied:
can a man remain steady on sinking ground,
and can anyone feel safe in a stormy sea?
Much accomplishes the man who patiently 12
bears the adversities he is not able to evade,
while living in this scorching world of ours.

In line 7, *staio* is a unit of capacity whose value differed from region to region. In line 12, *porta* stands for *sopporta*, from *sopportare*, meaning "to bear." Born into a prosperous family of Siena, Bindo Bonichi (1260—1338) occupied several important government positions, including that of governor. He was also a member of the Opera di Santa Maria, a committee of citizens who supervised the construction of the new cathedral. In old age, he entered religious life and became an oblate friar of the Virgin Mary. In "Fra l'altre cose non lievi a portare," Bonichi gives a description of society in which the rich, the poor, and the pretenders seem to mix and change places with the greatest ease.

Fra l'altre cose non lievi a portare
è 'l mercenai' veder tosto arricchito
e l'uom che di fiorini è mal guarnito
far del superbo e voler grandeggiare, 4
e 'l ricco stolto a la ringhiera andare
(vuol senneggiar e scendene schernito),
e femmina, che ha 'l quarto marito,
di castità volersi gloriare. 8
Ancora, ed è vie maggior ricadia:
a l'ignorante sentir dar sentenza
di quella la cosa che non sa che sia; 12
e 'l mal volpon, che par di penitenza
ed è vasello di ipocresia,
udir giurare in buona coscienza.

Among other things not easy to bear
is seeing a low-class man get rich quickly,
a man badly provided with florins strain
to show off and behave conceitedly, 4
a rich and stupid one become a politician
(acting as a know-it-all, then falling from grace),
and a woman who has had at least four
husbands trying to flaunt her chastity. 8
There is still an even greater bother:
to listen to a fool making a pronouncement
about matters of which he knows nothing,
and to hear an evil fox—who seems a paragon 12

of repentance but is vessel of hypocrisy—
making a momentous oath in all honesty.

In line 2, *mercenaio* refers to a man of the lower classes (Contini 1970, 448). In line 5, *andare alla ringhiera* means "to go to the railings"—that is, to run for public office. *Ringhiera* refers to the railings of the platform on which the ancient Roman lawyers delivered their pleas. In line 13, *vasello di ipocresia* means "vessel of hypocrisy," which recalls the "chosen vessel," or chosen instrument, by which, in the Acts 9:15, God refers to Saul of Tarsus, or Saint Paul, in saying: "This man is my chosen vessel who will bring my name before the gentiles, the kings, and the children of Israel." For the same word and context, cf. *Inferno* 2, 29.

2.5 Deaths of Dante and Immanuel Romano

Having refused to go back to Florence and plead his cause at humiliating conditions, Dante spent the rest of his life wandering from town to town in search of patronage. He was at the court of Della Scala in Verona from May 1303 to March 1309 and again from May 1312 to early 1318, when Cangrande was lord of the city. He then moved to Ravenna and placed himself at the service of Guido da Polenta, and there he died in 1321, having caught malaria while on a diplomatic trip to Venice. There is poetic justice in Dante's spending the last days of his life under the sponsorship of Guido Novello da Polenta, for Guido was a nephew of Francesca da Rimini, whom the poet had immortalized in canto 10 of *Inferno*. There is a kind of historical retributive irony, one might add, in his dying of malaria caught in exile, for Guido Cavalcanti, his friend, whose exile Dante must have approved when he was one of the priors in charge of the Florentine government, died the same way.

At the news of Dante's death, many sonneteers commemorated his life and achievements. Among them were Giovanni Quirini, Immanuel Romano, and Bosone da Gubbio.

Giovanni Quirini was a Venetian merchant who served Venice in diplomatic and military capacities in the decades from 1300 to 1330. In "Segnor, ch'avete di pregio corona," he entreats Cangrande della Scala to release Dante's *Paradiso* to the public. When living in Verona, Dante dedicated the last *cantica* of *The Divine Comedy* to the lord of the city and, in doing so, made him both sponsor and testamentary heir.

Segnor, ch'avete di pregio corona
per l'universo e fama di prodeza,
di onor, di cortesia e di largheza
e di iusticia, che meglio ancor sona,   4
e di virtù vostra gentil persona
ornata fulge e splende in grande alteza,
sì ch'ogni nazion vi dotta e preza
udendo ciò che di voi si ragiona.   8
Io sono un vostro fedel servitore

bramoso di veder la gloria santa
del Paradiso che 'l poeta canta,
onde vi prego che di cotal pianta   12
mostrar vi piaccia i bei fioretti fore,
ché e' dian frutto degno al suo fattore,
lo quale intese, e so ch'intende ancore,
che di voi prima per lo mondo spanta   16
agli altri fosse questa ovra cotanta.

My lord, you wear a great crown of virtue,
in the whole universe you enjoy fame of valor,
of honor, of courtesy, of munificence,
and of justice, which resound even higher;   4
your noble person, bedecked in virtue,
shines and sparkles at great heights,
and people regard you with respect,
hearing the virtues that of you are sung.   8
I am a faithful servant of yours
who yearns to see the blessed glory
of the paradise that the poet has sung:
therefore, I pray that it may please you   12
to display the amiable flowers of that plant
so they may give due glory to their author,
who did expect, and I know still expects
that now you should be the first to make   16
known his great work also to others.

In line 1, the phrase *di pregio corona* is a reminiscence of Dino Compagni's *Canzone del pregio* (song about merit), which enumerates and illustrates the qualities a prince must acquire if he wants to be esteemed and honored.[35] With regard to line 11, in his *Life of Dante*, Giovanni Boccaccio wrote that whenever the poet had completed six or seven cantos of *Paradiso*, he sent them to Cangrande for his approval and sponsorship. A long propitiatory address to Cangrande occupies the first eight lines, the poet's request begins on line 9, and it flows along acquiring persuasive power and clinches the argument in the tail. For the tailed sonnet, see the introduction.

Literary historians tell us that Bosone da Gubbio and Immanuel Romano (1.6 and 2.4) were friends. Romano resided in several towns of the Marche and might have met Bosone, a local public official, at Gubbio, in the home of his sponsor.[36] Besides sharing an admiration for Dante and writing under his inspiration,[37] the two men had been at the court of Della Scala: Romano might have been one of the many literati received by Cangrande, and Bosone must have lived in Verona when his father, Bosone di Guido d'Alberico, was *podestà* of that city, at the time of Alberto della Scala, Cangrande's father.

The Della Scala court had been open to a variety of cultural influences since the time of Ezzelino III, son-in-law of Emperor Frederick II Hohenstaufen. Cangrande, as lord of Verona (1308–29), continued the cultural policy of his family, making the city a refuge for artists and writers of all religions and backgrounds. As Giorgio Battistoni suggests, the concept of a multinational empire—championed by Dante in *De Monarchia*—might have taken shape or might have strengthened in Ghibelline Verona, thanks to the encounter of the Christian world with texts of Islamic and Hebrew origin. In his Italian *frottola*, called *bisbidis* (69–76), Romano enthusiastically described the marvels of the Veronese court, where, among other things, one could "hear people discuss about astrology, philosophy and theology. Here Germans, Italians, French, Flemish, and English debate with one another" (*Quivi astrologia / con filosofia / e di teologia udrai disputare. / Quivi Tedeschi / Latini e Franceschi / Fiamenghi e Ingheleschi / insieme parlare*). It is not, therefore, surprising that when Dante died in 1321, Bosone sent Immanuel the following sonnet.

Due lumi son di novo spenti al mondo,
in cui virtù e bellezza si vedea;
piange la mente mia, che già ridea,
di quel che di saper toccava il fondo.   4
Piange la tua del bel viso giocondo
di cui tua lingua tanto ben dicea;
o me dolente, che pianger devea
ogni uomo che sta a questo tondo!   8
E pianga dunque Manoel giudeo,
e pianga prima il suo proprio danno,
poi pianga il mal di questo mondo reo,
ché sotto il sol non fu mai peggior anno;   12
ma mi conforta ch'io credo che Deo
Dante abbia posto in glorioso scanno.

Two lights have vanished from the world:
in them, one could admire beauty and virtue;
my mind, which once rejoiced, now mourns
for the man that plumbed the depth of knowledge.   4
Your mind bemoans the pleasant features
that your tongue used to praise so much.
I grieve, alas, because all the human beings
who live on this round world should weep!   8
And may Immanuel the Jew also weep,
weep first for his own misfortune, and then
for the adversity befallen to this evil world,
for under the sun never was a year worse than this.   12
What comforts me is my belief that God
must have assigned to Dante a heavenly seat.

In line 1, *due lumi*, means, literally, "two lights." It is usually used to refer to the eyes of the beloved, here Dante's eyes. Some interpreters think that one eye indicates Dante and the other refers to Immanuel's wife, who was alive at the time and had several more years to live. *Di novo* connotes novelty and surprise, for the original meaning of *novo* is "out of the ordinary," hence "newsworthy." Regarding line 2, *virtù e bellezza* were the requisite qualities predicated of any person of merit but especially of one's beloved. Regarding line 4, Dante's contemporaries admired him above all for his encyclopedic knowledge and philosophical expertise (Sapegno 1966, 113). Battistoni suggested a plausible explanation of lines 4–5: while Bosone would primarily admire Dante's erudition (*saper*), Immanuel would instead appreciate his poetic accomplishment (*bel viso giocondo*). In line 8, *tondo*, meaning "round," is possibly a recollection of Dante's "round ether," meaning the earth, in *Paradiso* 22, 132. With *il suo proprio danno* in line 10, we see that while subsuming his own sadness under that of the public mourning, Bosone imagines Immanuel to be lamenting the loss of not only a great poet but also a personal friend (Battistoni 57). In line 12, the *peggior anno* is 1321, the year Dante died. This was also the year when the Christian authorities expelled Roman Jews from their city.

"Io, che trassi le lacrime dal fondo" is Romano's answer to Bosone's sonnet. Besides repeating his correspondent's rhyme scheme and making use of the six rhyming words of his sestet—*giudeo, scanno, reo, anno, Deo*, and *danno*—Romano takes up Bosone's ideas section by section.

> Io, che trassi le lacrime dal fondo
> de l'abisso del cor, che 'n su le 'nvea,
> piango; ché 'l foco del dolor m'ardea,
> se non fosser le lacrime, in che abbondo; 4
> ché la lor piova ammorta lo profondo
> ardor, che del mio mal fuor mi traea;
> per non morir, per tener altra vea
> al percoter sto forte e non affondo. 8
> E ben può pianger cristiano e giudeo,
> e ciaschedun sedere 'n tristo scanno:
> pianto perpetual m'è fatto reo,
> per ch'io m'accorgo che quel fu il mal anno, 12
> sconfortomi, ben ch'i' veggio che Deo
> per invidia del ben fece quel danno.

> Drawing tears from the deep recesses
> of my heart, which send them mounting,
> I weep; for the fire of grief would have burned
> me, except for the tears that in me abound; 4
> their rain has extinguished the deep-seated
> ardor which would have released me of pain;
> in order not to die, I choose a different way,
> I stand firm under the blows and I do not drown. 8
> May every Jew and every Christian weep,
> may everyone be seated on a mourning chair;
> but to me a perpetual grief seems unworthy,
> because, while I recognize this as a luckless year 12
> and deeply grieve, still I see that God for envy
> of our good luck has brought such calamity on us.

Per lines 2–6, the poet is perilously caught between fire and water, between the heart-felt pain for the loss and the flood of tears, which has the power to alleviate his deep-burning grief. Romano's imagery takes after the paradox of the lover perpetually caught between two extremities, tortured as he is by the fire of his passion on one side and the coldness of the reception he receives on the other. Per line 6, by extinguishing the fire, his tears have saved him from dying, death being the release from pain. In line 8, Romano says, "I remain four-squared firm under the blows of fortune," just as Dante had declared to be (*tetragono ai colpi di fortuna*) when his future misfortunes were forecast (*Paradiso* 17, 24). In line 12, the bad year, *mal'anno*, is 1321, the year also mentioned in the previous sonnet. Dante's death (the *danno*, meaning "damage," of line 14) is God's will: the great poet, says Immanuel, has been called to heaven by the Omnipotent, because God envied human beings for having such a great man among them, just as, in Dante's *La Vita Nuova*, Beatrice dies because the angels, envious of her presence on earth, summon her back to paradise. Alternatively, by following Romano's syntax closely, one can interpret the sestet as follows: "a perpetual grief sternly [*reo*] comes to me, for I recognize this to be a luckless year and I deeply mourn, though I see that God for envy of our luck brought such calamity on us."

After Romano's death in 1331, Cino da Pistoia and Bosone da Gubbio exchanged the following sonnets.[38]

Messer Boson, lo vostro Manoello,
seguitando l'error de la sua Legge,
passato è ne lo Inferno e prova quello
martir ch'è dato a chi non si corregge.   4
Non è con tutta la comune gregge,
ma con Dante si sta sotto al cappello
del qual, come nel libro suo si legge,
vide coperto Alessi Interminello.   8
Tra lor non è sollazzo, ma corruccio,
del qual fu pieno Alessi com'un orso
e raggia là dove vede Castruccio.
E Dante dice: "Quel satiro morso   12
ci mostrò Manoello in breve sdruccio
de l'uom che innesta 'l persico nel torso."

Sir Bosone, your Emmanuel,
erroneously persisting in his Law,
has ended up in hell and now he suffers
the pain of those who did not repent.   4
However, he is not with the common herd;
he is with Dante, covered by the same hat
that Dante saw—as it's written in his book—
covering Alessio degli Interminelli's head.   8
There is no rejoicing there, only anger,

> of which Alessio is as full as a bear, groaning
> as he does when casting an eye on Castruccio.
> Dante says, "In a short *sdruccio* Manuello   12
> showed us how worthy of scorn a satire can be,
> like grafting a peach branch on a pear tree."

The sonnet does not explain why Dante and Manuello should be in hell together—only Immanuel's persistence in the old law is mentioned in line 2—and no interpreter has wondered, supposedly because it is ironic and amusing to think that two poets who visited hell when alive should find themselves permanently in it when dead. What critics have been arguing about at length is why Dante and Manuello should specifically find themselves in the eighth circle of *Inferno* (17, 118–26), which is reserved for flatterers and seducers. Regarding lines 6–8, in Dante's *Inferno*, the flatterers are fittingly plunged in human excrement. Regarding line 11, being a Guelf, Alessio would naturally be angry at the sight of his relative Castruccio Castracani degli Interminelli, who was a Ghibelline leader and, after defeating the Tuscan Guelfs, became lord of Lucca (see 2.3). Per line 14, trying to reconcile things that do not go together would be like grafting a branch of a peach tree on a pear tree.

Commentators have suggested that the irreconcilable things Dante and Immanuel tried to put together are religion and courtly love, or even Christian and Jewish doctrine. The contradiction mentioned by the sonnet can only refer to Dante and Immanuel pretending to be both Guelfs and Ghibellines, and flattery, therefore, would be the sin that has fittingly brought them to that specific section of hell. Indeed, by flattering Cangrande and other princes, Dante tried to reconcile his old Guelf party affiliation with his newly found Ghibelline leanings, sympathies that his declared hope in Emperor Henry VII and praise of Cangrande in *Paradiso* 17 clearly attest. As to Romano, he openly and flippantly described himself as a political turncoat (see 2.3) who agrees with any powerful person he happens to be facing. To what poem line 12 of the sonnet refers is more difficult to establish. I suggest that by *sdruccio*, Cino might have meant Romano's *bisbidis*, a poem that, in the manner of the classical Roman satire, displays a variety of scenes and topics and describes Cangrande's court in vivid onomatopoeic and multilinguistic details.[39]

Here is Bosone's answer to Cino.

> Manoel, che mettete 'n quell'avello
> ove Lucifero più che altri regge,
> non è del regno di colui rubello
> che il mondo fe' per riempir sue segge.   4
> E ben che fosse in quello luogo fello
> ove 'l ponete, ma non chi 'l vel regge,
> n'avea depinto il ver vostro pennello
> che lui e Dante cuopra tal lavegge.   8
> Alessi raggi sotto tal capuccio
> ma non se doglia se con lui è corso
> lo quell fece morir messer Guerruccio.
> Dante e Manoello compiono lor corso   12
> ov' è loro cotto lo midollo e 'l buccio,
> tanto che giunge lor lo gran soccorso.

> Immanuel, whom you placed in that vault
> where Lucifer legislates above all others,
> does not belong in the kingdom of him who,
> to fill his seats, enticed the world to revolt.   4
> Even if he were in a place as foul as where
> you put him—but not who holds him there—
> your brush did not depict the truth correctly
> by painting him and Dante under that sludge.   8
> May well Alessi roar under such hat,
> but he may not complain, if with him is placed
> the man who caused Sir Guerruccio's death.
> Dante and Immanuel will follow their course   12
> where they are to burn their skin and mellow,
> until the day of their great release shall dawn.

Dante and Immanuel might be expiating their sins in a place that is as unpleasant as hell, says Bosone, but not under Lucifer (line 4). In hell are fittingly found Alessi and the man who killed Guerruccio. Dante and Immanuel are on the seventh corniche of purgatory, where their bones will be burned to the marrow until forgiveness comes from heaven, and they, purged of all sins, will enter paradise. Regarding lines 9–11, I have not been able to discover who killed this Guerruccio. By the logic of this sonnet and of *Inferno* 17, it ought to be Castruccio Castracani. For many critics, the fact that Cino and Bosone, who were Dante's and Romano's contemporaries, paired them in the same after-death destiny is a confirmation that in life, they had been friends.

2.6 Town and Country

Town and country play a role in the poetry of this section either as a theme or as a setting. They set the stage for the spontaneous realism with which the sonneteers describe their own and other people's activities and moods. All sonnets by Pucci are caudate, as are "Oggi abbian lunedì" by Tedaldi and "El mi rincresce" by Nuccoli. In Nuccoli's poem, the coda consists of two hendecasyllable lines. The codas of other sonnets consist of two hendecasyllables preceded by a *settenario* that rhymes with the last line of the sonnet proper. In all cases but one, the coda is independent of the sonnet but brings to it an added point, a clinching finish to its argument. For a lengthier explanation of the caudate, or tailed, sonnet, see the introduction.

Pieraccio Tedaldi wrote the upcoming poems between 1327 and 1328, when he was guardian of the Castle of Montopoli, a Florentine stronghold at a strategic crossroad of Valdarno, a valley of the Arno River.

> Se colla vita io esco de la buca,
> ov'io son castellano pel discreto
> messer Filippo da Santo Gineto,

vece in Firenza per messer lo duca,
ch'egli, o su' oficial, mi riconduca,
quand'io arò il termine colleto,
se io accetto, ciò non glielo veto,
frustato io sia con aspra marmeluca.
Però che io ci sono assedïato
da' forti venti e da la carestia,
ed ogni cosa m'è porto e collato;
di quel ch'è vaga più la vita mia,
ciò è di veder donne, son privato,
in chiesa, a li balconi o ne la via.

    4

    8

   12

Should I come out of this hole alive,
where I am Castellan in the name
of our illustrious Sir Filippo da Santo Gineto,
Vicar in Florence of our Lord the Duke,
and should he or his officials ask me back
when my prescribed term expires,
and, should I accept—for so am I inclined—
may he lash me with a prickly whip!
Here I am besieged by strong winds
and by shortages of food; and everything
must be brought and hoisted up to me;
but of what I am most keen in life, I am
deprived, which is to say, of looking at women
in church, on balconies, and in the street.

      4

      8

     12

In line 1, the hole (*la buca*) is Montopoli. Regarding lines 2–4, Filippo da Santo Gineto was general vicar, representing Carlo, duke of Calabria. The Florentines, fearful of Castruccio Castracani, had accepted the lordship of the duke, who was the son of Robert Anjou, king of Naples. In line 6, *colleto* means "completed"—that is, "when I shall complete or reach the end of my term." In line 10, *collato*, from *collare*, is to pull up by a cord.

I' truovo molti amici di starnuto,
e chi di "Bene andiate" e "Ben vegnate,"
chi di profferte e piccole derrate,
mostrando ognun ver me il volere acuto.
Ma tal fiata io ho bisogno aiuto
aver da lor, denari ovver derrate,
chi gambero diventa piccolo, frate,
chi sordo o orbo, o chi diventa muto.
Sì ch'io son fermo di trasnaturare

    4

    8

e di più non aver la man forata,
e quel che m'è rimaso ben guardare,
e spender sempre secondo l'intrata: 12
e l'animo è seguace al migliorare,
ch'oggi la gente è troppa iscozzonata.

I find many friends worth a sneeze,
a "God bless you" or a "You're welcome!"
who are good for promises and small handouts,
and others who swear they are at my full disposal.   4
However, every time I need their help,
either in form of money or in provisions,
then, brother! one withdraws like a crawfish,
one turns deaf, another blind, another dumb.   8
So I am firmly resolved to change nature,
to have no holes going through my hands,
to pay full attention to what I have left,
and to live strictly within my income: 12
my mind is well disposed to improve,
for nowadays people are far too astute.

Oggi abbiam lunedì, come tu sai;
domani è martedì, com'è usato;
mercoledì è l'altro nominato;
poi giovedì, el qual non falla mai.   4
L'altro so che cognosci, per che sai
che carne non si mangia in nessun lato;
sabato è l'altro, i' non l'ho smenticato;
l'altro è quel dì che a bottega non vai.   8
Qualunque s'è di questi, mille volte
hai detto del fornir del fatto mio,
e poi mi dì che hai faccende molte.
Tu hai faccende men che non ho io;   12
le tue promesse tutte vane e stolte
le truovo, con sustanza men che un fio.
Dimmi s' tu credi ch'io
ne sia servito innanzi al die iudicio;   16
quando che non, rinunzio al beneficio.

Today is Monday, as you well know;
tomorrow is Tuesday, as the custom is;
the next day is called Wednesday;

then comes Thursday, which is never missing.	4
Of the next day I know you are aware,	
because people don't eat meat anywhere;	
Saturday is the other, I have not forgotten;	
and the next is when we don't go to work.	8
Whatever the day, a thousand times	
you told me you'll give me what you owe me,	
then you say you have so many things to do.	
You have less to do than I, and I do find	12
your promises to be empty and senseless,	
and to be worth far less than a farthing.	
So let me know if you really do think	
you will pay me back before judgment day;	16
if not, I shall give up what is due to me.

Corretto son del tutto e castigato	
di non giacer con femmina nessuna,	
o bella o brutta o bianca o rossa o bruna,	
infino che io avrò punto del fiato.	4
Così mi foss'io tosto riposato,	
ch'i' ebbi quanrant'anni, in ciascaduna,	
e la mia opra ne fosse digiuna	
ben quindici che io v'ho poi peccato.	8
Però che saria bene a l'alma mia	
e poscia al corpo ed anche al mio borsello,	
se raffrenato avessi mia follia.	
Ch'io l'ho per un gran matto ed un gran fallo	12
chi non corregge sé di tal risìa	
in prima ch'e' diventi vecchiarello.

I am chastised and strongly determined	
not to lay with whatever woman any longer,	
may she be pretty, ugly, white, brown, or red,	
as long as I shall be able to draw a breath.	4
Now I wish I had given it up, and	
with everyone, the day I turned forty,	
and that my works had been inactive	
all the fifteen years I went on sinning.	8
Had I been able to restrain my folly,	
it would have been good for my soul,	
for my body, as well as for my wallet.	
For I believe anyone is wicked and mad,	12

who cannot get free of such like sacrilege,
before turning into a weakened little man.

Opra, or *opera*, is used in line 7 euphemistically to indicate Pietro's reproductive apparatus. Besides indicating the work of a writer or a composer, *opera* often refers to the construction and maintenance of a public building and to the committee supervising them, as in the expression *Opera di San Michele*—that is, the work carried on in the Church of Saint Michael and the citizens' committee that controlled it. For another poem by Pieraccio, see 2.4.

Antonio Pucci (ca. 1310–88) was born, lived, and died in Florence. He started his working life as a foundry man, and in 1334, he progressed to become the city's bell ringer. Because of his literary proclivities, in 1349, the Florentine government promoted him to town crier.[40] Much of what he wrote was tied to that public position. Some of his poems, in the form of the narrative *cantare* or *sirventese*, describe momentous events in the history of the town: the flood of 1333, the famine of 1346, the plague of 1348, and the 1362–64 war against Pisa. Achille Tartaro sees him as a kind of city reporter mediating between the governing body and the city's less prosperous classes. His sonnets, which are all caudate, allow a good glimpse into the life of ordinary citizens, most of them vivacious, literate people and habitual participants in community activities and public events.

Pucci addressed "Dante Alighier ne la sua Comedia" to a friend running for city office.

Dante Alighier ne la sua Comedia
narra d'un fiume che si chiama Lete,
del qual qualunque si toglie' la sete,
ogni suo fatto di mente gli uscia.   4
Dimenticava amore e compagnia
e le cose palesi e le secrete,
perché quell'acqua gli facea parete
a la memoria e a la fantasia.   8
Così color che salgon a gli ufici
paiono inebriati di quel fiume
dimenticando parenti o amici,
e del passato non veggon più lume,   12
le lor promesse non hanno radici
e straccian di memoria ogni volume.
Deh fa' che tal costume,
caro compare mio, non regni in te,   16
ma se tu puoi, ricordati di me.

In his Comedy, Dante Alighieri
tells of a river whose name is Lethe,
in whose water anyone quenching his thirst
would have all facts come out of his head.   4

He would forget lovers and friends,
both secret and well-known events,
because that water becomes a barrier
to imagination and to remembrance. 8
Similarly, those who rise to public spheres
seem to get intoxicated with such a river:
they quickly forget relatives and friends,
and no longer can throw any light on the past; 12
their promises turn out to have no substance,
for tomes are ripped off from their cognizance.
Please, take care that such habit,
dear friend, does not take roots in you, 16
and try to remember me, if you could.

Regarding line 2, Lethe is the river of oblivion found in *Inferno* 14, 136–38 and in *Purgatorio* 28, 121–32. The tomes of memory in line 14 are reminiscent of *La Vita Nuova* 1.1, in which Dante, recollecting his early love for Beatrice, speaks of his "book" of memory. The whole sonnet is taken up with the behavior of public officials who forget the promises they have made during their electoral campaigns. Finally, in the coda, Pucci turns to his friend and asks to be remembered.

"Deh fammi una canzon, fammi un sonetto"
mi dice alcun ch'ha la memoria scema,
e parli pur che, datomi la tema,
i' ne debba cavare un gran diletto. 4
Ma e' non sa ben bene il mio difetto
né quanto il mio dormir per lui si strema,
ché prima ch'una rima dal cor prema
do cento e cento volte per lo letto. 8
Poi lo scrivo tre volte alle mie spese,
però che prima corregger lo voglio
che 'l mandi fuori tra la gente palese.
Ma d'una cosa tra l'altre mi doglio: 12
ch'i' non trovai ancora un sì cortese
che mi dicesse, "Te' il denai' del foglio."
Alcuna volta soglio
essere a bere un quartuccio menato, 16
e pare a loro aver soprapagato.

"Please, write me a song, write me a sonnet,"
says to me someone with a defective brain,
thinking that, when I am given a subject,
I can draw from it a huge entertainment. 4

He does not know at all what it costs me,
how much he is impinging on my sleep, how
to squeeze one rhyme out of my heart,
I have to turn in bed more than a hundred flips.   8
Then, to my exhaustion, I write it thrice,
because I want to improve it to perfection
before sending it to the world loud and wide.
Among other things, what most pains me   12
is that I find no one yet so considerate
as to say, "For the paper, here is some cash."
Once in a while,
someone offers to buy me a drink,   16
and thinks to have somehow overpaid!

In line 16, *quartuccio* is a unity of capacity that varied in size but was usually a quarter of a liter. Pucci had many fans among people of his class, members of the so-called *popolo minuto* (the little people), who apparently did not appreciate the pains his literary parturitions gave him. Neither did they think of compensating him for the trouble they caused. "I' fui iersera, Adrian, sì chiaretto" is amicably addressed to Adriano de' Rossi, also a sonneteer, after a night spent together drinking.

Io fui iersera, Adrian, sì chiaretto
ch 'n verità e' non vel potre' dire,
ché mi parea si volesse fuggire
con meco insieme la lettiera e 'l letto.   4
E abbracciando il piumaccio molto stretto
Dissi: "Fratel mio, dove vuo' ire?"
In questo il sonno cominciò a venire
e tutta notte dormii con diletto;   8
e esser mi parea alla taverna
là dove Paolo vende el buon Trebbiano
che per tal modo molti ne governa,
e avendo un bicchieri di quel sano   12
in su quell'ora che 'l dì si discerna,
e voi venisti a tòrlomi di mano.
Deh non esser villano!
poi che stanotte mi togliesti il mio,   16
vieni a dar ber, ché quello accorda' io.

Adrian, last night I was so tipsy
that in truth I cannot tell you.
I felt as if I were about to fly away
together with coverlets and bedstead.   4
Holding my pillow very tight, I said,
"Brother, where do you want to go?"

At this point, slumber overcame me;
I slept peacefully through the night, 8
and I thought I was in a tavern
—where Paolo sells a good Trebbiano
and takes good care of so many—
drinking a glass of the most genuine 12
when, at the very first light of day,
you appeared, and took my drink away.
Please, stop being so rude! Last night
you got away with mine, now come and pay 16
for a drink, because the other was on me!

Trebbiano is a white wine. After four lines of introduction setting the locale of the story, the sonnet goes on describing an agitated night after a bout of drinking. In the tail, the witty retort plays on the belief, widespread since ancient Roman times, that all dreams that occur at dawn are truthful, hence Adriano's obligation to pay for the next round of drinks.

Amico mio barbier, quando tu meni
al viso altrui così grave il rasoio,
faresti me' filar a filatoio
che rader per segare altrui le veni; 4
ché quando tu mi radi tanto peni
che di malinconia tra man ti muoio
e par che tu mi metta al tiratoio
tanto piegar mi fai drieto le reni. 8
Però quando tu radi, non esser lento
e per non intaccar la man provvedi,
come facesti a me di sotto il mento.
Deh come tu se' sciocco se tu credi 12
che a radermi da te più sia contento,
s'i' avessi la barba infino a' piedi.
È ver, come tu vedi,
che 'nfino a qui alcun guadagno t'ho dato: 16
sonne pentito, ond' io non ho peccato.

Barber, my friend, you push down
the razor over my face so ponderously!
You should be working in a spinning mill,
istead of shaving and cutting people into bits. 4
When you shave, you slog about so heavily
that I almost die of anguish in your hands,
and feel like being tied to the stretching rack,

so far back I am forced to bend over my back. 8
When you shave, please, do not dawdle!
Watch out, don't let your hand slice people up,
as you did with me, here, just under my jowl.
You are indeed foolhardy, if you believe 12
I shall be glad to be sheered by you again,
should my beard grow all the way to my feet.
It is true, and you know it, that until this day
I made you earn quite a bit of money, 16
but I repent, though I am guilty of no sin.

Regarding line 7, the *tiratoio* was an instrument of torture used to pull limbs apart. Per lines 15–17, the bell ringer was known and well liked by everyone in town. Thanks to a story by a contemporary, Franco Sacchetti (*Novelle* 175), we know that Pucci owned a small house in Via Ghibellina. Behind the house was an orchard where he grew flowers, mostly jasmines, as well as fruit trees, many of which were fig trees. He also planted a number of young oaks, which he called "my forest."

Po' che no' fummo ne la zambra entrati,
non crederesti mai la nobil festa
che noi facemmo, essendo manifesta
a tutti voi se drento fussi stati, 4
sentendo i dolci baci innamorati
che le dona' dal piè fino a la testa,
e ella a me dicendo: "Ben è questa
la bocca e gli occhi ch'i' ho disïati." 8
A poco stante ella si fu spogliata,
nel letto se n'andò la graziosa,
la qual vi dico ch'io ho tanto amata.
Com'io la vidi tanto dilettosa, 12
dov' ell'entrò i' l'ebbi seguitata
e allor colsi una aulente rosa;
e fu sì graziosa
a lasciar correr a mio dimino, 16
che più d'otto ne colsi anzi mattino.

After we went into the bedroom,
you cannot believe what a glorious fun
we had, which would have been obvious
to all who had been inside with us, 4
and saw the sweet loving kisses
with which I covered her from head to foot,
while she was saying to me, "Yes, this is

> the mouth, these are the eyes I so desired!" 8
> As soon as she took off her clothes,
> the pretty one jumped on the bed,
> the girl, I say, for whom I longed so much!
> When I saw her so desirable, 12
> I followed her the way she went
> and there I picked a fragrant rose;
> and she was so gracious
> in letting me run to my pleasure, 16
> that more than eight I picked before dawn.

Last in a crown of sonnets exchanged between a man and a woman, the sonnet sets the final stage of a much-labored courtship. For Pucci, as for most sonneteers of the less erudite classes, love was not an experience needing the accompaniment of abstract speculations. The delicate metaphor of the rose, first mentioned in line 14, is reprieved in the tail to underscore the hyperbolically successful outcome of the protracted dalliance.

After the Battle of Benevento in 1266, Charles of Anjou took possession of southern Italy and moved the capital from Palermo to Naples. Under his son Robert (1308–42), Naples became a vibrant city crowded with foreigners, many of whom were businessmen and bankers. The city also had an outstanding university. Among the teachers invited from other parts of Italy was Cino da Pistoia, Dante's friend, who lectured on jurisprudence. In town was also Giotto, who had just completed the bell tower of Santa Maria del Fiore in Florence and was now painting a cycle of frescoes on the walls of Castel dell'Ovo.

Giovanni Boccaccio (1313–75), the future author of *The Decameron*, arrived in Naples from Certaldo, Tuscany, in 1327 at fifteen years of age. He worked first as apprentice with his father, Boccaccio di Chelino, and later as a middleman for the Bardi bank.[41] All the while, he wrote romances in verse and in prose and, of course, sonnets. In his writing, he gave a fictionalized version of himself as a young man about town who moved in the elegant society of the Angevin court and who was in love with the wife of a count of Aquino.[42] This, or another, was presumably the woman he called Fiammetta, who, in the following two sonnets, we see moving against a background of beaches and sea rocks.

> Discinta e scalza, con le trezze avvolte,
> e d'uno scoglio in altro trapassando,
> conche marine da quelli spiccando,
> giva la donna mia con altre molte, 4
> e l'onde, quasi in sé tutte raccolte,
> con picciol moto i bianchi piè bagnando,
> innanzi si spingevan mormorando
> e ritraênsi iterando le volte. 8
> E se tal volta, forse di bagnarsi
> temendo, i vestimenti in su tirava,
> sì ch'io vedeo più della gamba schiuso,

oh, quali avria veduto allora farsi,
chi rimirato avesse dov'io stava,
gli occhi mia vaghi di mirar più suso!

Ungirded, barefoot, her braids pinned up,
hopping from one rock to another,
and picking seashells here and there,
my woman went about with many others,
while the waves, spiraling up onto the shore,
bathed her pale feet with caressing motions,
advancing with a murmur, then withdrawing
and repeating their comings and goings.
When, perhaps in fear of getting wet, now
and then she pulled up and up her skirts,
letting me get a glimpse of her naked leg,
oh! to those who were there, looking at me
where I was, what my eyes must have seemed,
as eager as they were of seeing higher!

In line 4, *con altre molte* means "with many other young women" skipping on the beach of Baia. The style is courtly and gracious, but the woman is not idealized, and the landscape has no supernatural reflections. Fiammetta and her companions go about their games naturally, engaged in activity and in surroundings that strike us as surprisingly modern.

Se io temo di Baia e il cielo e il mare,
la terra e l'onde e i laghi e le fontane,
le parti domestiche e le strane,
alcun non se ne dee meravigliare.
Quivi s'attende solo a festeggiare
con suon e canti e con parole vane
ad inveschiar le menti non ben sane,
o d'amor le vittorie a ragionare.
Ed havvi Vener sì piena licenza,
che spess' avvien che tal Lucrezia vienvi
che torna Cleapatra al suo ostello.
Ed io lo so, e di quinci ho temenza,
non con la donna mia sì fatti sienvi,
che 'l petto l'aprino ed intrinsi in quello.

If I have a dread of Baia, of its sea and sky,
of its earth, waves, lakes, and fountains,
of its deserted spots and the frequented,

 no one indeed should be surprised.   4
 There, the people are keen on having fun,
 on music and songs, on snaring with empty
 words the minds of the undiscerning,
 and on boasting of their amorous triumphs.   8
 There, Venus displays such license
 that a woman who has arrived as honest
 as Lucretia, might go back home a Cleopatra.
 And I know it, and therefore I fear   12
 such things might happen to my woman,
 enter her heart, and take roots in there.

Baia, a small town on the Bay of Pozzuoli, in ancient Roman times, was a celebrated seaside resort, apostrophized by Ovid and Martial for its licentious lifestyle. Regarding line 2, near Baia, there are two small lakes, Averno and Lucrino. In line 7, *invischiare* is a term pertaining to hunting, meaning "to catch (birds) with birdlime." In line 9, Vener, Venus, stands for lovemaking. Regarding line 10, the Roman Lucretia was considered the perfect model of female virtue. Raped by Sextus, son of Tarquinius Superbus, the seventh king of Rome (486–510 BCE), she denounced her seducer publicly and then killed herself. Regarding line 11, Cleopatra, queen of Egypt, Caesar's and Anthony's mistress, was considered the prototype of the loose and wayward woman. Dante calls her "lascivious Cleopatra" in *Inferno* 5, 63.

In "El mi rincresce sì lo star di fuore," Cecco Nuccoli, a lawyer who lived in Perugia in the first half of the fourteenth century, contrasts the inconveniences of country living with the advantages of city life. Detained by business out of Perugia, he feels nostalgic for the friends and games he has left behind, notably the pleasures and displeasures provided by his young lover, Trebaldino Manfredini.[43]

 El mi rincresce sì lo star di fuore
 dai mura de colei ch'ogni ben mostra,
 ch'io con Tristan ne prendiria la giostra,
 sol per veder gli occhiucce ner' co' more   4
 di quel furel, che m'ha 'nvolato el core
 e tiènlosi in pregion dentro ai suoi chiostra;
 ond'io so' certo ch'a me molto costra
 prima ch'io de pregion nel cave fore.   8
 El gran diletto ch'io abbo in contado
 si è d'odir cantar rane e saleppe
 e le lucerte correr per le greppe.
 E tu in Perosa el ciamprolino e 'l dado   12
 e la taverna, con le borse ceppe;
 ed io in essa m'artrovo di rado.
 Molto divisa l'essere mio dal vostro;
 saluta 'l ciamprolin, ch'usa col nostro.

I loathe so much being outside the walls
of the town that in all good things abounds,
that with Tristan I would be ready to joust,
just to see the lovely eyes, as dark as berries,   4
of that little thief who stole my heart
and holds it prisoner within narrow fences;
and I am quite certain that a lot will cost me
before I'll be able to draw it out of prison.   8
In the country, the highest pleasure I may have
is to listen to the sounds of frogs, of crickets,
and of lizards as they swish down the ditches.
In Perugia, you can enjoy the boy, the dice,   12
and the tavern—with pocketfuls of money—
a locale that one is that I can rarely frequent.
Very different is my lifestyle from yours:
so say hallo to your boy, pal of that boy of mine.

In line 2, *Colei* is Perugia. Regarding line 3, Tristan of Cornwall is the most famous knight of the Round Table. In lines 4–5, the terms describing the object of his desire are familial and affectionately diminutive. The charming eyes of his beloved (*occhiucci* is a diminutive of *occhi*) are as dark as blackberries, and he is a little thief (*furel* is diminutive of *fure*, meaning "thief") who has snatched his heart. *Chiostra* are the walls of town. In line 7, *costra* is Perugia dialect for *costerà*, meaning "will cost." In line 9, *abbo* is dialect for *ho*, meaning "I have." In line 10, *saleppe* is dialect for *grilli*, or crickets. In line 11, *lucerte* stands for *lucertole*, or lizards, and *greppe* for *greppi*, or banks of ditches. In line 13, *ceppe*, or *piene*, means "full." In line 15, *divisa* comes from *divisare*, meaning "to be different."

Nuccoli's sonnet is a pleasant amalgam of regional terms, educated vernacular, and high-style phrases. There are references to concrete objects and localities, such as the walls of Perugia and all the good things (*ogni ben*) they contain. The self-ironizing reference to Tristan is not inconsistent with the regional familial style. The self-mockery continues in the second part of the sonnet: the only pleasure Nuccoli can find in the country is listening to the songs of frogs and crickets and the noise of lizards rustling down ditches. The two-hendecasyllable tail is an afterthought and an envoy. About Trebaldino Manfredini, the none-too-faithful object of Nuccoli's passion, we know that he, later in life, was exiled from Perugia because of his involvement in a plot to overturn the city's democratic government. He too wrote poetry. On Nuccoli, see more in the next section.

2.7 The Other Face of Love

The sonnets of this section open a window on the lives of some men of Perugia, mostly lawyers, who, for professional reasons, mingled freely with the city and country nobility. One such man was Cecco Nuccoli, the author of the following two sonnets.

Ramo fiorito, el di ch'io non te veggio,
mio lieto cor di doglia se trafigge
e la smarrita mente se refigge
con quel signore Amor ch'I' sempre chieggio.   4
Ond'io ne prego voi, prima ch'io peggio
stia, ch'io vegna so' la tua merigge;
se non, la morte dal corpo defigge
l'alma, che nel mio cor per voi posseggio.   8
Donque ve piaccia, per Dio, signor caro,
di farme grazia, prima ch'io sia morto,
ch'io non ne spero mai altro conforto
se non 'l suo dolce frutto, per me amaro;   12
ma, se per lui mia vita non riparo,
girò nell'altro mondo da te scorto.
Sì me prendeste, Amor, con novo ingegno,
ch'io sempremai so' stato vostro segno.

Flowery bough, the day I do not see you
my quiet heart is pierced through by pain,
and my mind, bewildered, turns obsessively
to Love, the despot I beseech incessantly.   4
Therefore, I beg you, before I waste away,
do let me take refuge in your shade,
or else, from this body, Death will tear away
my soul, which only for you is still in my heart.   8
So for God's sake, may it please you,
dear sir, to grant me grace before I die,
for I shall never hope for any other comfort
than the comfort of your love, so harsh to me.   12
But if that will not restore me back to life,
driven by you I shall pass on to yonder world.
You took me, Love, by such startling ruse
that I have been your target ever since.

In line 1, *ramo fiorito* (flowery bow) is a *senhal* for Trebaldino Manfredini. *Ramo* is an anagram of *amor* (love). In line 3, *smarrita* (bewildered) indicates the mind's failure to control itself, while *smarrita mente* is a close copy of Cavalcanti's *perduta mente*. In fact, many of Nuccoli's personified abstractions are reminiscent of Cavalcanti's spirits and the part they play in man's psychological undoing. In line 7, *defigge* comes from *defiggere*, meaning "to tear away." Regarding line 8, in medieval physiology, the soul—or *anima*, the vital spirit—and the sense of self resided in the heart. In line 12, *dolce frutto* (sweet fruit) is a continued metaphor for love, for its consummation. In line 14, *scorto* translates to "accompanied by the unappeasable passion for you" (Mancini 1, 127).

Felicitous in Nuccoli's poem is the coming together of the physiological analysis with some engagingly graceful images—the bough, the shade, and the fruit—as well as the balanced mixture of local dialect and courtly expressions. The two-hendecasyllable tail—exceptional for a high-style sonnet—is in the manner of a *congedo*. That is, it is the type of ending that sends off the poem to its recipient—in this case, Love.

Ogni pensier, ch'i' ho in te, se dispera
poi che con crudeltà te se' compliso,
e Dio a tal gente non dà paradiso,
ance i descaccia: e questa è cosa vera.   4
Se ben racordi il salutar di sera,
mi rispondeste: "Or va, che tu sie ucciso!"
Sempre col fin de tuoe parole un riso
t'uscìa di bocca con allegra cera,   8
ond'io, mirando a voi, foi sì contento,
che non m'increbbe le villan parole,
ma rischiaraste, com l'aere 'l vento
fa, se da nuvoli è coverto el sole: 12
sì ch'io di tal disio ognor mi pento;
poi ch'ascaran se' fatto e 'l cor m'invole.
Ma quell signor Amor, ch'amar mi trasse,
non vuol ch'io retro ritorne coi passe.

Every thought of you drives me to distraction,
ever since you became cruelty incarnate;
to people like you God grants no paradise,
he turns them away instead, and that is a fact.   4
If you remember my greeting you that night,
when you answered: "Go, go off, drop dead!"
But at the end of each word, your mouth hinted
at a smile, and you put on it a gleeful cast.   8
Hence, looking at you, I felt so happy
I did not mind your offensive words;
you cheered me up, just as the wind does
in clearing the air when clouds obscure the sun: 12
now I regret again and again my loving, since you
have become a thief and ripped off my heart.
But Love, the lord who drove me to adore you,
does not allow me to fall a single step behind.

Marino Ceccoli was a lawyer and a jurisprudent of renown. Documents attest that he practiced his profession in Perugia around 1320 to 1350. He deals with homosexual love in the high courtly style—more specifically, in the stilnovo manner—and with no less passion than we find in Cavalcanti's sonnets and no less delicacy than some sonnets penned by Dante.

A la dolce stason ch'ei torde arvegnono,
e dietro i volan glie sparvier' seguendogli,
e 'nfra le verde selve remettendogli,
quando per l'àire descendendo vegnono, 4
color che vita de deletto tegnono,
per la riviera fuor sen van veggendogli,
de colpo tal con loro arco ferendogli
quali esse spesso con Amor sostegnono. 8
Ed io che già percosso li sentivame,
mirando gl'uccelette andar piangendose
ch'a dolce lagremar con lor movìvame,
vidi un uccel da ciel ver me scendendose, 12
che 'l petto, per grimire el core, aprivame:
se non che per pietà vegnìa rendendose.

In springtime, when the thrushes return
and the falcons fly in pursuit behind them
and, plunging precipitously through the air,
force them all the way into the green forest, 4
the people who lead a life of pleasure,
when they see them, come out into open country
and with their bows inflict on them such blows
as they themselves suffer by the hand of Love. 8
But I—who already felt equally wounded
to look at the tiny birds fly away weeping,
as to be shedding with them pitying tears—
saw a bird fly down from the sky toward me, 12
wrench open my chest, and snatch out my heart,
but then, out of compassion, he slowly withdrew.

In line 6, a *riviera* is a meadow bordering on a forest. The repeated gerund (*seguendogli, remettendogli, veggendogli, ferendogli, piangendose, scendendose, rendendose*); the internal cadences; and the rhymes accented on the third vowel before the last (*-éndogli, -égnono, -ívame*) create an elegiac cadence, while terms and inflections characteristic of the Perugia area (*ei, glie, torde, esse*) bestow on the old motif of Love's cruelty a tender, familiar local flavor.

Poi che senza pietà da te m'escacce,
almen me di, signor, che via io tenga,
ch'io non so du' me stia né du' me venga,

e volontier morria su glie toi bracce. 4
E s'ucciderme déi, prego che spacce,
ché mei' m'è morir vaccio ch'io sostenga,
vivendo, morte ed infra me desvenga
a poco a poco, pur co' fanno i ghiacce. 8
S'io so' senza mercé da te fuggito,
e con glie desperate a star me mande,
fuor de speranzia, do' trovare aito?
Famme esta grazia, che de me demande 12
alcuna volta poi ch'io sirò gito:
sì che deserto al tutto no m'armande.

Since you push me away from you so cruelly,
at least tell me, sir, which path I ought to take,
for I don't know where I am and where I am to go,
while I would rather die in your arms contentedly. 4
If you must kill me, I pray, do it in a hurry:
for I prefer to die quickly, rather than suffer
a lingering death, and waste away inside
very slowly, just as glaciers are known to do. 8
If I have run away from you disconsolate,
if you cast me off among the jilted lovers,
who have no hope, where am I to find support?
At least concede me one grace and ask 12
after me sometimes when I am gone,
so I won't go bereft, deprived of everything.

In line 5, *spacce* is dialect for "hurry." In line 6, *vaccio* is another dialect word standing for *subito*, meaning "at once." Some interpret *glie desperate*, or *i disperati*, meaning "the desperate ones"—here translated as "jilted lovers"—to mean "the damned in hell" in line 10.

The sonnet "Come per' giaccio, fòre andando, sdruce" is Ceccoli's deeply felt meditation on love and is as concise a reprise of Cavalcanti's philosophical description of passion as the sonnet form could allow.

Come pèr' giaccio, fòre andando, sdruce
nostro intelletto, contemplando fiso
quest'accidente, per cui pianto e riso
e altre passion' nove l'alma aduce, 4
per che oltra natura te produce,
e il razional sentir devèn sommiso;
e quanto più se 'n vede, men proviso
è ciascun atto suo, ch'en noi induce; 8

donqua foll'è chi nostra forza crede
scrimir dai colpe che sì dolce trànno
che spesso morte—parer vita fanno.
De ciò molte consorte—a noi stanno,   12
e sì giocando, sé provar concede,
perché sua cognizion nel ciel resede.

As ice liquefies when it is exposed to air,
our intellect perishes when obsessively fixed
on that accident that forces the soul to yield
tears, laughter, and other unusual feelings;   4
because, turning us into something contrary
to nature, our rational faculty is impaired.
The more conscious of it, the least prudent
is each movement that it provokes in us;   8
therefore it's foolish to believe we may parry
the blows that can wound us so sweetly
making us believe that our dying is like living.
This way, we acquire many fellow travelers,   12
for we all may experience love only in this game,
while the real knowledge of it resides in heaven.

Per lines 1–4, just as ice perishes by liquefying, our reason fails when we love intensely. Like the "fearful accident" in Cavalcanti's "Donna me prega" (1.6), Ceccoli's love is an accidental quality, for the passion of love and other such strange cravings are products of the sensitive soul. When the rational faculty is overpowered, humans are forced to live in a way contrary to natural principles, the principles of reason. In line 7, the subject of *quanto più se 'n vede* (the more conscious of love) is *intelletto* (intellect) of line 2, meaning that the more taken by love our mind is, the less wise are the actions that love forces upon us. Regarding lines 12–14, *consorte* (fellow traveler) has the etymological meaning of "companion in misadventure." *A voi stanno* means "you have." Does the last line reinforce the impossibility for humans to know love, since only heavenly creatures know what it is, or does it suggest that an understanding of love will be possible in the life beyond?

2.8 The Divided Self: Petrarch

Petrarch—Francesco Petrarca in Italian—the master of the sonnet form, was born in Arezzo in 1304 and died in Arquà in 1374. When his father, a Florentine notary exiled from Floence at the same time as Dante, found employment at the papal court, the whole family, and young Petrarch with it, moved to Avignon. Francesco grew up in a cosmopolitan, multilingual ambiance; learned to enjoy the gay life it offered; and dropped out of law studies at the University of Bologna. After spending the money inherited from his father, he decided to take minor orders, and under the financial patronage of the church, he dedicated the rest of his life to study, poetry, and fame. On occasion, he traveled on diplomatic missions on behalf of several sponsors, but wherever he was, he remained aloof from politics and local affairs.[44] Democratic Florence offered to reinstate him in the life of the city, and he refused, choosing instead to live as a lionized guest and protégé of several potentates, such as King Robert Anjou of Naples, the Da Carrara lords of Padua, the Visconti of Milan, and as a guest of the most aristocratic Republic of Venice. Illustrative of such deliberate choices is his acceptance of the invitation that Giovanni Visconti made in 1353.[45] He chose to live at the Visconti court—as he explained in a letter of the *Variae* collection—because that lord wanted nothing from him except his presence, which he thought would give luster to himself and his domain.

Petrarch participated in different cultures—he spoke Italian and French, did his thinking in Latin, and wrote Latin and Italian—but remained alone in his intellectual and emotional world. What made him famous in Italy and abroad was the novel character of the lyrics he wrote in Italian beginning in 1327. That year, he told friends and readers, he fell in love with Laura, a woman of Avignon whom he saw for the first time in church on Easter Sunday. From then until his death in 1374, he worked on his Italian rhymes, correcting, revising, arranging, and rearranging them in a sequence known as *Canzoniere* (Songbook).

For previous poets, love had been a phenomenon impending on all human beings with the same power and set of manifestations, an experience they analyzed objectively and of which they sought to give a description philosophically correct. Petrarch did not generalize or theorize; he described the moment-to-moment thoughts and moods of one individual: himself. On their theories of love, his antecedents built a system reflecteing the values of their culture and class. Petrarch created a system of values and a fantastic world for himself alone. The eight poems that follow—chosen out of 317 sonnets of *Canzoniere*—focus on three main thematic points: the poet's fluctuating emotional state, the myth he created around Laura, and his proud awareness of a unique destiny of sensibility and fame.

The first four sonnets—numbers 30, 61, 62, and 145 in *Canzoniere*—are a reflection of his recurring, often contradictory thoughts.

Quanto più m'avvicino al giorno estremo
che l'umana miseria suol far breve,
più veggio il tempo andar veloce e leve,
e 'l mio di lui sperar fallace e scemo.   4
I' dico a' miei pensier: "Non molto andremo
d'amor parlando omai, ché 'l duro e greve
terreno incarco come fresca neve
si va struggendo, onde noi pace avremo: 8
perché con lui cadrà quella speranza
che ne fe vaneggiar sì lungamente,
e 'l riso e 'l pianto, e la paura e l'ira;
sì vedrem chiaro poi come sovente   12
per le cose dubbiose altri s'avanza,
e come spesso indarno si sospira."

As closer and closer I get to the final day
—which is to shorten all human misery—

I consider how lightly and quickly time goes by,
how hopeless and vain have been my expectations.   4
I say to my thoughts, "Not for much longer
we shall now talk of love, because the harsh
and heavy earthly burden of life, like new snow,
will swiftly vanish, and then peace we shall have;   8
because, with it, will also die the hope
that kept us raving for so long, the laughter
and the crying, the fears and all the anger;
and then we shall clearly see how often   12
people strive toward dubious aims,
and how frequently we sigh in vain."

In line 9, *con lui*, meaning "with it," refers to *greve e terreno incarco*, or the body. Real peace can be obtained only at the point of death, when all hope and passions are spent. In line 10, *vaneggiar*, commonly translated as the English "raving," indicates the wasteful imaginings and longings that typically characterized Petrarch's inner life. Per lines 12–14, with death approaching, life appears in retrospect a short-lived misery, all desires and longings a pointless anguish. There is no anger in the poet's awareness; tone and rhythm are distributed measuredly, rising somewhat with the antithesis of line 11, descending soon after, and remaining subdued in the disenchanted conclusion. By the last line, time and love—lines 3 and 6—have acquired a rich connotation and become symbols for longing, denied and reciprocated love, and all the pleasures and displeasures life may give.

Benedetto sia 'l giorno, e 'l mese, e l'anno,
e la stagione e 'l tempo e l'ora e 'l punto
e 'l bel paese e 'l loco ov'io fui giunto
da' duo begli occhi che legato m'hanno;   4
e benedetto il primo dolce affanno
ch' i' ebbi ad esser con Amor congiunto,
e l'arco, e le saette ond'i' fui punto,
e le piaghe che 'nfin al cor mi vanno.   8
Benedette le voci tante ch'io
chiamando il nome de mia donna ho sparte,
e i sospiri, e le lagrime, e 'l desio;
e benedette sian tutte le carte   12
ov'io fama l'acquisto, e 'l pensier mio,
ch'è sol di lei, sì ch'altra non v'ha parte.

Blessed be the day, the month, the year,
the season, the time, the hour, the moment,
the beautiful country, and the site where
two beautiful eyes lured and entrapped me;   4

blessed be the first sweet pang I felt
when I became one with Love, and the arch
and the arrows that did pierce me, and
the wounds that go deep into my heart.   8
Blessed be the many words that around
I spread calling the name of my woman,
and the sighs, the tears, and the desires;
and blessed be all the papers by which   12
I made her famous, and my thoughts that are
only hers, of which no other has any part.

The poet's exultation is due to his surrender to an unusual destiny of joy and suffering, of solitude and self-imposed isolation. In line 3, the country is Provence, and the place is the Church of Saint Claire, where Petrarch saw Laura for the first time. In line 7, *l'arco e le saette* are the bow and arrows that, in the iconography of love, are hidden in the woman's eyes. The equivocal rhymes (*anno, hanno*), the rich rhymes (*sparte, parte*), and the derivative ones (*giunto, congiunto*) progressively underscore the intensity of his desire and the anguished condition of his being (Amaturo 271–78). The enumeration of events advances chronologically and with a progressive intensity of meaning: from the moment he saw her and fell in love to his celebration of her to his exultation in his own exceptional destiny. As Gesualdo and Castelvetro already pointed out in the sixteenth century, there is variety in that inventory.[46] Time first is considered according to the movement of the planets, from minor to major: day, month, and year. Then it is divided according to man's enumeration and in reverse order, from major to minor: season, time of day, morning and afternoon, and then hour and moment. The use of the adjective *benedetto* in both quatrains and tercets and the contrast between the singular, which opens the quatrains, and the plural (*benedette*), which opens the tercets, create a structure that is varied and tight. Calculated words' arrangements such as these are constantly present in Petrach's verse. They produce harmonious balances. They develop a thought, explore the changing facets of a state of mind, and shed light on the poet's existential condition. They generate a soothing rhythm that confers on the acceptance of his condition a sort of liturgical fervor.

Padre del ciel, dopo i perduti giorni,
dopo le notti vaneggiando spese,
con quel fero desio ch'al cor s'accese,
mirando gli atti per mio mal sì adorni,   4
piacciati omai col tuo lume ch'io torni
ad altra vita e a più belle imprese,
sì ch'avendo le reti indarno tese,
il mio duro adversario se ne scorni.   8
Or volge, Signor mio, l'undecim'anno
ch'i' fui sommesso al dispietato giogo
che sopra i più soggetti è più feroce.
Miserere del mio non degno affanno;   12

redùci i pensier vaghi a miglior luogo;
ramenta lor com'oggi fusti in croce.

Father in heaven, after the loss of days,
after the nights I spent vainly raving
with a fierce desire blazing in my heart,
conjuring up her graces, so enticing to my shame,   4
may it now please you that, led by your light,
I might turn to new life, to worthier undertakings,
and, having set out his traps in vain,
my cruel Adversary may be repulsed.   8
The eleventh year is coming, my Lord,
since I was forced under that ruthless yoke,
which is harshest on those who most comply.
Take pity on my unworthy suffering; guide   12
my wayward thoughts to a better purpose;
remind them that on this day you were crucified.

Regarding line 11, exactly eleven years had gone by since Petrarch saw Laura for the first time on Holy Friday of 1327. The sonnet—for which I follow the commentaries of Chiorboli 371 and Amaturo 277–78—is a feat of contrasts and balances. The keynote to the poet's prayer is given by the *miserere* of line 12, which is also a constant motif in Petrarch's *Psalmi penitentiales* 3: "Have pity, O Lord, of my suffering; enough, more than enough have I turned and wearied, alas, in the filth of my sins" (*Miserere dolorum meorum, Domine; satis superque volutatus sum, et in ceno peccatorum meorum marcui miser*). A play of reprieves, delays, and echoes give the sonnet a lulling rhythm. The prayer starts in the first quatrain slowly, purposefully delayed by the remembrance of a past wasted vainly in desires and anguish—a delay kept securely in place by the vocative *Padre del ciel* at the opening and by the optative *piacciati omai* at the beginning of the second quatrain. The entreaty takes off at that point, quickly rising to the reassuring protection of the divinity, whose comforting illumination is prospected in opposition to the darkness of nights spent obsessing about Laura. A new reference to the misspent past ties the first tercet back to the first quatrain, while the second tercet echoes the invocation and prayer of the second quatrain. There is also a connection between the two tercets: the day of his falling in love is mentioned first in line 9 and again in line 14 as the day of Christ's passion. The prayer ends in a quasimournful tone, with the ejaculatory progression of verbs: *miserere, reduce, rammanta* (have pity, guide, remind).

Notwithstanding the ever-present wish of renovation, underneath Petrarch's disconsolate prayers, his passion remained unchanged, and his divided identity always reasserted itself.

Ponmi ove 'l sole occide i fior e l'erba,
o dove vince lui il ghiaccio e la neve;
ponmi ov'è 'l carro suo temprato e leve,
et ov'è chi cel rende, o chi cel serba;   4
ponmi in umil fortuna od in superba,
al dolce aere sereno, al fosco e greve;
pommi a la notte, al dì lungo ed al breve,

a la matura etate od a l'acerba; 8
ponmi in cielo, od in terra, od in abisso,
in alto poggio, in valle ima e palustre,
libero spirito, od a' suoi membri affisso,
ponmi con fama oscura, o con illustre: 12
sarò qual fui; vivrò com' io son visso,
continuando il mio sospir trilustre.

Place me where the sun burns herbs and flowers
or wherever ice and snow overcome it;
where its chariot advances moderate and light,
where the sun appears or where it hides; 4
place me in low or in high estate, in sweet
balmy air, or in one that is heavy and dark,
plunge me into the night, where the days are short
or where they are long, in young or mature old age, 8
place me in heaven, on earth, into the abyss,
on a high hill, in a low and marshy valley,
either a free spirit or a slave to bodily limbs,
bestow on me bright fame or obscurity: 12
I shall be, as I was; I shall live, as I have lived,
as ever carrying my fifteen-year-old load of sighs.

Petrarch might have drawn inspiration for this sonnet from several Roman authors. Two passages from Horace will suffice for the purpose of comparison. In *Odes* (1.22.17–24), Horace confirms his love for Lalaga: "Place me in infertile fields where no summer wind revives the trees; place me in a part of the world where rigid weather and clouds persevere; place me under the chariot of too-near a sun, on a land denied to habitation. I shall always love Lalaga, who smiles and speaks so lovingly" (*Pone me pigris ubi nulla campis / arbor aestiva recreatur aura, / quod latus mundi nebulae malusque / Juppiter urget, / pone sub curru nimium propinqui / solis in terra domibus negata: / dulce ridentem Lalagen amabis, / dulce loquentem*). In *Satires* (2.1.57–60), Horace avows his dedication to writing: "No matter whether a quiet old age awaits or Death flies around me with his dark wings, rich or poor, in Rome or, if destiny wants it, in exile, whatever will be the tenor of my life, I will always write" (*Seu mea tranquilla senectus expectat seu mors atris circumvolat alis, dives, inops, Romae, seu fors ita iusserit exul, quisquis erit vitae scribam color*). The Latin lines are quoted by Chiorboli (371).

Petrarch does not proclaim his love for Laura, nor does he directly declare that he will forever be a writer. He multiplies Horace's antithesis: *sole/ghiaccio* (sun/ice), *chi cel rende/chi cel serba* (where is shown to us [where the sun rises]/where it is taken away and saved for us [where it sets]), *umil/superba* (humble/haughty), *sereno/fosco* (clear/foggy), *matura/acerba* (ripe/unripe), *cielo/terra* (heaven/earth), *poggio/valle* (hill/valley), *libero/ai suoi membri affisso* (free/tied to its limbs), *oscuro/illustre* (unknown / famous). In so doing, he creates the impression of an unalterable psychic state. He accepts and confirms life as a self-contradictory passion and this passion as a condition for poetry.

His declaration is locked in the crossed rhymes of the quatrains, ABBA ABBA, and in the rare chained rhymes of the tercets, CDC DCD. The enumeration receives variety by the chiastic arrangement of lines 1–2 and lines 3–4, while quatrains and tercets are tied together by the anaphora of *ponmi* (place me) at the beginning of each strophe. Again, the selected language and the frequent departures from the ordinary order of words are the devices that vary, expand, and specify memories and feelings. Again, the conflicting passions locked in protracted, indecisive battle—the bitterness for wasted years, the pride in his poetic calling, the weariness of many contradictory feelings, the longing for a final revitalizing peace—are all summarized and included in that final "fifteen-year-old load of sighs," the years he has wasted longing for Laura.

The Myth of Laura

The following two sonnets, numbers 90 and 185 in *Canzoniere*, celebrate the myth and magic of Laura. Here too, rather than giving a description of the woman, Petrarch described the changing perception of his emotions. Laura remains in the background as the symbol of all that is desirable, the elusive image of the feelings that forever linger in the poet's psyche. She is the seduction of beauty, love, and glory. She is a phantasm, a haunting mirage, something the poet tries to reach or achieve; she is what he cannot express and explain, a lure he evokes with obsessive persistence.

> Questa fenice de l'aurata piuma
> al suo bel collo, candido, gentile,
> forma senz'arte un sì caro monile,
> ch'ogni cor addolcisce, e 'l mio consuma: 4
> forma un diadema natural ch'alluma
> l'aere d'intorno; e 'l tacito focile
> d'Amor tragge indi un liquido sottile
> foco che m'arde a la più algente bruma.   8
> Purpurea vesta d'un ceruleo lembo
> sparso di rose, i belli omeri vela:
> novo abito, e bellezza unica e sola.
> Fama ne l'odorato e ricco grembo   12
> d'arabi monti lei ripone e cela,
> che per lo nostro ciel sì altera vola.

> This phoenix, with her golden plumes
> she artlessly styles so precious a necklace
> around her fine, tender snow-white neck
> that all hearts she softens and mine consumes.   4
> She fashions a natural diadem that lights
> the air around, from which the silent fuse
> of Love draws a rarefied stream of fire
> that scorches me in the most frigid weather.   8
> A crimson dress with a blue border
> scattered with roses veils her fine shoulders:
> a garb unseen before, a beauty singular and rare.

Fame has it that she lives and hides 12
in the rich and scented mountains of Arabia:
but in our skies, so magnificently she flies!

Regarding line 1, the legendary phoenix has the shape of an eagle, a tuft on its head, golden feathers around its neck, crimson (*phoeniceus*) plumage on the body, and a blue tail. Per line 3, some of Laura's curls, falling around her neck, take on the semblance of a necklace, or a *monile*. In line 5, this diadem is Laura's golden hair. In line 6, *focile* refers to flint, and *acciarino*, or *pietra focaia*, refers to a variety of calcedonium capable of producing sparks and used to start a fire (as in the flintlock gun). Regarding line 12, the bosoms (*grembo*) of a mountain are its valleys. The vales of the Arabian Peninsula were celebrated for plants giving incense, myrrh, and cinnamon cassia. The phoenix—the bird that prepares its own death by collecting wood and setting it on fire; sings while burning; and, from its own cinders, comes back to life—was used in courtly poetry to symbolize the power of love that transforms, obliterates, and re-creates the lovers anew. Throughout the sonnet, the images of the phoenix and Laura intermingle, each one transmuting inadvertently into the other. The repeated switch from her colorful dress to the plumage of the fantastic bird and from the bird back to her transports this woman of Avignon into the realm of the fabulous. Similarly, the continuous metaphoric performance generates the impression that it is not the image of a woman the poet fantasizes; it is the magic accomplishments of his own artistry, for in the phoenix's wide range of possible symbolisms, the suggestions multiply.

Laura's name is a reverberation of resonances, of insisted echoes and allusions. Laura is *auro*, or *oro* (gold); she is *l'aura* (air), the air that Petrarch breathes and lives by; she is as unstable and unreachable as the breeze; she is the richness of dreams; and she is as unattainable and remote as a myth.

Erano i capei d'oro a l'aura sparsi
che 'n mille dolci nodi gli avolgea,
e 'l vago lume oltra misura ardea
di quei begli occhi, ch'or ne son sì scarsi; 4
e 'l viso di pietosi color farsi,
non so se vero o falso, mi parea:
i' che l'esca amorosa al petto avea,
qual meraviglia se di sùbito arsi? 8
Non era l'andar suo cosa mortale,
ma d'angelica forma; e le parole
sonavan altro, che pur voce umana.
Uno spirto celeste, un vivo sole 12
fu quel ch'i' vidi: e se non fosse or tale,
piaga per allentar d'arco non sana.

Her golden strands of hair wafted in the breeze,
which twisted them in a thousand entrancing
waves; a radiance beyond measure sparkled
in those fine eyes, which seldom shine so now; 4
her face seemed to take on a pitying tinge,
I do not know if it was false or true:

is it then any wonder that I, who had love's
tinder in my heart, so swiftly caught on fire? 8
Her gait was not that of a mortal creature,
an angelic form she was; and her words
did not sound like those of any human voice.
A celestial spirit, a lively sun was what 12
I saw, and, if she is not so now, a wound
does not heal when the bow unbends.

In line 1 is an instance of Petrarch's frequent wordplay between Laura's name and *l'aura* (the air). There is also the suggestion of a shift from Laura to *auro* (gold). In lines 3–4, the word *vago* has the multilayered meaning of "charming, beautiful, vague, and indefinite"; on the subjective side, it takes on the connotation of longing. Per line 7, the lover was already disposed to love. In line 10, *forma* has the technical Aristotelian meaning of "immaterial being," or a spiritual substance.

The first quatrain evokes a luminous apparition; the second one concentrates on the warmth of sympathy emanating from it. The apparition is then reprieved in the first tercet—we see an immaterial form, and we hear a disembodied voice—and the sonnet closes in epigrammatic fashion: his love will never wane, just as a wound produced by an arrow does not heal when the bow that shot it has slackened. The structure is simple; the images are dynamic: they expand from one chain of meaning to another, multiply, and oscillate from one temporal dimension to another. The image of Laura moves through increments of attraction: from two luminous eyes and an impression of gold to an immaterial vision, a divine sound, a living sun. There is a constant switch from objective to subjective consideration: from Laura, the attention moves to the feeling she causes in her lover; her face is described as colorful, and then it turns into an expression of sympathy. The switch from the sight of an object to subjective impression continues in the last tercet; from her unearthly apparition, we are taken to the awareness of it: "a celestial spirit … a lively sun was what I saw." There are also restless temporal shifts. From the past tense of "the golden hair was" (*Erano i capei d'oro*) and "a lovely radiance shone" (*'l vago lume … ardea*), the sonnet moves to the present tense of "now they are so scarce" (*or ne son sì scarsi*). Line 5 takes us back to the past, into the sphere of remembrance: "her face was taking on a pitying tinge … it seemed to me" (*il viso di pietosi color farsi … mi parea*). The tercets shift from the vision of the past—"a celestial spirit … was what I saw"—again to the present: "a wound does not heal." A doubt—"were she not so now"—is thrown in at the end for one additional restless swing (the analysis is Amaturo's, 282).

An Exceptional Destiny

Cantai, or piango, e non men di dolcezza
del pianger prendo che del canto presi,
ch'a la cagion, non a l'effetto, intesi
son i miei sensi vaghi pur d'altezza. 4
Indi e mansuetudine e durezza
et atti feri, et umili e cortesi,
porto egualmente, né me gravan pesi,

né l'arme mie punta di sdegni spezza. 8
Tengan dunque ver' me l'usato stile
Amor, madonna, il mondo e mia fortuna,
ch'i' non penso esser mai se non felice.
Viva o mora o languisca, un più felice 12
stato del mio non è sotto la luna,
sì dolce è del mio amaro la radice.

I sang, and now I weep, and no less pleasure
I take from the weeping than I took from the singing,
because on the cause, not on the effect,
my senses are intent, desirous only of sublimity. 4
Hence, both mild and harsh, rude as well
as courteous and kindly gestures I bear,
and burdens do not weigh me down,
nor shafts of disdain can break my armor. 8
Love, my lady, the world, and Fortune too,
may well keep toward me their usual ways,
for I cannot ever be anything but happy.
Might I live or die or languish, a kinder state 12
than mine does not exist under the moon,
so very sweet is the root of my anguish.

This is sonnet 229 of *Canzoniere*. Per lines 3–4, the poet's desire is to keep alive his transcendent state of being. He does not mind its effects, as anguishing as they may be, because he is interested only in their cause—in what brought them about. Was it the woman? Poetic creativity? In line 8, *vaghi pur d'altezza* refers to being desirous only (*pur*) of that exhilarating experience. The conceptual and emotional development of the sonnet follows an ascending line. What is of no interest to him at the start is specified in the second quatrain and then expounded upon in the sestet: "both mild and harsh, rude as well as courteous and kind gestures I bear," and "I do not intend ever to be anything but happy, might I live or die." The sonnet closes with a summary of the contradictory character of his condition: "a kinder state than mine does not exist under the moon, so very sweet is the root of my bitterness." His life is destined to be filled with joy and suffering; it gives him certainties and doubts, persistence and despair. It is the happy task of his poetry to interpret that manifold feeling.

Sonnet 229 of the *Canzoniere* was written in 1351. Years had gone by. Laura was now dead. In this sonnet, there is an idyllic and lonely spot in the countryside. The birds, the river, the sight, and the sounds made by the tree branches lull the poet. Here, the image of Laura floats into his memory in a sort of magic epiphany. The passing of time has intensified his fantasy; the reality of a past of anguish has transmuted into pleasant imaginings. The once unsympathetic woman has become warm and understanding.

Se lamentar augelli, o verdi fronde
mover soavemente a l'aura estiva,
o roco mormorar di lucide onde
s'ode d'una fiorita e fresca riva, 4
là 'v'io seggia d'amore pensoso e scriva,
lei che 'l ciel ne mostrò, terra n'asconde,
veggio, et odo, et intendo ch'ancor viva
di sì lontano a' sospir' miei risponde. 8
"Deh, perché inanzi 'l tempo ti consume?
—mi dice con pietate—a che pur versi
degli occhi tristi un doloroso fiume?
Di me non pianger tu, ché' miei dì fersi 12
morendo eterni, e ne l'interno lume,
quando mostrai de chiuder, gli occhi apersi."

If birds lamenting or green leaves
gently swaying in the summer breeze
or shining waters raucously murmuring
are heard on a flowery streamside bank 4
where I sit and write thinking of love, then
I see and hear her, whom the heavens revealed
to us and the earth now hides, and I feel that,
though afar, she responds, still alive, to my sighing. 8
"Oh, why do you waste away before your time?"
concernedly she says. "Why do you pour from
those sad eyes so painful a stream of tears?
Do not weep for me, for in dying, my days 12
became eternal. When I seemed to close my eyes,
into a radiance within I did open them wide."

Each stanza of the sonnet develops a distinct thematic segment: in the first quatrain is the description of the landscape; in the second, Laura appears; in the first tercet, she questions his sadness; and in the closing one, she reveals her transfiguration and his. She no longer is the object of a distressing yearning. Thanks to her, he has discovered a range of new possibilities, the forever-rewarding field of poetic creation. Remarkable again is the orchestration of formal balances, anticipations, and antithesis: "gently swaying" and "huskily murmuring" (*mover soavemente* and *roco mormorar*), "I sit and write" (*seggia … scriva*), *revealed* and *hides* (*mostrò* and *asconde*), *dying* and "became eternal" (*morendo* and *fersi eterni*), and *close* and *open* (*chiuder* and *apersi*).

3
From Democratic Commune to Princely Court

3.1 Literati and Scientists.

By the second half of the fourteenth century, the democratic communes of central Italy were slowly turning into hereditary principalities. South of Rome, the kingdom of Naples had strengthened its feudal character. In the north, new regional states had come into being. Their political and hegemonic power was in the hands of single families who had made their states flourishing centers of culture. Besides the prominent Visconti family, which had ruled Milan since the beginning of the century, there were the Della Scala of Verona, the Da Polenta of Ravenna, the Ordelaffi of Forlì, the Pepoli in the city of Bologna, and the Da Carrara in Padua. In the north were also the universities of Bologna and Padua. There were new public libraries and private ones that kept their doors open to all.

Many writers and intellectuals who flocked to these centers of culture were provisional and transient courtiers. To lords, they provided services that dithered between those of literary factotums and those of the court entertainers. Their social position was different from the one enjoyed by the literati of the communes in previous decades, most of whom were members of the governing class. Sonneteers, such as Antonio Beccari da Ferrara and Francesco di Vannozzo of Padua, who are featured in this section, were vagrant men of all trades, compelled to move from town to town in search of employment and patronage.

Antonio Beccari (1315–70) was born in Ferrara, hence his more common appellation of Antonio da Ferrara. He was born and grew up in Bologna, but in 1344, after wounding a singer during a quarrel, he ran from the police and took refuge in towns farther north. He lived in Padua, Ravenna, Milan, and Verona. Wherever he resided and worked, part of his function was to write verse that expressed the policy and intent of his employers. When, in 1354, Azzo da Correggio, captain general of the city of Verona, attempted to dethrone Cangrande della Scala, Beccari wrote the following sonnet.

Se Dante pon che Giustizia Divina
mandi giù nello 'nferno, ove ogni uom plora,
i traditor, poi che Morte li accora
(chi trade 'l sangue suo ne la Caina,   4
chi trade sua città ancor declina
in altro luogo detto l'Antenora,
chi trade suo signor ancor dimora

in Tolomea a prender disciplina), 8
qui se può fare una bella domanda:
"Chi trade sua città, sangue e signore,
la divina giustizia dove 'l manda?"
Dico per messer Azzo traditore, 12
quel da Correggio, ch'è de simil razza:
che parrà ch'abbia, s'i' non metta Azza?

If Dante posits Divine Justice to hurl
all traitors, after Death has killed them,
down to hell, where everybody weeps,
—the betrayers of their families go to Caina, 4
the betrayers of their city are plunged
into another place called Antenora,
while the betrayers of their lord
remain for their penance in Tolomea— 8
then we can ask a good question:
those who betray city, family, and lord,
where does Divine Justice send them?
I am talking about Sir Azzo, the traitor 12
from Correggio, who is such a man: which place
does he deserve, if not a new one named Azza?

In line 3, *accora*, or *uccide*, means "kills." In line 4, *trade*, or *tradisce*, means "betrays." In line 5, *declina*, or *precipita*, means "hurls down." In line 8, *prender disciplina*, or *fa penitenza*, means "does penance." Regarding lines 4–8, in Dante's *Inferno*, the deepest part of hell, called Cocito, is divided into three sections, each reserved for a specific type of traitor and named after a traitor of that type famous in history or literature: the traitors to kindred are in Caina, the traitors to country in Antenora, and the traitors to lords and benefactors in Tolomea. Azzo da Correggio, therefore, should be sent to a new section named after him, for he is a traitor who combines in himself all three kinds of treason.

As numerous as were Beccari's residences, so were his thematic and stylistic choices. The above political sonnet is in high style and rich in erudite allusions. A familiar stance, with traces of Venetian, is used in the tailed sonnet "E' me ricorda, cara mia valise." Being in trouble and in urgent need of cash, Antonio apologizes to his suitcase because he is about to sell it at the Rialto market and, with the money, run out of Venice. For the tailed sonnet and other metrical extensions, see the introduction.

E' me recorda, cara mia valise,
che già de molti vai t'ho fatto onore,
de drappi, de zendadi de valore,
de perle, de cinture e d'altri arnise. 4
Ma tu sai ben quel che 'l proverbio dise:
che 'l se conosce al tempo del merore
colui ch'è amico de perfetto amore,
come demostra el frutto la radise. 8

Or tu se' vota e non te posso empire
né da Venesia posso far lo salto,
perch'io non ho moneta da partire.
Però te prego che tu vadi a Realto   12
e diete tosto al primo profferire,
sì che non m'abandoni in questo assalto.
Io zuro a Dio, se non son preso o morto,
novarte tosto e vendicar 'sto torto.

I do remember, my dear suitcase,
when I regaled you with many furs,
with robes, with silks of great value,
with belts, precious objects, and pearls.   4
But you know what the proverb says:
at the time of trouble, one finds out
who really is the friend that loves you,
just as a fruit will always reveal its root.   8
Now you are empty and I cannot fill you,
nor can I make a swift retreat from Venice,
for I have no money for any leave taking.
Therefore I pray you, go on to Rialto   12
and offer yourself to the first buyer;
do not abandon me in straits so dire.
I swear to God, if I am neither jailed nor dead,
I will make up for this wrong, I will buy you back.

In line 2, *t'ho fatto onore* means, literally, "I honored you," or "I treated you sumptuously." The phrase *de molti vai*, or, in Italian, *molti mantelli di vaio*, refers to coats decked out with fur of squirrel, usually worn by magistrates and doctors. Regarding line 12, usurers and secondhand dealers carried on their transactions at the market near the Rialto Bridge. In line 10, *fare il salto* means, literally, "to jump," or "to run out of town."

Francesco di Vannozzo (ca. 1330/40–89), poet, musician, and, on occasion, jongleur, spent his life wandering from one town to another: from Bologna to Venice; Padua, where he was around 1340; Verona; and, finally, Milan. There we find him after 1389. In the following sonnet, he feigns regret for having moved to the west and asks for the protection of the local lord, Giangaleazzo Visconti.

Quand'io mi volgo atorno e pongo mente
al mio cor alto e alle scarpe rotte,
bramo la febre, mal de fianchi e gotte,
e maledico Dio ch'a ciò consente;   4
biastemo el dì che mi spinse a ponente

e 'l tristo mar ch'affogar non mi puotte,
la terra che non s'apre e non me 'nghiotte
come ranochia in boca di serpente.   8
Però, sonetto, fa delle gambe ali,
e dì con reverenzia a meo signore
che ponga fine a questi nostri mali.   12
Seco m'ha ritenuto el grande amore,
né in papa spero più, né in cardinali:
s'egli è gran conte, io son gran servitore.
Più non dico: schietto a lui t'accosta,
ma guarda non tornar senza risposta.

When I look around and earnestly reflect
on my great dreams and my broken shoes,
I wish for myself fever, lumbago, and gout,
and I curse God, who allows this to occur;   4
I curse the day that swayed me to go west,
the wretched sea that would not drown me,
the earth that did not open to swallow me
like a bullfrog into a snake's mouth.   8
Therefore, sonnet, turn your legs into wings
and, with all due respect, beseech my lord
to put an end to these misfortunes of ours.
My great affection for him has kept me here,   12
since I lost all hopes in cardinals and pontiffs:
if he is a great lord, I shall be a great servant.
I will say no more: pray to him in all sincerity
and mind not to come back without an answer.

Vannozzo couched this self-portrait in a mixture of low and high style, with a sprinkling of Latin, Venetian, and Paduan words. Regarding lines 8–14, some critics think the man referred to here is Giangaleazzo Visconti, whom, elsewhere, Vannozzo celebrates as "Count of Virtues." Others believe him to be Marsilio da Carrara, lord of Padua, who became count of the Campagna Romana in the first half of 1371. The picture Vannozzo draws of himself is typical of the realistic-satirical tradition, but that model well fit the conditions of neglect in which he lived and the many peregrinations he endured throughout life. In the two-hendecasyllable tail, syntactically independent of the sonnet, the poet turns to the poem and gives it his last instructions in the manner of the traditional envoy.

El poder basso col voler altiero
m'ha fatto roder osse e gollar spine,
tal ch'io son oggi d'ogni ben confine,
di pena carco e di piuma leggiero.   4

E non mi val armonico mestiero
o por con lingua nero in albe brine,
né di natura mi val medicine,
ch'io son converso d'omo in un sparviero.   8
Ben che tra gli altri uccelli io vivo adorno
de getti, de braghette e de sonagli,
con le promesse assai di giorno in giorno,
e coronato con creste di gagli,   12
le longhe e 'l ben-farem mi va d'attorno
più ch'a lèvere brocche de bresagli.

My lowly prospects and my lofty ambitions
have made me gnaw at bones and swallow thorns,
so today I find myself at the end of my tether,
weighed down by troubles and as light as a feather.   4
The musical profession is of no help to me,
and neither is the pen dropping black on white;
no natural remedies are of value whatever
since from man to kestrel I have changed my nature.   8
Although I am festooned, among other birds,
with jets, with hoods, and with ringing bells,
and many promises are made from day to day,
and although I am crowned with rooster's combs,   12
delays and "We'll take care of it" swirl round me
more abundantly than arrows aimed at hares.

Per line 8, once, the poet dreamed of being a free man; now he is a prisoner of a lord, and like a hawk trained for the hunt, he must obey the whims of his owner.

Vannozzo wrote a garland of eight sonnets entitled *Cantilena pro comite virtutum* (Songs for the Count of Virtues) in praise of his patron, Giangaleazzo Visconti. Giangaleazzo was called Count of Virtue because his wife, Isabelle de Valois, daughter of King John of France, had brought him in dowry the county of Vertus in Champagne. Giangaleazzo was an intelligent man and a good soldier. He succeeded in uniting a large territory that included the towns of Pavia, Alessandria, Bergamo, Brescia, Como, Cremona, Piacenza, Parma, Reggio, Vicenza, and Verona. Under his leadership, the creation of an Italian monarchy strong enough to face foreign invaders seemed possible. He was also a sagacious businessman and competent administrator. Milan, which had been razed to the ground by German emperors twice, was rebuilt to unprecedented splendor and prosperity. The city now counted fourteen thousand homes, fifteen hospitals, and more than two hundred churches. The inhabitants were 250,000. Among them were 150 surgeons, 40 doctors, about 100 elementary school teachers, and 1,500 lawyers. By Giangaleazzo's initiative and with his large contribution, the Milanese started to build their Duomo. Giangaleazzo was much abhorred by the Florentines, against whom, in a few years, the secretary of the commune, Coluccio Salutati, would unleash—as we will see in the next section—his demonizing propaganda.

In each sonnet of Vannozzo's *cantilena*, the voice is that of an Italian town of central and northern Italy. In the following caudate sonnet, which is the last poem in that sequence, the voice is that of Rome.

> Italia, figlia mia, prendi diletto,
> prendi conforto, lieta, e prendi lena
> ché in breve tu sarai tratta di pena,
> immaculata senza alcun difetto.   4
> Io son la negra Roma, che l'aspetto
> per farmi bella con pulita lena;
> e non dubitar che zò che a te lui mena
> è il priego mio ch' al cielo ogni dì zetto,   8
> però che senza lui far non si puote
> azal che duri a raconzar le lime,
> che fazan tonde to' fiaccate rote
> con tale equalità, che a terze e prime   12
> nel grado suo tassato fie la dote.
> Donque correte ensieme, o sparse rime
> e zite predigando in ogni via
> ch'Italia ride ed è zunto 'l Messia.

> Italy, dear daughter of mine, rejoice,
> be comforted, be happy and courageous,
> for shortly you will be free of all your pains;
> unscated you shall be again, with no blemish.   4
> I am Rome, downcast, waiting for him
> to restore my beauty and my fragrant breath;
> and have no doubt: what makes him come to you
> are the prayers that I daily raise to heaven,   8
> because, without him, there is no steel
> strong enough to sharpen the files
> able to repair the slackened wheels,
> so that the weight will be distributed   12
> equally between the front and the back.
> So run together, o scattered rhymes,
> and go to announce on every highway
> that Italy smiles, for the Messiah has come.

Vannozzo's encomium of Visconti takes the form of an enraptured prophecy and makes the characteristic use of figurative language and obscure references. In line 5, *negra* means "black"—that is, in mourning. Regarding lines 9–13, without Visconti's help, says Francesco, no army can establish peace in Italy. The complex metaphor of the wheels refers to the supposed plan conceived by Visconti to mediate between the belligerent Italian powers. Without him, no steel (*azal*, in Milanese) can be made strong enough to sharpen (*raconzar*) the files that would reshape (*fazon tonde*, or make round again) Italy's cart so that its weight may be distributed in right proportions between the front and the back wheels—and justice and power may be fairly distributed to the various regions of Italy. Vannozzo wrote the sonnet in 1388, when Visconti was about to annex Padua and its lands.

Giovanni Dondi dall'Orologio (1318–89) wrote verse in praise of Giangaleazzo Visconti from a higher social footing than did either Beccari or Vannozzo. Dondi was a medical doctor also renowned for his proficiency in mathematics, astronomy, and science. He taught at the universities of Florence and Padua. From Padua, he moved to Pavia in order to cure Visconti's son. He was subsequently appointed professor at the local university. Today Dondi owes his fame to his pioneering work in clock making (his father had also been an inventive clockmaker, hence the addition of "dall'Orologio" [of the clock] to the family name).[47]

In "Ogni cosa mortal convien che manchi," Dondi, the doctor, meditates on the physical transformations brought on the human body by old age: deteriorated skin tone, weak elasticity and motion, shrinking of the bone structure, and a general progressive asthenia.

> Ogni cosa mortal convien che manchi,
> ben che tal men e tal più tempo dura,
> unde, crescendo al fin di sua statura,
> l'uom prima avanza et po' par che se stanchi.   4
> El capo langue, el ventre, i piedi, i fianchi;
> de giorno in giorno cade la natura;
> la pelle increspa e perde sua figura
> e i capil biondi inbrunan e poi vien bianchi.   8
> Ed è sì breve et ratta la dimora
> nostra nel mondo qui pien di difetto,
> che la maor parte si ritrova a l'ora
> de la partita senza alcun profeto.   12
> Ma quel è saggio che sol s'inamora
> di Dio, sì ch'abbia pace in suo cospetto.

> Every mortal thing must in the end fail,
> some lasting for a while, others much longer,
> so that, after reaching their full potential,
> men first run and then seemingly decelerate.   4
> The head weakens; feet, hips, belly sag;
> from day to day all natural properties decay;
> the skin gets wrinkled and loses elasticity;
> blondish hair first darkens and then turns white.   8
> So short and speedy is our sojourn
> in this world, so marred by imperfections,
> that, at the time of departure, most of us

will find to be with no compensations. 12
Only the man who worships God is intelligent,
for in the end he'll have peace in his presence.

In Dondi's time, the sonnet form was the favorite means to make a point with a friend, communicate a thought, or memorialize a personal situation or event. In "Hora prov'io che l'è ben vero el detto," Dondi, the scholar, describes to a friend the inconvenience of having distracting neighbors.

Hora prov'io che l'è ben vero el detto
del gran morale, là dove mostrava
ch'al studioso uom non besognava
quel ocio e quel silentio che fi cretto. 4
Però ch'el studio mio s'è posto e dretto
ad aspro sòn d'una campana prava:
di sotto stan gramatici che grava:
sì ch'io tra du' fastidi son constretto. 8
E per la fenestruccia alcuna volta
mi occore agli occhi, alicitivo obiecto,
una fangiula con la coma sciolta,
che mi dà noglia con alcun dilecto; 12
tal che la mente m'ha talor rivolta,
trahendo in altra parte l'intelecto.
Or pensa quand'io son qui studïoso,
qual i' sarei dov'io fosse ocïoso!

Now I have proof of how true is what
the great moralist said, when he maintained
that the studious man does not need all
the free time and silence that is presumed. 4
For my study is so situated as to face
the ugly sound of a nasty bell, while below
are some very vexing schoolteachers:
so I am stuck between two great bothers. 8
Besides, through my little window, at times
comes into view a forbidden object:
a young woman with her hair undone.
She is a nuisance, but somewhat a pleasure; 12
sometimes my mind becomes so distracted
as to direct my mental faculties elsewhere.
Then think how studious I can be this way,
and how I would be, were a lazy man instead!

Dondi uses a mixture of Italian, Venetian, and Latin: *alicitivo*, *obiecto*, *dilecto*, and *intelecto* are from the Latin *alicere*, *obiectus*, *dilectus*, and *intellectus*; *besognava*, *ocio*, *ocioso*, and *s'è posto e dretto* are Venetian words. In line 2, the *gran morale* is Seneca, the Roman philosopher who expounded on the time and tranquility needed by the scholar (*De tranquillitate animi* 17, 3). The *coda*, syntactically independent, wraps up Dondi's description into a finish of self-directed and self-indulgent irony.

In the upcoming sonnet, the professor presents himself as a moralist who reproaches a friend for making the mistake, not for the first time, of falling in love with a dangerous woman. Some interpreters maintain the friend in question is the lord of Carrara.

Io temo che tu non doventi cervo
sì come Atteon quand'el vide Diana
con le altre belle nuda in la Fontana
per qual cangiò la pelle e l'osse e 'l nervo,   4
però ch'io sento che fato sei servo
novelamente d'una bella eguana,
tal che poristi uscir de forma umana
se non prendi rimedio qual ti servo.   8
Pensa che tu sei uom per la ragione,
la qual convien che ti sia principale
duce e governo; e s'el ti ven a meno
questa parte, tu sei bruto animale: 12
seguendo il senso corri senza freno
e d'uom in cervo fai la traslazione.

I am afraid you might become a stag,
just like Actaeon, who, after looking at Diana
naked, with her fetching nymphs, at the spring,
changed his bones, his sinews, and his skin;   4
for I hear that once again you have become
very infatuated with a beautiful *iguana*,
so you might soon slit out of the human figure,
if you don't follow the remedy I recommend.   8
Remember you are a man thanks to reason;
this must be your main guide and master.
That part failing, you shall turn into a brute:
if you follow your sensual instincts and run   12
without restrain, from the man you are
you shall soon metamorphose into a stag.

Regarding line 2, in punishment for having surprised the goddess Artemis, who was bathing naked in the river, the mythological Actaeon was changed into a stag and devoured by his own dogs (Ovid, *Metamorphoses* 3.155.252). In line 5, *fato sei servo* means "you have become the servant." In courtly terms, this means to have fallen in love. In line 7, *eguana*, or, in Italian, *iguana*, refers to an undine, or water nymph. It is a Venetian term indicating a woman of insidious allure, or a siren.

3.2 Wisdom and Desires

The subject matter in the sonnets of this section varies greatly, but in each case, it is expression of popular wisdom and common desires. The authors, often using the caudate sonnet, deal with love in a light, realistic vein without the intellectual sublimation characteristic of high-style verse. They draw scenes of everyday life and intimate domestic situations and tell charming animal fables, the latter being a genre used in textbooks to teach children how to read and write. We do not know who the authors of some of these sonnets were.

> Pover al mondo over chi è mal vestito
> non parli tra la gente o faccia motto,
> che, se fusse più prò che Lancillotto
> o Seneca 'n saper, sì fie schernito.   4
> Il vizio è sopra altrui tanto salito:
> chi ha, di chi non ha, crede di botto
> ogni suo dir, per torgli, torni in motto;
> così non è il suo ben per bene udito.   8
> Oh quanti ci ha che nudi son di panno,
> ch'hanno più indosso che tal ch'ha mantello!
> Così in capo molti tosi vanno,
> che tal sopra 'l cappuccio tien cappello,   12
> perch'hanno indosso in capo quel che sanno,
> non chi l'ha carco e vòto di cervello.

> In this world, a poor man, one poorly dressed,
> is not expected to talk to people or utter a sound,
> because, were he braver than Lancelot or wiser
> than Seneca, no matter what, he would be scorned.   4
> Nowadays, this vicious habit is very widespread.
> Those who have believe they can turn into a joke
> what the have-nots say, in order to steal their words:
> thus, the good they have to say cannot be heard.   8
> Ah, how many there are who are naked of dress,
> but have more in them than those wearing a cloak!
> And how many youths who are better endowed
> than those who on their little heads wear a hat,   12
> because inside they have what it takes to think,
> unlike some who wear a hat and are devoid of wit.

In line 7, *per torgli* means "to take away from him"—that is, to prevent him from saying what he has to say. Per lines 9–14, the rich believe they can ridicule what a poor man wishes to say and prevent him from being heard. In line 11, *tosi* is northern dialect for "young men." Per line 13, in their heads, they have what it takes to reason properly.

The poet is Niccolò Soldanieri, son of Neri de' Soldanieri, who was exiled from Florence at the same time as Dante. Documents show that Niccolò was active between 1350 and 1370. This sonnet is one of several he wrote and set to music for Opizzo degli Alidosi of Massa, the nobleman for whom he worked.

The next sonnet is from *Saporetto*, a collection of sonnets by Simone Prudenzani, citizen of Orvieto, who was active in the political life of his town in the years 1387–1440.

"Le tue parol mi paion cosa vana,
—dic'ella a me—io voglio una fiata
esser vestita per essere onorata,
et altresì vogl'i' un mantel di grana,   4
ché la mia dota è tutta quanta sana
in un tenere, e tutta l'è stimata;
per quattrocento livre te fo data
con tre pedon' d'olive e la fontana.   8
Che vuol dir questo e quante scuse mette?
Io vo' la fante per essere servita
e voglio le pianelle e le scarpette!"
Guardate pur omai a la mia vita,   12
che solo in un mantel vuol vintesette
braccia di panno, e la sua dote è gita.

"As far as I am concerned, your words
are nonsense," she says to me. "For once, I want
to be well dressed and feel I am respected;
besides, I want a mantel of crimson cloth,   4
becasue my dowry is a good patch of land
all in good condition, punctiliously appraised;
I was married to you for four hundred liras,
with a fountain and three yards of olive trees.   8
And what does he say? What are his excuses?
I want to have a serving maid at my disposal,
and I want slippers and some very nice shoes!"
Consider what my life has now become: 12
just to make a cloak, it takes twenty-seven
yards of cloth, and then her dowry has gone!

In line 4, *mantel di grana* refers to a mantel of crimson cloth. A cloth of that color was of Florentine manufacture and very expensive. In line 6, *tenere* means "land holding." Regarding line 8, the number of trees on a lot was counted by *pedoni*.

The dates and authors of the next four sonnets are unknown.

Se io 'l potessi far, fanciulla bella,
la tela che tu tessi fare' d'oro
e le tue spuole con sottil lavoro
d'un zaffino che luce più che stella.   4
E d'argento farei cento cannella
tutte smaltate con sottil lavoro,
e lo spoletto che metti nel foro
di diamante che sta ne le anella.   8
Le casse e le banche farei di corallo,
pettine e liccio d'avorio commessi,
calcole e subbio farei di cristallo,
e per lucerna vorre' che tu avessi   12
due carbonchi che lucon sanza fallo
e balsimo per olio vi mettessi,
e io con voi istessi ad imparare
cent'anni e più ni penassi a 'nsegnare.

If I could do it, my charming girl, the cloth
you are weaving I would turn into gold,
your shuttles I would turn into finely carved
sapphire, far more shining than any star.   4
A hundred spools I would make of silver,
all glazed with art superfine, the spindle
that you insert in the hole I would make
of the very diamond that is set in rings.   8
Boxes and seats I would make of coral,
the comb and the heddle of inlaid ivory,
treadle and beams I would make of crystal;
and for your lanterns, I would want you   12
to have two rubies, unfailingly resplendent,
and balsam I would pour in them instead of oil;
and with you I would want to stay on, learning
and tutoring for a hundred years, and on and on.

This sonnet's voice is that of a tutor-supervisor working in a weaving mill. In line 3, the *spuola*, or shuttle, is the device used, by hand in this case, in passing the thread of the weft between the threads of the warp. In line 10, the *liccio*, or heddle, is a set of parallel wires or cords used to guide the threads into place. In line 11, the *calcola* is the lever that the weaver handles to operate the loom. The *subbio* is the beam, or roller, on which the finished product is wound. The enumeration of the many wonderful things with which the man imagines regaling the woman runs smoothly into the coda, and there it turns into a clear, almost defiant, declaration of love.

Un abate avea un suo bel catellino,
che per suo trastullo molto l'amava,
e davagli di ciò ch'esso mangiava
la parte sua da sera e da mattino.   4
L'asino suo, veggendo il sonaglino
come ciascun di casa il vezzeggiava,
pensò che tutto l'anno someggiava
e mai non gli era serbato un lupino.   8
E disse "I' vo' veder s'i' so saltare."
Trovando in un praticel dormir l'abate,
saltogli addosso com' il can solia fare.
Se l'abate il sentì or lo sappiate!   12
Come leone incominciò a mughiare:
onde il miccio ebbe molte bastonate.
Perciò non v'impicciate
di voler far quel ch'a voi non s'aviene;   16
lasciatel fare a cui più si conviene.

An abbot owned a charming little dog,
which for his amusement he liked a lot;
he gave to it a portion of everything
he ate, in the morning and at night.   4
Seeing that everybody in the house petted
that rattle of a dog, the donkey considered
that he carried heavy weights all year long,
but never got for it as much as one lupine. 8
He said, "I want to see if I too can jump."
Finding the abbot asleep on a patch of grass,
he jumped on him, just as the dog had done.
Now you can imagine how the abbot felt!   12
Just like a wounded lion he began to howl:
and the donkey got a good tasting of the belt.
So do desist from wishing to do
what turns out to be too difficult for you, 16
let it be done by those it most becomes.

Catellino stands for *cagnolino*, meaning "little dog." In line 5, *sonaglino*, or rattle, refers to the dog itself as object of entertainment. In line 7, *someggiava*, meaning "carried weights," comes from *soma*, meaning "weight." In line 8, *legume* refers to the edible seed of the lupine plant. The idiomatic expression "not a lupine" equals the English "not a sausage." In line 13, *mughiare* means "to bellow" or "to howl." In line 14, *muccio* means "donkey." Regarding lines 15–17, the coda is an expression of popular wisdom, a warning to all those who are unwise enough to try what they are not capable of carrying to completion.

Nel tempo che 'l leone era infermato
ogni animale lo scoccoveggiava:
il porco gli togliea quel che mangiava,
el tor col corno 'l pungea da lato, 4
e dall'asino era scalceggiato;
el lupo la sua morte disiava
e la volpe cogli altri ragionava:
"Se si morisse, migliorenno stato 8
e fuor saremmo di sua tirannia,
ché voi sapete com'egli è feroce
verso di noi per la sua gran balia."
Considera, lettor, ch'ogni mal nuoce; 12
però quand'hai alcuna signoria
acquista amici, che 'l contrario nuoce:
vedi la mala boce
che gli animali davano al lione, 16
e chi aveva il torto e chi ragione.

At the time when the lion was ill,
all the other animals derided him:
the pig robbed him of his food, the bull
poked him on the side with his horns, 4
the donkey kicked him here and there,
the wolf wanted him to give up the ghost,
and the fox reasoned with the others:
"If he died, our condition would improve 8
and we would be free of his tyranny,
for you know how ferocious he can be
with us, because of his ascendency."
Consider, reader, all bad luck is bad, 12
so when you have power, make friends,
for the opposite is surely going to hurt.
See what a wicked fame
those animals gave the lion, and while 16
some were right, others were by far less.

In line 2, *scocoveggiare*, or *burlare*, means "to scorn, disdain, and deride." In line 5, *scalceggiare*, or *prendere a calci*, means "to kick around." In line 11, *balia* refers to power, domain, and supremacy. In line 14, *cuoce* means "it cooks," "it burns," or "it hurts." In line 15, *boce*, or *voce*, means "fame"—in this case, bad name.

Prima ch'io voglia rompere o spezzarmi,
quando la piena vien, le spalle chino
e per lasciarla andare al suo cammino
a qualche sterpo ingegno d'appiccarmi.　　　　　　　　　4
E s'ella vuol pur al tutto affondarmi
nel suo andare e mettermi a ruino,
io mi lamento e chiamomi tapino,
ma non però ch'io voglia disperarmi.　　　　　　　　　8
Speranza mi conforta e dice "Tienti,
non t'annegar, ch'io pur t'aiuterò:
non sieno i tuoi pensier al tutto spenti."
E io m'attengo e non so se io potrò;　　　　　　　　　12
ma se Fortuna tempera i suoi venti,
com'io fui ritto ancor mi rizzerò:
ch'io veggio il salcio che per forza piega
poi se derizza e gli altri legni lega.

Before I am ready to shatter or to break,
when the flood comes, I shall bend my back
and, letting it run its course, I shall try hard
to hold on securely to some tree stump.　　　　　　　　4
If the flood still insists in sinking me
in its overflow and in ruining me entirely,
then I shall wail, calling myself a wretch,
but for that, I shan't be ready to despair yet.　　　　　　8
Because Hope comforts me and says,
"Hold on, do not drown, for I will help;
please, do not give up completely."
So I hold on, not knowing how long I'll last;　　　　　　12
but if Fortune curbs her winds, as up I was once,
so I shall straighten out on my two feet again:
for I see the willow as he is forced to bend,
but then he's up and ties other trees good and fast.

In line 6, *nel suo calare* means "in its coming down." In line 11, *non sieno al tutto i tuoi pensier spenti* means "may your thoughts not be completely smothered." In line 13, *fortuna*, or *fortunale*, is a storm. In line 17, *gli altri legni* means "the other woods," or timbers. The tail brings in, as a separate addendum, a popular example of resilience: the willow tree bends but does not break and proves to be stronger than all the other trees.

3.3 The Sonnet as a Political Weapon

After the 1378 uprising of the Florentine salaried workers and their failure to establish a more democratic regime,[48] the political and economic power rested again in the hands of the arti maggiori, the guilds representing industry and banks. Under their leadership, the city embarked on a policy of expansion aimed at acquiring a solid territorial base and ensuring easy access to highways and the sea. The major obstacle to the Florentine plan was Milan, a princely state with comparable expansionistic ambitions. Its lord was Giangaleazzo Visconti, an intelligent man and effective ruler who was, at times, unscrupulous and cruel.[49] After centralizing the administration and reorganizing its finances, Giangaleazzo promoted the economy and modernized the agriculture. Having established peace and security in his territory, he proceeded to take over Bologna and Perugia. He came in open conflict with the Florentines when he annexed the Tuscan towns of Pisa and Siena. The battle between Florence and Milan was fought not only on the field but also, more effectively, in the chancelleries. There, the struggle was waged with rhetorical guile and erudite fervor by their respective chancellors, Coluccio Salutati for Florence and Antonio Loschi on behalf of Milan.

In demonizing the enemy, Coluccio Salutati (1331–1406) gave proof of a ferocity worthy of a biblical prophet. He cast Visconti as an apocalyptic, evil tyrant who, through cunning and deceit, was about to devour all Italy.

> O scacciato dal ciel da Micael,
> ruina della sede d'Aquilon,
> o venenoso serpent Fiton,
> o falso ucciditor del giusto Abel,   4
> o mal commettitore Architofel,
> o successor d'incanti d'Eriton,
> maladìcati l'alto Iddio, Sion,
> che benedisse i figli d'Israel.   8
> Contro ti sia la fede d'Abraam,
> e l'orazion che fe' Merchisedech,
> e l'angel che diè storpio a Balaam;
> nascer possa per te nuovo Lamech,   12
> che 'l sangue vendicò del fi' d'Adam,
> tal sia tuo fin qual fu d'Abimelech.
> Contro ti sia la grazia di Jacob,
> poi che procacci crescer pene a Job.

> You, expelled from heaven by Michael,
> you, who ruined the house of Aquilon,
> you, venomous viper, you Phaëton,
> you, deceitful assassin of the fair Abel,   4
> you, evil sinner Archithophel,
> you, heir to the conjurer Erechto,
> be cursed by the high God of Zion,

> who sanctified the children of Israel. 8
> May be against you the faith of Abraham,
> the prayer invoked by Melchizedek,
> the angel who thwarted Balaam's intent;
> may rise against you a novel Lamech, 12
> who vindicated the blood of Adam's son;
> may your end be like that of Abimelech;
> and may turn against you Jacob's grace,
> so hard you try increasing Job's plagues.

Regarding line 2, Aquilone is a north wind, harbinger of disasters and ruin, mentioned by Dante in *Purgatorio* 4, 60. Regarding line 3, the serpent was the Visconti symbol in the family's coat of arms. In Greek mythology, Phaëton was the sun, son of Helios. Allowed to drive his father's chariot across the sky, Phaëton was unable to check his horses and ran off the prescribed track, almost setting the earth on fire (Ovid, *Metamorphoses* 2, 178–324; *Inferno* 17, 107). Regarding line 5, Archithophel, or Ahithophel, sided with Absolom in his conspiracy against his father, David (2 Samuel 15:12, 31). With regard to line 6, Erichto was a Thracian sorcerer who, according to Lucan, resuscitated a dead man in order to predict for Pompey the outcome of the battle of Pharsalia (*Pharsalia* 6, 508; *Inferno* 9.23.10). Melchizedek, a high priest of Salem, went out to meet Abraham, who was returning victorious from the battlefield, and blessed him. The *orazion* of line 10 must therefore be his blessing (Hebrews 7:1–2). Regarding line 11, the prophet Balaam was asked to curse the Israelites, but an angel prevented him from doing so (Numbers 22–24). Regarding line 12, Lamech was a descendant of Cain and therefore accursed (Genesis 4:18). Regarding line 14, Abimelech killed his brothers, seventy of them; became the king of Shechen; and died when a millstone crashed his head during his siege of Thebes (Judges 9:1–6, 50–57). Regarding line 15, Jacob bought Esau's birthright for a pottage of lentils and won Leah and Rachel through his service to their father. His sons founded the twelve tribes of Israel (Genesis 27–35). According to the book of Job, Job went through a period of rigorous testing with great patience. This last and better-known biblical reference brings Salutati's series of curses to their portentous conclusion.

From an artistic viewpoint, Salutati's sonnet is nothing short of a disaster, but the forceful hammering of its sixteen lines, all accented on the last syllable, drives the curses effectively, albeit monotonously, on. Apparently, the chancellor's poetic effort was a successful piece of political propaganda, judging from the high number of manuscripts that have preserved it.

Salutati was a famous humanist, a man in which intellectual and literary interests tallied neatly with political convictions. He wrote treatises on politics, morality, and grammar. He collected books and created the richest private library of his time. As chancellor of Florence, a post he occupied from 1375 to 1406, he was in charge of relations with other communes, princely states, and the pope; in case of war, he saw to the hiring of mercenary captains. Salutati condemned Giangaleazzo Visconti's regime as a tyranny and defended Florence in name of the Roman ideal of republicanism. Many followed, admired, and feared his official correspondence. Giangaleazzo was known to have declared that he was more fearful of one of the Florentine chancellor's letters than of a thousand cavalrymen in the field.

The answer to Salutati's sonnet came from Antonio Loschi, the Milanese chancellor. Overflowing with comparable condemnation and curses, Loschi's poem exhibited a public relation zest as great as that of the Florentine secretary. A respectable humanist in his own right, Loschi had been a pupil of

Salutati. It is reported that during the propaganda campaign they carried out in name of their respective states, the two chancellors maintained their customary cordial relation with each other.

Giangaleazzo Visconti died suddenly in 1402, and his plan of unifying the greater part of northern and central Italy into a single state collapsed. None of his successors was able to maintain the Milanese domain at the level to which he had raised it. In 1406, Florence succeeded in conquering Pisa and reaching the sea. In 1421, the city of Livorno too was added to the Florentine territory.

Throughout the peninsula, the character of most states had been changing. In the face of the recurrent hostilities between party factions, the old democratic regimes proved to be unable to guarantee order. When the power fell into the hands of one family and one party, the commune evolved into a stronger form of government and became de facto a hereditary principality. Besides stopping sectarian struggle and establishing better administration and fairer jurisdiction, these new forms of government were able to ensure the political continuity necessary to a coherent foreign program. The expansionistic policy of the more powerful among them would change the city-states into regional entities.

In Florence, the transformation from commune to principality occurred slowly. The acumen of the Medici saw to it that it would also occur surreptitiously. The head of the family was Cosimo de' Medici, a banker. His chief opponents were the Albizzi, aided by the Gianfigliazzi and the Peruzzi, other banking families. The Albizzi party prevailed in the elections of 1433, and Cosimo, who, up to that time, had dominated the political scene, was condemned to ten years of exile. The next year, however, new elections reversed that decision, and the Signoria allowed Cosimo to return.

When, in 1434, the Signoria decided to recall Cosimo from exile, Domenico di Giovanni, called Burchiello (1404–49), penned the following sonnet for the party opposing the Medici. An urgently felt need to have that decision revoked pervades his poem and allows his plea to overflow into three tails, each consisting of a *settenario* (seven-syllable line) followed by two hendecasyllables.

Oh umil popol mio, tu non t'avvedi
di questo iniquo e perfido tiranno,
quant'aspramente con sua forza e 'nganno
tien nostra Signoria sotto a suoi piedi.   4
O triofal già Signoria! Or siedi
bassa, al presente per tua verga e scanno
levati presto, il tuo e 'l nostro danno
vendica, il fior gentil, stato richiedi.   8
Per costui ti verrà di dì in dì meno
la forza e 'l senno; e del tuo gran tesoro
ti vota sempre ed empie a Marco il seno.
Costui tocca il suo nido, e fra costoro   12
è or colombo e dopo, il gozzo pieno,
diventerà falcon marino e soro.
Giunto è già il Bucintoro
a Chioggia per levar lui, e' suoi Medici,   16
sicché prudentemente omai provvedici.
Il nostro aiuto chiedici,
che sarà vero alfin ch'io ti scrivo:
noi piglierem la preda e il lupo vivo.   20

Con corona d'ulivo
coronerem la testa di Marzocco
c'ha 'l cercin' or di Niccolò di Cocco.

My poor dear people, you are not aware
of this iniquitous and perfidious tyrant,
of how harshly, by violence and by deceit,
he has trampled our seigniory under his feet.   4
Oh, once triumphant signoria! How low
you lie now! In name of your throne and staff,
do rise quickly, your injury and ours do redress,
claim your status and your noble flower!   8
Because of him, your wisdom and power
will falter from day to day; he will deprive you
of your treasure and fill with it Marco's coffers.
He is getting near his nest; now, with his people,   12
he behaves like a dove; later, with his gizzard full,
he will become a sea hawk and a ruinous leader.
The *Bucintoro* is already
at Chioggia, to let him and the Medici   16
on board; so now you decide judiciously.
Ask for our help,
for in the end, what I write will come to pass:
we shall catch alive the wolf and its prey;   20
with an olive wreath,
we shall crown the head of Marzocco,
who now wears the hat of Niccolò di Cocco.

In line 1, *umil popol mio* means "my humble people." In line 4, by *signoria*—the top executive body of the government—the Florentines meant Florence itself. In line 6, *verga* (staff of command) and *scanno* (the seat reserved for high officials) are symbols of authority. In line 8, the *fior gentil* is the lily, the heraldic symbol of Florence. In line 11, *seno* means "breast" or "lap." Marco (St. Mark) stands for Venice. In line 14, I take *soro* to mean "inexpert," hence "ruinous." I deduce it from the usage of the word made by Giovanni Cavalcanti, Burchiello's contemporary, and given as example in Battaglia's *Grande dizionario* 19, 497: "*un altro soro, che teneva la signoria di Piombino.*" In line 15, the *Bucintoro* is the Venetian state barge. Cosimo spent his exile in Venice and there acquired useful connections. Regarding line 16, Chioggia is a port town at the southern edge of the Venetian lagoon. Regarding line 22, Marzocco is the lion on the heraldic device of Florence. In line 23, *cercine* is the name of the thick cloth that people placed on their heads when carrying weights. Here it indicates, jokingly, the hat of Niccolo' di Cocco Donati, a Medici follower, who, in 1434, was gonfalonier of justice, the highest public office in Florence. Pucci essentially says, "If you accept our help"—the help of the Albizzi and other bankers, that is—"the Medici government will be overthrown, and we shall become democratic again." See Battaglia 2, 996, where line 23 is quoted.

The year of Cosimo's return marked the beginning of the long Medici ascendency. While no member of the family ever occupied a public position, the Medici exercised decisive political influence through their followers. Most officers of the Balia degli Squittini were members of their party. The balia was the committee that reviewed and approved the names of the men chosen to run for election; the balia's officers, and therefore the Medici, thus controlled the electoral system and the political life of the city. For other sonnets by Burchiello, see the next section.

The function of giving voice to the government's views was assigned to a city employee called *araldo della signoria*, or *araldo di palagio* (herald of the government, or herald of the palace). In Florence, in the 1330s, such public-relation man was Antonio di Matteo di Meglio. His task was to make official announcements, compose celebratory verse on special events, and be the mouthpiece for the signoria's political views.

In 1438, Pope Eugene IV organized and opened at Ferrara an ecumenical council aiming at reconciling the Eastern and the Western churches. He also intended to reassert his authority over a council of bishops that had been gathering in Constance, Germany. In January of the following year, the plague broke out in Ferrara, and Eugene, accepting the financial support offered by Cosimo de' Medici, who was now back in power, moved the council to Florence. With the council arrived the emperor of Byzantium, John VII Palaeologus, Patriarch Joseph of Constantinople, and a large retinue of bishops. In Florence, these high prelates approved a plan for the reunification of the two churches and recognized the primacy of the Roman pontiff. Soon, however, Pope Eugene became annoyed with Cosimo for having allied himself with Francesco Sforza, the lord of Milan, who had invaded lands belonging to the church. In 1440, when the council reached a satisfactory conclusion, the expectation was that the council would leave Florence, and everything and everybody would be moved to Rome.

At this news, Antonio di Matteo di Meglio affixed two sonnets on the door of the papal residence. One of them, "Foll'è chi falla per l'altrui fallire" (A fool is he who fails because of other people's foolishness), consists, in the form that has come down to us, of a rather incoherent series of harsh accusations aimed at the pontiff. The other sonnet, "O puro e santo padre Eugenio quarto," which is the tailed poem reported here, is a continuous, more coherent flow of patronizing admonitions, well sprinkled with the customary bashing of the Roman citizenry.

> O puro e santo padre Eugenio quarto,
> per dio, vogli pensar quel che tu fai,
> ché dove accenni andar, vi troverai
> guerre, ruine, incendi e sangue sparto.   4
> Entra un po' nel pensar: s'io di qui parto
> che seguir può? dove chiaro vedrai
> che qui senza sospetto o spesa istai;
> misura sette e taglia una il buon sarto.   8
> Per prova sai come è fidata Roma,
> e qual sieno i costumi dei Romani,
> che ben figli or di Troia il ver gli noma.
> Tu dunque, o capo e guida de' Cristiani,   12
> non metter a pericol tanta soma:

son dopo i danni i pentimenti vani.
Greci Etiopi e Russiani
ha' teco uniti in pace e in concordia;
non cercar or d'Italia la discordia.

O pure and holy father Eugene the fourth,
you ought to think, by God, what you are doing!
Wherever you intend to move, you will surely
find burnings, bloodshed, wars, as well as ruin.
Do, I pray, a little thinking, "If I leave,
what will come next?" and you will clearly see
that here you suffer neither danger nor expense;
good tailors take seven measures and cut once!
You have proof of how reliable Rome can be,
and how good the customs of the Romans are,
whom Truth calls authentic sons of Troy.
Then you, head and guide of Christendom,
do not expose so great a charge to danger:
misgivings are vain, when the damage is done.
Greeks, Ethiopians, and Russians
you reconciled to you in peaceful harmony;
so now, do not throw down Italy into disorder!

Regarding line 11, after the destruction of Troy by the Greeks, Aeneas, the hero of Virgil's *Aeneid*, escapes with family and friends and arrives in Latium. Here, his descendants found the city of Rome. Virgil's fable thus connected the origin of Rome to the celebrated legends of the Greeks, just as his sponsor, Emperor Augustus, desired. In the sonnet, therefore, the Romans are properly called sons of Troy. The word *troia*, however, besides indicating, when capitalized, the city of Troy, when not capitalized, means "sow" and "whore."

As was the custom, the pope rebutted Antonio's literary-political parturitions with two sonnets penned by his own public-relation sonneteer, who also packed his message with a good measure of "concerned" advice and accusations.

In 1443, Eugene moved to Siena, and in September of the same year, he was back in Rome. The union of the two churches was not achieved. The patriarch of Constantinople died in Florence two days after approving the agreement with Pope Eugene, and later, in Constantinople, the new patriarch rescinded it. Even so, Eugene could boast of having welcomed back to the Church of Rome the Christian Syrians, the Maronites, and the Chaldeans and reasserted his ascendency over the dissenting bishops and over Christendom.

3.4 Literate Citizenry

Realistic poetry, with its great variety of topics, was a long tradition in Florence. It ran the gamut of satire, from witty mockery and literary parody to loutish burlesque and offensive scorn. The sonneteers had an interest in the political destiny of the city or were concerned with problems of personal nature. They could be polemical, satiric, surreal, or simply descriptive.

In the first half of the fifteenth century, the economy of Florence was flourishing, and the Florentine zest for profitable activities and the enjoyment of life was evident everywhere. Many new private homes and public buildings were going up. Everywhere in Italy, architects, painters, and sculptors were receiving more commissions than ever before; engineers were planning fortifications, canals, and dams. They also wrote books on various techniques and on the history of their professions, thus attaining cultural and social prestige. As their public standing grew, so did the competition among them.

The rivalry between Filippo Brunelleschi and Giovanni Gherardi da Prato is well known. Giovanni Gherardi (1367–1446) was a notary, archivist, and judicial consultant for the Orsanmichele and the Opera del Duomo, societies that planned and supervised those two building projects. He lectured on Dante at the university and was the author of an allegorical poem and a rather strange treaty "on an angelic happening due to a very devout vision" (*trattato di un'angelica cosa di mostrata per una divotissima visione*).[50] He was also the author of a project for the yet-to-be-constructed cupola of the cathedral.

Filippo Brunelleschi (1371–1446), the object of Gherardi's enmity, was a man destined to become the most important architect of his time. His theory and use of perspective would give the start to Renaissance architecture. A first dispute between them arose a propos of a shallow-draft propeller-motored barge that Filippo designed to transport merchandise on the Arno River. When Brunelleschi's boat lost its cargo, Gherardi criticized the invention scathingly (Brunelleschi-Battisti 323), and the enmity between the two spilled into an exchange in verse. In this sonnet, Gherardi argues that what is impossible—Brunelleschi's barge—cannot be made possible by clever rationalizing.

> O fonte fonda e nissa d'ignoranza,
> pauper animale ed insensibile,
> che vuoi lo 'ncerto altrui mostrar visibile,
> ma tua archimia nichil habet possanza;   4
> la insipida plebe sua speranza
> omai perduta l'ha, ed è credibile:
> ragion non dà che la cosa impossibile
> possibil facci uom sine sustanza.   8
> Ma se 'l tuo Badalon che in acqua vola
> viene a perfezion, che non può essere,
> non ched i' legga Dante nella scuola,
> ma vo' con le mie man finir mio essere,   12
> perch'io son certo di tua mente fola,
> ché poco sai ordire e vie men tessere.

> Fountain and deep pit of ignorance,
> o miserable and irrational animal

who wants to make visible the invisible,
there is no substance in your alchemy; 4
when all other hopes are lost, simple
and fickle people may still believe in you,
but reason does not allow the impossible be
made possible by a man without substance. 8
Should your *Badalon*, the one flying on water,
ever be perfected—and that will never be—
I wager to end my life by my own hands,
let alone keep lecturing on Dante in the school, 12
for I am certain of your folly, because you are
hardly capable of warping, let alone of weaving.

Gherardi's use of Latin words—*pauper, nichil habet, sine*—and the reference to his lessons on Dante turn the sonnet into a haughty reprimand, which he, an erudite man, is addressing to a man with no formal education. Regarding lines 5–6, this is the meaning given by Eugenio Battisti (whose interpretation I follow throughout): the wishy-washy ignorant plebs, having lost faith in other means, trust him (Brunelleschi-Battisti 324). Regarding line 9, Brunelleschi's patented barge—the *Badalon*—was supported by floats and moved by propellers, some of which were in the water, while others were in the air. Gherardi launches his attack by accusing Brunelleschi of being deeply muddled, or trying to present as truth what is uncertain, but false science (Brunelleschi's alchemy) has no power, he maintains. "Should the *Badalon*"—a word that, in familiar parlance, means dim-witted—"which is supposed to fly over the water, ever be perfected, which is impossible, I," goes on Gherardi, "will not only renounce my Dante lectureship at the university but also take my life by my own hands, so certain I am that you are deranged, for surely you hardly know your own profession."

Brunelleschi rebutted Gherardi's attack with this sonnet:

Quando dall'alto ci è dato speranza,
o tu c'hai efigia d'animal resibile,
perviensi all'uom, lasciando il corruttibile,
e ha da giudicar Somma Possanza. 4
Falso giudicio perde la baldanza,
ché sperienza gli si fa terribile:
l'uom saggio non ha nulla d'invisibile,
se non quel che non è, perc'ha mancanza. 8
E quelle fantasie d'un sine scola,
ogni falso pensier non vede l'essere
che l'arte dà quando natura invola.
Adunque i versi tuoi convienti stessere, 12
c'hanno rughiato in falso la carola,
da poi che 'l mio impossibil viene all'essere.

When hope is given to us from above—hear me,
you who have the looks of the laughing animal—

> we rise above corruptible matter and become men;
> after that, the Highest Power does the judging. 4
> Bad judgment is bound to lose its power,
> for experience will strongly contradict it:
> but to a perceptive man nothing remains invisible,
> except what does not exist, for it has no reality. 8
> As to the fantasy of an unschooled man,
> wrong thinking won't let you see what is there,
> if nature hides it, but the artist is able to unveil it.
> Therefore, unravel the tangle of your verses 12
> for they strike discordant notes in your jingle,
> because my "impossible" will come to life!

Line 1 begins, essentially, "When there is some sort of inspiration from heaven." Regarding the term *animal risibile* in line 2, Aristotle defines man as the animal capable of laughing. Brunelleschi is saying that Gherardi has only the appearance of a human being, for he cannot reason. Elliptic lines 9–11 might mean Filippo is unschooled, but the opinion held by Gherardi, who is an educated man, might nonetheless turn out to be wrong if he cannot see what is under his eyes. On the other hand, Brunelleschi, the artist with the imagination (*fantasia*) of an intelligent experimenter, can see things even when they are not made obvious by nature. Filippo's sonnet is a paean to human endeavor and the value of intelligence and art. When inspired, the artist gets free from the limitations of the physical world and acquires great powers of vision. Art is superior to scholarship, for it can wrench secrets from nature and compete with her by creating life out of imagination, thus turning the possible out of what seems impossible.[51]

The enmity between Brunelleschi and Gherardi continued for several years. In 1417, the Opera del Duomo, the committee charged with the upkeep and completion of the cathedral, invited plans for the construction of the dome. Both men submitted plans. Brunelleschi's project became the object of wide ridicule, but the opera approved his idea, and construction began in 1420. Opposition and criticism continued because Brunelleschi went on modifying his work-in-progress. One fear was that the cupola would curve too precipitously toward the center, with the danger of falling into the space below; another was that with his new changes, there would not be enough light down in the cathedral.

Brunelleschi won the battle with his critics; the construction of the cupola progressed as planned, and his project was completed in 1436. His freestanding, self-sustaining dome became one of the most celebrated constructions in architectural history. Gherardi eventually lost his position at the university—due to budget cuts—and retired to his native Prato. Brunelleschi, although trained as a sculptor, continued to produce architectural works: for the Medici, he reorganized the church and the sacristy of San Lorenzo; for the Pazzi, he built a chapel in Santa Croce; and for the Rucellai and the Pitti, he designed palatial homes. The porticoes of the Ospedale degli Innocenti, then a foundling hospital and now a university building, are another architectural work of his. These works remain prime examples of fifteenth-century Renaissance architecture.[52]

Domenico di Giovanni, whom the Florentines called Burchiello (1404–49), was a barber and a poet. His nickname derived from the shop he had on via Calimala—the street of the rich guilds—over which hung a sign depicting a *burchiello* (a type of small boat).[53] The place had become a gathering point for artists, writers, and sundry admirers. A man of scant erudition but considerable talent, Burchiello took pleasure in ridiculing, in tailed sonnets, the pedantry of unimaginative schoolmen.

> Questi ch'andaron già a studiare a Atene,
> debbono essere stati licenziati,
> e che sia ver, più parte n'è tornati
> e van col capo chino e colle rene.   4
> Questo si è che gli han patito pene
> a star tanto in su' libri spenzolati,
> sicché meritan d'esser dottorati,
> e ser Pecora faccia questo bene.   8
> E questi altri studianti più moderni
> si vorrebbon mandar dove che sia,
> ch'a Firenze n'è fatto troppi scherni;
> vorrebbonsi mandare in Balordia,   12
> che v'è buona derrata di quaderni,
> se già non rincrescessi lor la via.
> Or quel che si sia,
> per mio consiglio vadino a Barbialla,   16
> e tutti col Buezio in su la spalla.

> These guys who went to study in Athens
> have undoubtedly obtained their degrees;
> it must be so, for most of them are back here
> and walk with bent-down heads and kidneys.   4
> That is due to the great pains they suffered
> in dangling over their books for so very long;
> they undoubtedly merit to be made doctors,
> and Professor Sir Sheep may perform the deed. 8
> As to these others, students of modernity,
> they ought to be sent away, no matter where,
> for too much fun is made of them in Florence.
> They ought to be shoved off to Dullsville,   12
> where they can find a supply of writing pads,
> though I regret their showing up even there.
> Whatever their place may be,
> my advice is that they all ought to go to hell, 16
> each carrying the book of Boethius on his back.

Burchiello's satire is directed not only against the bookish knowledge of humanist scholars who felt gratified by their privileged status of experts but also against the enfeebled verse of Petrarch's imitators (the students of modernity). Regarding line 1, the ancient Romans, not the Florentines, went to Athens to study. Burchiello's joke is about both the contemporary humanist interest in ancient life and the custom, on the part of learned institutions, courts, and wealthy families, of playing the host to Byzantine scholars. Many Greek-speaking learned men had arrived in Italy in the wake of the council organized by Pope Eugene IV in 1434, and many more would arrive after the fall of Constantinople in 1453. In line 2, the *licenza* was the lowest academic title. Regarding line 4, Sir Sheep was customarily the name given to unimaginative professors. Regarding line 7, the title of doctor was a higher academic degree. In line 9, the modern scholars are the vernacular poets who practiced the Petrarchan style of poetry. In line 16, *Barbialla*, in *vadino a Barbialla* (translated as "may they go to hell"), was apparently chosen because it rhymes with *spalla*. Regarding line 17, *De consolatione philosophiae* (The Consolation of Philosophy), the influential work of sixth-century Roman poet Boethius, stands here for abstruse and useless knowledge. The coda, independent of the sonnet, is in the guise of a humorous imprecatory recommendation.

In this sonnet, images, words, nouns, and metaphors tend to detach themselves from their conceptual structure, increase their semantic value, and—as Achille Tartaro points out—take on an existence of their own in a satirical-fantastic world where a puppetlike humanity—Professor Sheep, the humanist scholars, the Petrarchists—move about with automatic and grotesque gestures, carrying on their backs the book of Boethius as a sign of their mental deformation.

Burchiello's landscape becomes a veritable surreal invention in "Nominativi fritti e mappamondi." Diction and phrasing create a topsy-turvy world visually wild and mentally unconceivable. Phonic associations, incorrect analogies, and a jocular, imaginative virtuosity nonetheless transform the nonsense into an arabesque of meaningful suggestions and fragments that hint at some profound and mysterious poetry.

Nominativi fritti e mappamondi,
e l'arca di Noè fra due colonne
cantavan tutti Chirieleisonne
per l'influenza de' taglier' mal tondi.   4
La Luna mi dicea: "Ché non rispondi?"
ed io risposi: "Io temo di Giasonne,
però ch'io odo che il diaquilonne
è buona cosa a fare i capei biondi."   8
Per questo le testuggini e i tartufi
m'hanno posto l'assedio alle calcagne,
dicendo: "Noi vogliam che tu ti stufi."
E questo sanno tutte le castagne: 12
pei caldi d'oggi son sì grassi i gufi,
ch'ognun non vuol mostrar le sue magagne.
E vidi le lasagne
andar a Prato, a vedere il Sudario,   16
e ciascuna portava l'inventario.

Fried nominative cases, world maps,
Noah's ark floating between two columns

were all together singing the kyrie eleison
under the influence of dishes not quite full.   4
The Moon said to me, "Why don't you reply?"
and I answered, "I am afraid of big Jason,
for I have heard that the diachylon
is also very good to dye the hair blond."   8
For this reason, tortoises and truffles
have built a blockade around my heels,
and "We want you to give up!" they say.
All the chestnuts are in the know: 12
thanks to our prosperous times, the owls
are very fat and no one wants to show his rot.
And I saw the lasagnas
go to Prato, to contemplate the Shroud,   16
and each one walked carrying a catalog.

In line 1, *nominativi* stands for pedantic grammarians. *Fritti*, meaning "fried"—as in the idiomatic expression *fritti e rifritti*, meaning "fried and refried"—indicates that they, the grammarians, tend to stultify their students with pedantic and repetitive teachings. In line 3, *Chierieleïsonne* is a malapropism of *kyrie eleison*. In line 4, *tagliere* could be either the potter's wheel or the wooden board on which, in preparation of a peasant meal, polenta (cornmeal mush) was poured. Afterward, everybody dug in with his or her spoon. In line 6, *Giasonne*, meaning "big Jason," is another malapropism, for *Giasone*. Jason was the Greek hero who went on an expedition to capture the Golden Fleece. The gold of the fleece is echoed by the *capei biondi* (blond hair) of line 8. Regarding line 7, *dïaquilonne* was a pharmaceutical poultice made of oil and protoxide of lead, usually applied on abscesses and wounds. It was also used to bleach hair. Regarding lines 15–17, there are several disconnected, nonsensical images throughout the poem, but the most inventive and vivid vision is in the coda, with the *lasagne* (plural) marching off on a pilgrimage to Prato. The *sudario*, or the Holy Shroud, is the linen with which a woman by the name of Veronica wiped the bleeding face of Christ as he walked to Calvary. The displacement in this line is that the Veil of Veronica was venerated in Rome, not Prato. *Inventario* is literally inventory of merchandise—replaced in my translation by "catalog"—an indication that many people who are outwardly religiously pious cannot take their minds off making money.

Several critics have been tempted to elicit some coherence from this sonnet. Most suggestive is again the analysis offered by Achille Tartaro (1971, 97–99), which I paraphrase in part.

A dynamic plot propels the sonnet from the start. There is a provocation and then a menace, with an ongoing effect of danger and persecution. The situation is solemnly reminiscent of Dante's *Inferno* 5, 111–12: "Che pense? Quando rispuosi, cominciai …" (What are you thinking about? When I answered, I began …). Such infernal association creates a sense of impending cosmic hostility. The sonnet is shot through with phonic relations that generate beguiling semantic analogies. The word *dïaquilonne* suggests the name *Giasonne*, Jason, in line 6 and is mentally connected with *Sansonne*, popular distortion of Samson, whose demise was due to his hair. If taken to refer to food, *taglier mal tondi* could signify dishes without or with little food in them (Orvieto, in Segre 266)—that is, authorities without substance. Alternatively, by analogy with *moon*, *taglier* could indicate "celestial body," meaning the ascendancy (*influenza*, or "influence") of abusive powers. *Sudario*, or Holy Shroud, makes a good alliteration with *sudatorium*, or the sweat room where, in public baths, the Romans had their sauna; the allusion, therefore, is to the sweating that the faithful must endure during religious pilgrimages and celebrations. The expressions "nominative cases," "world maps," and "Noah's ark"—the latter being taken in textual exegesis as a prefiguration of the Christian community—could indicate that the satire is aimed at the grammatical, philosophical, and geographic pedantry of the highbrows.

Burchiello, like Dante, is a pilgrim in a world that transcends him menacingly. In his sonnent, the beneficent guide is the moon; in Dante's *Inferno*, it is Virgil. The impending danger becomes a reality in lines 9 and 10, where strange objects lay siege to the sonnet's persona, pressing close on his heels and asking him to give up. Soon the grandiosity created by the association with Dante's text is dissipated, the tone becomes farcical, and the chosen symbols are vulgarized, brought to a familiar domestic level—that of plates, truffles, tortoises, and owls. In line 13, the satirical attack is renewed and becomes stridently anticlerical, for here, they, the *gufi* (owls), are said to have grown fat on the prosperity of the times, and they are hiding their vices. A denunciation of rottenness is also in *castagne* (chestnuts), proverbially fine outside and rotten inside. It is a rich social class—that of lasagne. It is one that goes on pilgrimages, holding an inventory of merchandise instead of a book of prayers.

Un topo e una topa e un topetto
m'hanno, con lor assedio, consumato:
e', quand'io dormo, escono de l'agguato:
un va da' piedi e l'altro dal ciuffetto,   4
l'altro mi piscia adosso per dispetto;
e quando senton ch'io sono svegliato,
l'un qua e l'altro là subito entrato,
e' non li veggio, che sian benedetto.   8
E per pigliar li topi maladetti,
trappole ho teso lor e risogallo
arsenico con lardo ed altri archetti;
ed ho due gatti, da fame costretti,   12
che non li piglian, vedendoli al ballo,
sì tosto d'imbucar par ch'e' s'affretti.
E con questi dispetti
io vivo: pensa se ho da consumarmi,   16
che da tre topi non posso aitarmi.

A mouse, a lady mouse, and a little mouse
have, with their siege, totally worn me out:
when I sleep, they come out from their hiding,
one runs to my feet, the other up to my tuft,   4
the third mouse pees on me out of spite,
and, when they see that I am wide awake,
one rushes off and the other quickly hides,
and I can't see them, may they be blessed!   8

In order to catch these blasted mice,
I set out many traps, with poisonous bites,
arsenic with lard, and sundry other tricks;
I also have two cats, driven by appetite,   12
that cannot catch them when they dance about,
so fast they seem to run off to their hideout.
With such aggravations
I live: think whether I have reasons to be riled,   16
as I cannot hold my own with three tiny mice.

Jokingly exaggerating the misery of his life, Burchiello gives us a charming picture of his feckless fight against a rather charming family of mice. Typical of Burchiello's subject matter are amusing scenes, realistic details, and extravagant and obscure allusions, as well as captivating images, realistic witticisms, and plebian language wittily presented. In line 4, a *ciuffetto* is tuft of hair or a hair lock. In line 10, *risogallo* refers to bisulfide. The conclusion, in the form of a morality, comes in the tail, as it often does in caudate sonnets.

Drawn into the hazardous politics of the city, Burchiello sided with Rinaldo Albizzi, the leader of the bankers and the rich business families hostile to the Medici. (For the political sonnet he wrote for Albizzi and his followers, see the previous section.) On the other hand, Cosimo de' Medici, who also was a banker and a businessman, enjoyed the favor of the working classes. This was mainly due to his father, Giovanni di Bicci de' Medici, who, in 1321, as gonfalonier of justice, had imposed a 7 percent tax on capital. Cosimo, his political fortunes firmly established, went on to levy a progressive taxation on all the citizens of the commune. In 1424, the Albizzi faction had him arrested and condemned to death. Cosimo managed to have the sentence commuted to a ten-year exile. When, the following year, the Medici returned to Florence, Burchiello, who had sided with the Albizzi faction, left the city. Documents attest that in 1439, in Siena, the outspoken barber was imprisoned for theft, because supposedly, he was caught climbing a ladder into the room of a German couple, whose clothes he intended to filch. By now, he was without money and miserably ill.

Son diventato in questa malattia
come un graticcio da seccar lasagna,
l'un viso agro sospira e l'altro piagne,
sì son duro in sul far la cortesia.   4
Sento cadermi, andando per la via,
le polpe dietro giù per le calcagne,
e le ginocchia paion due castagne,
sì son ben magre da far gelerìa.   8
Fuoco ho il fegato, e diaccio la sirocchia;
tosso, sputo, anso, e sento di magrana,
e in corpo mi gorgoglia una ranocchia.
Cresciuta m'è un palmo la fagiana,   12
e scemato un sommesso la pannocchia:
nol trovo, èssi smarrito infra la lana.
Non mi da più mattana,

erbolaio è, non istrologo piùe,   16
e pisciommi fra i peli, come il bue.

Thanks to this disease, I have become
a rack on which to dry pasta for lasagna;
in seeing me, some people sigh, others weep,
so stiff I get when I try to drop a curtsy.   4
Walking in the street, I feel my buttocks
hanging all the way down to my heels;
my knees look as big as chestnuts
and are soft enough to be made into jelly.   8
I have fire in the liver, ice in the spleen:
I cough, I spit, I pant, I suffer from migraines;
a frog gurgles inside my frame.
My scrotum has lengthened by a span,   12
my dick has shrunk by a pointing fist;
I cannot find it; it is lost in the woolies.
It does not bother me any longer,
it is now a herbalist, no longer an astrologer;   16
and it pees in the hair, just as an ox does.

In line 9, *sirocchia* means "sister." Here it indicates the spleen, the liver's sister. In lines 12–13, *fagiana* and *panocchia* are popular jargon for scrotum and penis. *Sommesso* is the length of a fist with the thumb up. Per line 16, now his organ keeps its head down like an herbalist intent on preparing his mixtures; it does not look up like an astrologer, who scrutinizes the stars. The climax of Burchiello's self-denigration is in the coda, where a series of metaphorical revelations creates a fanciful animalistic finish.

Io ho il mio cul sì forte rinturato,
che se sciroppo fusse il Po e 'l Tevere,
pria tutto quanto mel' converria bevere,
che ogni budel di me fusse bagnato.   4
E s'io avessi rubarber mangiato
con mille pille non potrei mai credere,
che mi facessimo una volta petere:
pensa a bell'otta ch'i' sarò purgato.   8
Ben ho fatto al mi cul cento cristieri,
sopposte, medicine, e non mi vale;
che stitico non sia più oggi che ieri.
Che s'io avessi in culo uno speziale,   12
e 'l medico ci fusse anche in tal loco,
non posson far ch'io cachi un poco poco.

> Ben darei bando e 'l fuoco
> a qual medico si vuol dottorare, 16
> se primamente non sa far cacare.

My asshole is so securely plugged up
that, if the Tiber and the Po were laxatives,
I would have to swallow them all up
before the tiniest tract of bowel got wet. 4
Were I forced to gulp down rhubarb
and a thousand pills, I would still doubt
they could make me fart even once;
imagine if they could fully clean me out. 8
I have given my ass so many enemas,
suppositories, medications, but nothing doing!
Today I am more constipated than yesterday.
If I had a druggist up my very ass, 12
or even a doctor, neither of them would
be able to make me go a tiny, weeny bit.
I would definitely exile and set on fire
anyone who wanted to become a specialist, 16
if he had not learned how to make people shit.

Regarding line 2, Tiber and Po are rivers crossing Rome and the northern plane, respectively. Regarding lines 15–17, Burchielo's expert suggestion for the qualification of a doctor is left for the coda. Later in life, the barber moved to Rome, where he tried to start another shop and failed. He died in 1449, the year of Lorenzo de' Medici's birth. His sonnets, especially those climaxing in the nonsense and the surreal, achieved great popularity in his lifetime and thereafter. Leonardo Dati, a humanist and pontifical secretary to Paul II, is known to have said, "Burchiello is a little nothing, but he enchants everyone." Anton Francesco Grazzini, who in 1552 and 1568 edited a collection of Burchiello's poetry for the Giunti publishing house, wrote that in the estimation of the Florentines, Burchiello came third after Dante and Petrarch. Besides the two Florentine editions just mentioned, his verse was published in Venice in 1480, 1522, and 1525.

3.5 The Medici and Their Circle

At the end of the fourteenth century, a new intellectual and literary movement, now known as the Renaissance, was about to sweep through the Italian peninsula. It began as a study of the classical world, including its literary culture and technologies. At the center of interest were literature, history, and philosophy, the disciplines called *humanae litterae* by the Romans, or humanities by us. The specific term for a proto-Renaissance man who studied such disciplines is *humanist*.

It was the custom of Florentine humanists to meet for conversation. One place for such gatherings was Salutati's home; another was the garden of Villa del Paradiso, a country house belonging to Antonio Alberti. The Alberti were an old family of merchants and bankers whose business had representatives in several Italian towns and abroad.[54] The topics of discussion varied, although popular were those that had been dear to the cultured Romans, such as friendship, intellectual solidarity, and the *otia litterarum* question—the latter dealing with how much time a man ought to take from business and political life to dedicate to literary studies.

A prominent member of the Alberti family was Leon Battista Alberti (1404–72), a celebrated architect as well as a humanist and author of treatises on a variety of subjects, Latin dialogues, and poetry.[55] He dabbled in realistic-satiric verse as well and carried friendly sonnet battles with the barber of Calimala Street. In general, however, his verse tended to maintain a sustained literary tone, as does this sonnet of his.

> Io già vidi seder nell'arme irato
> uomo furioso palido e tremare;
> e gli occhi vidi spesso lacrimare
> per troppo caldo che al cor è nato.   4
> E vidi amante troppo adolorato
> poter né lagrimar né sospirare,
> né raro vidi chi né pur gustare
> puote alcun cibo ov'è troppo affamato.   8
> E vela vidi volar sopra l'onde,
> qual troppo vento la sommerse e affisse;
> e veltro vidi, a cui par l'aura ceda,
> per troppo esser veloce, perder preda.   12
> Così tal forza in noi natura immise,
> a cui troppo voler mal corrisponde.

> Once I saw an impetuous man, ready
> to fight, turn pale and tremble; and I saw
> his eyes weep profusely, for too intense
> a passion was swelling in his heart.   4
> And I saw a very distraught lover
> who could neither weep nor sigh; and I saw,
> not rarely, some people unable to partake
> of nourishment, for they were too famished.   8
> I furthermore saw a sail flying over the waves
> get flooded and be drowned by strong winds;
> and I saw a hound, swifter than any breeze,
> lose its prey, for it ran at too great a speed.   12
> Such strength Nature has placed in us
> that is unable to respond to too strong a will.

The message of the sonnet is that moderation is needed in all human activities. This is the principle that Alberti championed in the famous *Libri della Famiglia* (Books on the Family). A regulated and measured life—he maintained—is the foundation of productivity and industriousness, a correct use of money, and a fair accumulation of wealth. The theme of the sonnet runs through three quatrains in a series of antitheses. It takes off with the word *vidi* at the beginning of lines 1, 5, and 11; is stressed by the repetition of *vidi* in the middle of the third verse of each quatrain; and is emphasized by the alliterations of *vela, vidi, volar, veltra,* and *vidi*. The series finds the finish in the aphorism of the closing couplet.

Among the many initiatives that Cosimo de' Medici undertook after his return from exile was a comprehensive plan of patronage of both humanistic studies and popular culture. At the time, the humanists wrote almost exclusively in Latin; the vernacular was used in popular poetry, especially in the sonnets penned by people of lower education. In 1441, in order to encourage the use of the vernacular by all and bring it to a higher literary level, by Cosimo's initiative and with his financial backing, Leon Battista Alberti organized a contest of lyric poetry in Italian. It was the Certame Coronario, or Contest for the Crown—a crown, in this case, made of laurel leaves.

The Alberti had consistently been on the side of *popolo grasso*, and Leon Battista had sided with the Albizzi. However, after a period of exile, during which he was a guest of the Visconti and the Sforza of Milan, Leon Battista was reconciled with the Medici. It was Cosimo's chosen practice to make friends with his former enemies and, rather than keep their enmity alive, put them to some good use.

The local university officially announced the contest, and on October 22, the eight poets chosen for the competition stood on a platform in the church of Santa Maria della Croce and read their verses before the Florentine audience. That was the church where it had become customary to recite cantos of *The Divine Comedy* to the public.

The theme assigned to the contestants was friendship, a subject much discussed by the ancient Romans and by modern humanists. It was also a subject that perfectly tallied with Cosimo's all-inclusive postvictory policy. For Marsilio Ficino and the other members of the Florentine Academy—a society that Cosimo had helped to establish—the concept of friendship was closely associated with those of Platonic and Christian love. Ficino liked to think that all the members of the academy were bound to one another by a tie of Platonic friendship, to be understood as a "spiritual bond between two persons who both participate in the contemplative life" (Kristeller 96). At the end of the competition, no poem was considered good enough to win the prize—or was this another of Cosimo's shrewd decisions? Even so, the contest itself and the reason for it aroused considerable interest, and soon copies of the competing poems began to circulate in the country.

Among the poems read during the contest, this sonnet by Ciriaco de' Pizzicolli of Ancona became a favorite.[56]

> Quel Sir, che sotto l'ideale stampa
> diè forma all'alme sustanze superne,
> a Delio, alla sorella, a l'altre eterne
> ninfe, che 'l cielo adorna e 'l mondo avvampa,   4
> con quei liquenti corpi, con che accampa
> Anfitrite la terra, ove concerne
> ogni animal che vive, sente e scerne
> sotto li raggi di sua diva lampa,   8
> per l'universo ornar d'ogni delizia,
> produsse in forma, in atto e in potenza
> tante diverse al mondo creature,

   sustanze e accidenti, miste e pure,   12
   dandoli in don più degno alla sua essenza
   util, gioconda, onesta, alma Amicizia.

   That Lord who, following an ideal model,
   formed the life-giving substances up above,
   as well as the sun, his sister, and the eternal stars
   that adorn the sky and warm up the universe,   4
   and the liquid bodies with which Amphitrite
   took residence on earth, where all the animals,
   which are living, have understanding and feelings
   and are cared for under the rays of his divine lamp,   8
   that Lord, in order to adorn the universe with all
   delights, produced in form, act, and potentiality
   the diverse creatures of this world, substances
   and accidents alike, mixed and pure; and to them   12
   He gave the prized, honest, nurturing, and joyful
   Friendship, a gift most worthy of his essence.

In Ciriaco's sonnet, the assigned theme of friendship becomes a celebration of the harmony that potentially exists among all created things. In line 1, *stampa* means "mold" or "model." God fashioned the creatures of this earth following an ideal model—that is, a Platonic idea. Regarding lines 2–4, Apollo, personification of the sun, is indicated by the name of Delos—here by the adjective *Delio*—for Delos is the island where the god was born. Apollo's sister is Artemis, the moon. The eternal nymphs are the stars, bodies that adorn the sky and warm the earth. In line 5, the *liquenti corpi* are the seas. In line 7, *scerne* is from *scernere*, meaning "to distinguish" or "to discern." In line 10, the subject of "has produced" (*produsse*) is "that Lord" (*Quel Sire*) of line 1. *Atto* and *potenza*, meaning "actuality" and "potentiality," are concepts used by scholastic philosophers to explain all physical and psychological changes. Potentiality indicates the qualities that a thing can possibly take on, while actuality is the change that has brought about the fulfillment of that possibility. In other words, God created the creatures as they are and as they can potentially become.

When Piero de' Medici, Cosimo's son, died, Lorenzo, later called the Magnificent (1449–92), became the de facto head of the Florentine state. The government of the city and its foreign relations were his main preoccupations, but he took time to befriend literati and intellectuals, continue the sponsorship of humanistic studies, and encourage the production of vernacular literature. He also proved to possess outstanding literary capacities and was able to display them in a variety of genres, in high and popular style. One hundred eight sonnets of his are extant.

   Belle e fresche e purpuree viole,
   che quella candidissima man colse,
   qual pioggia o qual puro aer produr volse

tanto più vaghi fior che far non suole? 4
Qual rugiada, qual terra o ver qual sole
tante vaghe bellezze in voi raccolse?
onde il soave odor Natura tolse,
o il ciel che a tanto ben degnar ne vuole? 8
Care mie violette, quella mano
che v'elesse infra l'altre, ov'eri, in sorte
v'ha di tanta eccellenzia e pregio ornate.
Quella che 'l cor mi tolse e di villano 12
lo fe gentile, a cui siete consorte,
quell'adunque e non altri ringraziate.

Beautiful blooming purple violets,
picked by that immaculate hand of hers,
what purity of air, what rain wished to produce
flowers far more enchanting than any others? 4
What dew, what earth, or what sun
gathered in you such perfect loveliness?
Where did nature or the heavens take this sweet
fragrance of yours, wanting to grace us so? 8
My dear flowers, a great excellence and worth
was bestowed on you by the hand that picked you
where you happened to be among many others.
The woman who took my heart and from vile 12
made it noble, and with which you now consort,
is the one you must thank, and no one other.

In line 10, *ov'eri* stands for the plural *ov'eravate*, meaning "where you were," and refers to *viole* or *violette*, a word that in those days, I understand, did not specifically indicate violets. In line 13, *lo fe gentile* is an obvious trace of the stilnovo theory according to which the man's heart is made *gentile* ("noble" in the original meaning of the word) by the love for an excellent woman. *A cui siete consorte(i)* means "to which you are consort." *Cui* refers to *'l cor* (the poet's heart). *Consort*—from the Latin *sors*, or *sortis* (destiny)—has here the original meaning of sharing a destiny, as in prince consort. From Lorenzo's *Comento de' miei sonetti* (Commentary on My Sonnets), we know that the flowers were sent by Lucrezia Donati, the friend to whom he dedicated his *Rime*. The sonnet applies to his appreciation of the flowery gift a concept drawn from Guinizzelli's doctrinal song "Al cor gentil rempaira sempre amore" (see section 1.3). Nature gave the flowers beauty and perfume, and then, by picking them, the hand of a woman with exceptional redeeming qualities conferred excellence and merit on them. Thus, Lorenzo's heart and the flowers were made consorts, for they shared the same destiny, having both been ennobled by Lucrezia.

The subtext of many of Lorenzo's sonnets is generally understood to be the Neoplatonic philosophy of love, as it was expounded by Marsilio Ficino, the reigning philosopher of the Medici circle.[57] Goodness and beauty are reflections of the greater beauty and perfection of the Creator. Human love is preliminary to the higher form of love that all humans must ultimately address to God. The authors of treatises on love and, subsequently, the writers of love poetry assumed the love for a beautiful and worthy woman to be the first step toward the perception of divine love. A trace of that theory is certainly in Lorenzo's *Comento de' miei sonetti*. The clear Ficinian distinction between human passion and the loving experience of the contemplative mind, however, is, in Lorenzo's verse, somewhat blurred. What we find most striking in his poetry are a new sensibility and a modern frame of mind.

> O veramente felice e beata
> notte, che a tanto ben fusti presente;
> o passi ciechi, scorti dolcemente
> da quella man suave e delicata;   4
> voi, Amor e 'l mio cor e la mia amata
> donna sapete sol, non altra gente,
> quella dolcezza che ogni umana mente
> vince, da uom giamai non più provata.   8
> Oh più ch'altra armonia di suoni e canti
> dolce silenzio! oh cieche ombre, che avesti
> di lacrimosa luce privilegio!
> Oh felici sospiri e degni pianti!   12
> Oh superbo desio, che presumesti
> voler sperare, aver sì alto pregio!

> Oh, truly happy and blissful night,
> which beheld my greatest happiness!
> Oh, hidden movements, so quietly guided
> by that soft and gentle hand of hers!   4
> Only my heart, my beloved woman,
> and you, Love, and no one else, have known
> such tenderness, which overcomes all human
> minds and never was felt by anyone before.   8
> Oh, silence, sweeter than any harmony
> of music and song! Oh, those dark shadows
> which were privileged to see her weeping eyes!
> Ah, those lovable tears! Ah, those contented   12
> sighs! Oh, supreme desires that presumed
> to wish and to hope for so high a prize!

Regarding line 11, in the phrase *di luce lacrimosa privilegio* (literally "privilege of a tearful light"), *luce* stands for "eyes," and *lacrimosa* is "tearful": in the dim light of the bedchamber, he could see her eyes full of tears. With their suggestion of her touch and her emotional reaction to lovemaking, lines 3–4 and 10–11 tenderly convey the lingering impressions of a night of love. The enjambments of lines 1–2 and 5–6 and the long inversion enjambment of 9–10 at the beginning of the sestet (*più ch'altra armonia … dolce silenzio*, or "more than any harmony … sweet silence") sustain the sonnet's long, quivering, pulsating recollection.

Più che mai bella e men che già mai fera
mostrommi Amor la mia cara inimica,
quando i pensier del giorno e la fatica
tolto avea il pigro sonno della sera.   4
Sembrava agli occhi miei proprio com'era,
deposta sol la sua durezza antica,
e fatta agli amorosi raggi aprica:
né mai mi parve il ver cosa sì vera.   8
Prima, al parlar, e pauroso e lento
stavo, come solea: poi la paura
vinse il desio e cominciai dicendo:
"Madonna …" E in quel partissi come un vento.   12
Così in un tempo sùbita mi fura
il sonno e sé e mia merzé, fuggendo.

More beautiful and less cruel than ever
Love showed to me my dear enemy,
as the concerns and weariness of the day
dissipated in the evening's lazy slumber.   4
To my eyes, she appeared as she really was,
except for the letting go of her usual cruelty;
now she was springlike, open to the rays of love:
no real thing ever appeared to me so real.   8
At first, I was hesitant and afraid to speak,
just as I used to be, but then my fears were
overcome by desire, and I began to say,
"Lady …" when, like wind, she disappeared.   12
Thus, by fleeing, all at once she robbed me
of my sleep, of herself, and of my desire.

Regarding line 1, in courtly poetry, *fera*, meaning "fierce," is a thematic word indicating a woman unresponsive to love. In line 7, *aprica* literally means "open to the sun," or, metaphorically, "well-disposed, pleasing, and ready to reciprocate." In line 14, *mia merzè* is another thematic term, signifying "the lover's reward"—that is, the return of love the man might finally succeed in obtaining.

Lorenzo's sonnet is reminiscent of "Levommi il mio pensier" by Petrarch, but the inspiration differs. Petrarch's exalted experience and ecstatic tone are absent here. Lorenzo's representation of the dream is realistic. There is in it a moment of intense happiness, but the magic illusion dissipates quickly. The accent is on the deception of the dream, on the final sudden, bitter awakening. The sonnet is a vivid yet delicate representation of the frustrating experience of an interrupted, unfulfilled fantasy.

As time went by, there appeared in Lorenzo's poetry an increasingly more poignant desire for solitude and tranquility. "Cerchi chi vuol le pompe e gli alti onori" is a sonnet penned sometime in the 1480s.

Cerchi chi vuol le pompe e gli alti onori,
le piazze, i templi e gli edifizi magni,

le delizie e il tesor, quale accompagni
mille duri pensier, mille dolori. 4
Un verde praticel pien di be' fiori,
un rivo che l'erbetta intorno bagni,
un augelletto che d'amor si lagni,
acqueta molto meglio i nostri ardori; 8
l'ombrose selve, i sassi e gli alti monti,
gli antri oscuri e le fere fuggitive,
qualche leggiadra ninfa paurosa:
quivi vegg'io con pensier vaghi e pronti 12
le belle luci come fussin vive,
qui me le toglie or una or altra cosa.

Let him who wishes seek pomp and honors high,
the piazzas, the temples, the stately palaces,
unusual pleasures, and those riches that go together
with a thousand unpleasant thoughts and worries. 4
A small verdant meadow full of flowers,
a rivulet that bathes the novel grass around,
one little bird singing of his unrequited love
can calm my unrest more soothingly by far. 8
Give me shaded forests, high peaks and rocks,
some shadowy caves and absconding animals,
and the vision of an alluring, fearful nymph:
there, with pleasing, friendly thoughts, I shall see 12
those lovely eyes of hers as if they were before me;
here, one thing or another drives them away from me.

In the country (*quivi* of line 12), the thought of his beloved is unimpeded and soothing. In the city (*qui* of line 14), people's race for rewards, rare pleasures, and riches makes any beatific contemplation impossible. Only a pastoral setting, in the quiet enjoyment of small pleasures—the diminutives *praticello*, *erbetta*, and *augelletto* emphasize the modesty of such desires—or, alternatively, the impressive features of an uninhabited landscape—mountains, rocks, caverns, and wild animals—can bring calm to his thoughts. Only there he might conjure the soothing image of his beloved.

The power of fantasy and the memory of happy moments were comforting balms to Lorenzo, so taken up by public life. But for him, such soothing experience of love was no initial step toward the ultimate contemplation of the divine. The calming effect was simply due to a momentary flight of the imagination. A comparison between human imagining and contemplation is here suggested, but one remains substantially different from the other: one is contemplation of the truth, and the other is "vain imagination, fathomed by human appetite," as he stated in *Comento* 21. What imagination produces is the greatest happiness humankind can obtain, and that is the same as saying that humankind can find happiness only in illusion, in dreaming.

The Platonic Academy and academies in general were cultural institutions that supported many writers and intellectuals; they were also important centers of political influence. In Lorenzo's old circle of friends, there was a man who did not feel comfortable with the highly intellectual company of humanists and Neoplatonic philosophers.

Luigi Pulci (1432–84), author of an irreverent mock-heroic epic poem, was long accustomed to entertain Lorenzo with antics and amusing writings. Feeling an outsider among the Magnificent's intellectual friends, he made fun of the philosophical beliefs they espoused.

Costor che fan sì gran disputazione
dell'anima, ond'ell'entri o ond'ell'esca,
o come il nocciol si stia nella pesca,
hanno studiato in su 'n un gran mellone.   4
Aristotile allegano e Platone
e voglion ch'ella in pace requiesca
fra suoni e canti, e fannoti una tresca
che t'empie il capo di confusione.   8
L'anima è sol, come si vede espresso,
in un pan bianco caldo un pinocchiato,
o una carbonata in un pan fesso.
E chi crede altro ha 'l fodero in bucato,   12
e que' che per l'un cento hanno promesso
ci pagheran di succiole in mercato.
Mi dice un che v'è stato
nell'altra vita e più non può tornarvi,   16
che appena con la scala si può andarvi.
Costor credon trovarvi
e beccafichi e gli ortolan pelati
e buon vin e letti sprimacciati;   20
e vanno dietro a' frati.
Noi ce n'andrem, Pandolfo, in valle buia,
senza sentir più cantare alleluja!

These people who carry on interminable
disputations on the soul, on how it comes in,
how it goes out, and how the pit stays in the peach,
have ponderously pondered on a giant melon.   4
They believe, taking after Aristotle and Plato,
that the soul will rest in peace among
music and songs, and they make a big noise
throwing our heads into a enormous muddle.   8
The soul is only found, it can be clearly seen,
in pine-seed jam spread on warm white pastry
or in roast pork inside a good chunk of bread.
He who believes otherwise has a hole in his head, 12

and those who promise a hundred percent,
will pay back in the market with boiled chestnuts.
One man told me, one who has been
in yonder life but has not been able to return,   16
that you can get there simply with a ladder.
Those people believe that over there
one can find plucked ortolans, many tasty
little birds, good wines, and soft, bouncing beds.   20
They take their lead from friars!
You and I, Pandolfo, will enter the vale of darkness,
and there we shall hear the hallelujah no more!

In line 3, the pit (*nocciolo*) stands for the soul. The discussion of the theologians had to do with the immortality of the soul (the pit) and with its relation to the body (the peach). Line 4 means that they have meditated on the problem deeply. *Mellone*, meaning "big melon," is a reference to the pupil's apple on which the teacher carved the letters of the alphabet. The pupil who recognized the letters on the apple could afterward eat it. There is also an association with the derivative word *mellonaggine*, or "great nonsense" (Orvieto, in Segre 22, 278). In line 7, *suoni e canti* is a jocular expression indicating paradise after death, as well as paradisiacal goings-on. The *tresca* is a dynamic dance; it stands for great fuss, or great song and dance. In line 10, *pinocchiato* is a soft mixture of sugar and pine seeds. Regarding line 12, to have *il fodero in bucato* (the lining in the wash) means not to be awake, or to be out of one's head. In line 13, there might be a reference to Mark 10:29–30. To Peter, who bemoaned that in becoming a follower, he had left everything he cared for behind, Jesus said, "There is no one who has given up home, or brothers, or sisters, or mother, or father, or children, or land for my sake and for the sake of the Gospel, who will not receive a hundred times as much." Regarding line 22, Pandolfo Rucellai was the friend to whom Luigi sent the sonnet. He answered by advising him not to antagonize people who really mattered (Nigro 66). The "valley of darkness" is the ground where the dead are buried. With the hallelujah, the hymn of Christ's resurrection, sung on Easter Sunday, Pulci implies that when he and his friend Pandolfo are buried, they no longer will hear about paradise and eternal life, for they will be really dead.

Pulci's apparent rigmarole is, in effect, neatly organized. The parody is dealt with within the space of the fourteen lines: the quatrains put forward, disrespectfully, the theory of immortality; the sestet opposes it with derisive objections. All is expressed, for added ridicule, in familiar language and images. After line 14, the attention shifts from the know-it-all to the uneducated. The three codas are anecdotal additions referring to the ridiculous proofs that simple-minded people entertain for such nonsensical beliefs as life after death. The last couplet is an open, jibing negation of afterlife.

Pulci's parody—strong in his major work, the *Morgante*—was directed in particular against Marsilio Ficino. At the time, Ficino lectured on the question of the soul and, a few years later, would uphold its immortality in *Theologia platonica de immortalitate animorom* (Platonic Theology on the Immortality of the Soul).

In earlier times, the existence of other sources of power than the church—such as the emperor—guaranteed a relative amount of freedom of speech, and the satire of religion was tolerated; it was no longer so in fifteenth-century Florence, where the Medici, in dire need of the largest consensus possible, thought it counterproductive to alienate the religious authorities and well-entrenched professorial class.

In Lorenzo's youth, Pulci had entertained him with his comic-satirical talk and verse and enjoyed his admiration and protection. When Lorenzo became the head of the state, he adopted a versatile cultural policy with the intention of pleasing the more prestigious and influential people as well as the lowbrows. The old friend's insistently disrespectful attitude toward high culture and their representatives was felt to be getting out of hand. Pulci's inconsiderate behavior finally provoked Ficino into accusing him of blasphemy. After alienating all the members of the Medici family as well, the poet left Florence for good.

3.6 Noblemen

The recurrent wars between Italian states officially ended with the Pace di Lodi, a peace treaty signed at Lodi, in Lombardy, in 1454. The second half of the century was a period of stability and peace, in great part thanks to the diplomatic skill of Lorenzo de' Medici. Ensconced in their resplendent courts, the Gonzaga of Mantua, the Este of Ferrara, the Sforza of Milan, and the Montefeltro of Urbino had long vied with one another in embellishing their domains and promoting humanistic studies, literature, and the arts. They established new schools, promoted academies, and opened libraries to the public. Their courts were centers of culture and of entertaining festivities and elegant life.

One such family was that of Leonello d'Este (1407–50), author of the first sonnet in this section. Son of Nicolò III d'Este[58] and his mistress, Stella dei Tolomei, and educated by Guarino da Verona, a celebrated educational innovator, in 1441, Leonello became lord of Ferrara, Modena, and Rimini. Besides being a shrewd politician capable of rising to a position of dominance in the region, Leonello proved to be a man of refined taste, a devotee of literature, and a patron of the arts.[59] He promoted the reformation of the local university, which had been founded by his father in 1391. He attracted to his court valued artists, such as Andrea Mantegna, Piero della Francesca, Iacopo Bellini, Rogier van der Weyden, and Pisanello. To him, Antonio Decembrio dedicated *Politica Letteraria*, a work discussing the courtly code of conduct and polite conversation to be expected from women and men of refinement.

Leonello's sonnet combines the traditional topic of the man helplessly in love with an amusing take on Love's irresponsibility. A psychological condition has become animated action. Love has blinded the unfortunate lover and has left him to his own devices in the middle of the street. Losing all sense of orientation, the man no longer knows where he is and where he is going; he stops forlornly at one corner, hoping that someone will come to his rescue. Elegant phrasing is maintained throughout the sonnet, in a mixture of high-style Italian and words inflected in the Milanese manner.

> Lo Amor me ha facto cieco e non ha tanto
> de carità che me conduca in via:
> me lassa per meo despecto en mea balia,
> e dice: or va' tu, che presciumi tanto.   4
> Ed eo, perché me scento en forze alquanto,
> e stimo de truovar chi man me dia,
> vado, ma puoi non sciò dove me sia,
> tal che me fermo dricto in su d'un canto.   8

Allora Amore, che me sta quatando,
me mostra per desprezzo, e me obstenta,
e me va canzonando en alto metro.
No 'l dice tanto pian ch'eo non lo senta,   12
ed eo respondo così borbottando:
mostrame almen la via che torna endietro.

Love has blinded me and does not have
as much charity as to escort me along the way:
to spite me, he has left me to my own devices
and said, "Now go on, since you presume so much!"   4
And I, feeling to be bursting with confidence
and expecting someone in time would help me,
moved on, but then I no longer knew where
I was; so I stopped, right at a corner of the street.   8
Now Love, who has kept an eye on me,
points me out in a contemptuous manner,
and ridicules me to a distasteful degree.
He does not speak too low and I can catch   12
his words, and in answer to him, I mutter,
"At least, show me the way I can go back!"

The patronage of literature and the arts continued under Borso d'Este, Leonello's brother and successor. Borso opened to the public his brother's library, which was rich in classical and humanistic manuscripts. Borso began the construction of Palazzo Schifanoia, and thanks to his numerous commissions, a school of painting took shape in Ferrara, headed by Cosmè Tura, Francesco del Cossa, and Ercole de' Robertis. Under Borso and under Ercole I, his successor, there began a new production of Latin and vernacular plays, while the old tradition of the narrative epic took a high literary turn with Matteo Maria Boiardo and Ludovico Ariosto.

Matteo Maria Boiardo, count of Scandiano (1441–94), was educated in the classics by Guarino da Verona and later at the University of Ferrara.[60] He was a nephew of the famous humanist Tito Verpasiano Strozzi and a cousin of the more famous Pico della Mirandola. In 1476, Boiardo began his career at the service of Ercole I, and he served in turn as the military governor of Modena and later as governor of Reggio. For the entertainment of his lord and court, he wrote a chivalric-romantic epic, the *Orlando Innamorato* (Orlando in Love). Inspired by his love for Antonia Caprara, a court lady, he wrote what is considered the best songbook of the century and called it, after Ovid, *Amorum Libri*. Its 150 sonnets tell a story of sexual longing, fulfilled desire, and tormenting jealousy, all against the background of the court, its society games, and its festivities. The poems presented here exemplify Boiardo's capacity for visual pleasure, tendency to disclose intimate feelings, and sensual celebration of life and all that is beautiful and refined.

Dàtime a piena mano e rose e zigli,
spargete intorno a me viole e fiori;
ciascun che meco pianse e mei dolori,
di mia leticia meco il frutto pigli. 4
Dàtime e fiori e candidi e vermigli;
confano a questo giorno e bei colori;
spargeti intorno d'amorosi odori,
ché il loco a la mia voglia se assumigli. 8
Perdon m'ha dato et hami dato pace
la dolce mia nemica, e vuol ch'io campi,
lei che sol di pietà se pregia e vanta.
Non vi meravigliati perch'io avampi, 12
ché maraviglia è piú che non se sface
il cor in tutto de alegreza tanta.

Give me lilies and roses full-handedly,
scatter violets and florets all around;
any one of you who grieved at my pains
today may partake of my happiness! 4
Give me flowers, white and vermilion,
—beautiful colors become a day like this—
sprinkle all over inebriating perfumes,
and let the place befit my mood for love. 8
My sweet enemy has forgiven me; she,
who only gentleness flaunts and claims,
granted me peace and wishes me to live.
So do not marvel if I am set ablaze: 12
it is a real wonder if my heart does not
totally melt down in a gladness so great.

Obvious in line 1 are the reminiscences of Virgil's "Manibus o date lilia plenis, purpureos spargam flores" (*Aeneid* 6, 883) and Dante's *Purgatorio* 30, 21. But the colorful touch becomes unmistakably Boiardo's thanks to the amplifications of lines 2, 5 ("flowers, white and vermilion"), 6 ("beautiful colors"), and 7 ("inebriating perfumes"). The Italian word translated as "inebriating" is *amorosi*, amorous in the sense that they give a sensual pleasure and are therefore well suited to the poet's longing for love. In line 8, the poet-lover invites his surroundings, the entirety of nature, to participate in his newfound happiness. The octave is a hymn to a joy that overflows in the many doublings and repetitions, frequent imperatives (*dàtime, spargete, dàtime, spargete*), and insistent use of first-person adjectives and pronouns (*me, a me, meco, mei, mia, meco, me*) that obsesses on the need for the lover to take on himself all the beauty and pleasure that nature can offer (Zanato 110–11). The sestet leads to the closing by explaining such rejoicing in simpler, more subdued courtly terms.

Già vidi uscir de l'onde una matina
il sol di ragi d'or tutto iubato,
e di tal luce in facia colorato
che ne incendeva tutta la marina;   4
e vidi la rogiada matutina
la rosa aprir d'un color sì infiamato
che ogni luntan aspetto avria stimato
che un foco ardesse ne la verde spina;   8
e vidi aprir a la stagion novella
la molle erbetta, sì come esser sòle
vaga più sempre in giovenil etade;
e vidi una legiadra donna e bella   12
su l'erba coglier rose al primo sole
e vincer queste cose di beltade.

Out of the waves, one morning, I saw
the sun rise with a flowing mane of gold;
of such splendor was its face adorned
that all the sea seemed to be set on fire;   4
and, in the morning dew, I saw a rose
open its petals in such a blazing color
that any faraway eye would have thought
a flame was burning on the greenish thorn.   8
In the springtime season, I also saw
the soft grass come up, growing most
lovely, as it does in its early days;
and, in the meadow, I also saw a beautiful   12
and charming woman pick roses in the early sun
and, with her beauty, outshine everything above.

In line 2, *Iubato* refers to being surrounded by a resplendent lion's mane, from the Latin *juba* (mane) and *jubar* (radiance). This mane is of a golden light. In line 7, *luntan aspetto* is metonymy for "someone looking from afar." The colorful natural images—the blazing sun, the morning dew, the rose petals, and the tender grass—are organized in parallel, symmetrical sections whose regularity is underlined by *vidi* (I saw) at the beginning of each section. However, there is great dynamism and vivacity inside that stable grid. The sun, rose, and grass are personified; have physiognomies of their own; and move about. The sun is coming out of the sea, and his face is highly colored; the rose is opening its petals, which are of so vivid a hue as to give the impression of a flame; and the grass is growing, soft to the touch (Ceserani-De Federicis 2, 502; Zanato 118).

La smisurata et incredibil voglia
che dentro fu renchiusa nel mio core,

non potendo capervi, esce de fore,
e mostra altrui cantando la mia zoglia.
Cingete il capo a me di verde foglia,
ché grande è il mio trionfo, e vie magiore
che quel de Augusto o d'altro imperatore
che ornar di verde lauro il crin si soglia.
Felice bracia mie, che mo' tanto alto
giugnesti che a gran pena io il credo ancora,
qual fia di vostra gloria degna lode?
Ché tanto de lo ardir vostro me exalto
che non più meco, ma nel ciel dimora
il cor, che ancor del ben passato gode.

The unbelievable and unmeasurable
desire that remained locked in my heart,
unchecked within, now overruns its bounds
and sings, revealing to the world my happiness.
Wreathe my head with greenish leaves,
my triumph is great, greater than Augustus's
or any other emperor's whose head
was ever decked with verdant laurel.
Oh, happy arms of mine, you have reached
such lofty heights that I can hardly believe it still;
what praise will be fitting so great a glory?
So exalted am I by your glorious daring
that no longer inside me but in heaven
is my heart, still feeling my jubilant past.

The poem bounces along with an impetuous rhythm, each section vibrant with joy for the return of love from a woman who appeared unreachable. It is a rejoicing more exalting than any emperor's triumph. In line 12, the *ardir vostro* (your daring) refers to the arms of the man in line 9, which dared to embrace her and enjoy a love he had so intensely desired.

Se passati a quel ponte, alme gentile,
che in bianco marmo varca la rivera,
fiorir vedreti eternamente aprile,
e una aura sospirar dolce e ligiera.
Ben vi scorgo sinor che v'è una fiera
che abate e lega ogni pensier virile,
e qualunqua alma è più superba e altiera,
persa la libertà, ritorna umile.
Ite, s'el v'è in piacer, là dove odeti

cantar li augei ne l'aria più serena
tra ombrosi mirti, e pini e fagi e abeti.
Ite là voi, che io son fugito a pena, 12
libero non, ché pur, come vedeti,
porto con meco ancora la catena.

If you walk over that bridge, gallant souls,
the one of white marble over the river,
you shall find April in eternal flower,
and an air that sings softly and sweet. 4
From here I can see a ferocious creature
that thwarts and hinders all manly feelings;
any soul that might be haughty and proud
she will humiliate and deprive of all liberty. 8
Go there, if it pleases you, and you shall
hear birds singing in the most serene air,
in shady myrtles, in beeches, in pines and firs.
You go there; I have managed to escape, 12
but I am not free: because, as you can see,
I still carry my very heavy chains with me.

The bridge takes the incautious lover to a fabulous island, where mysterious dangers lurk. Is the danger a specific woman, the *fiera* (ferocious creature) of line 5? A woman who thwarts and hinders all manly feelings (*che abate e lega ogni pensier virile*)? To some critics, the danger is the passion of love itself—a kind of passion that is too powerful to be controlled, hence the warning to any man who might be far too inclined to loving (Piemontese 147; Zanato 407). The fairylike atmosphere and the exciting mystery are due to what is suggested rather than what is being said. The magic persists, no matter if the bridge is a real one that took the Este courtiers to the delights of a villa on an island of the Po River or if we prefer to see in the sonnet a preview of the magical entrapments that alluring witches will prepare for the unsuspecting knights in Boiardo's *Orlando in Love*.

Gasparo Visconti (1461–99) was of a cadet branch of the Visconti family and lived at the court of Ludovico Sforza. The Sforza had succeeded the Visconti as lords of Milan when Francesco Maria Sforza took over the duchy in 1450.[61] Ludovico, called il Moro because of his black hair and dark complexion, was married to Beatrice d'Este, daughter of Ercole I, duke of Ferrara. Gasparo dedicated his collection of poetry to Beatrice and Bianca Maria Sforza. There are 210 sonnets. "Io vidi belle adorne e zentil dame" gives a cinematic vision of a courtly dance.

Io vidi belle, adorne e zentil dame
al suon de suavissimi concenti
con lor amanti mover lenti lenti
i piedi snelli accesi in dolce brame. 4

E vidi murmurar sotto velame
alcun de gli amorosi suoi tormenti,
dividersi, e tornare al sòno intenti
e cibar d'ochi l'avida sua fame.   8
Vidi stringer le mani e lassar l'orme
dolcemente stampate in lor non poco
e trovarsi in dui cor desio conforme,
né mirar posso così lieto gioco   12
ch'a pensier lieto alcun possa disporme
senza colei che nocte e giorno invoco.

I saw beautiful, genteel, and stylish ladies
and their lovers slowly, slowly dance
at the sound of pleasant melodies, their
slender feet burning with sweet desire.   4
And I saw them confide in furtive
murmurs the anguish of their loves,
separate and return, heedful of the melody,
and greedily nourish their hungry eyes.   8
I also saw the tightening of hands,
the marks on them so amorously pressed,
and each two hearts unite in one desire:
but I cannot look at any joyful game   12
that might turn my mind to happy thoughts,
without her, for whom I pine day and night.

The first three sections of the sonnet visualize three successive moments of the dance: the slow stepping forward of the couples, their separating and turning, and their holding hands. Each frame, each controlled movement, tells a story: the feet suggest longing; their coming and going becomes a means of exchanging glances and murmuring sweet words; and the touching and pressuring of hands allows the dancers to communicate their desires. The concluding section opposes the flirtatious games that take place on the dance floor to the joyless isolation of the lonely lover who is looking on. Each section is forcefully marked, the first three by the repetition of *vidi* (I saw) and the concluding one by the opposing *né mirar posso* (but I cannot look), which stresses a condition of lovelessness and separateness.

Chi se dilecta udir gran meraviglie
in la mia nova sorte il penser ferme,
e vederà s'io ho causa de tenerme
sopra ciascun de cui stupor se piglie.   4
Per le fenestre c'ho sotto a le ciglie
intrato al cor mi sento un dolce verme,
al cor che più che mai nudo ed inerme

poco pensava a simigliante artiglie.
E quel che mi par più, de lui si pasce
e lo dismembra mille volte l'ora,
poi che, smembrato, uno altro cor renasce;   12
renato, il serpe subito il divora,
né par che un ponto sol quieto il lascie.
Così il mio duol sempre immortal dimora.

Whoever delights in hearing of marvels
may stop to consider my strange condition,
and he shall see whether I have cause to think
I am above anyone at whom they greatly wonder.   4
Through the openings that are under my lashes
a sweet worm I feel has been entering my heart,
a heart that, forever startled and defenseless,
could hardly think of claws so strongly clasping.   8
And the worm, it seems to me, feeds on it
and dismembers it a thousand times an hour,
and, once dismembered, a new heart is born,
which, once born, the snake quickly devours,   12
and not for one moment, it seems, lets it be.
Thus, my anguish keeps going on, endlessly.

In line 2, *nova* is used in the sense of "extraordinary" or "prodigious." In line 5, *per* is used in the Latin sense of "through." The first quatrain states the situation. The second tells us of its antecedents. Then, in a rapid, dramatic crescendo, lines 9–12 describe the unrelenting suffering of the lover and the disintegration of his heart. The last line seals the drama.

Gasparo could enjoy the comforts of his courtly position and, at the same time, serenely consider the necessity to assuage the man in power, as this ironic sonnet and its moralizing tail tell us. For Gasparo Visconti, see also 4.2.

Un dì il leon, tra bruti il gran signore,
per solenne decreto par facesse
ch'ogni subiecto suo che corna avesse
subito de la selva uscisse fuore.   4
Onde ciascun cornuto, a gran furore,
per obedir partirse quindi ellesse.
La volpe tra costor par se mettesse,
fugendo anche ella pien di terrore.   8
A cui un cervo disse: "Torna, torna,
ché come a noi non ti convien partire,
perché animal non sei che porti corna!"
Et ella a lui "E se 'l leon vol dire   12
che d'alte corna sia mia testa adorna,

chi serà quel ch'ardisca contradire?"
Se vol sempre fugire
ciò che dei re possa noiare il gusto
ché quel che piace a lor quel par sol iusto.

16

One day the lion, lord of all beasts,
by high decree, it seems, gave order
that all his subjects wearing horns
should come out of the forest deep.

4

All horned animals decided to exit
and obey his demand in great hurry.
Among them, it appears, there was a fox,
who too was running off full of fear.

8

To her, a deer said, "Go, go back,
you are not obliged to leave with us,
you are not an animal wearing horns."
She answered, "If the lion wants to say

12

that there are high horns on my head,
who will ever dare to contradict him?"
One must always be careful to shun
what goes against the fancy of a king,

16

for only what he likes will seem correct.

Niccolò da Correggio (1450–1508), soldier, diplomat, and writer, was born in one of those Po Valley noble families who depended on the patronage of more powerful lords for their fortunes. He was at the service of the courts of Ferrara, Milan, and Florence. He was a friend of Lorenzo de' Medici and Boiardo. Isabella d'Este, whose cousin he was, described him as the "most correct and, in poetry and in behavior, the most gracefully accomplished knight and baron that can be found in the whole of Italy."[62]

Sì como el verde importa speme e amore,
vendetta è el rosso e il turchin gelosia,
fermezza el negro e ancor melanconia,
el bianco mostra purità di core;

4

el giallo avere extincto ogni suo ardore,
e chi veste morel secreto sia,
teneto puoi fastidio e fantasia,
travaglio il beretin, carneo, dolore.

8

Di questo ultimo volse a te venire
coperto el libro mio, se ben chi 'l manda
voria più presto lui i suo' casi dire.

In quel non legerai cosa nefanda,
né ti chiede ancor fine al mio martire,

12

ché un bon servir, tacendo, assai dimanda.

Just as green signifies hope and love,
red is vendetta, and blue is jalousie,
black firmness and also melancholy,
while the white shows purity of heart, 4
and yellow the suppression of all ardors.
By wearing a dark tint, one is secretive;
brown can be bother and flight of fancy,
gray indicates trouble; flesh-color, anguish. 8
Wrapped in that last color, my book wished
to come to you, though he, who does the sending,
would rather have presented his case himself.
You shall read in the book nothing aggressive, 12
nor does it ask for an end to my anguish,
because fine service stakes its claim silently.

In line 6, *morel* indicates a dark color, as in *cavallo morello* (a darkish horse). In line 7, *taneto*, or *tané*, is a reddish-brown color like the color of chestnuts. In line 8, *beretin*, or *berrettino*, is blue gray, and it indicates trouble. *Carneo* (flesh colored) means anguish. Society games were ceremoniously controlled but allowed men and women to communicate and flirt. The symbolism of colors, flowers, gestures, and gifts played a great part in courtly dalliance, and the books on the use of such means of communication were widely consulted (Tissoni Benvenuti 140).

L'ordito che Natura a prova cresce
tutto a ornato dil secul si lavora;
se un arbor secca, alor un altro infiora,
secondo il voto suo tutto riesce. 4
Che senza alito in aqua viva il pesce
e talpa in terra, è la Natura ancora
che fa che de aria uno ucel s'inamora,
e l'altro l'odia sì che 'l dì non esce. 8
Taccia chi sol per l'om tant'opra crede,
ché l'è commun: l'un mangia un fructo e poi,
morto, di quella pianta aiuta il piede.
Se utile abbiam di lor, lor l'han di noi; 12
un falso dir, "L'è mio: el fia de l'erede,"
fa l'omo servo a capre, a vache e a boi.

The fabric that Nature so wisely creates
is woven to cover and adorn the whole world;
if a tree dries up, presently another will bloom

and, according to her wish, everything prospers.	4
If, without breathing, fish live in water	
and moles in earth, it is Nature that compels one	
bird to love the air and another animal to hate it	
so as never to come out into the light of day.	8
Those who think such work is for man alone	
should be quiet, for all is communal: we eat a fruit;	
then, once dead, of that plant we nourish the root.	
If we profit from them, they profit from us;	12
a lie such as "it is mine, all will then be my heir's"	
will make us slaves to goats, to oxen, and to cows.	

In line 4, *secondo il voto suo* means "according to nature's vow," or "according to nature's plan." Lines 1–8 develop the theme—what exists in the world is for the benefit of everyone—in relation to nature; lines 9–12 reprieve it in reference to humankind. The final line concludes sententiously: if we believe to be the owners of nature, we will become prisoners of what we think we possess.

3.7 Courtiers

The land south of Rome continued to constitute a territorial block ruled by a succession of dynasties. In 1442, with the death of the last Anjou sovereign and after the war of succession that followed, the kingdom passed on to the House of Aragon. Alfonso, the first Aragon king (1442–58), established contacts with humanist centers throughout the peninsula, and soon a renewed interest in classical literature animated the city. Members of both the aristocracy and the upper middle class embraced the new trend. Under Alfonso's successor, Ferdinand I (1458–94), called Ferrante by his subjects, the old university was reorganized, and renowned humanists, such as Giannozzo Manetti, Lorenzo Valla, and Antonio Beccadelli, were invited to come to Naples to teach.

A retrograde economic system, however, lay behind the brilliant facade of Neapolitan life. The merchants and bankers who had flocked to Naples under the Angevin kings had stifled local industry and commerce. In the countryside, the administrative and jurisdictional privileges that the Angevins had granted to the members of the provincial nobility in order to ensure their political backing remained intact. The wealth of these barons consisted of large land holdings that subsisted on the export of natural resources, while their workers lived in conditions of near serfdom. When, in the 1480s, Ferrante tried to promote the economic development of the kingdom, the barons objected strenuously, for they saw the royal initiative as a threat to themselves and in favor of the manufacturing enterprises in the city. In 1485, the landed gentry, most of it still loyal to the Anjou, organized a plot against Ferrante. It was the famed Conspiracy of the Barons.

The first four sonnets of this section are by Giannantonio Petrucci (1456–86). His father, Antonello, had been the most powerful minister of the kingdom. From peasant origins, Antonello became a great landowner; a humanist—he had been a student of Valla; a patron of the arts; owner of a rich library; and sponsor of the local university. His son Giannantonio was made count of Policastro, the king's secretary, and then councillor. Following his father's ambitious family plan, Giannantonio married Sveva Sanseverino, niece of the prince of Salerno and daughter of Bernabò Sanseverino, count of Laurìa. Both Antonello and Bernabò Sanseverino—the latter was Giannantonio's father-in-law—were among the plotters of the conspiracy. Through his family's entanglements, Giannantonio too became involved in the plot. On August 13, 1486, father and son were arrested. Giannantonio was decapitated in December of that year, and his father was decapitated the following May.

While in the prison tower of Saint Luigi, waiting for the day of his execution, Giannantonio composed eighty-three poems. Seventy-eight are sonnets. They are all imbued with a feeling of predestination and resigned acceptance, all contain a strong patina of Neapolitan dialect, and all are in one metrical form: ABBA ABBA CDC DCD.

De sutto al Fato sta ciò che è creato
e tutti sutto de esso li elementi:
lo sole con la luna e con li venti,
lo celo con le stelle è sutto al Fato.   4
È sutto al Fato ciò che è generato
ed hasse a concepire, e li sementi,
de quisto mundo li piaciri e stenti:
tutto dal Fato sta predestinato.   8
In terra non si move alcuna fronde,
né ucello alcuno ne l'äer pennato,
né men se move pescie in liquide unde,
che jà da prima non sia ordinato: 12
e questo, como accasche o venga donde,
ancora ingengnio nullo ha retrovato.

All that is created is subject to Fate,
all elements are under his domain:
the sun, the moon, and the winds,
the sky and the stars. All bow to Fate.   4
Under Fate's sway are the seeds,
what is created and what is conceived,
the pleasures and the hardships of the world:
all that exists has been so destined by Fate.   8
Neither can a tree branch move on earth,
nor can a plumed bird go fly in the air,
nor can a fish swim in the liquid waves,
if it had not been decided beforehand: 12
but how and for what reason this occurs
no mind has yet been able to comprehend.

In line 9, *hasse a concepire* (in Italian, *deve essere concepito*) means "it is still to be conceived." In line 13, *come accasche o venga donde*, or *come accada o da dove venga*, means "how it happens and where it comes from." The articles *lo* and *li*; the preposition *sutto* (*sotto*); the nouns *sementi*, *piaciri*, and *pescie*;

and the verbs *sta* (in place of *è*), *hasse* (in place of *ha*), and *accasche* (in place of *accada*) are Neapolitan words. The sonnet transcends the specification of place and political and personal situation and rises to become a general reflection on the power of destiny: in nature, all elements, from the stars, moon, and sun in the heavens to everything that grows on earth, cannot move a tad without been destined beforehand. The sadder becomes such realization when we consider that no human intelligence has yet been able to explain how and why this happens.

Fu alcuna volta loco da pescare
llà dove mo se seminan li grani,
e, dove mo so' munti, foro piani,
dove è mo terra, fo profondo mare.   4
El tempo fa onne cosa variare,
non lassa stato fermo tra li umani
corpuscoli, secondo per li inani
el dissoluto vanno ad condensare.   8
Mo umidi, mo sicchi, mesti o leti,
concurreno beati ed infelici,
quando coniunti e quando so' discreti.
Perciò non te ammirar, se li felici   12
imperii, che parïeno quieti
per lor grandezze, el tempo fa mendici.

Where, upon a time, one could fish,
now grains are being sowed; once, there
were valleys where now are mountains,
a deep sea was once where now is earth.   4
Time forces everything to change,
in the human corpuscles nothing stays
firm, because what is dissolved to almost
nothing tends thereafter to condensate.   8
Now humid, now dry, sad or glad,
they all run together, happy or unhappy,
what is conjoined and what is separate.
So do not marvel if time has made   12
beggars of what were jubilant empires,
which looked so stable in their grandeur.

From the intimate meditation on the power of fate in the previous poem, the attention shifts now to the ever-changing face of nature and the unpredictability and transitory character of man's life, which is part of natural evolution. The concept of nature has widened into an atomistic theory of the universe. Man is made of the same conglomeration of atoms as the rest of creation, and his life is subject to the same rules; his destiny is unpredictable and remains a mystery to the mind. Clear is the presence of both Lucretius's and Democritus's philosophies. In another poem, Giannantonio stated that in prison, he had taken up again the study of philosophy: "in this place I found again Lucretius, / Empedocles, Aristotle, and Plato; / Democritus is always to my side" (*Lucrecio in esto loco ho ritrovato, / Empedocle, Aristotele e Platone / Democrito me sta sempre al costato*).[63]

Quel che de' capitani fo lo fiore,
dotto, eloquente, placido e jucundo,
ch'intr' al Senato lo posse nel fundo
de' conjurati el perfido livore,   4
in questo poco bronzo, o viatore,
como tu vide, redutto in un tundo,
mo sta incluso, imperator del mondo,
Caio Cesare, divo dittatore.   8
Di tal signore li infiniti onori,
la crudel sorte co' lo iniquo fato
e la su' ciner, fa che qui demori.
De tanta gran potenzia e tanto stato   12
de so' ricchezze e tanti gran tesori
appena questo poco li è restato.

He, who was the flower of captains,
learned, eloquent, confident, serene,
whom, in the Senate, the envious deceit
of conspirators tossed into the empty deep,   4
inside this small bronze is now confined,
as you, passerby, can see; inside this small
round he is now enclosed, Caius Caesar,
emperor of the world, divine dictator.   8
His adverse destiny and an unfair Fate have
willed the endless honors and the last
vestiges of such great lord here to stay.
Of so great power, of such authority,   12
of such riches, and of such great treasures,
this little space is all that to him remains.

In the first edition, the title of the sonnet is *A la guglia dove sta Julio Cesare* (To the *guglia* where Julius Caesar is). It is not clear what the object prompting the prisoner's meditation was: *guglia* could have been an eagle, they say, or a spire. Petrucci might also have been looking at a coin or a plaque showing a profile of the Roman general. A disquieting sense of how suddenly human destiny may be reversed is all in the ascending sweep of the poem and in the suspense maintained throughout the octave. The subject *he*, placed at the start and separated from its verbal clause, "is now enclosed," by five lines of qualifying clauses, pushes the reading forward, until, in line 7, the identity of that *he* is revealed.

Caesar's exceptionality is forcefully stated by the two appositional ascending qualifications uttered with his name: emperor of this world and dictator with divine powers. In the sestet, the somber meditation on the downfall of any human being sounds like the toll of a death sentence.

O tempo, come presto si' volubile!
per te, al mondo non è cosa stabile;
in uno punto tu si' varïabile,
materie dure tu le fai solubile;   4
le cose liete le torni lugubile,
e lo omo in un momento miserabile;
per te imperii forti sono labile,
e le cità, che pareno insolubile,   8
consume con la immense tua voragine.
Dove sta ascosa preclara Palepole?
E dove è ita la inclita Cartagine?
Atene, Siracusa con Persepole,   12
Micene, de li libri ne le margine
ad pena haï lassate, e Filippopole!

Oh, time, how swiftly you can change!
Thanks to you, nothing in the world is stable,
in a few moments you become variable,
hard matter you quickly turn into soluble,   4
what was a happy thing you make regrettable,
and mankind in a moment miserable;
thanks to you, strong realms become perishable,
towns that one time seemed indestructible   8
you have consumed in your endless maelstrom.
Where is hiding now famous Paleopolis?
and where have gone the great Carthago,
and Athens, and Syracuse, and Persepolis,   12
and Mycenae? In the pages of books you
grudgingly have left them, with Philippopolis!

Regarding line 10, Paleopolis once next to the old Napoli and later uniting to it, gave origin to the present Napoli—that is, Naples (Ponte 1199). In line 11, Carthago is the famed Phoenician town on the northern coast of Africa, east of present-day Tunis. In line 12, Syracuse is a Sicilian town founded by Greek colonists in 734 BC. Persepolis was the capital of the Persian Empire. In line 13, Mycenae was an ancient town of Argolis, in the Peloponnesus. In line 14, Philippopolis was the capital of the Roman province of Thrace, now the town of Plovdiv, Bulgaria.

In Naples, the tradition of lyric poetry in the vernacular had been revived in 1476, when Lorenzo de' Medici presented Alfonso, King Ferrante's son, with the first Italian anthology of lyric poetry, a collection now called Raccolta Aragonese.

Among the humanists who wrote lyric poetry in Italian was a Catalan, Benedetto Gareth, called by the Neapolitan academicians Cariteo, or Chariteo. After arriving from Barcelona in 1467 when he was a teenager, Gareth entered the royal administration (King Alfonso too was a Catalan), and in time, he rose to occupy several responsible positions under three different Aragonese sovereigns. In 1495, he became secretary of state. When French troops invaded Naples in that year and again in 1501, Gareth remained faithful to the king and followed him into exile. He returned to Naples in 1503 and later was made governor of Nola by the viceroy who now represented Habsburg Spain. The first edition of his collection of poetry, classically entitled *Endimione* and containing forty-five sonnets, was published in 1506. The opening poem, "Costei che mia benigna e ria fortuna," explains the reason he has chosen the fictitious name of Moon for his beloved.

Costei che mia benigna e ria fortuna,
e la mia vita e morte tene in mano,
per cui tanti suspiri spargo in vano,
è con iusta cagion chiamata Luna,   4
non sol perché nel mondo è sola et una
e ha divino il volto più che umano,
ma perché basta ad agghiacciar Vulcano,
quando tutte le fiamme inseme aduna.   8
Fu preso il suo candor da l'alto cielo,
dov'è la lattea via del paradiso,
non nota a la volgare e cieca gente.
Quanti col raggio tocca, muta in gelo,   12
ma 'l scintillare e fulgurar del viso
me, misero!, converte in fiamma ardente.

This woman, who my kind and evil fortune,
my life and my death holds in her hand,
for whom so many sighs I pour out in vain,
for good reasons, I call Moon: not only   4
because she is unrivaled in the world
and has a face more heavenly than human,
but for the power she has to freeze Vulcan
when all his flames in one fire he gathers.   8
Her whiteness was conceived in heaven,
where is the milky way of paradise,
unknown to unseeing common people.
All the men her ray touches turn into ice,   12
but the light and splendor of her face
have turned me, alas! into a scorching blaze.

The poem, a reworking of tired clichés, gains a fresh allure thanks to several classical allusions. By grafting the symbolism of the moon on the conventional praise of the beloved as a creature of heaven, Gareth has created an atmosphere of myth and classical decorum. Luna is the equivalent of Cynthia, the Roman name for the moon and the name of Propertius's beloved woman. By reflex, the poet becomes the Endymion of legend, the mythical youth and lover of the moon, whom she visited by night on the slopes of Mt. Latmus (Barbiellini Amidei 57). Regarding lines 1–4, a woman in command of the lover's destiny is an idea already found in Horace's *Letters* 12, 73–74, and in Petrarch: "My fortune, my destiny, all my good and evil, my life and my death He (Love) who can do it has placed in her hand" (*Canzoniere* 170). In lines 5–8, the hyperbole of the woman's uniqueness goes on in a cascade of antithetical qualifications: she is both life and death; she is human and divine; and her icy nature is paradoxically capable (*basta* in line 7) of freezing all the flames spewed by Vulcan. The theme of the quatrains is then briefly reprised in the sestet, and the last three lines close the poem with an epigrammatic ending.

"Ecco la notte: el ciel scintilla e splende" describes a silent lunar landscape. The sky sparkles with stars. Everything is tranquil in the Neapolitan countryside.

Ecco la notte: el ciel scintilla e splende
di stelle ardenti, lucide e gioconde;
i vaghi augelli e fere il nido asconde,
e voce umana al mondo or non s'intende.   4
La rugiada del ciel tacita scende;
non si move erba in prato o 'n selva fronde;
chete si stan nel mar le placide onde;
ogni corpo mortal riposo prende.   8
Ma non riposa nel mio petto Amore,
Amor d'ogni creato acerbo fine:
anzi la notte cresce il suo furore.
Ha sementato in mezzo del mio core   12
mille pungenti, avvelenate spine,
e 'l frutto che mi rende è di dolore.

Here is the night: the sky is all aglow
with bright, glittering, and cheery stars;
beasts and roving birds hide in their nests,
and not a human voice is heard on earth.   4
The heaven's dew is descending silently:
no grass moves in the fields, no twig in the forest;
the placid waves rest quietly in the sea;
all mortal bodies lie peacefully and rest.   8
But in my heart Love does not repose,
Love, the bitter fate of every creature:
at nighttime, he fires up his wrath instead.
In the center of my heart, he has flung   12

a thousand venomous, piercing thorns,
and the fruit they give me is one of pain.

The sonnet is a mosaic of descriptive fragments taken from Petrarch and classical authors. In line 1, *Ecco la notte* is a reminiscence of Virgil's *Nox erat* in *Aeneid* IV, 522 (Vitale 498). In line 5, the detail of falling dew is from Ovid, *Fasti* 1, 312.5.10. In lines 12–13, the idea of venomous thorns derives from Catullus, 64, 72. *Sementato*, meaning "seeded," is from Latin *sementamentum*. The motif of the night that brings peace and repose to humanity, but not to the lover, is found, among others, in Dante's *Inferno* (2, 1–3), Politian's *Stanze* (1, 6), and Sannazaro's *Arcadia* (7), but stronger are the trace of Virgil's *Aeneid* (4, 522–32) and the suggestion of Petrarch's *Canzoniere* (50, 15; 164; 216, 1–4). In line 14, *rendere* means "to yield." The lover says the fruit yielded to him is one of sorrow, of suffering.

Gareth makes ample use of antithesis, alliteration, conceits, and symbolism. The cumulative effect is that of an idyllic night scene brought to an epigrammatic close in a tone of subdued passion. The next sonnet, witty rather than effusively contemplative, was much liked and widely imitated.

Voi, Donna, et io per segni manifesti
andremo inseme a l'infernal tormento,
voi per orgoglio, io per troppo ardimento,
ché vagheggiare osai cose celesti.   4
Ma, perché gli occhi miei vi son molesti,
voi più martiri avrete, io più contento,
ch'altro che veder voi gloria non sento,
tal, ch'un sol lieto fia tra tanti mesti.   8
Ch'essendo voi presente a gli occhi miei,
vedrò nel mezzo inferno un Pardiso,
che 'n pregio non minor che 'l cielo avrei.
E, si dal vostro sol non son diviso,   12
non potran darmi pena i spirti miei:
chi mi vuol tormentar, mi chiuda il viso!

You, woman, and I, by all manifest signs,
shall descend together to the tortures of hell,
you because of pride, I because of recklessness,
since I dared to yearn for things divine.   4
But since my sight is bothersome to you,
you shall have an immense pain, I much pleasure,
because, feeling no other bliss than seeing you,
I shall be the happy one amidst great displeasure.   8
As you will be present to my eyes,
being in no less regard to me than heaven,
I shall enjoy in mid inferno a paradise.
So if I am not removed from your sight,   12
my spirits will give me no pain: whoever wishes
to inflict a torture on me must shut my eyes!

Contento, in line 7, stands for *contentezza*, meaning "contentment" or "gladness." In poetry, *viso* is *sguardo*, meaning "sight" or "glance." *Gloria* (glory) indicates the perfect happiness one can only experience in paradise. The sonnet, from lines 1 to 13, is one unit of progressive reasoning: the lovers will be condemned to hell, with a different punishment being meted out to each. Line 14 gives the explanation and concludes in quick epigrammatic fashion.

3.8 Commoners

I call commoners the sonneteers of this section because they were neither lords nor courtiers of high standing. Suardi and Sommariva were trained professionals who worked and lived among people of the less advantaged classes and observed them keenly. Their poems are concerned with immediate problems and tangible things. Pistoia, a man of humble origins, worked as a general factotum at the service of anyone who would employ him. He viewed himself and the world around him with dry realism, flavored at times with agreeable bonhomie and at other times with acerbic criticism. In the tradition of the popular type of poetry, most of these sonnets are caudate.

Gian Francesco Suardi (1422–69) was born near Bergamo, now Lombardy, then in territory belonging to the Venetian Republic. When a child, he became a student in the experimental school called *La Casa Gioiosa* (the House of Joy), established by the humanist Vittorino da Feltre (see section 3.6). After graduating from the University of Bologna, he embarked on the career of *podestà*—a mayoral position obtained by appointment—which took him to some minor towns of Lombardy, Romagna, and Marche. In "Io son pur quel predicto," he gives a dispassionate evaluation of his position, the privileges it entailed, and the type of work he found himself doing as the administrative head of the small community of Massa Lombarda.

> Io son pur quel predicto e onorevole
> podestà de la Massa de' Lombardi,
> misser Giovan Francesco de' Suardi,
> cavaliere e doctore convenevole.   4
> L'officio è bono et assai ragionevole
> fra gli altri di Romagna, se ben guardi:
> senza bandere e spesa di stendardi;
> la stancia è bona e 'l loco assai piacevole;   8
> chi va al mercato io mando a tuor de l'olio
> e di quel che bisogna a la mia corte,
> ch'è bella assai secondo i precessori.
> A posta di ciascun io scrivo un foglio   12
> per tre dinari, e pargli troppo forte
> a spender tanto e solvere i suoi errori.
> Io son vice-signore,
> e scuso per vicario e per notaro,   16
> e qualche volta anche per piagiaro.

> ℐ am the above mentioned, honorable
> mayor of Massa Lombarda,
> Sir Giovanni Francesco Suardi,
> a knighted man and a serviceable doctor. 4
> The position, if you consider, is good and quite
> reasonable, compared to others in Romagna:
> there are no expenses for flags or standards,
> the residence is good, the place rather pleasant; 8
> whoever goes to market is charged to get me
> some oil and what else is needed in my lodgings,
> which are fine indeed, in my predecessor's view.
> At anyone's request, I will write a document 12
> for three cents; to them, it seems a lot to pay
> for such a task, and for correcting their errors.
> I am vice lord,
> and I substitute the vicar and the notary; 16
> at times I act also as a peace maker.

Regarding line 3, the university degree in jurisprudence qualified Suardi as doctor of law. The first three lines announce name and title with a solemn, official sweep, which is ironically toned down by that ambiguous *serviceable* of line 4. The description of this mayoral condition appears at first unbiased—"my position is reasonable"—but the list of the advantages it entails colors it with a tinge of ever-increasing irony. As *podestà*, he does not have to pay for office expenses (for flags and standards). His residence is fine, or so it was described when offered. Scarcely provided with servants, he must beg for small favors of any citizen who happens to come by. For little change, he consents to write for those who do not know how, and he must sort out the quarrels among the most litigious of his subjects. A sardonic coda adds a few more high-flown titles to his enviable position. For the caudate sonnet, I repeat, see the introduction.

Giorgio Sommariva (1435–97) was born in Verona and, like his contemporary Suardi, was educated in the classics and the law. He held public office, and for the Venetian Republic, he carried out many tasks of political and military nature. His literary education prompted him to translate several works from Latin, produce a history of the kingdom of Naples, and write poetry in the Petrarchan manner. His fame endures thanks to his *Sonetti Villaneschi* (Rustic Sonnets), which were written in the dialect spoken in the area between Verona and Bergamo.

In the north of the peninsula, thanks to an enlightened patrician class, the use of the land had been improved considerably: swampy areas were drained, irrigation systems were created, and modern methods of cultivation and a more efficient organization of production were adopted. The condition of those who worked on the land was unaltered. The tenant farmers remained indebted, usually to the landowners, from whom they constantly needed to borrow money. Sommariva's "Duò, messer me, mo que volì-vu fare" is the parody of a peasant's lamentations over his hard life, obligations, and financial difficulties.

Duò, messer me, mo que volì-vu fare
d'i fati mie' a darme tante spese?
Eh, mao de l'angio! Aspeté ancora un mese
che verò pur compirve de pagare.   4
Vu me mandé agna dì a pegnorare
e mi me vegno a sgarbar de le cese
a far solcàli e a segarve le prese;
e vu non me volì un poco aspettare?   8
Pota che ve sa muò! Vu sì crudelo
a far sto malo incontra del Mesiàgia!
Mè son pur sempro mè sta vostro frèlo.
Duò, mal del cigno! Non me dé più batàia,   12
se desso vendrò el gaban, el ziupèlo
e i miei scufúni, el versór e la tràia
e tuta la mia pàia.
Ve vuò' pagar fina a un bel bagatin,   16
pur che non me facié vendro el me vin.

Oh, my lord, what do you want to do
to me, that you pile on me so many charges?
For heaven's sake! Wait one more month,
and I shall see to pay you back to the full.   4
Every day you force me to pawn my things,
although I come to you to trim your hedges,
to do your ploughing and cut your grass;
and you, can't you wait for me a little longer?   8
Blast you! You are so hard, you behave
so unkindly against your poor Mesiàgia!
But I am God's creature as well as you are!
May the plague get you! Don't give me   12
more trouble! For I am about to sell my coat,
my jacket, my cap, the plough, and the hoe,
as well as all my straw.
I am sure I shall pay you back to the last dime,   16
as long as you don't make me sell also my wine.

In line 3, *mao de l'àngio* means, literally, "by the sickness of the snake." Regarding line 10, Mesiàgia is the peasant's name. Line 11 actually says, "Even so, I am your brother (*frèlo*)," which, if translated literally, would suggest, wrongly, a family relationship. In line 12, *mal del cigno* means, literally, "the swan's sickness," whatever that was. Regarding line 14, there are other dialect terms: *gaban* is *mantello*, or a cloak; *ziupelo* is *giubbetto*, or a doublet; *scufuni* are *scuffioni*, or caps; *versor* is *aratro*, or a plough; and *traia* is *erpice*, or a harrow (Ponte 1133). The sonnet belongs of the tradition of the satire of peasant life, a tradition carried on by those who did not have to share the hard life of the peasants. In this sonnet, however, the hardships endured by Mesiàgia— the exploitation to which he is subject and the debts he has incurred with the owner of the land—and the naturalness of his ways are rendered with a considerable degree of empathy. Even so, and not surprising in the case of a city dweller living in relative comfort, as the poet was, the lamentations of the beleaguered worker come to an end in the coda with what may be interpreted as a submissive, self-condemning prayer.

In the upcoming sonnet, "Se tu te trovi in galia, o in bordel," Sommariva's angle of vision on contemporary society opens up considerably.

> Se tu te trovi in galia o in bordel
> e dì: "Puta cornuta!" di per totto;
> e se tu fusti in tavern condotto:
> "Synch goth Bayn, liver Chesel!" 4
> Se de sforceschi tu fussi in tripel:
> "La putanaza straza, via di boto!"
> e se de giostra sentesti far moto:
> "Portami lo caval, o mio gianel." 8
> Se tu ti trovi là dove si danza:
> "Dames, el votro amor m'ha sì ferì,
> che tout in vous ho posta mia speranza."
> Se ad interesse volesti per ti: 12
> "Lapo con lenzo," e fali mescolanza
> di cremosino, e serai ben servì.
> E se ad alcun convì
> rasonar tu sentesti de prelatis, 16
> e tu respondi sempre de portatis.

> If you find yourself in a galley or in a brothel,
> say, "Dirty whore!" everywhere you turn.
> If, instead, you are taken into a tavern, say,
> *Synch goth Bayn, liver Chesel!* 4
> If you are in a squad of Sforza soldiers,
> say, "Big ragged whore, bugger off quick!"
> If you hear people speak in a joust, say,
> "Bring me my horse, my darling groom!" 8
> If you are where there is some dancing,
> say, "*Dames*, your love *m'ha sì feri*,
> that *tout en vous* I placed my hope."
> If you want to borrow at interest, say, 12
> "Lapo, that cloth from Reims," and "add
> some *chermosino*," and you'll be well served.
> And if, at some dinners,
> you hear people talk about *prelatis*, 16
> do always answer *de portatis*.

In line 1, *galia* may mean "galley" or, by extension, "prison," for a ship's oars were customarily handled by men condemned to hard labor. The words in line 4 seem to be mangling the German words *Schink gutes Wein, lieber Geselle!* (Pour some wine, dear host!), interpreted by Tissoni Benvenuti (21). Others understand *lieber Geselle* to mean "dear comrade." Regarding line 5, the soldiers of the Sforza, lords of Milan, were one of the first professional armies in Europe. In line 8, *gianel* means "groom." Regarding lines 13–14, *Lapo* is a typical Florentine first name. *Lenzo* was the wool imported from Reims, which, like other imports, was then treated with expensive Florentine dyes. *Chermosino*, or *chermisi*, was the red coloring made with the cochineals that Florentine manufacturers imported from the east. In lines 16–17, *prelatis* and *de portatis* are mock Latin. *Prelatis* is an equivocation of the classical Latin word meaning "favorite" and of the medieval Latin word meaning "prelates" (supposedly, priests sitting at dinner). *De portatis* would then mean "about dinner courses" (from Italian *portata*), suggested by favorite dishes implied in *prelatis* and by prelates—that is, members of the clergy. The sonnet's coda would therefore suggest that if you were having dinner in the company of prelates, the talk would surely be about favorite dishes.

The sonnet offers a landscape historically suggestive of what must have been Italy at the middle of the fifteenth century, a mixture of cultures existing side by side. Language, dialect, and slangy expressions vary according to place and people: vulgar expletives for a brothel; mock German for mercenary soldiers ordering wine in a tavern; polished language for courtly gatherings, such as jousts and dances, and descriptions of merchandise by shopkeepers; and, finally, Latin for high clerics discussing gourmet food during a banquet. The mercenary soldiers, or landsknechts, hired by the Italian states, were mostly from Bavaria and what had recently become the German part of Switzerland. Their largest contingent was at the service of the Sforza. "Borrowing at interest" in lines 13–14 refers to the need merchants had to borrow money from banks and private investors, hence the necessity of showing off their competence in trade and the value of their goods.

Antonio Cammelli, called Il Pistoia (1436–1502) because he was born in Pistoia, Tuscany, immigrated with his family to the north of the country in search of employment. He was first at the service of Niccolò, lord of Correggio, and then Ercole I Este, lord of Ferrara. At Ferrara, besides entertaining the court with his satirical poetry, he worked in the kitchens and the dispensary. He was also made captain of the guards, overseeing one and then another door in the city of Reggio. Fired by Ercole for insubordination in 1497, he was in Milan for two years at the service of Ludovico il Moro. Ludovico's wife was Beatrice d'Este, Ercole's daughter and sister to Isabella, whose protection Pistoia enjoyed. He dedicated to Isabella his verse collection *Sonetti faceti*, as well as *Panfila*, a tragedy. Many of his poems are caudate sonnets. For other sonnets by Cammelli, see 4.2.

The sonnet "Belle donne a Milan, ma grasse troppe" describes the physique and fashions of Milanese women and, indirectly, the comfortable city life. Pistoia probably wrote it for the enjoyment of Isabella, whom he always tried to amuse and who—I may add—was much interested in, besides many loftier matters, clothes and jewelry.

> Belle donne a Milan, ma grasse troppe:
> il parlar tu lo sai, sai che son bianche,
> strette nel mezo, ben quartate in l'anche,
> paion capon pastati in su le groppe.
> Porton certe giornee e certe cioppe
> che le fan parer emple nel petto anche;

4

basse hanno le pianelle, vanno stanche,
tutte le più son colme in su le coppe. 8
Le veste lor di seta e di rosato,
le scoffie d'or e nel petto il gioiello,
maniche di ricamo o di broccato.
In spalla hanno il balasso ricco e bello, 12
tutto il collo di perle incatenato,
con un pendente o d'intaglio o niello:
ogni ditto ha lo anello.
Quando le vidi poi mangiare ai deschi, 16
paion tutte botteghe da tedeschi.

The women of Milan are lovely but far too fat;
you know how they speak, how white they are,
how slender at the waist, how well provided on the hips;
like fattened capons they are shaped on their backs. 4
They wear some corsets and some vests
that make them ample also around the chest;
they wear flat mules, they walk a tired walk,
and most of them are bulging in the cups. 8
Their dresses are made of silk and of satin,
the bonnets of gold, a jewel is on their breast,
sleeves embroidered or made of fine brocade.
A splendid ruby is pinned on their shoulder, 12
their necks are all enchained in pearls,
with a pendent that has a carving or inlay;
and on each of their fingers rests a ring.
Then, when at table you see them eat, 16
you might think you are in a German inn.

Pistoia's tone becomes stridently political in the sonnet "A Roma che si vende?" The customary accusation of corruption hurled at the Roman administration acquires here a specific urgency. Considering Pistoia lived at the Milanese court at least until 1499, I surmise his denunciation of the curia and the pope to be a reflection of the enmity that had just flared up between Ludovico Sforza and Pope Alexander VI. The pontiff, his son Cesare Borgia, and Louis XII of France had made a reciprocally expedient pact, one term of which was Alexander's endorsement of Louis's claim to the lordship of Milan and his plan to invade the Milanese territory.

"A Roma che si vende?" "Le parole."
"Del vero e de la fè?" "C'è carestia."
"Che mercanti vi son?" "Di simonia."
"Che vita si gli fa?" "Com' l'uom vòle." 4
"Che se blastema piú?" "Chi formò il sole."
"Che vizi sonvi?" "Incesti e sodomia."

"Dove si fa iustitia?" "In beccaria:
de la ragion son serrate le scole."   8
"U' vanno i benefizii?" "Fra' denari."
"Bisognavi altro?" "Poca coscienzia."
"Che altro?" "Amici bon, ma qua son cari."
"Vendevisi altro?" "Sì, la indulgenzia."   12
"Il vostro dio perdona a questi avari?"
"Sì, se confesson ogni lor fallenzia."
"Vuolse altro?" "Penitenzia."
"Altro?" "Restituzion di fama e d'oro: 16
la nostra legge poi perdona a loro."
"È di questi il tuo Moro?"
"No: che, antivisto Dio il suo iusto stato,
lo elesse prima in ciel che fusse nato."

"What do they sell in Rome?" "Words."
"What about truth and faith?" "There is a shortage."
"What kind of merchants are there?" "Of simony."
"What life do they lead?" "The kind that pleases them."   4
"Whom do they curse more?" "Him who made the sun."
"What vices are there?" "Incest and sodomy."
"Where do they administer justice?" "In butchers' shops:
the schools of jurisprudence are locked up."   8
"Where do the benefices go?" "To those with money."
"Is there need of anything else?" "Of a little conscience."
"Of what else?" "Of good friends; they fetch high prices."
"Do they sell something else?" "Yes, indulgencies."   12
"Does your God forgive these grasping people?"
"Yes, if they confess all their sins."
"Is anything else necessary?" "Penitence."
"Anything else?" "To return money and repair reputation;   16
then our law forgives them."
"But your Moor, is he one of them?"
"No, because having foreseen his virtuous character,
God picked him out in heaven before he was born."

Piú de cent'anni imaginò Natura
di farmi piú quanto poté diforme:
fatte e disfatte piú di mille forme
in fin tolse il disegno alla Paura.   4
Gli occhi mi fece e la bocca a ventura,
come fa chi, scrivendo, o sogna o dorme;

non è ad alcun il mio viso conforme,
né in triangol, né in torno, né in misura.   8
Il naso è con la punta al mento accosto,
la faccia è dalla Notte colorita,
il petto fu, dove le spalle, posto.
Da la cintura in giú non son dua dita,   12
l'un piè guarda settembre e l'altro agosto,
son dritto come va in arbor vita.
Quando sarà finita,
la mia figura, in cima a una bacchetta,   16
piglierà più uccei che una civetta!

More than one hundred years having tried
to make me as ugly as she could, Nature
made and unmade more than a thousand molds;
then, finally, for me drew a model from Fright.   4
Haphazardly she made my eyes and mouth
as if drawn while one is asleep or dreaming;
my face does not resemble anyone's at all,
either in size, as a triangle or as a round.   8
The point of my nose approaches the chin,
the face has been painted by the dark of Night,
the chest is where the shoulders ought to be.
From the belt down, there is hardly an inch: 12
one foot looks at September, the other at August,
I walk as straight as a vine wound on a tree.
Thus completed,
my figure, on top of a high pole,   16
can catch more birds than does an owl.

For this sonnet, I followed the order of lines suggested by Ponte (1068). In line 12, *vita* stands for *vite*, meaning "vine." Per line 13, his feet seem to be going in different directions. Regarding line 14, owls were used as decoys for catching larks. Pistoia could unleash his satirical talent on himself, but having exercised it on others was probably the cause for losing the protection of the lords he served and being reduced to live the rest of his life in great financial distress.

"Danza già in cielo" was written at Christmastime. Its benevolent, tranquil mood and a few naive surrealistic touches conjure an impression of magical, childlike enchantment.

Danza già in cielo ogni immortal farfalla
per allegrezza, grandi e piccioline,
e le bianche e le rosse e le turchine,
e intorno al Padre una Colomba balla;   4
l'asino e il bue, la mia casa, ogni stalla,
le selve ombrose, boschi, tronchi e spine;

sonano i peccorar' per le colline,
e in oriente chi incassa e chi imballa. 8
La bambola del ciel lustra più lieta;
con lo specchio del giorno in concistoro,
hanno formato una nova cometa,
che mostri salvo il camino a costoro, 12
quai cercan dove è nato il gran profeta
per presentagli incenso, mirra et oro.
Adamo, Eva e gli loro
figli e parenti L'aspettan che mora, 16
acciò ch'El torni vivo a trargli fora.

All immortal butterflies of heaven are already
dancing for joy, the small and the big ones,
the whites, the azure, and the red ones;
around the Father a fine Dove is turning. 4
Here is the donkey, here the ox, here my house,
and the stable, shady forests, woods, trunks,
and thorns; the shepherds play pipes on the knolls;
in the East some are wrapping, others are packing. 8
The doll in the sky sparkles more happily;
with the mirror of the day in consistory
a brand-new comet is being born,
which will show a way to those who search 12
for the place where the Great Prophet was born,
in order to offer him incense, myrrh, and gold.
Adam, Eve, their children,
and relatives are waiting for him to die, so he will 16
be able to return and bring them out into the light.

In line 1, the immortal butterflies are the angels. In line 4, the Dove is the Holy Spirit. Per line 8, in the East, the Magi are preparing for their journey. In line 9, the doll of the sky is the sun, and the mirror of the day in line 10 is the moon, because like a mirror, it reflects the rays of the sun. Regarding line 17, on his second coming, Christ will free all the souls of Limbo. In Dante's *Divine Comedy*, Limbo is an area at the entrance of hell where reside the souls of people who lived either before the coming of Christ or after and, through no fault of their own, did not receive baptism. In Limbo are also the great characters of the Old Testament, who will enter paradise at the Savior's second coming.

The sonnet's persona looks on the scene of the crèche with a calculated sense of childish wonder. Certain touches—the angels described as colorful butterflies; designations like "doll of the sky" (*bambola del ciel*) for the sun and "mirror of the day" (*specchio del giorno*) for the moon; and the disconnected enumeration of people, animals, and plants—suggest the presence of a child admiring, pointing at, and naming the varied wonders of a Nativity scene.

4
Invasions, Reversals, and Reformations

4.1 A Raging Fashion

In the last decades of the fifteenth century, a new kind of sonnet became all the rage. It was organized in a series of witty similes and metaphors and ended with a surprising turn of thought. Behind its success was the interest the humanist scholars had in the classical epigrams, the most admired being those authored by Martial.[64] Antonio Tebaldeo and Serafino Aquilano were prominent among the champions of the new style. Their rare conceits and epigrammatic endings seem to most critics consistent with the taste of the courts they frequented, where literature had become an entertainment and poetry was expected to satisfy a desire to be amused and surprised. Scholars have argued that poetry and cultural context are so intrinsically connected in the work of these authors that it is difficult to decide whether it was their social milieu or their idiosyncratic inclination that created the taste generally described as courtly. Judging by the many editions of Tebaldeo's and Aquilano's verses, the popularity of the courtly manner continued well into the sixteenth century and was widely imitated abroad.

Marco Antonio Tebaldi (1463–1537) of Ferrara, called Tebaldeo in academic circles, was in the service of the Este court as tutor to young Isabella and then as secretary to her younger brother, who became Cardinal Ippolito. Later, from 1504 to 1508, he served as secretary to their sister-in-law, Lucrezia Borgia, wife of Duke Alfonso. When Isabella married Francesco II Gonzaga, Tebaldi spent some time at her court in Mantua. He moved to Rome when, in 1513, Giovanni de' Medici became pope with the name of Leo X. At the Vatican, he produced several Latin works and became familiar with Pietro Bembo, Baldesar Castiglione, and Raphael. His features can be seen in one of the frescoes that Raphael painted in the papal apartments. In 1527, during the sack of the city, Tebaldi lost all his property and lived until his death in financial straits. His Italian lyrics—of which three hundred are sonnets—were published to great acclaim in 1498 and, between that year and 1557, had as many as thirty-three editions (Tebaldeo: Basile and Marchand 90–109).

> Del foco che per voi m'arde et incende
> mandovi dentro questa palla accesa,
> che sia a la vostra man scudo e difesa
> contra il freddo crudel, quando l'offende.
> Pensati in me che forza il foco prende,
> se in un metal sì dur tanta n'ha presa!

4

Ma nulla l'ardor suo mi grava o pesa,
poi che a sì bella man soccorso rende; 8
e se avien che in la palla il calor mora,
di nuovo riscaldar la poterete
al mio cor, che cum vui sempre dimora.
Ma se del foco aver da me volete, 12
fàte ch'io arda pian pian, ché gli è a quest'hora
poco a brusar di me, se ben vedete.

Some of the fire that for you inflames
and burns me I send to you inside this ball,
that it may be a shield and cover to your hand,
when the cold weather brutally offends it. 4
Imagine what power that fire may have in me,
if such is its strength in so hard a metal!
But I do not mind and do not regret its power,
if it can comfort a creature as fine as thee. 8
If in the ball the fire should ever die down,
you will be able to warm it up again
at my heart, which remains with you always.
But if you wish to get more fire from me, 12
see to it that I burn slowly, because by now,
as you can see, there is little left to burn in me.

The poet has sent the woman a hand warmer, one made of metal and containing a fire as strong as the fiery love he feels for her. In line 14, *brusar* is northern dialect for *bruciare*, meaning "to burn." Here are all the technical devices typical of the courtly style: paradoxical situations, extravagant metaphors, and content organized according to the epigrammatic formula.

Io vidi la mia ninfa anci mia dea
girsene per la neve, e vidi lei
di tal bianchezza che giurato avrei
che fosse neve se no si movea. 4
La neve che fiocando discendea,
vedendo esser più candida costei,
più volte in ciel contra il voler dei dei
stette, né al basso più venir volea. 8
Stava pien ciascun di maraviglia
vedendo che fioccava e che sole era:
il sol che facea lei con le soe ciglia.
Vincer la neve e l'aria oscura e nera 12
far lucida, gli è laude, e onor ne piglia:
ma, lasso, in vincer me che gloria spera?

𝓘 saw my nymph, I should say my goddess,
walk by when it was snowing, and I saw her
so white that, had she not been moving,
I would have sworn she was made of snow.   4
When the Snow, which was coming down
in flakes, saw her whiter than herself, more
than once demurred in the sky, against
the gods' desire, wishing no longer to descend. 8
Everyone stopped in amazement to watch
the flakes come down, while the sun was shining,
the sun created by the brightness of her eyes.
To triumph over snow, to turn dark shadows   12
into light is her boast, and reason to be praised:
but in defeating me what glory can be claimed?

The three first sections of the sonnet contain a conceit. The first quatrain is taken up by a comparison between the woman and the snow—here personified—that is found in an epigram attributed to Petronius in *Anthologia Latina*.[65] In the second quatrain, the idea of the snow being envious of a woman goes back to a poem by Petrarch, in which the sun in the sky is envious of Laura's resplendent eyes (*Canzoniere* 156, 5–6). Tebaldeo has pushed the hyperbolic element of the metaphor further than his predecessors: the snow refuses to come down, upset by the competition from a woman. A third conceit combining the preceding two is in the first terzina: the splendor of the woman's eyes is so intense that the sun seems to shine even while the snow is falling. The last three lines contain the epigrammatic ending.

𝓢e avien che 'l ciel mi dia viver tant'anni
che quella trezza d'or veggia d'argento
e il vermiglio color del viso spento
e il corpo in altra scorza e in altri panni,   4
ricorderotti tanti oltraggi e inganni;
e come ora tu ridi del mio stento,
così anch'io riderò lieto e contento
del tuo color deforme e de' toi danni;   8
né temerò questi tuoi fieri sguardi,
ché gli occhi non avran più foco ormai,
e Amore altrove temprerà suoi dardi.
Allor di sdegno il specchio spezzerai;   12
ma sì forte mi struggi e sì forte ardi
che quel giorno veder non credo mai.

𝓢hould the heavens grant me to live so many
years as to see those golden braids of yours

turn into silver, the pink of your face fade away,
and your body hide beneath other skin and clothing, 4
then I shall remind you of your wounding
deceptions and, gratified by your disfiguring
colors and devastations, I shall gleefully laugh
at you, who now make such fun of my suffering. 8
No longer will I fear your alarming glances,
because by then, your eyes will have no fire,
and Love will hone his burning arrows elsewhere.
Then you will break your mirror in a rage: 12
but now so fiercely you consume and burn me
that I don't believe I shall ever see that day.

In line 4, Petrach uses the term *scorza*, meaning "bark," in place of *skin*. Per line 11, Love will sharpen his darts in other women's eyes, and younger women will cause men to fall in love. The traditional warning to the woman reluctant to reciprocate love receives here a new twist. The man is in a vindictive mood and looks forward to the time when the ravages of age will perform their destructive action on her and turn the irresponsive young beauty into an old hag. The poetic charge gravitates toward the closing, and there, the lover has an unforeseen change of feeling: he has lingered so longingly and so long on her that the possibility of a future vindication can no longer be a comforting idea.

The courts that most enthusiastically welcomed artists and writers were those of Urbino, Mantua, and Milan. Many of their cultural doings were directed by a woman: at the court of Milan, by Beatrice d'Este, married to Ludovico Sforza; at the court of the Gonzaga in Mantua, by her sister, Isabella—the two sisters vied with each other in patronage and entertainments; and at the court of Urbino, by Elisabetta Gonzaga, wife of Guidobaldo of Montefeltro.[66]

At these courts, the star of Serafino Ciminelli, called Aquilano (1466–1500), shone more brightly than anyone else's. A man of versatile talent and great charm, Serafino set his verse to his own music and sang it on the lute. Born in the city of L'Aquila, hence his nickname, he grew up in Naples and there was trained in music by Wilhelm Guarnier and Josquin des Près. In 1491–94, he became a page to Innico de Guevara at the court of Potenza. Later, in Rome, he was at the service of Cardinal Ascanio Sforza, and then, at Urbino, he was at the service of Guidobaldo of Montefeltro. In Mantua and Milan, he scored his greatest successes: there he entertained not only with his poetry and music but also with games and theatrical productions. He became a sensation in 1495, when, at Mantua, he staged his *Rappresentazione allegorica Della Voluttà, Virtù e Fama* (Allegorical Representation of Voluptuousness, Virtue, and Fame), and playing the character of Voluptuousness, he appeared before the courtly audience stark naked. Aquilano's book of verse, rich in technical virtuosity and metaphorical wit, became one of the best sellers of the day. Between 1502 and 1513, it had twenty editions (listed in Rossi 173–74). From that year to 1568, thirty-three new printings emerged.

Chi el crederia? Fra noi l'idra dimora
con sette teste e con so gran veneno,
che n'ha sette altre, poi se una vien meno,
già che fa quello la mia donna ancora. 4

Ha sette capi, i qual te nomino ora:
el sguardo, el riso de dolcezza pieno,
la fronte, i piè, le man, la bocca, el seno,
ed ognun morde, ognun strugge e divora.   8
Tronca una testa, n'ha sette altre fore:
sdegno, desperazion, vivace morte,
sospetto, gelosia, dubio e timore.
In questo solo han differente sorte;   12
l'idra col foco, a quel ch'io intendo, more,
e questa col mio ardor se fa più forte.

Who would believe it? A hydra lives among us,
one with strong poison and with seven heads,
and seven more she grows, if one evaporates:
this is exactly what my woman also does.   4
Her seven heads are weapons, and I shall name
them: her glance, her smile full of sweetness,
forehead, feet, hands, mouth, and breast;
each of them bites, each consumes and devours.   8
When one head is cut, seven more appear;
they are anger, desperation, brutal death,
suspicion, jealousy, distrust, and fear.
Only in this they have a different outcome: 12
the hydra, as far as I know, is killed by fire;
with my ardor, my woman stronger becomes.

Regarding line 1, the hydra is a mythological monster with nine heads—one of them immortal—who supposedly ravaged the countryside of Lerna, near Argos. Fighting the Lernean hydra was one of the labors of Heracles. The traits that the hydra and the woman share are listed and qualified in eleven lines. The last three describe the only way in which they differ, and the difference becomes the punching point that gives the sonnet its epigrammatic finish (Rossi 78).

Io iurarei che non te offesi mai
per l'alma ch'ogne senso in me comparte:
ma tu potresti dir ch'io non v'ho parte,
ch'ella obedisse te più di me assai.   4
Direi: per el mio cor; ma tu ben sai
ch'el mio non è, se mai da te non parte;
vorrei per questa lingua anco iurarte:
ma ella è pur tua, se tu ligar la fai.   8
Dirrei: per gli occhi; e tu farai risposta:

"Gli occhi son mei, per questo io nol concedo,
che gli apro, chiudo e abaglio ad ogne mia posta."
Orsù, per queste lacrime, ch'io credo   12
che 'l pianto sia pur mio, ch'assai mi costa,
poi ch'altro del mio corpo io non possedo.

On my soul, which bestows all sensibility on me,
I would swear that I never offended you.
But you could say that I have no right to it,
for my soul obeys you more than it obeys me.   4
Then I could say, "On my heart," but you know well
that my heart is not mine, for it never departs from you;
I would then like to swear on this tongue,
but that too is yours, since you can easily tie it up.   8
Then I could say, "On my eyes," but you will rebut,
"I do not concede it; the eyes are mine,
for I open, close, and dazzle them at whim."
So then, I shall swear on these tears, for, I think,   12
the tears I must possess, and they cost me greatly,
since nothing else in this body of mine belongs to me.

The idea that the lover is no longer in possession of himself because the woman has taken him over entirely is an old conceit going back to the Sicilian poets. Serafino extends that notion into a cascade of witty variations, as many as are the bodily parts and the functions by which he is ready to swear, functions and parts that he no longer controls. The poem proceeds speedily to its conclusion, and the end comes with a final oath: he will swear by the tears, the only ones he may claim as his own.

"O felice animal, felice dico" is addressed to a pet dog. Sonnets about beloved canines were popular with fifteenth-century sonneteers and their ladies. In this poem, the poet pushes the use of hyperbole to the threshold of caricature.

O felice animal, felice dico,
che godi de tal dea le labra e 'l fiato;
ah, chi te spinse a sì sublime stato
crudo, inumano, e de pietà nimico?   4
Tu de soe braccia cinto, et io mendico
(quanto me noce in miglior setta nato)
tu del suo dolce umor te pasci, io pato,
e sol per lei di pianto me nutrico.   8
Rigido can, tu più di me non l'ami,
ma veggio or ben che 'l ciel tutto governa
ch'io el cerco ognor, tu pur tal ben non brami.
Tua forma avessi, e tu mia pena eterna,   12
ché se 'l ciel dette a me gli uman ligami
fu a ciò ch'ogne dolor meglio discerna.

O happy little animal, happy I say because
of such goddess you enjoy breath and lips.
Ah! Who raised you to your sublime state, while
mine is so difficult for me, so cruel and inhumane?   4
You are wrapped in her arms, I am driven to begging
(so harmful is being born into a higher species!);
you feed on her sweet whims, I go on suffering
and only on yearning for her I am allowed to feast.   8
Unfeeling dog, you do not love her more than I do;
I see how the heavens keep everything so very fit,
for, while I crave it, you don't care for such a treat.
I wish I had your shape and you my eternal pain: 12
if the heavens bestowed human traits on me,
it was done more efficiently to hand out the suffering.

In the octave, where the hyperboles are kept in place by antithetical personal pronouns, the woman's affection for a pet indifferent to her attentions is juxtaposed with the suffering of the lover who hankers for her and is excluded from all forms of love. The sestet explains why this happens: by giving to each what is not wanted, the heavens fulfill to perfection their preordained plan of distributing punishment all around efficiently.

Se l'opra tua di me non ha già molto,
non da te, Bernardin, vien da colei
che l'immagine mia porta con lei;
l'aspetto mio non è donde m'hai tolto.   4
Son tutto un longo tempo in essa accolto:
Onde, per far del viso i membri mei,
prima te converria ritrar costei
e poi robbarmi intorno al suo bel volto.   8
Ma come la torrai che tu non ardi
al far degli occhi e lei quelli volgendo
che tutti i sguardi soi son foco e dardi?
Solo una via per tuo scampo comprendo: 12
pinger serrati i perigliosi sguardi,
ritrarre il resto, e dir ch'era dormendo.

If your portrait does not resemble me much,
it is not your fault, Bernardin, it is hers, for she
carries with her my image, therefore my features
cannot be found where you looked for them.   4
For so long I have been all enwrapped in her
that, if you wish to represent my lineaments,

you first would have to paint her portrait,
then steal me away from around her face. 8
But how will you paint her without being burned
when you sketch those eyes—the way they turn!—
and her glances, which are all fire and darts?
I see only one way to save yourself and flee: 12
paint her with her deceitful eyes shut tight,
then paint the rest, and say she was asleep.

Not surprisingly, many sonnets of this period are about paintings, whether of a mythological character, a scene, a friend, or a well-known personage. Aquilano writes about his own portrait and withdraws the customary praise of the artist. The portrait is not a good resemblance, he says. The fault is not the painter's, because Serafino's entire persona is now in possession of the woman he loves. She owns his body and soul. The painter should have looked at her, not at him, while painting. Another and somewhat strained witticism closes the poem: How can the painter extract his stolen features from her without being burned by her glances? The painter in question was the well-known Bernardino di Betto, called il Pinturicchio. Bernardino painted Aquilano in Rome. The poet then sent the portrait to his devoted friend, the duchess of Urbino.

For a change of mood and tone, here is a sonnet revealing Aquilano's unsuspected delicate feelings.

Non ti doler di quel che dato m'hai,
né dir che cagion sia s'io vivo absente,
ch'altra dolcezza el cor, donna, non sente
che ricordarsi de' diletti assai. 4
Io ben conosco el ben perché el gustai,
come l'infermo per gran sete ardente,
che in quel punto li tornan ne la mente
quanti surgenti d'acqua vidde mai. 8
Non tornan volontier sospiri e lutto
in la memoria, né dogliosa piaga,
ma ben torna alcun di felice al tutto.
Sì che, madonna, ormai di me te appaga, 12
ché amor non sazia quando gli è il frutto,
anzi amor con amor solo si paga.

Do not regret what you have given me,
don't say it is the reason I stay away from you;
for the heart, woman, there is no greater sweetness
than fondly recollecting a past of pleasure. 4
I know what goodness is, because I tasted it,
just as a sick man suffers a burning thirst,
and, at that moment, very vividly remembers
all the springs of water he has ever seen. 8
No sighs, no grief, no painful wound will come

naturally to mind, only the memory
of the happy days that once were there.
So, my lady, be pleased with me by now,
for love does not die when the fruit of love is given:
on the contrary, love can only be repaid with love.

12

Tebaldeo and Aquilano's peregrinations from one court to another—both ended their careers in Rome—show the trajectory of cultural hegemony followed by the Italian states. By the middle of the century, the states that mattered in Italy were five: Milan, Venice, Florence, Naples, and the Papal States. As time went by, it became increasingly clear that the balance of power and prestige leaned heavily toward the Roman curia.

4.2 Invasions and Reversals

For many years, thanks to his discerning diplomacy, Lorenzo de' Medici had succeeded in maintaining a fair equilibrium among the states and preserving the peace throughout the peninsula. The calamity prophesized by his enemy, Friar Girolamo Savonarola, and prophetically lamented by Matteo Maria Boiardo in *Orlando Innamorato* occurred after Lorenzo's death in 1492. It arrived in the form of the Italian Wars, when the Valois of France and the Habsburgs, who reigned over Spain, Austria, the Flanders, and will dominate vast territories of the Americas, began to fight their battle for supremacy on Italian territory.

There were several reasons that brought about the steady, albeit slow, decline of Italian fortunes. The fall of Constantinople in 1456 made the roads into the Middle and Far East increasingly precarious for Italian entrepreneurship. Later, with the discovery of the Americas in the same year of Lorenzo's death, the European states that faced the Atlantic entered a long period of economic hegemony. They also embarked on a policy of expansion on the continents of America and Europe. Led by the fame of the material and cultural riches of Italy, the armies of France and Spain, quickly followed by others, invaded the peninsula, bringing havoc to cities and countryside alike. Paradoxically, this time of political and economic disaster for the Italians coincided with their great epoch of literary and artistic achievement.

The first incursions of foreign armies occurred by direct invitation of Italian princes, who, in their quarrels with internal enemies and nearby states, looked at monarchs on the other side of the Alps as potential allies. The wars began in 1494 with the invasion of Charles VIII Valois, king of France, and ended in 1559 with the Treaty of Cateau-Cambrésis, which formalized the Spanish rule over most of the peninsula.

In 1494, when Gasparo Visconti (1461–99) wrote "A Milan che si fa?" "Chi il ferro lima," the lord of Milan was Ludovico Sforza. The Sforza had superseded the Visconti in the governance of the city in 1450. Needing support against the opposition of other Italian states, Ludovico urged Charles VIII to enter Italy at the head of an army and stake his claim to the throne of Naples in name of the ousted Anjou dynasty. Gasparo, who belonged to a minor branch of the Visconti family and, at the time, lived at the Milanese court (see section 3.6), became concerned about the new turn of events.

"A Milan che si fa?" "Chi il ferro lima,
chi 'l batte, e chi fa scarpe, o canta o sona,
chi mura, chi va a piedi e chi sperona;
questo la roba, e quel virtù sublima."   4
"Che se gli dice?" "Matutino e prima,
messa, compieta e terza, sesta e nona."
"Va' 'l diavolo; di' come se ragiona."
"In vulgare o in latino; o in prosa o in rima."   8
"Da senno, ormai di guerra c'è niente?"
"Qual guerra? Là se parla de la pace,
ché in pacifico stato ognun si sente."
"Donque del re di Francia là si tace,   12
che già passato l'Alpe ha tanta gente,
che appena Italia ne sarà capace?"
"Ogni lingua là giace;
però che questa patria sta sicura,   16
da poi che 'l Mor non sdegna averla in cura.
Né de l'altrui sciagura
più conto fa, che far conto bisogna,
ma lascia le onge aver a chi ha la rogna."

"What are people doing in Milan?" "Some hone iron,
others beat it, some make shoes, others sing or play,
some build walls, some walk, and others go by riding;
one is valued for his assets, another for his virtue."   4
"But what do they say?" "Matins and prime,
vespers, compline, terce, sext, and none."
"The hell with you! Tell me what they say!"
"They say it in vernacular or Latin, in prose or verse."   8
"Seriously! Nothing is being said about the war?"
"What war? There is talk only of peace here;
they feel all secure, in a peace-loving state."
"So they say nothing about the king of France,   12
who has already crossed the Alps with an army
that Italy will hardly be able to contain?"
"Here, all tongues are nice and quiet,
because their place feels very secure, since   16
the Moor is not above taking care of them.
Of other people's misfortunes
they make as much account as one must,
letting those who hitch do their scratching."

Regarding lines 4–6, these are the canonical hours for prayer. In line 17, the Moor is Ludovico Sforza, called il Moro because of his dark complexion. In line 20, *rogna* is rabies. The line would then be "let him who has the rabies scratch it." The opening scene of city activities and movements underlines the public unawareness of the disastrous initiative taken by the Milanese leader. The tone changes in the second quatrain, where the danger of the general nonchalance begins to surface. It is up to the first tercet to introduce a direct mention of the impending menace: the king of France is crossing the Alps with a powerful army. Only the three lines of the coda are a clear indictment of irresponsibility on the part of the leader and the entire population.[67]

To his predecessor's claim to the Kingdom of Naples, Louis XII of France added a claim of his own to the Duchy of Milan. He based his rights on the marriage of Valentina, daughter of Giangaleazzo Visconti, to his grandfather, the duke of Orleans. In preparation of his invasion of Italy, the king made a treaty with the son of Pope Alexander VI. In 1499, Cesare Borgia had arrived at the French court, bringing a papal dispensation that allowed Louis to divorce his first wife and marry his predecessor's widow, Anne of Brittany. In exchange, Cesare received Charlotte d'Albret in marriage, the French duchy of Valentinois (hence the Italian nickname of Valentino), and the promise that a French military contingent would be at his disposal in the campaign he was about to launch for the conquest of Romagna.

In "Il Duca Valentin, veduti i danni," Antonio Cammelli, called Il Pistoia (1436–1502), ironizes on Cesare's diplomatic and military exploits, all supposedly carried out in the interest of the church.

Il Duca Valentin, veduti i danni
ch'hanno già molti fatto al divin culto,
nella sua prima età, per questo insulto,
in un punto ha fatto quel che val mille anni.   4
A chi ha tolto gli sceptri, a chi gli scanni,
né mai stato è tra' suoi nimici occulto,
quale in exilio ha sperso e qual sepulto:
alcun non sii che 'l divin templo inganni!   8
Dato il Ciel gli ha la grazia e l'armi Marte
per difender la sposa del Signore,
ch'era squassata in più di cento parte.
O tu, che del ben d'altri sei raptore,   12
da la iustizia, dopo un tempo, guârte:
ché a chi nol pensa giunge il punitore.
Chi ebbe il frutto e 'l fiore,
di quel che mangiò mai, con gran sinestro,   16
ha reso il conto e pagato il maestro.

When Duke Valentino saw the harm
many did to the Holy Cult—he was so young!—
for that insult, in a second, he did what would be
great to achieve in a thousand years to come.   4
He deprived a few of scepter, others of bench;

no enemy of his was ever able to hide;
some he flung into exile, others he buried.
Never shall anyone deceive the Holy Church! 8
The heavens gave him grace, Mars the arms,
in order to defend the bride of our Lord,
who was ripped into a hundred shreds.
You, who are the robber of people's goods, 12
beware of justice! For after a while, the Punisher
will come to those who expect him the least.
Whoever stole the fruit and the flower
always gave an account of it—he paid the master 16
for whatever he ate—and suffered a great disaster.

In line 2, *divin culto* refers to Christianity. In line 5, the scepters and benches (*sceptri* and *scanni*) refer to the acts of violence committed by Cesare on holders of religious and secular offices. In line 10, *la sposa del Signore* means "the bride of the Lord," or the church. The sonnet is organized into two contrasting, uneven sections. In lines 1–11, the presentation of Cesare Borgia as the defender of the church is seemingly appreciative. The change occurs in line 12, where the feigned tone of poised appreciation switches into one of unequivocal condemnation. In the last tercet, the ironic description of the facts turns into the prophecy of a catastrophic punishment. The coda confirms it.

Taking advantage of the political and military turmoil generated by the Italian Wars, Valentino planned to appropriate parts of the papal territory in order to establish a state of his own. By 1503, he occupied the whole of Romagna and parts of Marche and Umbria.[68] Disaster soon arrived for the Borgia, however, just as Pistoia had prophesized. Alexander VI died in 1503. His death deprived Cesare of financial resources and foreign backing. His possessions quickly disintegrated. He was arrested and transferred to Spain, and there he died in a minor local skirmish in 1507 while fighting for the king of Navarre, his brother-in-law.

By the time Pistoia penned "Ecco 'l re dei Romani," the Italian Wars had flared up again. It was 1504. The new pope, Julius II (Giuliano della Rovere to the century), had persuaded Emperor Maximilian I of Austria, Louis XII of France, and the English and Spanish kings to form an alliance with him against the Venetians. At the demise of Cesare Borgia, Venice had annexed Faenza, Rimini, and other papal territories of Romagna. In his sonnet, Pistoia assesses the political situation and predicts that both the emperor and the French king will not fail in exacting heavy reparations from the Italian states they ostensibly have come to help.

Ecco 'l re de' Romani e 'l re de' Galli:
l'un per offender vien, l'altro in aiuto.
Prepara, Hesperia, il tuo ricco tributo
per pagar conduttier, barde e cavalli. 4
L'arme raccordarà li antiqui falli:
spesso è il vincitor vinto dal perduto.
Sia pur con Dio! Io non sarò creduto,
se non quando i padron saran vassalli. 8

Pensa al tuo fine, Italia! Italia, guärti!
L'Aquila e 'l Gallo dubito, ti dico,
ch'ancor se accorderanno a diciparti.
L'un ti dimanderà il suo censo antico,   12
l'altro la fede e suoi thesori sparti,
Napoli e la vendetta del nimico.
Se Marco e Ludovico
non apron gli occhi a gustar questa soma,   16
in breve si dirà: "Qui già fu Roma,
e lì Venegia è doma;
Genoa in ciner tutta si riserba;
Bologna rotta e Milan fatto in herba.

Here are the king of the Romans and the king of Gaul:
one comes to attack, the other to offer help.
Prepare, Hesperia, your rich tribute in order to pay
for their captains, their horses, and their armors.   4
The battles will even out the ancient errors:
often the victor is vanquished by the loser.
May it be God's will! For you will not believe me
until our princes have become their subjects.   8
Think, Italy, about your safety! Italy, beware!
Both the Eagle and the Rooster I fear; because, I say,
in plundering you, they will be of one mind.
One will demand your ancient tribute,
the other your loyalty and the money he spent,   12
also Naples and upom his enemies vengeance.
If Marco and Ludovico won't open their eyes
about getting a taste of this coming penance,
we soon shall say, "Once here was Rome,   16
over there Venice, totally subdued;
Genoa is preserved under her ruins;
Bologna is wrecked, Milan has turned into grass."

Regarding line 1, king of the Romans was Emperor Maximilian I, because Italy theoretically was part of the Holy Roman Empire. Maximilian entered Italy with the declared intent of aiding Milan. The king of Gaul in the sonnet is, of course, Louis of France. Regarding line 4, Hesperia is the ancient name of Italy. *Barde* (bards) are defensive coverings for the horse. Per lines 5–6, the new battles will even out, or compensate for the old ones lost, such as the 1495 Battle of Fornovo, in which the Italian Holy League fought Charles VIII, and the Italians, who had been the losers, seemingly turned out to be the victors. In line 10, *L'Aquila* and *il Gallo* (the Eagle and the Rooster) represent the empire and France, respectively. Regarding line 12, the ancient tribute is the tribute the German emperors periodically demanded of the Italian states, which jurisdictionally were within their territory. In line

14, the "enemy's vendetta" is the revenge that Louis will want for the defeat inflicted at Fornovo on his predecessor, Charles VIII. In line 15, Marco stands for Venice, whose patron saint is St. Mark. Ludovico is Ludovico Sforza, duke of Milan. For other sonnets by Cammelli, see 3.8.

No later than 1516, Niccolò Machiavelli (1469–1527) sent the sonnet "Io vi mando Giuliano alquanti tordi" to Giuliano de' Medici, duke of Nemours.[69] Giuliano, the grandson of the Magnificent, was then ruler of Florence, and Machiavelli, the former secretary of the Second Chancery, lived in exile.

Machiavelli had entered the Florentine bureaucracy in 1498, when the secular republic headed by Piero Soderini took over from the theocratic rule of Friar Girolamo Savonarola.[70] Foreign relations were among the concerns of the administrative branch in which Machiavelli had served. In 1512, Pope Julius II hired for the second time an army of Swiss mercenaries, and this time in alliance with Venice, Ferdinand II of Aragon and Holy Roman Emperor Maximilian I defeated the Florentines and forced their allies, the French, to withdraw across the Alps. At the pontiff's request, an army of Spanish and Swiss soldiers set siege to Florence. When the besieging army entered the city, the republican institutions were dismantled, and Giuliano de' Medici was installed as ruler. With the fall of the republic, Machiavelli lost his position, left Florence, and went to live in a small property he owned at San Andrea in Percussina, a few miles from the city.

> Io vi mando Giuliano alquanti tordi,
> non perché questo don sia bono o bello,
> ma perché del pover Machiavello
> Vostra Magnificenzia si ricordi.   4
> E se d'intorno avete alcun che mordi,
> li possiate nei denti dar con ello,
> acciò che, mentre mangia questo uccello
> di laniare altrui ei si discordi.   8
> Ma voi direte: "Forse ei non faranno
> l'effetto che tu di', ch'ei non son buoni
> e non son grassi: ei non ne mangeranno."
> Io vi risponderei a tai sermoni   12
> ch'io son maghero anch'io, come lor sanno,
> e spiccon pur di me di buon bocconi.
> Lasci l'opinioni
> Vostra Magnificenzia, e palpi e tocchi,   16
> e giudichi a le mani e non agli occhi.

> I am sending you, Giuliano, a bunch of thrushes,
> not because they are a good and handsome gift,
> but in order to remind Your Magnificence
> to ponder about poor Machiavelli in distress.   4
> And if some who bite are sitting next to you,

> you might push my gift between their teeth,
> so that, while they make feast of one bird,
> they might forget to rip another one to bits. 8
> You could say, "These may not have the effect
> you think, because they are neither flavorsome
> nor fat, and no one shall want to taste them."
> To such talk, I would then reply that 12
> I too am rather skimpy, as they well know;
> yet they pick out of me some godly morsels.
> Ignore other people's opinion, Your
> Magnificence! Do your touching and fondling, 16
> judge by your own hand and not only by sight.

In line 5, *alcun che mordi* (someone who bites) refers to the men who had denounced Machiavelli to the Medici, as further indicated by "they took some good bites out of me" in line 14. Regarding lines 15–17, poultry was sold with the feathers on, and in order to check how fat a bird was, buyers fondled it carefully before choosing. "Do not listen to what other people say," the poet concludes in the coda. "Consider yourself my worth, and trust your own judgment."

Contrary to what is popularly believed—a reputation that became well entrenched thanks to the anti-Roman Protestant propaganda—Machiavelli was a convinced republican and a strong advocate of democratic institutions.[71] While living at Percussina, he produced the writings that made him famous, notably the *Discorsi sulla prima deca di Tito Livio* (Discourses on the First Decade of Livy) and *The Prince*. The *Discourses*, ostensibly a commentary on the Roman historian, are a study of the forces controlling the foundation and preservation of states, as well as a great theoretical work on republicanism. On the other hand, in *The Prince*, Machiavelli indicated how, in the current Italian situation, a resolute and ruthless leader could acquire power and decisively confront both internal obstacles and foreign invaders. He presented this pamphlet to the young Medici ruler, presumably in the hope of persuading him of his valuable experience and his possible usefulness in internal and external affairs.

While out of office, Machiavelli participated in the conversations that took place in the Orti Oricellari. The Orti were the gardens of Palazzo Rucellai, which had been built by Filippo Brunelleschi as the home of Bernardo Rucellai and his wife, Nannina de' Medici, sister of Lorenzo the Magnificent. The Rucellai were wealthy businesspeople and enthusiastic humanists. Their fortune and the name Oricellari were due to a wool-dying process that their firm carried out with a lichen called "oricello," which gave the fabric a much-admired red-purple color. The Orti Oricellari conversations, which were of both literary and political character, often dealt with the concepts of republicanism and tyranny and with the encroachment of finance and morality. In these gatherings, Machiavelli read passages of his *Discourses*. In 1522, the Medici uncovered a conspiracy somehow connected with the Orti. Machiavelli, suspected of treason, was arrested again and tortured. The gatherings in the Rucellai gardens were suppressed.

In order to hold off the invaders as long as possible, Pope Clement VII (1523–34) allied himself in turn with Francis I of France and Charles V of Spain, now emperor of the Roman Holy Empire. After a period of ambiguous neutrality, in an attempt to free the papacy and the country from the stifling imperial influence, Clement turned again to Francis for help. The result of his belated move was the disastrous sack of Rome in 1527.

Giovanni Guidiccioni's "Da questi acuti e dispietati strali" is one in a garland of fourteen sonnets lamenting what happened in 1527. In May of that year, the imperial army, made up of regular Spanish soldiers and mercenary German landsknechts, unchecked by their leader, Charles de Bourbon, entered Rome and sacked it. Churches and public and private buildings were ransacked, men were tortured, and women were raped.[72]

Da questi acuti e dispietati strali,
che Fortuna non sazia ognora avventa
nel bel corpo d'Italia, onde paventa
e piange le sue piaghe alte e mortali,   4
bram'io levarmi ormai su le destr' ali
che 'l desio impenna e di piegar giá tenta,
e volar lá dove io non veggia e senta
quest'egra schiera d'infiniti mali.   8
Ché non poss'io soffrir chi fu giá lume
di beltá, di valor, pallida e 'ncolta
mutar a voglia altrui legge e costume,
e dir versando il glorioso sangue: 12
"A che t'armi, Fortuna? A che sei volta
contra chi vinta cotanti anni langue?"

From these sharp and merciless blows
that Fortune, yet unsatisfied, keeps thrusting
on the beautiful body of Italy, making her quake,
weep, and bend over her deep, deadly wounds,   4
I long to rise myself on the capable wings
that my desire unfolds and, turning away, I try
to fly where no longer I may see and hear
of this appalling number of endless ills.   8
For I cannot bear to see this land, once a splendor
of beauty and boldness, now neglected and enfeebled,
change customs and laws at other people's bidding
and say, while spilling her glorious blood, "Fortune,   12
why do you inveigh so? What is your purpose toward
one that is beaten, one that has languished for so long?"

A citizen of Lucca, Guidiccioni had embarked on a successful ecclesiastical career and eventually became bishop of Fossombrone, papal legate to Spain, commissioner of the papal army, and, finally, governor of Romagna. Among his many prose works, especially memorable is the oration he delivered before the government of Lucca in defense of the poor of the city who had rebelled against the leadership of the noble class.

In the Orti Oricellari, Machiavelli sympathized and often confabulated with a much younger man by the name of Luigi Alamanni. He dedicated to him the *Vita di Castruccio Castracani* and made him one of the interlocutors in his *Art of War*.

Luigi Alamanni (1495–1556) was of a distinguished Florentine family. As a young man, he became a presence in the political life of the city, but accused of plotting against Giuliano de' Medici, in 1522, he was deprived of his property and forced into exile. He took refuge in France, and on behalf of the French king, he paid several diplomatic visits to Italy.[73] In 1527—the republic had been reinstalled in Florence—Alamanni returned to take part in the defense of the city during the ten-month siege set by Charles V of Spain. When Florence surrendered, Alamanni left Italy forever.[74] He wrote the following sonnet in Paris around 1530.

Quanta invidia ti porto, amica Sena,
vedendo ir l'onde tue tranquille e liete
per sì bei campi, a trar l'estiva sete
a' fiori e l'erbe onde ogni riva è piena! 4
Tu la città, che 'l tuo gran regno affrena,
circondi e bagni, e 'n lei concordi e quete
vedi le genti sì, che per te miete
utile e dolce ad altrui danno e pena. 8
Il mio bell'Arno (ahi, ciel, chi vide in terra
per alcun tempo mai tant'ira accolta,
quant'or sovra di lui sì larga cade?)
il mio bell'Arno in sì dogliosa guerra 12
piange suggetto e sol, poi che gli è tolta
l'antica Gloria sua di libertade.

What envy I feel toward you, o friendly Seine,
when I see your tranquil and happy waters flow
through lovely fields, slaking the summer thirst
of herbs and flowers, so abundant on every bank! 4
This city, which regulates your great power,
you surround and bathe; in it you see people living
in peaceful harmony and gathering, thanks to you,
sweet returns, but painful and hurtful to others. 8
My lovely Arno (ah, heavens! who on earth
ever saw so much anger gathered at one time,
as now is so abundantly falling on that river?),

my beautiful Arno, in such a doleful war	12
weeps subjected and alone, since from it	
has been taken its ancient glory of liberty.	

Regarding line 5, the city is Paris. Regarding line 9, the Arno is the river that flows through Florence. Rancor toward the enemies and nostalgia for the homeland always remained in the men whom internecine struggles had made hopeless exiles. Besides the wistful melancholy typical of the banished, Alamanni's sonnet is imbued with bitter regret for the political devastations of Italy and with nostalgia for a democratic, secular world that no longer existed. After the sack of Rome, the republican communes gave way to new aristocratic regimes and a strong clerical culture, Venice being the exception. The warfare that for decades brought devastation and disease to the country continued until 1556. Peace between France and Spain, the two main contenders for supremacy in Europe, was finally stipulated that year at Cateau-Cambrésis. By that treaty, Milan and all southern Italy became part of the Spanish empire, a domain extending from Austria and the Flanders to Italy, Spain, and, beyond the ocean, Florida, California, and South America. Alamanni died in the Castle of Amboise in 1556, the year of the treaty.

4.3 At the Curia

In the sixteenth century, the people of Rome could take the political pulse of the curia by reading the pasquinades. These were brief anonymous poems satirizing and attacking men in power and in the news. They were found glued or hung on the figure of Pasquino, a mangled statue positioned at a corner of Piazza del Parione, now Piazza Pasquino, near Piazza Navona. The ancient Roman custom of publicly berating the members of the opposite faction had continued to flourish among students of La Sapienza University, who liked to ridicule their professors and the academic system. More recently, fueled by the competitive spirit reigning in the curia, the custom spread among the general population. The first pasquinades were in Latin; later, when a wider circulation was desired, they appeared in Italian, oftentimes in the form of the regular or the tailed sonnet.[75]

At the news of Pope Alexander VI's death in 1503, the hostile faction celebrated with enthusiasm, and Pasquino came up with the following sonnet.[76]

Belzebù mughia, e nel mughiar si dole	
che sì per tempo è giunto al terzo regno	
el gran vicario che fu d'alma pregno,	
l'orribil loco che non vide il sole.	4
El teme che chi regge esta ampla mole	
non lo exponga del seggio, e che più degno	
Roderigo ne sia: onde ira e sdegno	
affligge quel che l'alme affligger sole.	8
All'ombre ancora duol cangiar governo	
e giunge all'urbe lor nuovo languire,	

che chi el mondo turbò, turba or l'inferno.
Ah Belzebù, tu sei più nobil sire: 12
almen più lieve sia 'l tormento eterno:
tutti i demon son pochi al suo martire.

Beelzebub bellows and in bellowing complains
that the great vicar, endowed with so great a soul,
has arrived far too early in the third kingdom,
the dreadful place that never sees the sun.   4
He fears that God, who oversees this large edifice,
might deprive him of his seat, considering Roderigo
to be more deserving: so wrath and indignation
aggravate him, who is used to aggravate all souls.   8
The shades too dislike to change their regime,
and new sorrow descends upon their city, as he,
who once upset the world, now perturbs the abyss.
Ah, Beelzebub, you are a much nobler lord: 12
may your eternal torture be much lighter,
and all the devils be not enough to punish him!

In line 4, *ampla mole*, meaning "large edifice," refers to the earth, in whose deep center is hell. In line 8, *quel*, used to aggravate the souls, is Satan or Beelzebub. Regarding lines 10–11, *urbe lor* (their city) is hell. The subject *of giunge* is the pope, *chi el mondo turbò* (he who distressed the world). Per lines 13–14, the author wishes for Satan a lighter torture, in the hope that he will inflict on Alexander the heavist punishment that hell can provide. Light traces of Romanesque dialect—*mughia, mughiar, afflige*—give the comparison between Pope Borgia and Satan a local flavor and a much-needed humorous touch.[77]

Pasquino authored the sonnet beginning "Padre dell'universo, almo pastore" during the pontificate of Julius II. Cardinal Giuliano della Rovere succeeded Rodrigo Borgia as Julius II in 1503. His bellicose character and personal participation in several military campaigns gave him the sobriquet of Warrior Pope. Julius's first concern was to establish a closer control over the papal lands, which had fallen into anarchy and disarray, and repossess the territories appropriated by Venice at the demise of Borgia. Determined to recover them, Julius marched north at the head of the papal army and supervised the war operations personally. In 1511, after accomplishing that mission in alliance with Louis XII, Alexander decided to get rid of the overbearing French king and organized against him a league comprised of Emperor Maximilian I, Ferdinand V of Spain, Henry VIII of England, and the Swiss Cantons.

The upcoming caudate sonnet, also by Pasquino, sees in Pope Julius the restorer and defender of the state and prestige of the church. Was that expression of enthusiasm the creation of the pope's publicity office?

Padre dell'universo, almo pastore
che rappresenti Jesu Christo in terra,
che tieni 'l loco di quel che apre e serra
la porta del sacro regno maggiore;   4

mira l'Italia tua, che a tutte l'ore
dinanzi ai sacri tuoi piedi s'atterra,
gridando: "Padre Sancto, ormai disserra
la spada contra 'l barbaro furore." 8
Guarda il suo corpo tutto lacerato
dalle mani d'esti cani amaramente:
soccorri, padre mio più che beato,
per amor della patria tua excellente, 12
porgi soccorso al popul flagellato,
scaccia questa barbarica aspra gente.
Vedrai poi incontinente
Italia farsi bella e rinverdirsi 16
e contra i tuoi nimici teco unirsi.

Father of the universe, o Holy Shepherd,
you who are in place of Jesus Christ on earth,
who represent the One who opens and closes
the door of the great heavenly kingdom, 4
look at your Italy, who at all hours
throws herself down at your blessed feet
and cries, "Holy Father, unsheathe by now
your sword against this barbaric furor." 8
Do look at her body so painfully torn
to pieces by the bites of these ugly dogs:
come to the rescue, Father more than holy;
do it for the love of your superb homeland! 12
Give your help to these trodden people;
throw out this barbaric, pitiless throng!
Then you shall instantly see that Italy
has become green and beautiful again 16
and will unite behind you against your foes.

The Father in line 1 and in lines 7 and 11 is Pope Julius. In line 8, *barbaro furore* means "barbaric furor." The battle cry of the pope's league was "Out with the barbarians!" Regarding lines 10–14, *esti cani* (these dogs) and *questa barbarica gente* (these barbaric people) were the French, against whom the pope's league had been organized. It's interesting to remember that the church had condemned Gallicanism, a movement inspired by the French king, which advocated the French clergy's administrative independence from papal controls.

The Romans admired Julius for his warlike deeds and respected him for his strength of mind and determination to clean the church of corruption and abuse. Upon becoming pope, he had initiated several reforms: he had published a bull against simony, suppressed nepotism, and legalized charitable pawnshops for the benefit of the poor. He was also one of the great patrons of the Renaissance, the commissions he assigned to Raphael, Michelangelo, and Bramante being the best known. Nonetheless, on February 20, 1513, soon after he died, Paquino displayed the following epitaph on his bust.

Io fui un Iulio Rover de Savona,
o viator, pontefice secondo,
che finzendo conzar, ruinato ho il mondo,
per pormi in testa una maior corona.   4
Ma la spada del ciel non mai perdona
a qualunque hom del sangue sitibondo;
m'ha posto qui, come tu vedi, al fondo.
Non men del precessor mia fama suona: 8
quel ruinò Italia, io e mare et terra;
quel fece grande un figliol Valentino,
e spogliò la Chiesa; io la tenni in guerra
e ho fatto grande 'l mio duca de Urbino.   12
Ma sol sta differrentia in noi si serra:
che lui lassò un thesor, io sangue e vino.

I was, o passerby, a certain Julius Rovere
the Second, the pontiff from Savona, who,
wishing to place on his head a greater crown,
and feigning to mend the world, led it to disaster.   4
But heaven's sword, which never forgives,
no matter who the bloodthirsty man may be,
hurled me, as you can see, into deeper hell.
My renown is greater than my predecessor's,   8
for he ruined Italy, I ruined earth and seas;
he made powerful a son of his, the Valentino,
and spoiled the church; I held it on the warpath
and have aggrandized my duke of Urbino.   12
Only one difference is between us:
he left a treasure, I left wine and blood.

In line 3, *conzar* (or *conciare, acconciare, aggiustare*) means "to adjust," "to mend," or "to put in order." In line 4, *una maior corona* (a larger crown) refers to Julius's territorial enlargements. In line 10, the Valentino is Cesare Borgia, who married a French princess, received from the French king the duchy of Valentinois, and was allowed by the pope to carve for himself a territory out of papal lands. In line 12, the *duca de Urbino* is Francesco Maria della Rovere, nephew of Pope Julius II. He was also the nephew and adopted son of Guidobaldo da Montefeltro, duke of Urbino. In lin 14, reference is made to the administrative talents of Pope Borgia.

Under Julius II, Rome had become a great cultural center; the curia was now the major source of employment for artists, literati, and educated members of the Italian upper classes. With Leo X,[78] who ruled the Papal States from 1513 to 1521, the prestige of the papal court among artists and intellectuals grew further.[79] Leo was Giovanni de' Medici, son of the Magnificent. His education, the best his family could provide, had emphasized the classics but had been also religious, mostly thanks to the supervision of his pious mother.[80]

As a monarch, Leo retained firm control over the church territories and removed from power many local families. He also tried to lessen foreign influence by allying himself alternatively with France and Spain, often by fighting with one against the other. This tactic was destined to fail miserably when his cousin, Pope Clements VII, used it in confrontation with the military powers of France and Spain.[81] Leo's greatest demerit was underestimating the seriousness of a German friar by the name of Martin Luther. In gauging the failure of the Roman clergy to appreciate the momentous importance of the German protest, one must consider the irreconcilable chasm that existed between the mostly secular upbringing of the Italian upper classes, from which popes and the upper clergy originated, and the religious mentality of the northern Europeans. Many had been the remonstrations against the corruption of the Roman church throughout history, but in the sixteenth century, the protests were for the first time backed by the political and economic interests of the local states. In his effort to persuade Luther to retract and then in an attempt to subdue him, Leo X allied himself with Charles V, thus setting in motion a series of complex events that led to the eventual division of Christendom and to the papacy's and Italy's subjection to Spain.

Well known was Leo's preference for the companionship of Florentines. His protégés roamed the corridors of the Vatican unimpeded, while other ambitious and resentful men remained outside the palace, siding with the adverse faction. The four-tailed sonnet "O musici con vostre barzellette," written when Leo died in 1521, confirms the discontent and the rivalries that had been festering in the Roman court.

> O musici con vostre barzellette
> piangete, o sonator di violoni,
> piangi e piangete, o fiorentin baioni,
> battendo piatti, mescole e cassette. 4
> Piangete buffon magni, anzi civette,
> piangete mimi e miseri istrioni,
> piangete, o frati, spurcidi ghiottoni,
> a cui dir mal la gola e 'l gettar dette. 8
> Piangete el signor vostro, o voi tiranni,
> piangi Fiorenza, et ogni tuo banchiero
> con qualcun altro offizial minchione.
> Piangi, clero di Dio, piangi su Piero, 12
> piangete, o sopradetti, i vostri mali,
> poscia ch'è morto el decimo Leone.
> Il qual d'ogni buffone
> e d'ogni vil persona era ricepto, 16
> tiranno sporco, disonesto, infetto.
> Et per chiarir meglio mio detto,
> impegnò per seguire un suo pensiero
> Fiorenza official, la Chiesa e Piero. 20
> E tengo certo e vero
> che se 'l viver ancor li era concesso
> vendeva Roma, Cristo e poi sé stesso.
> Ma sopra tutto, adesso, 24
> piangan Leon quei miseri mortali
> che 'l dinar non li ha fatti cardinali.

Weep, musicians, with all your ballads,
weep all of you, players of contrabasses,
weep and weep, o Florentines, o dullards,
by beating spoons, saucers, and boxes.   4
Weep eminent clowns, or rather buzzards,
weep mimes and miserable buffoons,
weep, you friars, weep, you filthy gluttons
driven to backstabbing by waste and greed.   8
Weep for your master, you despots,
weep Florence, with all your bankers
and some other foolhardy civil servants.
Weep, God's clergy, weep over Peter,   12
weep your misfortunes, all of you above,
for Leo the Tenth has expired his last.
Of every clown he was the refuge
and of every contemptible individual,   16
a filthy tyrant, dishonest and diseased.
And, to make my words even clearer,
in pursuing any whim whatever, he pawned
official Florence, the church, and Peter.   20
This I hold distinct and square:
had he been allowed to live a little longer,
he would have sold himself, Christ, and Rome.
But now, above all else,   24
let Leo be mourned by those sad mortals
whom money failed to make cardinals.

Regarding line 1, *barzellette* were a kind of minstrel song. In line 2, a *violone* is a bass viol, a deep-toned musical instrument belonging to the viol group and resempling a big violin. It is also called a double bass or contrabass. Regarding line 8, the pope was amused by clowns and minstrels of all kinds and generously remunerated their gossip. *Gettar*, meaning "to throw away," stands for "to waste." In line 12, Piero (Peter) is synecdoche for religion and Christianity. Regarding line 20, in order to finance his military campaigns, cultural projects, and expensive court, Leo borrowed heavily and indulged in the sale of offices, indulgencies, and dispensations.

The election of the new pope took a long time. No fewer than thirty-nine cardinals convened on December 1, 1521, and remained in session in the Sistine Chapel until May 9, 1522.[82] All throughout the conclave, the Romans placed bets on the outcome of the election. Inexorably, Pasquino carped about the unbecoming delay as murmured suppositions and contrasting news leaked daily out of the Sistine Chapel.

At the time, in Rome lived a Tuscan writer by the name of Pietro Aretino (1492–1556), a talented satirist and a scandalous and shameless provocateur. Aretino wrote the pasquinades that contain the sharpest invectives and strongest expressions of scorn. In becoming Pasquino's ghostwriter, favoring the election of Giulio de' Medici, he made no secret of either his preference or his authorship and insolently turned the caustic vein of the statue into viciously aggressive slander. This two-tailed sonnet is an example.

Non ti maravigliar, Roma, se tanto
s'indugia a far del papa la elezione,
perché fra' cardinal Pier con ragione
non truova chi sia degno del suo manto.   4
La cagion è che sempre ha moglie accanto
questo, e quel volentier tocca il garzone,
l'altro a mensa dispùta d'un boccone
e quel di inghiottir pesche si dà il vanto.   8
Uno è falsario, l'altro è adulatore,
e questo è ladro e pieno di eresia,
e chi di Giuda è assai piú traditore.
Chi è di Spagna e chi di Francia spia   12
e chi ben mille volte a tutte l'ore
Dio venderebbe per far simonia.
Sicchè truovisi via
di far un buon pastor fuor di conclavi,   16
che di san Pietro riscuota le chiavi
e questi uomini pravi,
che la Chiesa di Dio stima sì poco,
al ciel, per cortesia, balzi col fuoco.

Don't be surprised, o Rome, if the pope's
election is much delayed, because among
the cardinals, Peter understandably can
hardly find anyone worthy of his mantle.   4
The reason being that this one has a wench
close to him always, that one gladly fondles a boy,
one lectures at the table on whammy tidbits,
the other will boast of swallowing peaches.   8
One is a forger, the other a flatterer,
this one a thief, chock-full of heresy,
that one a traitor greater than Judas.
One spies for Spain, the other for France;   12
another would be quite willing to barter God,
indulging in simony a thousand times per hour.
So let us find a way
to elect a good shepherd out of conclaves,   16
one worthy to receive St. Peter's keys,
one who, for God's sake,
with fire will bounce to the sky these rotten
men, who do not esteem the church a whit.

In line 3, Pier refers to Peter; it stands for Christianity. Regarding line 5, some prelates lived with or regularly frequented courtesans. In line 8, *inghiottir pesche* (swallowing peaches) indicates great gluttony and is also an accusation of sodomy, as *peaches* stood euphemistically for "buttocks." It is not surprising that Protestant propaganda interpreted Pasquino's poetic efforts as the expression of popular opposition to the church. However, the pasquinades were the work of individuals, mostly university students, who wrote for men who were connected with the curia and who favored one or the other cardinal in the seat of power. The public—especially foreign visitors—eagerly bought the collections of pasquinades, turning Pasquino into a European celebrity.[83]

In 1522, the cardinals did not elect Giulio de' Medici, as Aretino had hoped. Unexpectedly, a teacher of Luvain, Adrian Florensz, became pope with the name of Adrian VI. Florensz, who had been a tutor to Charles V, was elected with the emperor's favor. The Romans, especially those who counted on a continued papal largesse, loathed the pious Netherlander, who suddenly obliged them by dying shortly after his election.

Francesco Berni wrote "Un papato composto di rispetti" presumably before 1527. At that time, he was working in Rome as secretary to Matteo Giberti, a much-respected datary and bishop of Verona. The sonnet makes fun of Clement VII, the pontiff who had succeeded Adrian VI in 1523. Clement had been Cardinal Giulio de' Medici, natural son of Giuliano, the Magnificent's brother who had fallen victim to the Pazzi conspiracy in 1478.

> Un papato composto di rispetti,
> di considerazioni e di discorsi,
> di pur, di poi, di ma, di se, di forsi,
> de pur assai parole senza effetti;   4
> di pensier, di consigli, di concetti,
> di conietture magre per apporsi,
> d'intrattenerti, pur che non si sborsi,
> con audienze, risposte e bei detti;   8
> di piè di piombo e di neutralità,
> di pazienza, di dimostrazione
> di fede, di speranza e carità;
> d'innocenza, di buona intenzione,   12
> ch'è quasi come dir semplicità,
> per no li dar altra interpretazione.
> Sia con sopportazione,
> lo dirò pur, vedrete che pian piano   16
> farà canonizzar papa Adriano.

> A pontificate replete with hesitations,
> with considerations and with fine speeches,
> full of "although," "then," "but," "if," "perhaps,"
> also of very many words without effect;   4
> of thoughts, advice, ideas, of very vague
> conjectures, which always fail to guess,

of keeping people distracted, of not having to pay,	
replete with audiences, with answers and wise	8
sayings, with feet of lead, with neutrality,	
with patience, with demonstrations,	
with faith, with hope, and with charity;	
with innocence and with good intentions,	12
which is almost like saying credulity,	
ignoring all other possible interpretations.	
Please allow me,	
I have to say it, bit by bit he will manage	16
to have Pope Adrian canonized, you'll see.	

In line 6, *conietture* suggests that Clement would make conjectures without compromising himself. In line 9, *piè di piombo* (feet of lead) stands for excessive caution. In line 13, *semplicità* is something between innocence and imbecility. Regarding line 17, used to the laissez-faire and lavishness of Giovanni de' Medici's style of papacy, bureaucrats, artists, and hangers-on resented the severity of Adrian VI, who did his utmost to curb their easygoing practices. The tail concludes the sonnet with an absurd prediction: Clement's maddening circumspection will drive the Romans to regret the passing of the Flemish pope.

The sonnet advances with an accumulation of terms of reticence, suspension, and concession, indicating a behavior consistently and purportedly used by the pontiff in order to delay a clear answer, get out of a difficult situation, or avoid risking a forced obligation. Nonetheless, Berni's raillery is no inconsiderate hostility to papal policies, for he was not an outsider. As Ghiberti's secretary, he stood at the center of the ecclesiastical administration.[84] For more sonnets by him, see 5.1.

The difficulties the papacy had to face under Clement were perhaps insurmountable. His desperate attempts to balance the power of the French with the might of Spain—he repeatedly reversed his alliances in favor of one or the other, following the outcome of battles and the humors of the curia—were, however, ruinous.[85] They contributed to bringing about the devastating sack of Rome, the decisive split between the church and Lutheranism, and the subjugation of the papacy and Italy to Spain.

4.4 A Pundit for All Courts

Throughout the sixteenth century, Rome remained an influential center of culture; the curia and the local aristocracy were the foremost providers of employment for artists and intellectuals from many parts of the peninsula and Europe.

Pietro Bembo (1470–1547) was the man who best navigated the tides of the time and most astutely interpreted the trends emanating from Rome. He was a man of flawless education; aristocratic bearing—he was born in an upper-class Venetian family; and a genial understanding of the Italian public. In 1501, he produced a critical edition of the *Canzoniere*. He wrote and, in 1505, published *Gli Asolani*, a dialogue espousing a Platonizing theory of love. He encouraged the Petrarchan fashion anew in 1525, when his treatise on style, *Prose della volgar lingua* (Prose Writings about the Vernacular

Language), came out of print, and again in 1530, when his own book of lyric poetry, *Rime*, was published. By giving, in the dialogue, a Platonic slant to the traditional repertory of love themes—in other words, by turning love poetry into the story of an exemplary life—he suggested the possibility of a restrained but free modus vivendi and gave the example of a public persona that responded with elegance and aplomb to any social situation.[86] Furthermore, by endorsing Petrarch's *Canzoniere* as a model for poetry, he popularized a literary language that all Italian versifiers, regardless of their spoken idiom, could adhere to and assimilate. For all these reasons, Bembo became a prominent literary pundit, and high literary circles, both in Italy and abroad, embraced the model he perfected.

He achieved success and satisfaction in both personal and public life as well. He enjoyed several love affairs, as well as a distinguished position in many courts. His literary prestige—he had no outstanding religious inclinations—prompted Pope Leo X to place him in charge of papal briefs in the Vatican, the Venetian government to nominate him librarian and historian of the republic, and Pope Paul III to reward him with a cardinalate.

Bembo probably wrote the sonnet "Sì come suol, poi che 'l verno aspro e rio" between 1497 and 1499, the years he spent at Ferrara, where he was sponsored by Lucrezia Borgia, then wife of Alfonso II Este, duke of Ferrara.

Sì come suol, poi che 'l verno aspro e rio
parte e dà loco a le stagion migliori,
giovene cervo uscir col giorno fuori
del solingo suo bosco almo, natio,   4
et or su per un colle, or lungo un rio
gir lontano da case e da pastori,
erbe pascendo rugiadose e fiori,
ovunque più nel porta il suo desio;   8
né teme di saetta o d'altro inganno,
se non quand'egli è colto in mezzo 'l fianco
da buon arcier, che di nascosto scocchi;
tal io senza temer vicino affanno   12
moss'il piede quel dì, che be' vostr'occhi
me 'mpiagar, Donna, tutto 'l lato manco.

When, at daybreak, as the unfriendly
and harsh winter is ending, leading the way
to kinder seasons, a young deer abandons
the quiet protected woods where he was born 4
and running now up a hill and now along a river,
away from shepherds and their shelters,
grazing on the dewy grass and flowers
wherever his vehement fancies take him,   8
he has no fear of either arrows or snares
until the dart of a skilled archer, who aims
from some hideout, shoots him on one side:
so did I, with no fear of pending danger,   12

walk out that day, and then your lovely eyes,
Lady, injured me over my whole left side.

In line 4, *almo* means "life giving," "soothing," or "quiet." Regarding line 14, the left side, *lato manco*, is where the heart is. The long comparison of the wounded deer has a more concise precedent in Petrarch's "I dolci colli, ov'io lasciai me stesso": "As a deer, wounded by an arrow, / runs away with a poisoned dart in his side, / the more he runs, the sharper his pain becomes; / in the same way I ..." (*e qual cervo ferito di saetta / col ferro avvelenato dentr'al fianco / fugge, e più dolsi quanto più s'affretta, / tal io ...*). Petrarch's simile catches the danger of the situation from the deer's point of view, making us feel its pain. In Bembo's sonnet, the standpoint is external to the animal; its effectiveness is in the grace of the natural description; the vision of the deer moving through the forest from grass to grass and from flower to flower; and the vision of the hunter hiding in the bushes, ready to strike.

Bembo mentioned the following sonnet in a letter to Lucrezia Bogia in June 1503.

Giaceami stanco, e 'l fin de la mia vita
venia, né potea molto esser lontano,
quando pietosa, in atto onesto e piano,
Madonna apparve a l'alma, e diemmi aita.   4
Non fu sì cara voce unquanque udita,
né tocca, dicev'io, sì bella mano
quant'or da me, né per sostegno umano
tanta dolcezza in cor grave sentita.   8
E già negli occhi miei feriva il giorno
nemico degli amanti, e la mia speme
parea qual sol vel che s'adombre.
Gìosene appresso il sonno, et ella, inseme   12
co' miei diletti e con la notte intorno,
quasi nebbia sparì che 'l vento sgombre.

I was lying down exhausted; the end
of my days was coming—it could not be far—
when gently, in modest and simple guise,
my lady appeared to my soul to comfort me.   4
A voice as dear as this was never heard,
I thought; so lovely a hand was never touched
as it was then by me, nor was such sweetness
of human comfort ever felt by a heavy heart.   8
Then the light of day, lovers' enemy,
wounded my eyes, and my hope began
to dim, like the sun when it is about to hide.
Afterward my sleep went, and she, together   12
with my joys and the all-embracing night,
vanished just like mist swept away by wind.

In line 3, *atto onesto e piano* (modest and simple guise) indicates the qualities traditionally praised in a woman: dignity and gentle simplicity, as in Petrarch's *Canzoniere*, 270, 83–84. In line 8, with *cuor grave*, the poet is saying, "A heavy heart never felt as great a sweetness as the one my heart felt when comforted by such kindness" (Pazzaglia). Regarding line 10, the daylight (*il giorno*) is lovers' enemy because it dissipates the dreams of the night, or brings to an end their lovemaking. In line 11, *qual sol vel che s'adombre* means, literally, "when a veil darkens the sun," or "like the sun that darkens when it is covered by the clouds." In line 14, *Nebbia … che 'l vento sgombre* refers to snow that the wind scatters away. The expression derives from Petrarch's *Canzoniere* 270, 36. If the theme of the sonnet can be traced back to Laura's after-death apparitions in the *Canzoniere*, the enchanted magic of Petrarch's phantasm and the emotional reverberations it produced in him are missing here. The grace of Bembo's poem is all in the literary veil enwrapping the reverie, the sweet gallantry with which the woman is evoked, and the soft sensuality transmitted by the touch of her hand.

Petrarch's revised love story was a good model for Bembo at the time of his involvement with the duchess. The program that he had prospected for himself at Ferrara is sketched out retrospectively in a poem sent to Bernardo Cappello, a young Venetian admirer, in the summer of 1528.

Arsi, Bernardo, in foco chiaro e lento
molt'anni assai felice, e, se 'l turbato
regno d'Amor non ha felice stato,
mi tenni almen di lui pago e contento.   4
Poi, per dar le mie vele a miglior vento,
quando lume del ciel mi s'è mostrato,
scintomi del bel viso in sen portato,
sparsi col piè la fiamma, e non men pento.   8
Ma l'imagine sua dolente e schiva
m'è sempre inanzi, e preme il cor sì forte,
ch'io son di Lete ormai presso a la riva.
S'io 'l varcherò, farai tu che si scriva   12
sovra 'l mio sasso, com'io venni a morte,
togliendomi ad Amor, mentr'io fuggiva.

I burned, Bernardo, in slow and clear fire
for many years and happily so, and even though
love's troubled kingdom has no happy state,
at least I held myself content and satisfied.   4
Then, to unfurl my sails to better winds,
when a light from heaven beckoned, I rid myself
of the lovely vision held in my heart, snuffing
the flame with my foot, and I do not regret it.   8
But the image of her, so sad and shy,
is always before me, haunting my heart so
persistently that Lethe by now I see nearby.
If I cross it, take care that on my tomb   12

it shall be written how I happened to die:
running away, trying to escape from Love.

Line 5 is reminiscent of *Purgatorio* 1, 1–2: "*Per correr migliori acque alza le vele la navicella del mio ingegno*" (the small vessel of my mind sets sails to navigate better waters). In line 6, *lume del ciel* means "the grace of God." Regarding line 7, consider Petrarch 266, 12–14: "*Un lauro verde ... / portato ho in seno e già mai non mi scinsi*" (A green laurel I carried in my heart, and I never broke loose from it). The laurel tree is a symbol for Laura. In line 9, *onesta* means "modest" or "shy"—that is, without arrogant forwardness. Regarding line 11, Lethe is the infernal river.

The choice of diction and sentence structure makes the poem consistently serene and gracious—or *leggiadro*, in Bembo's own terminology. The sonnet also confirms Bembo's plan to fashion the story of his life on the *Canzoniere*, but without the perturbing and elusive overtones of Petrarch's desires. The conflict that afflicted and exalted Laura's lover has turned into a calm, well-considered decision to order his thoughts and lifestyle in a slightly more ascetic direction. Significantly, as Gorni points out (2001, 177), 1528, when the sonnet was written, was an important year in Bembo's literary and public career. His *Rime* was about to be published, and the author was on the way to becoming a cardinal.

Emptied of its conflictual drama, what can be called "the Bembian model" became also a code to be used in correspondence and public contacts between the sexes. The sonnet "Io ardo, dissi" stages a flirtatious exchange between a man and a woman in a courtly background.

"Io ardo," dissi, e la risposta invano,
come 'l gioco chiedea, lasso, cercai;
onde tutto quel giorno e l'altro andai
qual uom ch'è fatto per gran doglia insano.   4
Poi che s'avide ch'io potea lontano
esser da quel penser, più pia che mai
ver me volgendo de' begli occhi i rai,
mi porse ignuda la sua bella mano.   8
Fredda era più che neve; né 'n quel punto
scorsi il mio mal, tal di dolcezza velo
m'avea dinanzi ordito il mio desire.
Or ben mi trovo a duro passo giunto,   12
ché, s'i' non erro, in quella guisa dire
volle Madonna a me com'era un gelo.

"I am burning," I said, and in vain, alas,
I waited for an answer, as the game required;
so all that day and the next I moved about
like one driven mad by a tormenting pain.   4
When she thought I had abandoned
that very thought, turning her fine eyes
toward me more feelingly than usual,
she extended to me her fine hand naked.   8
Her hand was colder than snow, but I did

not see my defeat, so agreeable was the veil
that desire had woven over my eyes.
Now I have reached an unbearable impasse,   12
because with that gesture, if I am not mistaken,
the lady wished to say that she felt as cold as ice.

In line 4, *per gran doglia insano* (made insane by a great pain) is the condition suffered by the lover in *Canzoniere* 43, 7. In this sonnet, it becomes the melodramatic gesture of a suitor during a society game. In line 8, *mi porse ignuda la sua bella mano* is a replica of Petrarch's *una bella ignuda mano* in the song 200, 1. In lines 10–11, *un velo di gran dolcezza* tells us that his desire had wrapped him up in a happy illusion of hope; therefore, he did not understand the woman's message. The story of the social mishap is enwrapped in a well-balanced oxymoron, with *io ardo* (I am burning) at the beginning and *era un gelo* (it was ice) at the end of the sonnet.

The game referred to in the second line required a number of players to sit in a circle and whisper a few words into the ear of the person close by. At the end, each whispered reply was repeated aloud, and the players who gave the wrong answer were fined. Bembo's sonnet might have been written in 1507, when he resided in Urbino, at the court of Guidobaldo da Montefeltro.[87] Plausibly, in the words *più pia che mai* of line 6, we may see a reference—in the word *pia*—to Emilia Pia, who, in Baldesar Castiglione's *The Book of the Courtier*—which describes the entertainments taking place at that court—assists Duchess Elisabetta in leading the men's discussions (Gorni 2001, 83). The connection between book and sonnet, I might add, is also suggested by the Bembo character itself, when, in the first pages of the *The Book*, Bembo proposes, as subject of conversation, what reason a man would prefer his woman to have for behaving coldly toward him.

Crin d'oro crespo e d'ambra tersa e pura,
ch'a l'aura su la neve ondeggia e vola,
occhi soavi e più chiari che 'l sole
da far giorno seren la notte oscura,   4
riso ch'acqueta ogni aspra pena e dura,
rubini e perle, ond'escono parole
sì dolci ch'altro ben l'alma non vole,
man d'avorio, che i cor distringe e fura,   8
cantar, che sembra d'armonia divina,
senno maturo a la più verde etade,
leggiadria non veduta unqua fra noi,
giunta a somma beltà somma onestate,   12
fur l'esca del mio foco, e sono in voi
grazie, ch'a poche il ciel largo destina.

Hair of curly gold, of flawless, shiny amber,
floating over snow, flying in the breeze;
two gentle eyes, more radiant than the sun,

that turn the dark of night into the light of day;	4
a smile that soothes any piercing, aching pain,	
rubies and pearls, wherefrom come words	
so sweet that no other balm the soul desires;	
an ivory hand that grips and steals the heart,	8
a voice that sounds like harmony divine,	
a mature mind in the greenest age,	
a loveliness never seen in our midst before,	
the highest beauty united to the highest good:	12
these were tinder to my fire, and in you they are	
graces the heavens bestow lavishly on a few.	

In line 1, the amber suggests the softness of the woman's hair. In line 2, the snow indicates the whiteness of her neck and shoulders. *A l'aura* is the famous Petrarchan play on words: *a l'aura* (in the breeze) / *a Laura* (to Laura). In line 6, the rubies and pearls (*rubini e perle*) are teeth and lips. Per line 10, although young—hers is "the greenest age"—the woman has the wisdom of an older person. In line 13, *fur* (were) is the verb that serves the subjects and qualifications mentioned in the preceding twelve lines. In line 14, *esca del mio fuoco* means "tinder of my fire"—that is, the qualities that made him fall in love. Bembo's sonnet is indeed a Petrarchan collage of a woman's celestial beauties, as Gorni says (2001, 60), and judging by a lovely sketch we have of Lucrezia Borgia, it could also be considered a description of her. The sonnet was imitated in Italy and abroad. It was also much ridiculed. The parody that Francesco Berni made of it is in section 5.1.

4.5 In a Platonic Frame of Mind

The model of love poetry promoted by Bembo found ideological support in the Neoplatonic theory popularized by many contemporary treatises on love. According to Platonic doctrine, the world issues by emanation from God. Man, God's creature, aspires to return to the principle that created him, and in order to achieve that end, he must go through several stages of purification, become free of all corporeal contamination, and thus acquire a capacity for pure contemplation. Among the sonneteers for whom such view was substance of life and poetry were Vittoria Colonna and Michelangelo Buonarroti.

Vittoria Colonna (1490–1547) belonged to the Roman and Neapolitan upper crust. She was the daughter of Fabrizio Colonna, grand constable of Naples and a general of the Holy League that fought for Pope Julius II against Louis of France at the Battle of Ravenna in 1512. On her mother's side, Vittoria was the granddaughter of Duke Federico of Montefeltro, ruler of Urbino. At four years of age, by express wish of the Neapolitan sovereign, she became engaged, and at nineteen, she was married to Ferdinando Francesco d'Avalos, marquis of Pescara, a relative of the king. In 1525, D'Avalos died of wounds received at the Battle of Pavia while fighting for Charles V. Determined not to marry again, Vittoria chose to reside with her retinue of servants in convents, including San Silvestro in Capite in Rome, San Paolo at Orvieto, Santa Caterina at Viterbo, and, finally, Sant'Anna in Rome. From such residences, where no one could reach her, she was able to sally forth on her many journeys and campaigns. She spent the rest of her life writing verse in celebration of her husband and doing her utmost to promote the reform of the Catholic church. Colonna's religious convictions and unexceptionable personal conduct made her an icon of womanly perfection.

In her celebratory sonnets, she defines Ferdinando Francesco, her dead husband, as a supreme example of virtue, the promoter of her spiritual perfection, and her mediator with God.

Quando io dal caro scoglio guardo intorno
la terra e 'l mar ne la vermiglia aurora
quante nebbie nel ciel son nate, allora
scaccia la vaga vista il chiaro giorno.   4
S'erge il pensier col sole, ond'io ritorno
al mio, che 'l Ciel di maggior luce onora;
e da questo alto par ch'ad ora ad ora
richiami l'alma al suo dolce soggiorno.   8
Per l'esempio d'Elia, non con l'ardente
celeste carro, ma col proprio aurato
venir se 'l finge l'amorosa mente
a cambiarmi 'l mio mal doglioso stato   12
con l'altro eterno; in quel momento sente
lo spirto un raggio de l'ardor beato.

When, from this dear rock, I look around
at the earth, at the sea in the reddish dawn
and the banks of mist still lingering in the sky,
the clear day drives away the pleasant view.   4
My thoughts rise with the sun, and I go back
to mine, whom heaven honors with a greater
light; and, from his height, he seems often
to be calling my soul to his sweet abode.   8
After the example of Elijah, not in a burning
celestial chariot, but in his own golden one,
my loving mind can see him coming
to change my miserable, painful condition   12
into the eternal one: and, in that instant, I feel
a beam of divine light piercing through my soul.

Regarding line 1, Vittoria was on the island of Ischia, which then belonged to the D'Avalos family. She had been there as a child, when she became engaged to Ferdinando Francesco, and she went back many times when she became a widow. The *scoglio* mentioned here is the rock on which the family castle stood, and its ruins still stand, connected to the main island by a short causeway. The first quatrain of the sonnet establishes a wide horizon: at dawn, from her window, Vittoria looks on one side at the sea and, on the other, at the sun rising in the eastern sky. The ascent, the passage from the earthly sun to her sun—her husband—in heaven, begins in the second quatrain and continues into the first terzina. The erotic and mystical metaphor of Elijah's burning carriage is at the same time used and rejected. With the golden chariot, Vittoria signifies the rational kind of love, the only one that allows her soul's flight to an unblemished, blissful heavenly glory. The idea of the carriage might have been suggested also by the chariot in Plato's *Phaedrus*, an allegory that had become central in sixteenth-century speculation about the soul. In line 12, Vittoria's sorrowful condition seems for a moment to cause an emotional downturn, but this is immediately overcome by the closing image of a sudden fulguration of bliss.

The soul's return to the divinity theorized by religious Neoplatonists is the subtext in "Sopra del mio mortal, leggiera e sola." Colonna's philosophical meditation seems to reach in this sonnet the ecstasy of a mystical fulguration.

Sopra del mio mortal, leggera e sola,
aprendo intorno l'aere spesso e nero,
con l'ali del desio l'alma a quel vero
Sol, che più l'arde ognor, sovente vola,   4
e là su ne la sua divina scola
impara cose ond'io non temo o spero
che il mondo toglia o doni, e lo stral fero
di morte sprezzo, e ciò che 'l tempo invola,   8
ché 'n me dal chiaro largo e vivo fonte
ov'ei si sazia tal dolce stilla
che 'l mel m'è poi via più ch'assanzio amaro,
e le mie pene a lui noiose e conte   12
acquetan alor che con un lampo chiaro
di pietade e d'amor tutto sfavilla.

Above this earthly sun, on wings of desire,
my soul, light and alone, opening its way
through the thick darkened air, often flies to that
true Sun, which burns it more and more;   4
and up there, in his divine school, it learns
of such things that neither I fear nor hope
the world could take or give, and death's
fearsome arrow I scorn, and what time may steal;   8
because into me, from that clear, rich, and living
Spring, at which he is sated, such sweetness flows
that, after it, honey tastes bitterer than gall,
and my sorrows, known and hateful to him,   12
are eased, and then everything within me blazes
in a vibrant lightning, full of kindness and love.

In this moment of paradisiacal bliss, every desire and worry falls away. The upward thrust of the octave continues in the sestet with the image of the heavenly spring, and the closing comes in a climactic flash of heavenly light. Many reminiscences of *The Divine Comedy* color the poet's mystical experience. *Divina scola* is a close copy of the *bella scola* of poets who, in Limbo, gather around Homer, the great poet of antiquity, in *Inferno*'s canto 4, 94. *Largo e vivo fonte* (rich and living spring) is reminiscent of *fonte di parlar sì largo fiume* (that spring pouring forth a stream of speech so large) of *Inferno*'s canto 1, 79–80. *Lampo chiaro di pietade e d'amor tutto sfavilla* is a good rendering of the last lines of *Paradiso*, wherein a lightning of knowledge flashes through Dante's mind, which is suddenly hit by the Love that moves the sun and the other stars. For a satirical sonnet on Vittoria Colonna, see Niccolò Franco in 5.1. For other sonnets by Colonna, see section 5.5.

Michelangelo Buonarroti (1475–1564) and Vittoria Colonna were among the people who, in the early 1530s, met regularly to discuss current events and common concerns in a small garden behind the Colonna palace in Rome. Michelangelo was then sculptor, painter, and architect to the pope. He had already painted the ceiling of the Sistine Chapel and now was working on *The Last Judgment*.[88] He wrote the following sonnet for Colonna around 1534.

> Non ha l'ottimo artista alcun concetto
> ch'un marmo solo in sé non circoscriva
> col suo superchio, e solo a quello arriva
> la man che ubbidisce all'intelletto.   4
> Il mal ch'io fuggo, e 'l ben ch'io mi prometto,
> in te, donna leggiadra, altera e diva,
> tal si nasconde; e perch'io più non viva,
> contraria ho l'arte al disiato effetto.   8
> Amor dunque non ha, né tua beltade
> o durezza o fortuna o gran disdegno,
> del mio mal colpa, o mio destino o sorte;
> se dentro del tuo cor morte e pietate   12
> porti in un tempo, e che 'l mio basso ingegno
> non sappia, ardendo, trarne altro che morte.

> The best of sculptors has no conception
> that a block of marble does not contain within
> together with surplus matter: and only at that
> arrives the hand that obeys the intellect.   4
> The evil that I shun and the good that I expect,
> both are hidden in you, o graceful, divine,
> most lofty lady; but to my distraction,
> my art goes against the effect that I desire.   8
> So neither can Love, nor can your beauty
> or severity, nor can chance, nor can great disdain
> be blamed for my faults, nor can my fate and luck,
> if death and compassion at the same time   12
> you carry within your heart, and if, from it, my poor
> wits, though burning, can draw nothing but death.

In line 2, *circoscriva* means "contains." The marble, Michelangelo maintains, already contains the idea of the statue that the artist is working on. A sculptor does nothing but chip away at it to reveal what is inside. This concept of the artistic process was based on the Neoplatonic theory that the real essence of a thing is the idea of it, which exists independently of its many possible applications. The theory went back to Plotinus's *Enneads* 1.6.9 and, some decades before the sonnet, had been reasserted by Masilio Ficino in his *In Plotinum* (M. Ariani, in Segre and Ossola). In line 4, *intelletto* is the intellect, where the idea of the work is conceived. In line 6, *donna leggiadra* is Vittoria Colonna, to whom the sonnet was addressed. In line 7, *tal si nasconde* tells us that in Vittoria, there is the possibility of both pleasantness and unpleasantness. In line 8, Michelangelo is politely saying that he is the one at fault, because while he can easily separate the conception of the statue from the surplus matter contained in a block of marble, he cannot separate the gentleness from the severity that is in her, thus removing her aversion and gaining her consideration.

The artist's feelings for Vittoria Colonna were unquestionably of great admiration and respect, which must have increased as time went by. His attitude toward her, however, was tinged at times with a touch of impatience—not unusual in Michelangelo, even when dealing with important people—perhaps caused by her demands. We can infer this much from the description of their discussions given by a Portuguese artist, Francisco de Hollanda, who, in 1538, attended the meetings in the Colonna gardens. In the above sonnet, therefore, it is possible to read, in my opinion, an apology rather than an answer to the lady's inquiry about art—an apology that is a polite way, with a simile from sculpture, to draw a distance between himself and the redoubtable lady. The sonnet became widely known in 1547, when Benedetto Varchi used it to illustrate his theory of the creating process during a lecture he gave at the Florentine Academy.

The person for whom Michelangelo formed a passionate attraction was Tommaso de' Cavalieri, a beautiful Roman aristocrat in his twenties.[89]

Tu sai ch'i' so, signor mio, che tu sai
ch'i' vengo per goderti più da presso,
e sai ch'i' so che tu sa' ch'i son desso:
e che più indugio a salutarci ormai?   4
Se vera è la speranza che mi dai,
se vero è 'l gran desio che m'è concesso,
rompasi il mur fra l'uno e l'altra messo,
ché doppia forza hann' i celati guai.   8
S'i' amo sol di te, signor mie caro,
quel che di te più ami, non ti sdegni,
ché l'un dell'altro spirto s'innamora.
Quel che nel tuo bel volto brano e 'mparo,   12
e mal compres' è dagli umani ingegni,
chi 'l vuol saper convien che prima mora.

You know that I know, my lord, that you know
that I come to take delight very near to you;
you know that I know you know I am the one:
then why still delay acknowledging each other?   4

If the hope that you give me is sincere,
if sincere is the great desire I am allowed,
then let us break down the wall between the two,
for a concealed distress attains double power.   8
If in you I only love, my dear lord,
what you most love in yourself, do not fret,
for it is one soul falling in love with another.
What I long for and learn from your fair sight   12
cannot be conceived by a human mind:
whoever wants to know, he first must die.

Regarding lines 1–2, see *Inferno* 13, 25: "*cred'io ch'ei credette ch'io credessi*" (I believe that he believed that I believed). Regarding line 12, in the language of poetry, *volto* means "sight." In line 14, *convien che prima mora* means "first one must die," in the Platonic sense of dying to the life of the senses. The repetition of *sapere* (to know) stresses the awareness of their mutual attraction and the intensity of Michelangelo's desire. The meaning of his message to the young man is predicated on the concept that "a soul falls in love with a soul" (*l'un dell'altro spirto s'innamora*). The human mind can understand such a marriage of souls only by transcending sensual perceptions.

Colui che fece, e non di cosa alcuna,
il tempo, che non era anzi a nessuno,
ne fe' d'un due e diè 'l sol alto all'uno,
all'altro assai più presso diè la luna.   4
Onde 'l caso, la sorte e la fortuna
in un momento nacquer di ciascuno;
e a me consegnaro il tempo bruno,
come a simil nel parto e nella cuna.   8
E come quel che contrafà se stesso
quando è ben notte, più buio esser suole,
ond'io di far ben mal m'affliggo e lagno.
Pur mi consola assai l'esser concesso   12
far giorno chiar mia oscura notte al sole
che a voi fu dato al nascer per compagno.

He who out of nothing created time,
which did not exist for anyone before,
of one made two, and gave one the faraway sun
and to the other he gave the close-by moon.   4
Then, in one moment, chance, destiny,
and fortune were born to everyone:
to me the murky time was given, as to one
that was like it in birth and in the cradle.   8

Just as someone who, compliant to his nature,
grows darker when the night grows deeper,
so I groan and grieve for turning good to bad.
Even so, my great comfort is that to my shady   12
night is allowed to make brighter the sun
that was given to you at birth as a companion.

The stated principle of the sonnet is the opposition between light and darkness, beauty and ugliness, heaven and earth—opposition that is the necessary premise of any Platonizing view of reality. It is also what creates and explains the artist's deep sense of inferiority toward as beautiful an object of love as Cavalieri. Such opposing duality between the two was decided at the time of creation, when God separated light from darkness and created the planets, and everyone's destiny was set.

The following poem, an exultant celebration of love, must have been written, like the other sonnets for Cavalieri, in the 1530s, the period of Michelangelo's most intense infatuation.

I' mi son caro assai più ch'i' non soglio;
poi ch'i' t'ebbi nel cor più di me vaglio,
come pietra ch'aggiuntovi l'intaglio
è di più pregio che 'l suo prio scoglio.   4
O come scritta o pinta carta o foglio
più si riguarda d'ogni straccio o taglio,
tal di me fo, da po' ch'i' fu' bersaglio
segnato dal tuo viso, e non mi doglio.   8
Sicur con tale stampa in ogni loco
vo, come quel c'ha incanti o arme seco,
c'ogni periglio gli fan venir meno.
I' vaglio contr'a l'acqua e contr'al foco,   12
col segno tuo rallumino ogni cieco,
e col mie sputo sano ogni veleno.

I am dearer to myself than I used to be
and far more precious, since I got you in my heart,
just as a marble when the carving is done
is of greater value than the original one.   4
As a page or a paper, written or painted,
is valued more than a scrap, more than a cut,
I too thought better of myself since I became
the target of your eyes, and I feel no regrets.   8
With such imprint of love, I go secure everywhere,
like a man who carries with him such talismans
and weapons that can ward off all dangers.
I triumph over water and over fire;   12
in your sign, I restore eyesight to the blind;
with my spittle, I heal all venomous sores.

Regarding line 6, paper was sold by a standard size, called *taglio*, meaning "cut." In line 8, *segnato* refers to being marked by a glance from the beloved's eyes. Regarding lines 13–14, Jesus restored light to the blind (Mark 8:22–23).

Vorrei voler, Signor, quel ch'io non voglio:
tra 'l fuoco e 'l cor di ghiaccia un vel s'asconde
che 'l foco ammorza, onde non corrisponde
la penna all'opre, e fa bugiardo 'l foglio.   4
I' t'amo con la lingua, e poi mi doglio
ch'amor non giunge al cor; né so ben onde
apra l'uscio alla grazia che s'infonde
nel cor, che scacci ogni spietato orgoglio.   8
Squarcia 'l vel tu, Signor, rompi quel muro
che con la sua durezza ne ritarda
il sol della tua luce, al mondo spenta!
Manda 'l preditto lume a noi venturo   12
alla tua bella sposa, acciò ch'io arda
il core senz'alcun dubbio, e te sol senta.

I wish I wanted, o Lord, what I do not want;
between your fire and my heart hides a veil of ice
that dampens the fire, so my pen does not equal
my deeds and makes my page a liar.   4
I love you with my tongue and afterward I wail,
for love does not reach my heart; yet I do not know
how to open the door to the grace that penetrates
the heart, so it might cast out my obdurate pride.   8
Tear away the veil, o Lord, tear down the wall
whose hardness obstructs the splendor of your light,
a light that on earth has grown so dark!
To your fair bride send the light that was   12
foretold to us, so that unhesitatingly I may set
fire to my heart and direct my feelings toward you.

In line 2, *il foco* is divine love. *Ghiaccio*, meaning "ice," represents the propensity for evil. In line 12, *a noi venturo* stands for "is predetermined" or "destined for us." In line 13, *bride*, or *sposa*, is a theological term referring to the soul. "Bride of Christ" is the expression used by the liturgy to indicate a nun entering the convent and by mystics to signify the church. The emotional intensity of this appeal for God's grace is in the repetition of the verb *volere* (to want) and in the direct address of the familiar *tu* (you) of line 5, which recurs again in lines 9 and 14.

4.6 Love Is an Onion

Born in Naples in 1520, Galeazzo di Tarsia became heir to his family estate of Belmonte, near Cosenza, Calabria, at ten years of age. The young baron proved to be of a tempestuous character and soon turned into a violent oppressor of the people on his estate. In 1547, when the local community complained about the treatment they received, the authorities deprived him of property and title and relegated him to the island of Lipari. Once back on his lands, having sought revenge, he had to face new legal procedures, and shortly afterward, at thirty-three years of age, he was murdered. Nobody ever learned by whom.

Not surprisingly, Tarsia's poetry suggests a restless and tormented personality, a proud and aggressive presence that, on the page, translates in complex, strong logical lines and rare and vigorous metaphorical designs.

> Te, lacrimosa pianta, sembra Amore,
> benché altrove i miei mal sien gemme e scogli;
> tu sola e nuda verdi germi sciogli,
> dal tuo grembo natio divelta fuore;   4
> ché è sì possente e di cotal vigore
> quella natura che da prima accogli,
> che nuovo parto a generar t'invogli
> allor che ogni altra si corrompe e muore.   8
> E' da la speme, onde si nutre e pasce,
> tolto lunga stagion, virtù non perde,
> ma spiega mille ognor freschi desiri.
> Lasso, né fredda pietra od erba verde,   12
> onda, rena, pratello, orto non nasce,
> che a tristo esempio del mio mal non giri.

> Love is like you, o tearful plant, even though,
> elsewhere, my woes are gems and rocks;
> you alone, when naked, grow green new shoots,
> even if you are uprooted from your native soil,   4
> because so powerful and so vigorous
> is the nature you possess from the start,
> that you are keen to generate new births,
> while all other plants die and putrefy.   8
> Love does not lose its power, even when
> the hope on which it feeds and lives is lost;
> for it still engenders a thousand new desires.
> Alas! Neither cold stone, nor green grass,   12
> nor wave, sand, meadow, nor orchard can be
> that I may not turn into a sad image of my ill.

In line 2, *altrove* means "elsewhere"—that is, in Tarsia's other poetic texts, where he describes the woman as a gem and, for her reluctance to reciprocate his love, compares her to a rock. He might have used precious imagery before, he says, but only the onion really resembles love. In line 3, the *verdi germi* are the greenish shoots that onions grow after they are pulled from the plant. In line 4, *grembo nativo* means "native womb," or the earth. In line 7, *nuovo parto* refers to the onion's new shoots. A simple, strong, logical structure sustains the analogy between love and the onion. The opening line declares the comparison. Lines 3–8 describe the performance of the vegetable. The first tercet explains the resemblance: just as the onion keeps growing new shoots when uprooted from the plant, love, even after rejection, continues to generate new desires. The closing three lines reassert the all-embracing power of love, which turns all elements of nature into symbols of the lover's condition.

Amor è una virtù che né per onda
pesce guizza, né crud'angue è in sentero,
né fende l'aria augel rapace e fero,
né crescse erbetta in riva o in ramo fronda,   4
né vento questa o quella agita e sfronda,
né stende corso umor, né s'erge al vero
angel puro làssu, quaggiù pensero,
né fuoco o stella spiega chioma bionda,   8
che non scaldi, addolcisca, prenda a volo,
rinverda, nutra, a mezzo corso affrene,
guidi, volga, risvegli, allume, indore.
Per sé si muove ed un oggetto ha solo: 12
bellezza e natural desio di bene;
nasce in noi di ragion, vive d'errore.

There is no fish darting through the waves,
nor a fierce snake lying on a country path,
nor a savage and rapacious bird slashing the air,
nor new grass growing on a bank nor leaf on a branch,   4
nor wind stirring and stripping this or that twig,
nor water meandering in its course, nor pure angel rising
to the truth above, nor a thought down here descending,
there is no fire, nor a star unfolding a golden tail   8
that the power of Love may not warm up, assuage, capture
in midflight, make green, nourish, refrain in the stream,
guide, turn, awaken, illuminate, and gild.
Love moves by itself and has only one aim: 12
beauty and a natural desire for good.
In us it is born of reason; it lives by error.

In line 1, *virtù* is power in the Roman sense of determination and capacity to conceive and carry a project through. The term is used in religious language to signify divine power. For reason of clarity, *Amor è una virtù* in line 1 (literaaly "Love is a power") does not appear in the translation, as "the power of Love," until line 9. In line 8, *chioma bionda*, literally "blond air," is translated here as "golden tail," for it refers to both star and fire. The subject of *scaldi* of line 9, and of all the verbs that follow, is *Amor* in line 1 of the Italian text; the things mentioned in lines 2–8, from *pesce* (fish) to *stella* (star) are the objects: there is nothing that the power of Love cannot renovate.

The concept of love as an unrestrainable presence and a force that animates all aspects of creation—a power, the poet says, that warms, nourishes, and guides everything in nature—is found in many Renaissance treatises on love. What makes Tarsia's depiction new and vibrant is the repeated exemplification of lines 1–8, which represent nature in many dynamic actions—fish darting through waves, birds slashing the air, winds stirring the branches of trees—and the logical structure that in lines 9–11 ties those images to the corresponding examples of love's power. The closing underscores the opposition between the undisturbed route of love in the natural world and the insecure, error-strewn paths it takes in the hearts of humankind.

⊱✦⊰

Come in limpido vetro o in onda pura,
se il destr'occhio del ciel risplende in lui,
mirar si può quel che ne' raggi sui
debil vista mirar non s'assicura,   4
così la mia, ch'altro veder non cura,
perde, donna real, mirando in vui
che siete un nuovo sole oggi fra nui:
ch'occhio non sano a gran splendor non dura.   8
Ma se mi volgo al cor che d'ogni parte
riceve il fogorar del vago viso,
non splende raggio in lui ch'ei non mi mostri.
Dunque a che tormi il sol de gli occhi vostri   12
se il veggio assai via men se in lui m'affiso
e lo scopro in me stesso a parte a parte?

As in a clear glass or in clean water,
when the sharp eye of heaven shines into it,
we can gaze at what, directly, in the heavenly
rays our feeble sight does not dare to stare,   4
so my sight, which to look at nothing else cares,
is overcome, o regal lady, when I look at you,
who are now a new sun among us: because
a weak eye may not sustain so great a splendor.   8
But if I turn to my heart, which receives the blaze
of your beautiful presence from everywhere, no beam
of light can shine in it that is not known to me.
Then why take fom me the sun of your eyes,   12
when I may see it much less if I stare at you,
but I can look at it in myself from side to side?

In line 6, *perde* means "vanquished." In line 10, more than the meaning of "face," *viso* has the meaning of "appearance" or "presence." In line 14, *a parte a parte* may mean either "thoroughly" or "in every part." This is a sonnet of homage to Vittoria Colonna, indicated as *nuovo sole* (new sun) in line 7. She had just arrived in Naples and had joined the society that Tarsia also frequented. His homage to her makes use of the Neoplatonic topos of the soul's transmigration from the body of the lover into that of the beloved, a theme here enriched and vigorously structured by the comparison between the power of the sun and the light in the woman's eyes: as human beings cannot stare into the sun but may look at it indirectly when it's reflected in glass or water, so the poet, who may not look directly at the lady, who is as splendid as the sun, can nonetheless see her reflected in his heart, where he keeps her always. In the last tercet, the poet reveals the reason that the preceding analogy intends to validate: there is no point in her running away from him.

Vinto da grave mal uom che non posi
in sua antica magion, debole e infermo,
cerca sotto altro ciel riparo e schermo,
ove d'arte sperar altro non osi: 4
tal io gli ostri, le gemme ed i famosi
alberghi, ove a ferir braccio ha più fermo
Amor, fuggendo in loco alpestro ed ermo
ricercai le mie paci e i miei riposi.   8
Ma perch'io vada dove folto e spesso
stuolo si prema, o dove uom non s'annide,
il mio fiero tiranno ognor m'è presso:
e s'io cavalco, ei su gli arcioni s'asside;   12
se l'onde solco, in su del legno istesso
mel veggio al fianco, e che di me si ride.

Just like a man who, weak and overcome
by serious illness, finds no rest in his old home
and looks for respite and repose under a new sky
where he can no longer look for skillful care,   4
so I—in flight from all pompous display of riches
and the famed mansions where Love can sport
a mightier arm with which to strike—have sought
rest and peace in remote and rugged places.   8
No matter: either where large and thick
crowds press on or where no man is found,
the cruel despot remains forever close by:
if I ride a horse, with me he sits on the saddle;   12
if I plough the waves, on the very boat I see
him standing by my side, laughing at me.

In line 4, *d'arte* means "by artificial means"—that is, by medical expertise. In its etymological sense, *art* indicates anything created by human skill, as opposed to what is produced by nature. The tyrant in line 11 is, of course, Love. In line 13, *legno*, meaning "wood," is a synecdoche for ship. The idea of the unhappy lover, who looks in vain for peace of mind in remote places, takes after Petrarch's lines "Yet I cannot find places so remote and savage that Love will not follow me always, speaking to me and I to him" (*Ma pur né sì aspre vie né sì selvagge / cercar non so, ch'Amor non venga sempre / ragionando con meco, et io con lui*) in "Solo e pensoso i più deserti campi" (12–14). In Tarsia's sonnet, the topos is reinvigorated by the image of Love, who keeps appearing either on the rider's saddle or at the pilot's side and laughs derisively at the man in love.

Già corsi l'Alpi gelide e canute,
mal fida siepe alle tue rive amate;
or sento, Italia mia, l'aure odorate
e l'aere pien di vita e di salute.   4
Quante m'ha dato Amor, lasso, ferute
membrando la fatal vostra beltate,
chiuse valli, alti poggi ed ombre grate,
da' ciechi figli tuoi mal conosciute!   8
O felice colui che un brieve e colto
terren fra voi possiede, e gode un rivo,
un pomo, un antro e di fortuna un volto!
Ebbi i riposi e le mie paci a schivo   12
(o giovanil desio fallace e stolto):
or vo piangendo che di lor son privo.

I've crossed the gelid and snowy mountains,
an untrustworthy barrier for this beloved land,
and now I feel again, dear Italy, your scented breezes,
your air so rich with life and with well-being.   4
Ah! How much anguish Love poured into me
whenever I remembered your fatal beauty,
your cozy valleys, your lofty hills and pleasing shades,
by your blind children so scarcely appreciated!   8
Happy is the man who in any of your lands
owns a small tilled acre, or enjoys a brook, or a cave,
or an apple, and can receive a smile from fate!
Once, I scorned my peace and my slumbers   12
(ah, foolish and rash desires of youth!);
now that I am deprived of them, I weep.

Regarding line 1, besides indicating the specific mountain range that separates Italy from the rest of Europe, the word *Alpi* has the general meaning of mountains. As Cesare Bozzetti points out, the poem is the expression of the poet's general regret for all that had been a source of happiness and was lost. It is nostalgia for the beauty of the country, the contentment with small things, and the peace they give.

There are great novelties in Tarsia's poetry. The exemplary love story, popularized by Bembo, that progressed from sinful passion to repentance and dedication to God has disappeared; so has the symmetrical, well-balanced structure of the periods. We no longer find the loveliness (*vaghezza*) and the pleasantness (*piacevolezza*) so keenly theorized by Bembo, nor can we really call Tarsia's manner *gravitas*, as some critics do, which is the manner and tone of any somber and serene meditation. Tarsia favors a fiercely consequential phrasing—a direct expression of feeling that relies on the translation of anything abstract into strong, concrete, dynamic images.

4.7 A Confessed Sensualist

Gaspara Stampa (1523–54) was a *virtuosa*—that is, an expert in some artistic field—in writing poetry and in musical performance, especially, it seems, of madrigals. A Paduan by birth and daughter of a jeweler, she lived in Venice with her mother, a sister, and a brother, who also was a poet. The family maintained a salon frequented by artists, musicians, and literati, as well as by men of the Venetian nobility. In the past, literary historians argued about Gaspara's status, whether she was really a courtesan. There are no indications that she was. She had unquestionably more than one love affair, but it was social class, not sexual morality, that, in the well-stratified Venetian society, kept her separate from the aristocratic men she loved and whose salons she frequented. In the home of the nobleman-poet Domenico Venier, Stampa met Callaltino di Collalto, a count from the Friuli region, north of Venice. Their love affair lasted three years, and most of Stampa's sonnets are expressions of her passion for him.

Stampa's poetry is usually cataloged as that of a Petrarchist. Readers can accept this only with the understanding that the mythologizing fantasy of Petrarch, Bembo, and their followers created a veil in which to hide all realistic data and biographical elements, while Stampa, when making use of phrases and similes common in love poetry, brought them into a new dimension where they acquired a performative power, open and clear confirmations of her predicaments and emotional life.

> Vieni Amor a veder la gloria mia,
> e poi la tua, che l'opra de' tuoi strali
> ha fatto ambeduo noi chiari, immortali,
> ovunque per Amor s'ama e disia.   4
> Chiara fe' me, perché non fui restia
> ad accettar i tuoi colpi mortali,
> essendo gli occhi, onde fui presa, quali
> natura non fe' mai poscia né pria;   8
> chiaro fe' te, perché a lodarti vegno
> quanto più posso in rime ed in parole
> con quella, che m'hai dato, vena e ingegno.
> Or a te si convien far che quel sole,   12

che mi desti per guida e per sostegno,
non lassi oscure queste luci e sole.

Come, Love, to see my glory and yours,
for the work of your arrows has made the two
of us immortal and legendary, wherever
there are lovers and those who long for love.   4
They made me famous, because I was not
reluctant to accept your mortal blows,
the eyes that enslaved me being so, the likes
of which Nature created neither before nor after.   8
Famous they made you, for I come to praise
you as much as I can in rhymes and words,
with the desire and talent you bestowed on me.
Now it befits you, Love, to see that the Sun   12
that you gave me for support and guide won't
leave these eyes in loneliness and in dark.

Io non v'invidio punto, angeli santi,
le vostre tante glorie e tanti beni,
e que' disir di ciò che braman pieni,
stando voi sempre a l'alto Sire avanti;   4
perché i diletti miei son tali e tanti,
che non posson capire in cor terreni
mentr'ho davanti i lumi almi e sereni,
di cui conven che sempre scriva e canti;   8
e come in ciel gran refrigerio e vita
dal volto Suo solete voi fruire,
tal io qua giù da la beltà infinita.
In questo sol vincete il mio gioire,   12
che la vostra è eterna e stabilita,
e la mia gioia può tosto finire.

I do not envy you one bit, o holy angels,
for your many glories and countless blessings,
for those longings you can entirely satisfy,
being forever present before the High Lord: 4
because my delights are so many and such
they cannot be contained in a human heart,
as long as I may gaze at the serene, soothing
eyes of which I must forever sing and write.   8
And, as in heaven you draw solace

and life from the sight of God, so can I
down here, from his unbounded beauty.
Only in one thing you exceed my happiness: 12
yours is preordained and everlasting,
while my pleasure may quickly reach its end.

Per line 3, because they wish to be in the presence of God and are, the longings of the blessed souls are satisfied in the moment of desiring—and so is hers, as long as she is in the presence of her beloved. In line 9, *refrigerio* means "solace" or "fulfillment of desire." In line 10, *fruire* means "to enjoy" or "to be satisfied." In line 13, *eterna e stabilita* is hendiadys for *stabilita in eterno*, meaning "preordained for eternity."

Per le saette tue, Amor, ti giuro,
e per la tua possente e sacra face,
che, se ben questa m'arde e 'l cor mi sface,
e quelle mi feriscon, non mi curo;   4
quantunque nel passato e nel futuro
qual l'une acute, e qual l'altra vivace,
donne amorose, e prendi qual ti piace,
che sentisser giamai né fian, né furo;   8
perché nasce virtù da questa pena,
che 'l senso del dolor vince ed abbaglia,
sì che o non duole, o non si sente appena.
Quel che l'anima e 'l corpo mi travaglia   12
è la temenza ch'a morir mi mena,
che 'l foco mio non sia foco di paglia.

On your arrows, Love, on your mighty
and sacred torch I swear that, although
one burns me and destroys my heart
and the others wound me, I do not care.   4
However far you look into the past or future,
there never were or shall be women in love
—pick whom you wish—who feel as much as I do
the power of one and the sharpness of the others: 8
for a power is born from this suffering
that overcomes and dulls any feeling of pain,
so it no longer hurts and can scarcely be felt.
What does indeed torture my body and soul   12
is the fear—a fear that drives me to distraction—
that my fire might prove to be a blaze of straw.

Here again, an abused cliché, the god of love with arrows and torch and with other traditional paraphernalia, becomes a living emblem that gives justification and weight to Gaspara's emotions. In line 6, *l'une acute*, meaning "the sharp ones," are Love's arrows, and *altra vivace* is his torch. Regarding line 8, the rather elliptical quatrain emphasizes the strength of her feeling: however far one looks into the past or the future, nowhere will one find women who felt or will feel the passion of love as strongly as she does. In line 9, *virtù* (virtue) has the etimologial Latin meaning of "power." Per line 14, Gaspara does not fear the pains of love; she is rather afraid that love might suddenly end.

⁂

O notte, a me più chiara e più beata
che i più beati giorni ed i più chiari,
notte degna da' primi e da' più rari
ingegni esser, non pur da me, lodata;   4
tu de le gioie mie sola sei stata
fida ministra; tu tutti gli amari
de la mia vita hai fatto dolci e cari,
resomi in braccio lui che m'ha legata.   8
Sol mi mancò che non divenni allora
la fortunata Alcmena, a cui sté tanto
più de l'usato a ritornar l'aurora.
Pur così bene io non potrò mai tanto   12
dir di te, notte candida, ch'ancora
da la materia non sia vinto il canto.

O night, for me more splendid and blessed
than the most blessed and splendid day,
night worthy to be praised by the first
and rarest minds, let alone by one such as I,   4
only you have been the faithful minister
of my joys; all the bitterness of my life
you made sweet and dear, returning to me,
into my arms, the man who has enchained me.   8
I only missed to be as fortunate
as Alcmene, for whom the dawn delayed
appearing well past the customary hour.
Even so, I shall never be able, o splendid night,   12
to sing so deservedly of you that still my singing
will not be exceeded by the subject of my song.

The sonnet is a celebration of the enjoyment of sexual love, a kind spurned by the authors of Platonic treatises and rarely sung in lyric poetry, especially by a woman. Regarding line 10, according to Greek legend, when Jupiter slept with Alcmene, wife of Amphitrion, he asked the sun god, Apollo, to delay the dawn so that he could prolong the night with her. Per line 14, her verse is inadequate to describe the pleasures of that night; her song, no matter how beautiful, will not come up to the beauty of the night she spent with her lover.

Collaltino di Collalto left Venice and his Venetian lover when he entered the service of the French king. Henry II was then engaged in carrying on his father's war against the emperor, Charles V, and had allied himself with the Lutheran princes who had rebelled against imperial authority. By and by, Stampa's feelings were engaged elsewhere. In time, she addressed some sonnets to Bartolomeo Zen, the Venetian nobleman with whom she was having an affair. In "Amor m'ha fatto tal ch'io vivo in foco," she proclaims that her emotional condition is not the temporary one of the lovelorn woman but a permanent, existential condition, one to which she is irremovably destined. She is proud of her passionate nature, which is as essential to her as fire is to the salamander and the phoenix.

Amor m'ha fatto tal ch'io vivo in foco,
qual nova salamandra al mondo, e quale
l'altro di lei non men stranio animale,
che vive e spira nel medesmo loco.   4
Le mie delizie son tutte e 'l mio gioco
viver ardendo e non sentire il male,
e non curar ch'ei che m'induce a tale
abbia di me pietà molto né poco.   8
A pena era anche estinto il primo ardore,
che accese l'altro Amore, a quel ch'io sento
fin qui per prova, più vivo e maggiore.   12
Ed io d'arder amando non mi pento,
pur che chi m'ha di novo tolto il core
resti de l'arder mio pago e contento.

Love has made me such that I live in fire
like a salamander, that unusual animal on earth,
and like the other no less extraordinary one
that breathes and lives in the same element.   4
All my delights and my game consist in living
by burning and not feeling any pain, nor caring
whether he, the man who has made me so,
will take pity on me, either great or small.   8
Barely was that first flame of mine extinguished
that Love kindled another, as much as I can feel
so far, stronger and sharper than the first one.
And this ardor of love I do not regret, so long   12
as he, who has made me lose my heart again,
is happy, gratified by the way I am burning.

Regarding line 2, the mythological salamander is able to remain in fire without burning. In line 3, the other strange animal is probably the phoenix. Regarding line 5, *gioco* is joy or happiness, but the word *game* better expresses what is implied here.

Stampa died in 1554. She was thirty-one years old. Her poems were published posthumously by her sister Cassandra, who gave them an order mimicking the Petrarchan spiritual itinerary from sin to redemption and dedicated the collection to the apostolic nuncio of Venice, Monsignor Giovanni della Casa, also a poet (for Della Casa, see section 5.4).

4.8 Women's Perspectives

We have seen that by adapting Petrarch's love story to the soul's Platonic ascent to the divinity, Bembo turned a poetic model into a code by which men and women could communicate with the restraint and decorum suitable to their stations in life. His strategic adaptation and example assume special historical importance also because they indicated to women how they could progress from being the objects of male writing to being subjects and authors of poetry. In 1538, the first collection of Vittoria Colonna's poems came out of the press, and afterward, publications of women's poetry began to multiply. Before the end of the century, more than two hundred volumes circulated that were either entirely authored by women or included women's verses.[90] The sonnets of this section give a glimpse of their expertise and of the perspectives that characterized their experiences in life as women and informed their poetry. I say "perspectives" in the plural because each of them saw the world from a different standpoint, according to her specific social status and personal circumstances.

Veronica Gàmbara (1485–1550) was born in a noble family of Prat'Alboino, near Brescia, Lombardy. Her father was Count Gianfrancesco Gàmbara, and her mother was Alda Pia da Carpi, sister of Emilia Pia, the woman celebrated in the pages of *The Book of the Courtier*. Veronica was also a direct descendant of two renowned female humanists, Ginevra and Isotta Nogarola. As was the custom for the daughters of the nobility, Veronica received a good humanistic education, and as we read in a letter written to her by Pietro Bembo in 1504, she began to write Italian verse at the age of sixteen. In 1530, she sent the famous literary pundit the following sonnet.

> A l'ardente desio che ognor m'accende
> di seguir nel cammin che al ciel conduce
> sol voi mancava, o mia serena luce,
> per discacciar la nebbia che m'offende.   4
> Or, poi che 'l vostro raggio in me risplende,
> per quella strada che a ben far ne induce
> vengo dietro di voi, fidato duce,
> che 'l mio voler più oltra non si stende.   8
> Bassi pensier in me non han più loco,
> ogni vil voglia è spenta: e sol d'onori
> e di rara virtù l'alma si pasce,
> dolce mio caro ed onorato foco,   12
> poscia che dal gentil vostro calore
> eterna fama e vera gloria nasce.

The burning desire that urges me
to follow the path leading to heaven
needed only you, my serene light,
to dispel the mist that conceals the way.   4
Now that your light shines on me,
I shall walk after you, my trusted guide,
on the road that goes toward the good,
for my desire is to advance no further.   8
Ignoble thoughts are in me no longer,
every vile wish is spent; only on honors
and exceptional virtues my soul is feeding,
my dear, honorable, and sweet fire,   12
because only from your noble warmth
can spring real glory and eternal fame.

Veronica proposes to become Bembo's spiritual follower. Her wish is predicated on the Platonic concept of master and disciple. Bembo replied to Gàmbara's overtures with "Quel dolce suon, per cui chiaro s'intende," a poem that is full of Platonic flourishes of reciprocation, each responding to a compliment proffered by the countess, but that courteously declines her invitation. Gàmbara and Bembo had met recently in Bologna during the ceremonies for the coronation of Charles V. That great event had occurred three years after the sack of Rome. By that time, the emperor's hold on the Italian peninsula had become unshakable, and Pope Clement VII found himself concluding a peace with him, with the coronation to follow.

In 1508, Veronica had married Giberto, count of Correggio, a condottiere who fought for the popes and for the king of Naples. The marriage had turned her into the perfect lady of the manor, patron of the arts and letters, pleasurably ensconced in her artistic home and fully appreciative of the pleasures that her social position offered. Her personality is best expressed in her letters, which exude reasonableness, elegance of manners and thought, and responsible behavior toward all, including her subjects. These traits are reflected also in the idyllic inspiration of her poetry, well suited to Bembo's norm of gracious elegance (*leggiadria*). She penned the sonnet "Sciogli le trecce d'oro" to celebrate the upcoming wedding of a family member.

Sciogli le trecce d'oro, e d'ogn' intorno
cingi le tempia de' tuoi mirti e allori,
Venere bella, e teco i santi amori
faccian concordi un dolce, almo soggiorno.   4
E tu, sacro Imeneo, cantando intorno
di vaghe rose e di purpurei fiori
col plettro d'oro in versi alti e sonori
rendi onorato questo altero giorno.   8
E voi tutti, o gran dei, che de' mortali
siete al governo, a man piena spargete
gioia, pace, dolcezza, amore e fede,

> acciò che i casti baci e l'ore liete,
> spese tra due, sieno felici e tali
> che dar non possa il ciel altra mercede.   12

> Untie your golden tresses and around us
> deck your temples with myrtle and laurel,
> o lovely Venus, and the blessed loves may always
> reside with you in sweet, life-giving harmony.   4
> And you, o sacred Hymen, singing around us
> of delicate roses and purple flowers,
> with high-sounding rhymes on the golden lire,
> do bestow on this day your greatest honors.   8
> And all of you, great gods, governors
> of us mortals, at full hand pour forth peace,
> happiness, love, fidelity, and pleasantness,
> and the chaste embraces and joyful hours   12
> spent together may be perfect and greater
> than any joy the heavens can provide.

Gàmbara has transformed a familiar event into a classical pastoral celebration. In line 1, the expression *trecce d'oro* comes directly from Petrarch's *Canzoniere* 37, 81. Regarding line 2, the myrtle was a plant sacred to Venus, and the laurel alludes to the goddess's love conquests. See *Canzoniere* 270, 65. In line 3, *teco* means "with you"—that is, with Venus. Here, Gàmbara makes a distinction between "blessed loves" and the sexual love the goddess symbolizes. Regarding line 5, Hymen, or Hymenaeus, was the god of weddings and marital love. In line 7, the plectrum is the ivory chip used for plucking the lyre. Regarding line 10, "*Manibus date lilia plenis*," says Virgil in *Aeneid* 6, 883. We may alternatively consider *rose e purpurei fiori* dependent on *rendi onorato* and read "honor this day with delicate roses and purple flowers." Roses and purple flowers may symbolize bashfulness and passion. This epithalamium, or wedding poem, was probably written in 1529 for the wedding of Brunoro, Gàmbara's brother, and Virginia Pallavicini, the widowed daughter-in-law of Alessandro Farnese, the future Pope Paul III.

When Giberto died in 1550, Veronica became the de facto ruler of Correggio and gave proof of being a shrewd diplomat. She defended her domain from direct military attack by balancing her negotiations between potential aggressors. Her idyllic vision of the countryside and her good classical education blend harmoniously in the upcoming sonnet, an erudite homage to Charles V. From Bologna, where the pope had crowned him, the emperor was traveling through her territory to a destination beyond the Alps.

> Là dove più con le sue lucid'onde
> il picciol Mella le campagne infiora
> de la mia patria, e che girando onora
> di verd'erbe e di fiori ambe le sponde,   4
> al gran nome real, che copre e asconde
> le nostre glorie e quelle antiche ancora,
> farò un tempio d'avorio, e dentro e fuora

mille cose vedransi alme e gioconde. 8
Sarà nel mezzo una gran statua d'oro,
e dirà 'l titol: "Quest'è Carlo Augusto,
maggior di quanti mai ebber tal nome."
D'intorno i vinti regi, e al par di loro 12
fuggir vedrassi il Turco empio ed ingiusto
giungendo a' suoi trionfi altere some.

There, where with its shining waves
the tiny Mella makes the meadows of my
homeland bloom and, in turning, creates
green meadows and flowers on either bank, 4
to your great royal name, which overshadows
our glories and the ancient ones as well,
I shall erect an ivory temple, and inside and out
a thousand happy inspiring things we will see. 8
In the middle, there will be a great statue of gold;
its inscription will proclaim, "This is Charles Augustus,
greater than anyone who bore that name before."
Around it, all the vanquished kings, as well as 12
the unjust and ungodly Turk, will be seen in flight,
adding a superior greatness to Charles's triumphs.

Regarding line 2, Mella is a small river crossing the territory of Correggio. Regarding line 11, Veronica's poetic monument to the emperor has a precedent in Virgil's *Eclogue* 3, 12–16, in which he says that in his city of Mantua—which is not far from Correggio—he will erect a temple covered by tender reeds near the meandering waters of the Mincio River, and in the middle of the temple, he will place a statue of Caesar Augustus (*viridi in campo templum de marmore ponam / propter aquam, tardis ingens ubi flexibus errat / Mincius et tenera praetexit arundine ripas. / In medio mihi Caesar erit templumque tenebit*).

Charles V was traveling to Austria and Germany. Trouble loomed in both countries: in Germany, his brother Ferdinand was having difficulties with the Lutheran rebellion; in Austria, the Turks were about to attack Vienna. The emperor made a stop to visit Gàmbara on his way north and on his way back. One of the attractions of Gàmbara's domain was the Palazzo delle Delizie, the so-called *casino*, which she had decorated expressly for the emperor's visit. In line 13, the Turk was Suleiman the Great. The idea of these added poetic ornaments, all illustrations of Charles's valor, is also straight from the third *Eclogue*, wherein Vigil's temple doors depict the Roman campaigns in Armenia, Persia, and Afghanistan (lines 26–36). The erudite references, hopefully not lost on Charles, and the passing description of Correggio's beautiful surroundings cloak the political flattery in gracious formality.

Tullia d'Aragona (1510–56) was a courtesan, albeit a high-class one—a point that she studiously endeavored to impress on people with her manners, lifestyle, and literary choices. She was renowned for intelligence, education, and wit. She entrusted her criticism of the dominant philosophical culture to a dialogue, *On the Infinity of Love*, and wrote poetry in the Petrarchan manner. The following sonnet is her expression of thanks to the duke of Tuscany, Cosimo de' Medici, who had decided a judicial controversy in her favor.[91] In 1547, when a new regulation prescribed that all courtesans were to wear a yellow veil when walking in the street, Tullia, who never wore one, was denounced as a common prostitute. The duke, appealed to by a literary friend of hers, exonerated Tullia on account of her being a poet and also versed in philosophy.[92] The relation between Aragona and her addressee was naturally different from the one existing between the aristocratic Gàmbara and the emperor or Bembo, but the intelligent courtesan, grateful for being saved from a humiliating regulation, made up for the disparity in social standing with much grace, literary skill, and wit.

> Se gli antichi pastor di rose e fiori
> sparsero i tempii e vaporar gli altari
> d'incensi a Pan, sol perché dolci e cari
> havea fatto a le ninfe i suoi amori,   4
> quai fior degg'io, o Signor, quai deggio
> sparger al nome vostro che sian pari odori
> a i merti vostri, e tanti e così rari,
> ch'ogni hor spargete in me grazie e favori?   8
> Nessun per certo tempio, altare o dono
> trovar si può di così gran valore
> ch'a vostra alta bontà sia pregio eguale.
> Sia dunque il petto vostro, u' tutte sono   12
> le virtù, tempio; altare il saggio core,
> vittima, l'alma mia, se tanto vale.

> If the ancient shepherds strewed roses and flowers
> in Pan's temples and scented the altars
> with incense only because he had made
> their loves agreeable and dear to the nymphs,   4
> what flowers should I then, o Lord, what
> perfumes must I scatter on your name
> that may be equal to your merits,
> which are so many and so rare, and on you,   8
> who pour over me graces and favors?
> No temple, no alter, no gift could surely
> be found so unlimited in worth that might be
> of a value equal to your great beneficence.   12
> May, then, your breast—which the virtues
> inhabit—be the temple, your wise heart the alter,
> and the victim my soul, should I be so deserving.

Regarding line 1, Pan, the Greek god of shepherds and flocks, was in the habit of wandering in the fields of Arcadia, playing the flute and leading the nymphs to the dance. Worshippers brought to his alter incense, flowers, and fruit. In line 2, the word *tempii* (temples), repeated in the singular in lines 9 and 13, has a well-known celebratory connotation, for *tempio* was used to indicate both a poem and an anthology of poems written to celebrate someone. Per line 14, Tullia offers herself as the sacrificial victim to Cosimo's alter.

The sonnet is a suggestive homage expertly constructed. Aragona presents her thankfulness in the form of a question and balances it on the correspondence between the classical scene of the first four lines and her own situation in the next four. In the first quatrain, a pagan landscape comes to life, where nymphs and shepherds in love, thankful for favors received, offer flowers and incense to the god Pan. In the second quatrain, Aragona's thanks and gratitude to the duke are flatteringly allusive. By wondering whether flowers and incense would be sufficient offerings for Cosimo, who has done so much for her, she metamorphoses the eighteen-year-old duke into a sensual pagan divinity. In myth, the god Pan was represented with horns and a goat's feet—a divinity, Tullia specifies, that allowed the shepherds to make love to the nymphs. The answer to the question of how she can thank him adequately comes in the sestet. In the first three lines, she praises him deferentially; her turn of phrase becomes subtly suggestive in the closing tercet, where her soul is offered as sacrificial victim on the altar of the duke's heart.

Qual vaga Philomela, che fuggita
è da l'odiata gabbia, et in superba
vista se n' va tra arboscelli e l'erba,
tornata in libertate e in lieta vita, 4
er'io da gli amorosi lacci uscita
schernendo ogni martire e pena acerba
de l'incredibil duol, ch'in sé riserba
qual ha per troppo amar l'alma smarrita. 8
Ben havev'io ritolte (ahi stella fera!)
dal tempio di Ciprigna le mie spoglie,
e di lor pregio me ne andava altera,
quand' a me Amor "Le tue ritrose voglie 12
muterò" disse, e femmi prigioniera
di tua virtù, per rinovar mie doglie.

Like fair Philomela, who just has flown
the hated cage and—a cocky sight to see—
hops about on grass and branches, I too,
going back to freedom and to a cheery 4
life, did escape all lovers' chains and did
jeer at the suffering, at the bitter hurts
and the incredible sorrows that chafe those
who have lost their souls for too much loving. 8
But from the Cyprian temple (ah, cruel
star!), I had barely retrieved my spoils,
feeling so very proud of their worth,

when Love said to me, "I shall change
your wayward ways," and, to renew my cares,
has made me a prisoner of your charms.   12

In line 1, Philomela stands for a nightingale. By comparing herself to that bird, the poetic bird par excellence, Aragona stresses her status as a poet. This nightingale has nothing to do with the gruesome Greek myth. According to that story, Philomela was the daughter of Pandion, king of Athens, and sister of Procne, who was married to Tereus, king of Thrace. When Tereus raped his sister-in-law, Philomela, and cut out her tongue to prevent her from complaining, the two sisters took revenge on him by killing Itys, Tereus and Procne's son, and serving the body of the child at the father's dinner table (Ovid, *Metamorphoses* 6, 424–674). Regarding line 10, the Cyprian goddess is the Greek Aphrodite, called Cyprian because she sprang from the sea foam near the island of Cyprus, which was the principle site of her worship. The practical Romans identified Aphrodite with Venus, their goddess of fertility and the harvest. The Roman generals deposited their trophies in the Temple of Mars when the war was over. Aragona instead took them out because she thought her battle with Love had been won.

A sense of self and a wish to acquire fame as a poet are strongly claimed in the following sonnet addressed to Piero Mannelli, a young man Aragona loved.

Poi che mi diè natura a voi simile
forma e materia, o fosse il gran Fattore,
non pensate ch'ancor desio d'onore
mi desse e bei pensier, Manel gentile?   4
Dunque credete me cotanto vile,
ch'io non osi mostrar cantando fore
quel che dentro m'ancide altero ardore,
se bene a voi non ho pari lo stile?   8
Non lo crediate, no, Piero; ch'anch'io
fatico ognor per appressarmi al cielo,
e lasciar del mio nome in terra fama.
Non contenda rea sorte il bel desio,   12
ché pria che l'alma dal corporeo velo
si sciolga, satierò forse mia brama.

Since Nature—or was it the great Creator?—
bestowed on me matter and form, as she did on you,
don't you believe, kind Manelli, that to me too
she granted lofty thoughts and a wish for fame?   4
Then do you think me so low-spirited
that I would not dare manifest in verse
how fiercely an ardor gnaws at me inside,
though my style may not be equal to yours?   8
Do not believe it, Piero, do not, for I too
persistently strive to get near the stars
and leave on earth a memory of my name.

> May no adverse fate contest my noble aim
> and so perhaps, before my soul is released
> by this bodily veil, my desire will be satisfied. 12

Regarding line 2, in Thomas Aquinas's interpretation of Aristotelian philosophy, matter and form are understood to be body and soul. In line 13, the poet uses "bodily veil" because the body is thought to be the veil of the soul.

Barbara Torelli (ca. 1475–1533), daughter of Marsilio II, fourth count of Montechiarugolo, was born at Guastalla, in northern Italy, in 1475. In 1491, she married Ercole Bentivoglio, and in Ferrara, their house became a gathering place for courtiers and literati. By 1503, Barbara found herself in the eye of a stormy scandal: she was legally separated from Bentivoglio, lived in an open relationship with Ercole Strozzi, and was embroiled in a complex and lengthy litigation with her husband in the attempt to retrieve from him her conspicuous dowry. In 1507, Bentivoglio died, and Torelli married her lover. One year later, Strozzi was murdered. The circumstances of the murder were never brought to light, and the culprit was not apprehended.

> Spenta è d'amor la face, il dardo è rotto,
> e l'arco e la faretra e ogni sua possa,
> poiché ha morte cruel la pianta scossa,
> a la cui ombra cheta io dormia sotto. 4
> Deh, perché non poss'io la breve fossa
> seco entrar dove hallo il destin condotto,
> colui che a pena cinque giorni ed otto
> Amor legò pria de la gran percossa? 8
> Vorrei col foco mio quel freddo ghiaccio
> intepidire, e rimpastar col pianto
> la polve e ravvivarla a nuova vita,
> e vorrei poscia, baldanzosa e ardita, 12
> mostrarlo a lui che ruppe il caro laccio,
> e dirgli "Amor, mostro crudel, può tanto."

> Extinguished is the torch of Love, wrecked are
> his dart, his quiver, his bow, and all his power,
> since cruel Death has shaken down the tree
> in whose shade I was so peaceably resting. 4
> Ah! Why, may I too not enter, with him,
> the narrow tomb where destiny has led him,
> the man whom Love had tied to me scarcely
> five days and eight, before the deadly blow? 8
> With my fire I would like to thaw that gelid
> ice, with my tears I would like to remold

> that dust and revive him to good new life;
> and afterward, challenging and daringly, to the 12
> one who broke the dear tie I would show him
> and say, "Cruel monster, Love can do this much!"

Regarding lines 1–2, Love was customarily depicted holding a torch that represented passion and carrying a quiver full of darts with which he shot people and made them fall in love. In line 3, the tree represents the man under whose protection the woman lived securely. Regarding line 6, Barbara gave birth to Strozzi's child—this is the new tie of love mentioned here—thirteen days before his murder. The child was a baby girl named Giulia, who, in 1518, was betrothed to Alberto Gazolo of Reggio Emilia by wish of Pope Leo X (Catalano 66, 95). After the first declarative quatrain, Barbara's passionate cry of grief takes off rapidly with some daring ideas and images: she would like to jump into her lover's tomb, warm up his cold body with the flame of her passion, and knead his ashes back to life, and then, pointing proudly at him, she would shout to the murderer that death cannot do anything against the power of love.

Besides being a diplomat, Ercole Strozzi was a renowned poet. He was ugly, small, and lame, but according to contemporaries, he was a brilliant conversationalist and a man of great charm. He had been the pupil of Aldo Manuzio and of his own father, the famed humanist Tito Vespasiano Strozzi. His Latin poetry is outstanding among much written in Latin during the Renaissance. He was a friend of Ariosto and Bembo. The latter made him a character in the dialogue *Prose della volgar lingua*. Lucrezia Borgia, the wife of Duke Alfonso d'Este, was a friend of Torelli, helped her in her affair with Strozzi, and protected her from the ire of Bentivoglio. After the murder, Barbara lived in impoverished circumstances—she never got any money from Bentivoglio, while the surviving Strozzi brothers contested her Strozzi inheritance. Even so, she took care of her children by both her husbands, as well as Strozzi's children from a previous marriage.

Torelli had also a tormented afterlife. Her poetry came out in print for the first time in *Rime scelte de' poeti ferraresi antichi e moderni*, a volume published in Ferrara by Pomatelli in 1713, but her work was soon forgotten, and even her existence was denied. Modern anthologies have attributed the above sonnet, which became famous among contemporaries and was included in several verse collections of her time, to Ludovico Ariosto.[93]

The following sonnet is by Isabella di Morra (1520–46), daughter of Giovanni Michele Morra, baron of Favale, in the southern region of Basilicata.

> D'un alto monte ove si scorge il mare
> miro sovente io, tua figlia Isabella,
> s'alcun legno spalmato in quello appare,
> che di te, padre, a me doni novella. 4
> Ma la mia avversa e dispietata stella
> non vuol ch'alcun conforto possa entrare
> nel tristo cor, ma di pietà rubella
> la salda speme in pianto fa mutare: 8
> ch'io non veggo nel mar remo né vela

(così deserto é l'infelice lido)
che l'onde fenda, o che la gonfi il vento.
Contra Fortuna allor spargo querela,   12
ed ho in odio il denigrato sito,
come sola cagion del mio tormento.

From a high mountain, where I can see
the sea, I, your daughter Isabella, often
look out for any shining ship to appear
and bring me news of you, dear father.   4
But my adverse, unyielding star does not
want any relief to come and comfort
my melancholy heart and, adverse to pity,
changes my strong hope into weeping,   8
for I see neither oar plowing the waves
nor a sail billowing in the wind,
so deserted is this forsaken shore.
Against Fortune I therefore pour forth   12
my lament, detesting this hideous place,
which is the single cause of my despair.

In line 1, *alto monte* is the high hill of Favale, on which the castle of the Morra barons was perched in a remote zone not far from a deserted seacoast.[94] There lived Isabella, her mother, and two of her brothers. Regarding line 4, Isabella's father, Giovanni Michele Morra, and two more brothers were then living at the French court. In 1528, Francis I of France had invaded the Neapolitan kingdom, and Giovanni Michele had sided with the French general, Odet de Foix de Lautrec, who was besieging Naples. After Lautrec's death and the defeat of his army, Morra and the two older sons took refuge in France, leaving the rest of the family at Favale. In lines 5–8, the vision of a ship appearing on the horizon embodies Isabella's anguished need for a better life and for compatible companionship. Her hope was that one day her father would ask her to join him in France. In lines 11–14, the anguish caused by a family unsympathetic to her needs is reflected in a nature seemingly desolate and hostile.

At the age of twenty-six, Isabella was murdered by the brothers who lived with her. Apparently, the correspondence she had started with Diego Sandoval di Castro, a nobleman and poet who periodically took up residence in a property nearby, aroused their rage. The police who investigated the case discovered Morra's small collection of poetry—ten sonnets and three songs—in the castle.

Chiara Matraini (1514–ca. 1597) was a citizen of Lucca, Tuscany, born in a family of well-to-do artisans. Lucca was an independent oligarchic republic in which political power was restricted to a few clans who owned extensive land and monopolized the city's commercial and banking interests. In 1531, Matraini's brother and an uncle were among the organizers of the *straccioni* rebellion, which sought to obtain access to public office for the middle and lower classes. During the uprising, the rebels held minor administrative positions, but when the rebellion was crushed, they had to surrender all their gains.

Widowed when still young, Matraini embarked on a relationship with Bartolomeo Graziani, a poet and son-in-law of a prominent citizen. Besides being shunned by her community because of her personal conduct, Matraini suffered from the continued hostility of relatives and political factions. Even so, she maintained a proud demeanor and a high tone in life and in her literary production. The poems she wrote for Graziani came out in 1555. She went on to live into old age, writing much verse and prose, all of religious character.

> Fera son di questo ombroso loco,
> che vo con la saetta in mezzo al core,
> fuggendo, lassa, il fin del mio dolore,
> e cerco chi mi strugge a poco a poco.   4
> E com' augel che fra le penne il foco
> si sente acceso, onde volando fuore
> dal dolce nido suo, mentre l'ardore
> fugge, con l'ale più raccende il foco;   8
> tal io fra queste fronde a l'aura estiva
> con l'ali del desio volando in alto,
> cerco il foco fuggir che meco porto.
> Ma quanto vado più di riva in riva   12
> per fuggir 'l mio mal, con fiero assalto
> lunga morte procaccio al viver corto.

> A wild animal am I in this eerie place,
> with an arrow driven through my heart,
> running away, alas, from what could end my pains,
> looking for him who is slowly destroying me.   4
> And like a bird who, feeling a flame ablaze
> in its feathers, flies off the beloved nest,
> and the more it runs away from that fire,
> the more with its wings it fans the flame,   8
> likewise in the summer breeze I fly high
> among the trees, on the wings of my desire,
> trying to escape the ardor I carry within me.
> But the further I run from field to field   12
> to elude my ills, more surely, in a brutal fight,
> I secure a lingering death to my short life.

Matraini's style is high, and her tone is tragic throughout. In lines 1–2, the image of the running deer with an arrow wedged in his heart is taken from Petrarch's *Canzoniere* 209, 9–11: "As a deer that, wounded by an arrow, flees and, the more he hurries, greater becomes his pain" (*e qual cervo ferito di saetta / col ferro avvelenato dentr'al fianco / fugge e più duolsi quanto più s'affretta*). It was also used by Bembo: see section 4.4. Per line 3, dying would be the end of the lover's pain. In line 13, *riva* is the poetic term for a pleasant spot in the country—a grassy meadow, for instance. *Assalto* means "attack" or "fight" and is a term from *Canzoniere* 148, 9–10. Notwithstanding the Petrarchan bucolic reminiscences,

Petrarch's idyllic, elegiac tone is missing. The nature Matraini describes is rather intimidating; strong are her sense of pain and her hopelessness of flight. The image of the deer that aimlessly tries to escape the pain he carries within poignantly emphasizes the paradox created by the two opposing properties of love: one that destroys and another that gives the strength to live and to hope.

Alti son questi monti et alti sono
li miei pensier di cui l'alma s'ingombra;
questi sol piante sterili gl'adombra,
le mie speranze senza frutto sono. 4
Scendon fonti da lor con alto suono,
contrari venti a le lor cime et ombra
di nubi stanno, e 'l duol da me disgombra
pianto e sospir di cui sempre ragiono. 8
Nemiche fere in essi, empie e rapaci
s'annidan solo, e nel mio petto alberga
fiera doglia, che 'l cor m'ange e divora.
Godon pur questi le superne faci 12
qualor vil nebbia almo seren disperga,
mai i' non vedo 'l sol che l'alma adora.

High are these mountains, and high
are the thoughts that burden my soul.
Only barren plants shade these summits,
and my hopes no fruit are destined to bear. 4
High-sounding rivers flow down their slopes,
contrary winds and dark clouds blow against
their peaks: for him, who is always in my mind,
my sorrow draws sighs and tears out of me. 8
Hostile, vicious, and rapacious beasts nest
in them: in my breast a brutal grief dwells
that distresses and devours my heart.
Yet these mountains enjoy the sun above, 12
when good weather dispels all shadowy mist:
I can never see the sun my soul adores.

In line 8, *ragionare* means "to talk." In line 5, *contrari venti* comes from *Canzoniere* 132, 10. In line 11, *angere* is an old form of *dolere*, meaning "to aggrieve." In line 12, *superne faci* means "torches above," or the sun. *Cor tristo ange* is from *Canzoniere* 148, 6. There is a new solemnity in Matraini's verse, a sense of impending tragedy; dark, almost threatening images are the counterpoint to her somber and stressed feelings.

5
Humankind, the Universe, and Death

5.1 Ironists and Subversives

In "Chiome d'argento fine," Francesco Berni has fun mimicking "Crin d'oro crespo," a sonnet of Pietro Bembo (see 4.4) admiringly and repeatedly quoted in sixteenth-century treatises on poetry.

Chiome d'argento fine, irte e attorte
senz'arte intorno a un bel viso d'oro;
fronte crespa, u' mirando io mi scoloro,
dove spuntan gli strali Amore e Morte; 4
occhi di perla vaghi, luci torte
da ogni obbietto diseguale a loro;
ciglia di neve, e quelle, ond'io m'accoro,
dita e man dolcemente grosse e corte; 8
labbra di latte, bocca ampia celeste,
denti d'ebano rari e pellegrini,
inaudita ineffabile armonia;
costumi alteri e gravi: a voi, divini 12
servi d'Amor, palese fo che queste
son le bellezze della donna mia.

Thin, bristling, entangled silvery hair,
artlessly encircling a fine goldish face,
a wrinkled forehead, which I gape at and pale,
in which Love and Death blunt their arrows, 4
delightful eyes of pearl, lights that turn away
from everything but from one another,
lashes of snow and—this breaks my heart!—
fingers and hands sweetly chubby and stumpy, 8
lips as white as milk, a mouth celestially wide,
with dispersed, dwindling teeth of ebony
—unspeakable, unheard-of symmetry!—

as well as a heavy and swaggering bearing.
These, I make clear, are, o divine servants
of Love, the many beauties of my woman. 12

In line 1, Berni ridicules Bembo's description of his woman by substituting and transposing words and characteristics so that the qualifications are the wrong ones or are attributed to the wrong object. In Bembo's poem, the woman's hair looks like *oro fino* (pure gold); in Berni's sonnet, *chiome d'argento fine* are the gray strands of hair of an old woman going bald. Regarding line 3, Bembo's piercing pains of love were soothed by the woman's smile; Berni pales because he is frightened by the woman's disagreeable looks. Per line 4, her ugliness has blunted the arrows of Love; even Death is frightened by her. Per lines 5–6, her pupils are as whitish as pearls due to thick cataracts. Bembo's woman would look away from anything unworthy of her. Berni's woman is cross-eyed. In lines 9–10, lips of milk and teeth of ebony that are rare and wobbly substitute Bembo's "rubies and pearls." Regarding line 12, the graceful and dignified demeanor of the beloved was traditional; this woman is rude and moves awkwardly on heavy haunches.

Critics widely agree that while Berni disapproved of the Petrarchan fad in poetry, he did not object to courtly principles and values. He seemed to propose a less artificial literary model, one more connected with life and everyday reality. Born in a good Tuscan family, Berni (1497–1535) moved to Rome to enter the service of Cardinal Bernardo Bibbiena, a relative of his, who, in his opinion, never did him anything bad or anything good (quoted by Borsellino 42). In time, he became secretary to Giovan Matteo Giberti, bishop of Verona and papal datary—head of the papal chancery. Giberti was a serious and religious man bent on reforming the church and the habits of its members. In that period, an intense enmity developed between Giberti and Aretino, the latter attacking the datary and the curia with a slanderous fury that infurated the authorities, who, in the end, forced him to leave Rome (for Aretino, see 4.3 and below). Berni's satire, on the other hand, although impatient with hypocrisy and selfishness, is never destructive toward a society whose values and taste he shared. The following two-tailed sonnets were penned in February 1529, during the illness of Pope Clement VII.

Questo è un voto che papa Clemente
a questa Nostra Donna ha sodisfatto,
perché di man d'otto medici un tratto
lo liberò miracolosamente. 4
Il pover'uom non aveva niente;
e se l'aveva, non l'aveva affatto;
questi sciagurati avevan tanto fatto,
che l'amazzavan resolutamente. 8
Al fin Dio l'aiutò, che la fu intesa;
e detton la sentenza gli orinali,
che 'l papa aveva avut'un po' di scesa.
E la vescica fu de' cardinali, 12
che per venir a riformar la chiesa
s'avevan già calzati gli stivali.
Voi, maestri cotali,
medici da guarir tigna e tinconi, 16

sète un branco di ladri e di castroni.

> This is due to a vow that Pope Clement
> made to Our Lady, who, with one stroke,
> miraculously, has liberated him
> from the nasty grasp of eight doctors. 4
> The poor man had no diseases whatever;
> and if he had one, he did not have it;
> those scoundrels had so manipulated
> they were about to kill him resolutely. 8
> God helped him in the end, for it was clear
> —the chamber pots gave their verdict—
> the pope suffered from a touch of the runs.
> So all the bother was for the cardinals, 12
> those who were about to put on their boots,
> eager to come here to reform the church.
> You, doctors and experts,
> good to cure nothing but pimples and boils, 16
> you are a bunch of robbers and boobs.

In lines 5–8, the ridicule falls on the often confusing, cautious, and sometimes contradictory pronouncement of the doctors: the pope had a disease; he did not have that disease. In line 17, *castrone* means "dolt" or "moron." The sonnet brings the pope down to the level of any common sick old man, but the satire is gentle, and the tone is almost affectionate. In the tail, Berni apostrophizes doctors and specialists as boobs because they do not know how to cure the pontiff and as robbers because they take advantage of their position to boost their reputation and fill their pockets.

In the sonnet "Fate a modo d'un vostro servitore," the denunciation of the medical profession continues, but Berni's voice takes on an even more familiar tone toward the suffering old man.

> Fate a modo d'un vostro servitore,
> il qual vi dà consigli sani e veri:
> non vi lasciate metter più cristeri,
> che per Dio vi faranno poco onore. 4
> Padre santo, io vel dico mo di cuore:
> costor son mascellari e mulattieri,
> e vi tengon nel letto volentieri
> perché si dica: "Il Papa ha male, e' muore;" 8
> e che son forte dotti in Galieno,
> per avervi tenuto allo spedale,
> senz'esser morto, un mese e mezzo almeno.
> E fanno mercanzia del vostro male: 12
> han sempre il petto di polizze pieno,
> scritte a questo e quell'altro cardinale.
> Pigliate un orinale

SONNET • 267

e date lor con esso nel mostaccio:
levate noi di noia, e voi d'impaccio.   16

Do what a servant of yours tells you,
one who gives you good and healthy advice:
don't let them give you any more enemas,
which, for heaven's sake, do you little honor.   4
My Holy Father, I speak from the heart:
these are butchers! They are mule drivers,
they are pleased to keep you in bed,
so they can say, "The pope is ill; he's dying;"   8
that they themselves are versed in Galen's art
because they have kept you in hospital almost
a month and a half, and you have not died!
They make a trade of your illness,   12
their chest pocket is always full of notes
addressed to this and to the other cardinal.
Now, take a chamber pot
and whack it on their faces: free us   16
of this nuisance, and yourself of shame.

Berni's report on the cure administered to the pope continues. He denounces the practice of doctors for being disrespectful toward His Holiness; nonetheless, on his part, he talks about the condition and the treatment received by the eminent patient rather cavalierly. The coda concludes with a fitting suggestion. Behind Berni's outburst is the view of a crowd of people—one would be tempted to say a multitude of reporters—standing around the doors of the Vatican, waiting to hear the upcoming medical bulletin.

In order to give free rein to his satire in "Non vadan più pellegrini o romei," Berni needed as many as six tails, each a more pungent postscript to the entertaining descriptions preceding it.

Non vadan più pellegrini o romei
la quaresima a Roma alle stazzoni,
giù per le scale sante ginocchioni,
pigliando l'indulgenze e i giubilei;   4
né contemplando li archi e' colisei,
e ponti, li aquedutti e' settezzoni,
e la torre ove stette in doi cestoni
Vergilio, spenzolato da colei.   8
Se vanno là per fede, o per desio
di cose vecchie, vengan qui a diritto,
ché l'uno e l'altro mostrerò lor io.
Se la fede è canuta, come è scritto,   12
io ho mia madre e due zie e un zio,
che son la fede d'intaglio e di gitto.

Paion gli dei d'Egitto,
che son de gli altri dei suoceri e nonne, 16
e furno inanzi a Deucalionne.
Gli omeghi e l'ipsilonne
han più proporzion ne' capi loro,
e più misura, che non han costoro. 20
Io li stimo un tesoro,
e mostrerogli a chi gli vuol vedere
per anticaglie naturali e vere.
L'altre non sono intiere: 24
a qual manca la testa, a qual le mani;
son morte, e paion state in man de' cani.
Questi son vivi e sani,
e dicon che non voglion mai morire: 28
la morte chiama, et ei la lascian dire.
Dunque chi s'ha a chiarire
dell'immortalità di vita eterna,
venga a Firenze nella mia taverna.

Neither pilgrims nor Romei should
any longer travel to the stations in Rome,
go up and down the holy stairs on their knees,
in order to pick up indulgences and jubilees, 4
and gape at arches and at coliseums,
at bridges, aqueducts, and *settezzoni*,
at the very tower from which a woman
left Virgil hanging in two chests. 8
If they go for their faith or out of a yearning
for old junk, they should come here instead,
where I would show them one and the other.
If Faith is white-haired, as they write, 12
here I have mother, one uncle, and two aunts
who are Faith sculpted in bronze and stone.
They look like some Egyptian divinities,
like grandparents and parents-in-law of gods; 16
they were alive far long before Deucalion!
The epsilon and the omega show
better measurements and proportion
in their shapes than these ones do. 20
I do treasure them a lot and,
to all who desire to see, I'll show
them as real and natural antiquities.
Those over there are not intact, 24
in some the head, in others the hands are missing:

they're dead; they seem to have been gnawed by dogs.
Mine are alive and kicking,
they say they never want to die: 28
Death calls them, and they let him call.
So whoever needs to clarify his ideas
about immortality (i.e., eternal life), he ought to come
to Florence and take a look into my modest house.

Regarding line 1, *Romei* were the pilgrims bound for Rome. Regarding line 2, to pick up indulgences, pilgrims had to visit a prescribed number of churches, called stations (*stazzoni*). The stations were, and still are, the basilicas of St. Peter, St. Paul Outside the Walls, St. John in Lateran, and Santa Maria Maggiore. Regarding line 3, in St. John in Lateran, a *scala santa* (holy stair) leads up to a relic supposedly taken from Pontius Pilate's quarters in Jerusalem. To get their indulgences, the pilgrims must go up the stairs on their knees, just as Christ is believed to have done when he was taken to Golgotha. Regarding line 4, pilgrims cannot pick up jubilees, of course; what the faithful who pray at the above-mentioned basilicas may obtain is the plenary indulgence that the pope grants every twenty-five years. Berni mixes up various terms for comic effect. In line 6, *settezzone* refers to an ancient seven-floor apartment building, where each floor exhibited a different style of column. Regarding lines 7–8, Virgil had been a popular figure throughout the ages, and many unlikely stories were told about him. One story was that the emperor's daughter promised to pull him up to her bedroom in a basket. However, she left him hanging midway outside the tower all night, and when morning came, he was still there, exposed to the gibes of his fellow Romans. Berni mentions two baskets, perhaps to make the word *cestoni*, in the plural, rhyme with *settezzoni*. In line 12, Faith is described as white-haired—*Cana fides*, per Virgil in *Aeneid* 1, 282—because Faith is old and difficult to eradicate. In line 14, *d'intaglio e di gitto* means, literally, "by carving and by casting." *Getto* is the jet of metal and, by extension, the foundry.[95] Regarding line 17, Greek mythology too had a universal flood legend. Deucalion, son of Prometheus, and his wife, Pyrrha, were the only mortals that Zeus saved when he decided to flood the world. When the water withdrew, Deucalion and Pyrrha repopulated the world, just as Noah and his wife do in the Bible. Regarding line 18, the Greek epsilon is thin, and the omega is wide. In line 26, *cani* means "infidels" (Longhi, in Gorni 2001, 861). Regarding line 32, *taverna* more often means "tavern," but here it describes a modest living quarter.

Berni's *sonettessa*—this is the name given to a sonnet with several tails—bruised the sensibilities of some critics who saw in it too disrespectful and gleeful a mockery of religion. Their disapproval might be due to the ambiguous comparison between the immortality enjoyed by the poet's relatives and the immortality strenuously sought by the pilgrims in Rome. For another sonnet by Berni, see 4.3.

By 1525, the Roman moral climate had changed. Pietro Aretino's ferocious attacks on high-placed people outraged the Roman authorities. While they could still tolerate Berni's mild satirical vein, they considered the vitriolic humors and scandalous behavior of the likes of Aretino beyond the limits of acceptance. The following caudate sonnet shows all the bitterness the writer felt for his failure to make a success of his pandering to the popes and for being forced to leave the city (most decisively, it seems, by an attempted assassination on his person).

𝕾ett'anni traditori ho via gettati,
con Leon quattro e tre con ser Clemente,
e son fatto nemico de la gente
più per li lor che per li miei peccati.   4
E non ho pur d'intrata dui ducati
e son da men che non è Gian Manente,
onde nel culo, se ponete mente,
ho tutte le speranze de' papati.   8
Se le ferite vacasser, ne avrei,
per diffender l'onor de' miei patroni,
motu proprio ogni dì ben cinque o sei,
ma benefici, office e pensioni   12
hanno bastardi e furfanti plebei
che i papi mangeriano in due bocconi;
e i suoi servitor buoni
muoion di fame come che facc'io,   16
cosa da renegar Domeneddio.

𝕴 waisted seven treacherous years,
four with Leo and three with Sir Clement,
and, less because of my sins than of theirs,
scores and scores of enemies I gathered.   4
My income is not as high as two ducats;
now I am worth less than Gian Manente:
if you well consider it, my expectations
in the papacy have all gone up my ass.   8
I wish beatings had been wanting, because
to defend my masters' honor, I have had
five or six of them *motu proprio* every day;
as to privileges, positions, and pensions,   12
they go to bastards and plebeian rascals
ready to eat up popes in one gulp or two,
while good servants
die of starvation, just as I do: something   16
to make one to forswear God the Almighty!

Regarding line 2, Pope Leo X and Pope Clement VII were Giovanni and Giulio de' Medici. In line 6, Gian Manente, a man known for organizing lottery drawings, was proverbially mentioned as a person of no importance. In line 9, *vacasser* comes from *vacare*, meaning "to be wanting" or "to lack." In line 11, *motu proprio* refers to a formula for a decree or assignment emitted by some high official. Aretino is saying that the many beatings he received were ordered by higher authorities. The coda flows syntactically from the preceding consideration and arrives at the closing with the shocking negation of God's existence.

After leaving Rome and lingering in the north for a while, Aretino set up residence in Venice. The

Very Serene Republic was then politically and jurisdictionally independent of church and empire; its institutions were stable, and its neatly stratified population remained at peace wth their institutions for centuries to come. The city was also one of the great cultural and editorial centers of Europe. There, Aretino found his ideal home: he was able to lead a free personal life and pursue with success an independent professional career. In time, he also learned to distribute blame and praise with shrewd consideration. Among the people he viewed as friends was Tiziano Vecèllio, the painter (1490–1576). In the following sonnet, he managed to flatter both Titian and the man who had posed for one of his paintings.

Se 'l chiaro Apelle con la man de l'arte
rassemblò d'Alessandro il volto e 'l petto,
non finse già del pellegrin subietto
l'alto vigor che l'anima comparte. 4
Ma Tizian che dal cielo ha maggior parte,
fuor mostra ogni invisibile concetto;
però 'l gran duca nel dipinto aspetto
scopre le palme entro al suo core sparte. 8
Egli ha il terror fra l'uno e l'altro ciglio,
l'animo in gli occhi e l'alterezza in fronte,
nel cui spazio l'onor siede e 'l consiglio.
Nel busto armato e ne le braccia pronte 12
arde il valor che guarda dal periglio
Italia, sacra a sue virtuti conte.

If the famous Apelles, with his artistic hand,
accurately depicted Alexander's face and breast,
he, nonetheless, was unable to represent the high
qualities of the soul in his extraordinary subject. 4
Titian, who had a greater talent from heaven,
can visibly represent all invisible potentials:
for in the features of the great duke he portrayed
he has shown all the virtues hidden in the heart. 8
The brows inspire owe and fear, while courage
is suggested in the eyes, dignity on the forehead,
and also, in that space, judgment and nobility.
On his arms at the ready, on his breast-plated chest 12
shines the valor that shields Italy from dangers,
Italy, which is sacred to his well-known merits.

Apelles, the acient Greek artist, painted a portrait of Alexander the Great. In line 7, the *gran duca* in question is Francesco Maria della Rovere, nephew of Pope Julius II and nephew and adopted successor of Guidobaldo da Montefeltro, duke of Urbino. Titian painted his portrait in 1537. In line 8, *palme*, meaning "palms," as in "to win the palm of victory," stands for "merits."

At the time, Titian enjoyed international fame. Aretino, who was interested in art, especially the relation of painting to literature, appreciated Titian's artistry and greatly admired his independence and professionalism. Aretino conceived his literary products as merchandise. This might explain his attempt to succeed in a variety of genres, including the religious ones. Nonetheless, his talent cannot be denied. His literary flair is evident in the scandalously famous *Dialogues* and perhaps more so in his correspondence. His personal letters came out of the press between 1538 and 1557, and the great acclaim they received started a vogue for the correspondence in the vernacular.[96]

We know little about Niccolò Franco (1515–70), born in Benevento, in the region of Campania. When still young, he became a friend and personal secretary to Pietro Aretino in Venice. Both friendship and employment vanished when Franco revealed embarrassing details of his employer's life, details that inspired Fortunato Spira to write a much-unauthorized biography. The following sonnet, insulting and bitterly derisive, is one of many that Franco wrote about his former friend.

Tizian, ritratto avendo l'Aretino,
mostrato avete ch'egli è il vero, e quello
che in mezzo il Canal Grande tien bordello,
e che scrisse la Nanna al babuino;   4
che non ha lettere, e chiamasi Divino,
che si scrive degli asini flagello,
che in sonettar concorre col Burchiello,
e che fa l'arte a dritto et a mancino.   8
Oh, s'in quell'attitudine che mostra
la schiena avesse volta, in guisa tale
che ne paresse in punto per la giostra,
cader possa in disgrazia del male,   12
se cosa aveste fatta in vita vostra
che avesse avuto più del naturale!

Titian, when you painted Aretino,
you showed the very person, the one who
holds a brothel midway on Canal Grande,
one who wrote the *Nanna* for a baboon,   4
who has no letters but calls himself divine,
one whose signature is "The Scourge of Donkeys,"
whose sonnets are a challenge to Burchiello,
one who plies his talents left and right.   8
Oh! If, given his well-known propensity,
you had turned his back in such a way
as to make him seem ready for the joust,
you, in your entire life, I swear you would   12
never—may I die, may the pox disfigure me—
have painted anything more lifelike than that!

Titian's portrait of Aretino was unveiled in 1545 and is now in the collection of Palazzo Pitti in Florence. Line 3 refers to the lifestyle Aretino maintained in Venice. In his living quarters, which looked out on the Canal Grande, he gave shelter to several courtesans. Regarding line 4, in 1534, Aretino wrote the *Ragionamento della Nanna e della Antonia*, a dialogue describing, in all their intimate details, the activities of some Roman courtesans. He dedicated the dialogue to his favored woman, whom he called "little monkey." In line 5, *non ha lettere* (has no letters) means that he is ignorant. Regarding line 6, Aretino used to sign himself as the Scourge of Princes, referring to his talent for keeping the nobility in line at his service. In line 8, this *arte*, or expertise, is sex—or, more specifically, the sexual propensity mentioned in the next line. *A dritto et a mancino* means "whichever way and with whomever." Regarding line 10, the accusation of homosexual inclinations was the utmost insult. In line 11, Franco refers to the sexual jousts, or roundabouts, that his former employer had described in his *Ragionamenti*. In lines 12–14, the poet says, "If you, Titian, had shown Aretino in the position for which he has great aptitude, you would have indeed painted something resembling life!"

Donne, m'è di bisogno ch'i' no 'l taccia:
di cotesti belletti ch' adoprate,
e tutta la muraglia intonacate,
cosa non è nel mondo che più spiaccia.   4
Talché temo d'avervi nelle braccia,
qualor vi veggio tanto infarinate,
e più tosto torrei le coltellate,
che con voi maneggiarmi a faccia a faccia.   8
Però che la cerussa con la biacca
a pena quel basciozzo n'ho pigliato,
che tutta intorno a i labbri mi s'attacca.
Di sorte, ch'i' mi son deliberato,   12
se 'l vostro imbellettarvi più m'intacca,
di farvi quella cosa da prelato.

Women, I cannot keep silent any longer
about all the makeup you put on:
enough to whitewash the city walls!
Nothing is more distasteful that that.   4
I am afraid to hold you in my arms
when I see you so smothered in flour!
I would rather be stabbed many times
than romp about with you face-to-face.   8
The reason is that I can hardly
give you one big kiss, that the white
of ceruse gets stuck all around my lips!
That is why I have definitively decided   12

that if your cosmetics smear me up again,
I shall have to take you the prelate way.

In line 3, *muraglia* means "city wall." *Infarinate*, from *infarinare*, means "to cover with flour (*farina*)." In line 9, *cerussa* is white lead, or ceruse. It was used to whiten the skin. In line 10, *basciozzo* means "big kiss," from *bacio* (kiss). In line 13, *imbellettarsi* is to put on *belletto* (makeup). Regarding line 13, sodomy was thought to be widely practiced in religious circles.

The upcoming sonnet praises Vittoria Colonna, the most celebrated female poet of the time, admired for her high moral standards and unflinching loyalty to the memory of her husband (for Colonna, see sections 4.5 and 5.5).

Priapo, io qui compaio ambasciatore
da parte d'una nostra poetessa,
con tutta quella riverenza espressa,
che converrebbe ad un imperatore.   4
Ella ti dice che t'ha sempre in core,
e la mattina, quando vede messa,
Dio sa se per te prega, ch'ella stessa
si meraviglia dond'è tanto amore.   8
E benché spenda l'intelletto e l'arte
in scriver rime, ed a te facci torto
co 'l farti tanta carestia di carte,
tutto questo riesce in tuo conforto,   12
e sei costretto a torlo in buona parte,
se piagne il cazzo del marito morto.

Priapus, I have come as ambassador
to you on the part of a poetess of ours,
with the expressed and utmost reverence
appropriate in dealing with an emperor.   4
She says she has you always in her heart,
and, in the morning, whenever she hears Mass,
God knows how she prays for you! She herself
wonders from where so much love may come.   8
And, although she wears out her intellect
and her art writing verse, while she wrongs you
in making great economy of paper,
yet you should count it to your satisfaction   12
and hold it in good stead, for she does only cry
for the cock of her husband, who is dead.

Regarding line 1, the Roman-carved image of Priapus, god of fertility and sexuality, exhibited an enormous phallus. Regarding line 2, besides being regarded for her high social standing, Vittoria Colonna was held in great esteem for the uprightness of her personal life. Born to a powerful Roman family whose sons had been, and still were, military men of high standing, Vittoria was connected on her mother's and father's side with the best Italian princely clans and, through her husband, with Neapolitan and Spanish royalty. In line 4, Franco directs his gibe at Vittoria's cordial personal relationship with Emperor Charles V. The reference in line 10 is to the avalanche of Platonic sonnets Vittoria wrote in praise of her husband, Ferrante d'Avalos, who had died of wounds received in 1527 while fighting at the Battle of Pavia on the side of the emperor. Per line 11, Colonna does not write any sonnet about Priapus and thus saves paper.

After breaking with Aretino, Franco wandered off for some time throughout Italy, making enemies wherever he went, especially in papal territory. In the end, after some injudicious railing against the Inquisition and after being mixed up with people ideologically dangerous, he was condemned to death for heresy. He died in Rome on the gallows.

Benvenuto Cellini (1500–71) was a sculptor, jeweler, and writer. Besides authoring a treatise on sculpture and one on metalworking, he wrote an autobiography that became famous for the description of the rambunctious, self-assured, self-asserting personality of the protagonist and for the vivid descriptions of Renaissance society and events. Cellini is also the author of no fewer than 147 lyrics. He lived at intervals in Rome. The first time, he worked in the Vatican mint under the patronage of Pope Clement VII. During the sack, he fought against the imperial army. A few years later, Pier Luigi Farnese, the nephew of Pope Paul III, had him arrested and jailed for pilfering from the mint years earlier. Cellini managed to escape in his usual spectacular fashion. For a while, he resided and worked in France. He wrote the sonnet "Porca Fortuna s' tu scoprivi prima" in Florence, his hometown, where he was jailed twice for homosexuality.[97]

> Porca Fortuna s' tu scoprivi prima
> che ancora a me piacessi 'l Genimede!
> Son puttaniere ormai, com'ogni uom vede,
> né avesti di me la spoglia opima.   4
> Dinanzi ai tuo' bei crin così si stima;
> né chi 'l merita gli dai, né chi te 'l chiede
> gli porgi a tal che non gli cerca o vede.
> Cieca, di te omai non fo più stima.   8
> Che val con arme, lettere o scultura
> affaticarsi in questa parte o 'n quella,
> poi che tu se' sì porca, impia figura?   12
> Venga 'l canchero a te, tue rote e stella;
> t'hai vindicata quella prima ingiuria:
> che nol facevi nell'età novella.

> Luck, you bitch, you should have discovered
> much earlier that I also enjoy the Ganymede!
> Now I am a well-known lecher, as all can tell,
> and you did not get any rich spoils from me!   4

That's how one is treated around those curls of yours;
you don't show your favor to those who deservingly
wish it, only to those who neither care nor look for it.
You are blind, and I no longer hold you in good esteem. 8
Why should one wear out in war, in writing,
or in sculpting, why labor in this or in that field,
when you are so bitchy and such an ungodly beast?
Blast you, blast your wheels, and blast your star: 12
you took revenge on that first wrong of mine,
something you did not do when I was young.

In line 2, Ganymede, the mythical young man loved and kidnapped by Jupiter, stands for homosexual love. In line 4, *spoglia opima* refers to the spoils that, at the end of the war, the victorious Roman generals brought to the temples and dedicated to the gods. Cellini perhaps intended to say that his love battles were not yet over. Regarding line 5, Fortune was depicted with long hair. Trying to get lucky, says Cellini, holding on to the goddess's hair, proved a waste of time. In lines 9–10, Cellini mentions all his activities and merits: in 1527, he had fought for the defense of Rome; he was active as a sculptor and writer. In line 13, the first injury, or wrong, could refer to some indiscretion or crime that Cellini committed in youth. Some commentators believe Cellini's error was coming back from France. Before writing the sonnet—that is, before 1557—he had resided in Paris twice. For Francis I of France, he had made the *Nymph of Fontainebleau*, which is now in the Louvre, and the famous saltcellar, the only work in gold to survive from the Renaissance, which is now in the Kunsthistorisches Museum of Vienna. In Florence, where he spent his last years under the patronage of Duke Cosimo I, he sculpted the *Perseus with the head of Medusa*, which can be seen in the Loggia dei Lanzi, in Piazza della Signoria in Florence.

5.2 The Benevolence of Critics

Benvenuto Cellini—who was, as we saw, a sculptor of renown besides being an author of 147 poems, some treatises, and a famous biography—did not hesitate to attack those who disparaged his poetic talents, using well-pointed denunciations about their professionalism and value system.

Già molti si son messi a far sonetti,
e molti pochi son quei che fan bene;
ogni uom conosce il ver da quel che viene,
ché le muse ognun chiama, e pochi eletti. 4
Non val l'esprimer bene i suoi concetti;
né ben d'Amor mostrar suo gaudio o pene;
né motti oscuri o parolette amene;
né dire: "Io feci, io fui, io andai, io stetti." 8
Al primo si domanda: "Chi l'ha fatto?"
E in sul nome di quel si fa 'l giudizio:

non avvien questo al pingere o scolpire.
Se l'opra è buona, si conosce a un tratto; 12
né importa aver del maestro prima indizio.
Sculpite or voi, e noi lascite dire.

Now many have started writing sonnets,
but only a few are those who do it well;
everyone knows their value from the result,
for the Muses lure many but choose a few. 4
It doesn't pay to express one's ideas effectively,
to confess one's joy or one's pains of love,
to employ rare conceits or lovely little words,
and to say, "I did, I was, I went, I stayed." 8
Right off, they will ask, "Who wrote it?"
Only by the author's fame they judge.
It's not this way in sculpture or in painting.
If a work is good, it is recognized at once, 12
with no need to know the author's name.
Now you do the sculpting, and let us write.

Benedetto Varchi (1503–65) wrote much literary criticism, a history of Florence, poetry, and a comedy by the title of *La suocera*. His erudition, his many interests, and the protection of Gran Duke Cosimo de' Medici made him the most authoritative member of the Florentine Academy. The following sonnet, a rather gracious example of Petrarchism, shows him to have been as derivative in poetry as he generally was in his philosophical and literary theories.

Ben mi credea poter gran tempo, armato
di pensier tristi e freddo ghiaccio il core,
girmen senza sospetto omai ch'Amore
fianco scaldasse più tanto gelato; 4
ma rimirando, io non so per qual fato,
donna, de' bei vostri occhi lo splendore,
voglia dentro cangiai, di fuor colore,
e trovami in un punto arso e legato; 8
ma qual ghiaccio è sì freddo, e quai cotanto
fur mai tristi pensier, ch'avvesser retto
al caldo stral che da' bei raggi uscìo?
Io vidi Amore: io 'l vidi da quel santo 12
lume ratto volando entrar nel petto
vostro, dirò, perché non è più mio.

For a long time I believed, armed as I was
with sad thoughts and a heart as cold as ice,
that I could go on living with no fear that Love
would warm up once again a breast so icy;   4
but in gazing, I know not by what destiny,
o woman, into the splendor of your eyes,
I changed inside the mood, outside the color,
and found myself, at once, tied and on fire.   8
But what ice could be so cold, how sad one's
thoughts could be, to be able to withstand
the fiery arrows shooting from your pretty eyes?
I saw Love: I saw him from that very blessed   12
light promptly fly and come into my heart,
your heart, I should say, for it is no longer mine.

Per line 2, sad are the thoughts alien to love. In line 4, *fianco*, meaning "side," is metonymy for "heart." In line 11, *raggi*, meaning "rays," stands for "eyes." In line 13, *petto*, meaning "breast," stands for "heart." Line 14 is a clear reminiscence of Aquilano's sonnet "Io iurerei che non t'offesi mai" in section 4.1

Anton Francesco Grazzini (1503–84) had been one of the original founders of the Florentine Academy—at the time called Accademia degli Umidi—and was better known by his academic appellation of Lasca. He was a successful writer of comedies, farces, short stories, and burlesque poems. He wrote this tailed sonnet when Varchi's play, preceded by great fanfare, was finally staged.

Con meraviglia e con gran divozione
era la vostra commedia aspettata;
ma poi ch'ell'è da Terenzio copiata,
son cadute le braccia alle persone.   4
Così sendo in concetto di lione
poi riuscendo topo alla gioranta,
di vo si ride e dice la brigata:
infine il Varchi non ha invenzione;   8
e in questa parte ha somigliato il Gello,
che fece anch'egli una commedia nuova,
ch'avea prima composto il Machiavello.
O Varchi, o Varchi, io vo' darvi una nuova;   12
anzi un ricordo proprio da fratello:
disponetevi a far più degna prova;
e dove altrui più giova,
attendete a tradurre e comentare   16
e dateci Aristotile in volgare.

With admiration and with great reverence
people looked forward to your comedy,
but as it turned out to be copied from Terence,
they were a great deal thrown off their balance.   4
Thanks to your having the repute of a lion
and on the battlefield behaving like a mouse,
many now laugh at you, and your friends say,
"Indeed, after all, Varchi has no invention;   8
in this respect, he is very much like Gelli,
who also wrote a comedy that was new,
but had been written before by Machiavelli."
O Varchi, Varchi! I will give you a bit of news,   12
or, rather, an admonition, as to a brother:
prepare to give of yourself a better proof,
and, whenever people find it useful,
do concentrate on translating, elucidating,   16
and reducing Aristotle's words into vernacular.

Regarding line 2, Varchi's comedy *La suocera* was imitative of ancient authors and had classical pretensions. The comedies written by Grazzini, on the other hand, had modern plots and characters. Regarding line 3, Terence, or Publius Terentius Afer, was an African (ca. 195–159 BCE) who took his name after Terentius Lucanus, the senator who brought him to Rome from Carthage as a slave, educated him, and granted him his freedom. Widely imitated during the Renaissance, he has inspired many modern playwrights, among them Molière, Thornton Wilder, and the authors of *A Funny Thing Happened on the Way to the Forum*. Line 4 means, literally, "they dropped their arms," an idiomatic expression signifying great disappointment. In line 7, *brigata* means "brigade," or group of friends. Regarding lines 9–11, the Florentine Giovan Battista Gelli (1498–1563) wrote *La Sporta*, a comedy he apparently concocted by making use of a draft left by Niccolò Machiavelli, who also wrote plays. Regarding line 17, any spoken language other than Latin was called *volgare*, from Latin *vulgus*, meaning "people." Latin was not the language of ordinary people—those who did not attended schools with classical programs. For some unspecified reason, in 1547, Lasca was expelled from the academy, where Varchi dominated. He was reinstated in 1566, after Varchi's death.

Michelangelo wrote "I' ho già fatto un gozzo in questo stento" around 1510. From 1508 to 1512, he was in Rome, painting frescoes on the ceiling of the Sistine Chapel. This *sonetto caudato* is addressed to Giovanni da Pistoia, chancellor of the Florentine Academy, to whom the artist had confided the extreme discomfort he had to suffer while painting. The manuscript containing the poem has on the margin the image of a bent-back figure straining to paint a ghostly shape above him.

I' ho già fatto un gozzo in questo stento,
come fa l'aqua a' gatti in Lombardia,
over d'altro paese che si sia,

ch'a forza 'l ventre appicca sotto 'l mento. 4
La barba al cielo, e la memoria sento
in sullo scrigno, e 'l petto ho d'arpia;
e 'l pennel sopra 'l viso tuttavia
mel fa, gocciando, un ricco pavimento. 8
E lombi entrati mi son nella peccia,
e fo del cul per contrappeso groppa,
e passi senza gli occhi muovo invano.
Dinanzi mi s'allunga la corteccia, 12
e per piegarsi addietro si ragggroppa,
e tendomi com'arco soriano.
Però fallace e strano
surge il giudizio che la mente porta, 16
chè mal si tra' per cerbottana torta.
La mia pittura morta
difendi orma', Giovanni, e 'l mio onore,
non sendo in loco bon, né io pittore.

I have already grown a goiter with this strain—
just as the water does to cats in Lombardy
or in whatever other country that may be—
for it is pushing the guts up under the chin. 4
I feel the beard up to the sky and the brain
on the hump, the chest like that of a harpy;
while the brush, which is above my face,
turns it, by dripping, into a decorated plain. 8
My loins have retracted inside the belly;
in counterbalance, my ass has shrunk;
and, with no eyesight, I take all steps blindly.
In the front, my skin is lengthening, lengthening, 12
and, in falling behind, has gathered into a lump,
and just like a Syrian bow I am stretching.
Henceforth, outlandish and false
becomes the judgment that my mind produces, 16
for a shot is badly aimed when the blowgun is bent.
Then, Giovanni, defend
my lethal way of painting and my honor,
for I am neither in a good position nor a painter.

Regarding line 2, Lombardy abounded in water. Rain and rivulets running through it were being channeled into canals according to plans drawn by engineers, among them Leonardo da Vinci. Contini tells us that *gatti* stood for local inhabitants, more specifically the citizens of Bergamo, who were frequently chided because of their goiters (Longhi, in Gorni 2001, 586). In line 4, the grammatical subject of *appicca* (pushes up) is understood to be *stento* (strain). In line 5, *memoria* (memory) stands for *nuca*, the nape of the neck. In line 6, *scrigno*, meaning "coffer" or "jewel case," stands for *gobba*, meaning "hump." In mythology, a harpy was a filthy bird with a hump extending from the upper chest to the back. In line 9, *peccia*, or *pancia*, refers to the belly. In line 17, a *cerbottana* is a blowgun, a tube through which a projectile is shot out by force of breath. It is a weapon used nowadays by so-called primitive people. In line 20, Michelangelo is saying that he was working in an unsuitable place and that he was not, after all, a painter. In fact, he thought himself a sculptor. For other sonnets by Michelangelo, see 4.5.

The next poem was found posted on the statue of Pasquino on All Saints Day of 1541, when Michelangelo's fresco *The Last Judgment* was unveiled. It is a caudate sonnet, and we may call it a guide to the painting. For Pasquino and his pasquinades, see 4.3.

O voi che riprendete 'l fiorentino,
considerate un poco la pittura:
vedrete che sta ben ogni figura
nella cappella di Gesù divino.   4
Sta Santa Caterina a capo chino,
nuda sì come fece la natura,
ed altri santi stanno con misura
a mostrar i lor culi a don Paulino.   8
Il coglion di Cesena come pazzo
sta con li muorti per suo mal governo,
tutt'ascosto in un certo cantonazzo.
Un altro sta ligato ne l'Inferno   12
con una serpe che li morde il cazzo
per peccato di rompere il quaderno.
Per questo, in sempiterno
Cristo condanna i bugironi al foco,   16
e star con una serp'al tristo loco.

You who reprimand the Florentine,
do consider his painting for a while:
you'll see how well conceived is every
figure in the chapel of Jesus, the Divine.   4
Saint Catherine, bending her head, is there,
as naked as Nature has made her;
the other saints stand very decorously by,
showing off their asses to Don Paulino.   8
The dolt of Cesena, looking like a madman,
is there among the dead, because of his bad
governance, hiding away in a dark corner.
Another fellow is tied up in Inferno   12
with a serpent that is biting his cock,

for his sinful practice of bursting quires.
For that sin, Christ
condemns buggers to burn in eternal fire   16
with a snake stuck up into their sad mire.

 Michelangelo's fresco met with much approval and much disapproval. The sonnet could be a mock rebuttal to the reaction of censorious critics. Some had stigmatized the presence of naked bodies, male and female. Among those who objected to the nudity was the scandalous Aretino. He seemed to have resented Michelangelo for refusing him the drawings he wanted. Other critics disapproved of Christ painted as a young man, beardless and, in their opinion, not sufficiently majestic. In line 4, *cappella* is the Sistine Chapel. Regarding line 5, Saint Catherine is depicted at the right of Christ, holding on to the wheel of her martyrdom. In line 8, Don Paulino is Pope Paul III, who commissioned the fresco. The use of the diminutive Paulino in place of Paolo has the effect of reducing the pope's importance to that of some little old man living perhaps in the working-class district adjacent to the Vatican. In line 9, the *coglion di Cesena*—*coglione* (testicle) stands for dolt—is Biagio Martinelli, the pope's master of ceremonies, who was from the town of Cesena on the Adriatic. In line 12, *un altro* is Pier Luigi Farnese, the pope's nephew, a well-known homosexual. Regarding line 14, *quaderno* has several meanings: a set of paper sheets, or quire; a piece of land assigned to a specific cultivation; and a notebook. Here it stands for "anus." In Dante's *Inferno* (14, 13–30), the homosexuals (called here and there *bugironi*) are condemned to walk on hot sand under a rain of fire.

5.3 An Alternative World

The sonnets of the previous section were addressed directly or indirectly to personal competitors, to antagonists, to holders of power, and against prescribed societal customs. The sonneteers of this section allow us a look into the wide world of ordinary people, including their passions and everyday situations. They advance their views and desires with bonhomie, in mild tones of irony, in a familiar idiom, and sometimes in dialect.

 In the early centuries, lyric poets had made use of dialect sporadically.[98] Dialect poetry proper took off at the beginning of the sixteenth century, when Bembo's regulations about high style produced a clear separation between highbrow and popular literature. Inspired by the life around them, many writers became aware of the value of local language, the world it represented, and its potential for expressiveness and authenticity of feelings. The examples given here are of the Venetian, Genoese, and Neapolitan dialects. The only exceptions are the poems penned by Camillo Scroffa, who created an erudite composite language, a mixture of Paduan, Italian, and Latinate words.

 Maffio Venier (1550–86) was born in Venice in a prominent patrician family. He lived as a courtier in Rome and Florence; visited the Middle East; and, inspired by his travels, wrote two works on the Ottoman Empire and how to confront it militarily. Later in life, he returned to Venice and entered public life. Shortly before he died, he became archbishop of Corfu, which is now Kerkira in Greece but was then Venetian territory. The Venier family counted several poet-writers among its members. Domenico, Maffio's uncle, and his son Marco were Petrarchan sonneteers who wrote in Italian. Their salon was frequented by artists and literati, among them Gaspara Stampa. Maffio was the only one of his family who wrote poetry in Venetian and described situations experienced by ordinary people, mimicking their way of talking and behaving.[99]

Fia mia, viseto belo inzucherào,
daspò che ho inteso che vegnì sta sera,
son vegnù belo e son muà de ciera
che pàro proprio un pèrsego mondào.   4
Sia laudà Amor, daspò che 'l mio mezào,
la mia corte, el mi orto, e la letiera
poderà dir da seno e da dovera:
"So che 'l nostro paron xé venturào."   8
Vegnì in bon'ora, caro el mio conforto,
e caso mò che me dassé l'impianto
doman sentiré a dir: "L'amigo è morto."
El desiderio che ho de vu xé tanto,   12
che se no vegnissé me fassé torto:
vu me fassé restar co l' cuor infranto.
Son de miel tuto quanto
daspuò che ho abbùo da niovo che vu, fia,   16
ve degné de vegnir in casa mia.

My dear, my beautiful, sugary face,
when I was told that you are coming tonight,
I got all spruced up; my looks have changed.
Now, I think, I look like a peeled peach.   4
Let Love be blessed, because my orchard,
my mezzanine, my courtyard, as well as
my bed, can judiciously and dutifully proclaim,
"I know our master has struck it lucky!"   8
Come early, my pleasure, my comfort,
and if tomorrow you are going to dump me,
you'll hear people say, "Your friend has died!"
The yearning that I feel for you is such   12
that it would be unkind, were you not to come:
you would leave me with a broken heart!
I have turned into a jar of honey
since I heard that you, my dearest,   16
will condescend to step into my house.

The whole sonnet is in Venetian. In line 2, *daspò*, Venetian for *dopo che*, means "since" or "as." In line 3, *muà*, Venetian for *mutato*, means "changed." *Ciera*, or *aspetto*, means "look" or "appearance." In line 4, *un pèrsego mondao* (in Italian, *una pesca sbucciata*) refers to a peeled peach. In line 8, *xè*, Venetian for *è*, means "is." *Venturào*, or *fortunato*, means "lucky." In line 10, *e caso mò che me dassé l'impianto* means "and then in case you dropped me." *Dassé* is the Venetian subjunctive of *dare*. The impossible word-for-word translation of the Venetial expression would be "in case you gave me the clearance," or, literally, "the dumping." Regarding lines 11 and 13–14, *no vegnissé* is Venetian for *non veniste* (you did not come). *Sentiré* and *fassé* are conditionals for *sentireste* (you would hear) and *fareste* (you would do). In line 16, *ho abbùo da niovo*, or *ho avuto la notizia*, means "I had the news." The tail, syntactically and thematically independent of the sonnet, contributes a final, stronger note of excited expectation.

L'esser ti, co' ti xé, senza cervelo,
e mi bestia futtùa senza rason
fa che quasi ogni dì femo custion
ti co mi e mi per ti, co questo e quelo. 4
Co' te vien vògia, ti me dà martelo
co 'l no vegnir, co 'l scampar dal balcon,
e mi con i sonetti e le canzon
te intòssego, cussì stemo in duelo. 8
Deh, dolce, cara e bella anema mia,
no pì sta giostra, no pì ste contese,
ma femo pase e bona compagnia.
E se 'l ciel fosse tanto descortese 12
che 'l ne inchinasse a sta furfanteria,
fémolo almanco una o do volte al mese.

Being you, the way you are, without a brain,
and I a fucked-up beast without any reason,
makes us quarrel almost every day, you with me
and I with you, either for this motive or for that. 4
When you are in the mood, you torture me
by not coming, or by jumping from the balcony,
while I keep poisoning you with sonnets
and songs: this way, we keep on fighting. 8
I beg you, my beauty, my sweet, dearest soul,
no more scenes, no more arguments,
let us make peace and be good friends.
And, if the heavens are so discourteous 12
as to incline us toward such skullduggery,
then let us fight only once or twice a month.

In line 3, *femo custion* (in Italian, *facciamo questione*) means "we argue." In line 5, *vogia* (in Italian, *voglia*) means "wish" or "want." *Ti me da martelo*, or *mi colpisci col martello*, means "you hit me with an anvil," or you nag or torture me. In line 7, *te intòssego*, or *ti avveleno*, means "I poison you." In line 14, *fèmolo*, or *facciamolo*, means "let us do it." This quarrel among lovers is different from the poetic diatribe

Maffìo engaged in with the courtesan and poet Veronica Franco, a diatribe so laden, on his side, with base vituperations as to gain Venier an infamous nook in feminist criticism.[100]

The following sonnet makes fun of courtly and literary mannerisms. Instead of lamenting his lovelorn condition and that of a nightingale, as any Petrarchan lover would do, Venier compares his condition to that of a pig, one being trussed up for the larder.

> Signora mia, vù manizé per tuto
> cussì sto porco infina a le buèle;
> donca per far salsizze e mortaèle
> vu ve degné d'un animal sì bruto? 4
> Mò mi, che son per vu morto e destruto
> no m'avé mai tocà nianca la pele;
> forsi che lu de quele man sì bele
> se sentì mai d'amor caldo un presùto? 8
> Orsù, s'ammazza el porco, e mi son morto
> mille volte per vu; ma ingiustamente,
> che lu muor a razon, mi moro a torto.
> Lu tuttavia ve 'l tegnì sempre arente, 12
> e mi non avì mai nissun conforto
> de sì longo servir con tante stente!

> Signora, you handle this pig every which way,
> far deep inside his bowels: so then, to make
> mortadella and sausages, you are ready to stoop
> so low, down to the level of a brutish beast, 4
> while with me, distraught and dying for you,
> you have never touched as much as the skin?
> Has, by chance, a prosciutto ever felt
> a tender love for hands as delicate as yours? 8
> So then, a pig is killed once, while for you
> I die a thousand times, and very unjustly,
> for the pig dies in a good cause but not I.
> You keep him always close to you, 12
> while I never receive any small reward
> for so devoted a service and so much suffering!

In line 3, *mortaèle* is Venician for mortadella, a big sausage made with pork meat. In line 7, *lu*, or *lui*, meaning "he," refers to the pig. In line 12, *arente*, or *accanto*, means "near."

The next poem shows Maffìo in a serious, meditative mood.

> Eccetto l'omo, ogn'altra bestia ha ben:
> l'altre vien governàe dalla natura,
> che è so mare, so nena, e che ghe ha cura,
> che ghe dà tutto quello che ghe vien. 4

L'omo d'ogni desgrazia è prima pien
che l'abbia, se può dir, preso figura;
l'è pur solo che sa, che ha sta paura,
de tornar a resòlverse in terren.   8
Esso ha per guida el senso e la rasòn.
e, si l'è da una banda partial,
l'altra el tien in continua passion.
Gramo sto viver misero e mortal,   12
se la natura e 'l Ciel ne fa sto don
perché el sia fondamento d'ogni mal.

With the exception of man, all animals
are well set: they are governed by nature,
which is mother, nurse, and provider
and gives them anything they may expect.   4
Man is laden with difficulties, even before
he has, so to speak, completely shaped up;
he is the only animal to know and fear
that eventually he will turn into dust.   8
His guides are his senses and reason,
and if this one always leans on one side,
the others keep him in restless confusion.
Meager is indeed this miserable life of man,   12
if nature and the heavens give us a gift
that becomes the foundation of every ill.

Camillo Scroffa (1525–65) was a count who made a living as a lawyer in both Venice and Vicenza, his native town. His literary fame is due to a collection of poetry entitled *I cantici di Fidenzio* (Fidenzio's Songs). Fidenzio is a schoolmaster, fashioned, it seems, after a real Piero Fidenzio Giunteo da Montagnana, who taught Latin at a local college. Besides his great love for the ancient language, Fidenzio has another great passion: he is infatuated with a handsome young pupil by the name of Camillo.

Cento fanciulli d'indole prestante,
sotto l'egregia disciplina mia,
i bei costumi imparano e la via
del parlar e del scriver elegante.   4
Ma come il ciel, benché di tante e tante
stelle al tempo nocturno ornato sia,
non posson la luce dar che si desia,
perch'è absente il pianeta radiante,   8
così il mio ampio ludo litterario,

poi che 'l gentil Camil non lo frequenta,
non mi può un sol tantillo satisfare.
L'essere pagato dal pubblico erario   12
et ogni giorno novo lucro fare,
heu me, che senza lui non mi contenta.

Under my very egregious discipline,
one hundred young men of vigorous build
learn the polite customs and the way
to write and speak in style elegant and neat.   4
However, just as in the nocturnal time,
which is adorned with many a star, the sky
cannot pour forth the light that is desired
because the radiating planet is absconding,   8
similarly, my outstanding literary school
cannot satisfy me even a tiny bit,
because gentle Camillo is not attending.
Being paid by the public treasury   12
and earning money every day does not make me,
without him, alas, at all contented.

In line 8, Professor Fidenzio describes the night sky in a tortuously erudite way: there is no light in the night sky because the sun, the radiating planet, is hiding. As we see in line 9, the sonnet is replete with precious Latin words. *Ludo litterario* is the Roman *ludus litterarum*—that is, "school." Other Latinizing words are *nocturne*, *absente*, *amplo*, *novo lucro*, and *satisfare*. A Latin exclamation is *heu me*, as in "*Heu me miserum!*" (Oh, poor me!). Scroffa's satire is addressed at the same time to the master's love for Latin, his cumbersome erudition, and his fixation on the handsome youth. Nonetheless, Fidenzio strikes us as a dear, if not pitiable, teacher who lives in a world of his own, a world kept aloft by the love of his discipline, and who cannot quite get the idea that erudition and the beauty of Latin are lost on the alluring Camillo (Orvieto 259).

Le tumidule genule, i nigerrimi
occhi, il viso peralbo et candidissimo,
l'exigua bocca, il naso decentissino,
il mento che mi dà dolori acerrimi,   4
il lacteo collo, i crimuli, i dexterrimi
membri, il bel corpo symmetriatissimo
del mio Camillo, il lepor venustissimo,
i costumi modesti et integerrimi,   8
d'hora in hora mi fan sì Camilliphilo
ch'io non ho altro ben, altre letitie,
che la soave lor reminiscentia.

>   Non fu nel nostro lepido Poliphilo
>   di Polia sua tanta concupiscentia
>   quanta in me di sì rare alte divitie.   12
>
> Those puffy little cheeks, those very dark
> eyes, that snow-white, spotless face,
> that tiny mouth, that most charming nose,
> that chin which gives me shrilling spasms,   4
> the milky neck, the soft hair, the very agile
> members, the fine, faultlessly shaped body
> of my Camillo, that charm of all charms,
> those modest and dignified ways of his   8
> make me hour to hour such a Camil-lover
> that no other good, no other joy is left to me
> than this dear, pleasurable recollecting.
> There was no such concupiscence for Polia   12
> in our gracious Poliphilus as there is in me
> for my Camillo's high and rarest treasures.

Regarding line 1, *genula*, Latin diminutive of *gena*, means "cheek." *Tumidulus*, diminutive of Latin *tumidus*, means "puffy." Regarding lines 2–3, *nigerrimi*, *peralbus*, *acerrimus*, *candidissinus*, and *decentissimus* are superlatives of *niger*, *albus*, *acer*, *candidus*, and *decens*, all Latin. *Exiguus* means "small." In line 5, *crinulus* is diminutive of the Latin *cris*, thus meaning "thin hair" or "soft hair." *Dexterrimus* comes from that Latin *dexter*. Regarding line 7, *lepor* is Latin for "grace." *Vetustus* is Latin for "lovely" or "alluring." With regard to line 12, *lepidus* is Latin for "charming." Poliphilus and Polia are the lovers, protagonists of *Hypnerotomachia Polyphili* (1499) by Francesco Colonna. Regarding line 14, *divitiae* is Latin for "wealth" or "opulence."

Fidenzio transplants Latin terms, many of them archaic, into the morphological and syntactical structure of Italian. This is not mock Latin, or *latino maccheronico*, which consists of adapting Italian words to a few simple Latin endings, a form of satiric language used by people with little or no Latin. Here, the poet has done the work of an expert, such as Fidenzio obviously was. Scroffa had acquired a good classical education as well as a law degree at the University of Padua. At that institution, he might have come across a professor such as Fidenzio. As Fidenzio's pupil is named Camillo, may we presume that the object of the professor's desire was young Scroffa himself?

>   Voi, ch' auribus arrectis auscultate
>   in lingua hetrusca il fremito e 'l rumore
>   de' miei sospiri, pieni di stupore
>   forse d'intemperantia m'accusate.   4
>   Se vedreste l'eximia alta beltate
>   de l'acerbo lanista del mio core,
>   non sol dareste venia al nostro errore,
>   ma di me avreste, ut aequum est, pietate.   8
>   Hei mihi! io veggio bene apertamente

ch'a la mia dignità non si conviene
perditamente amare, e n'erubesco:
ma la beltà antedicta mi ritiene   12
con tal violentia, che continuamente
opto uscir di prigion, e mai non esco.

You who, in the Tuscan language, listen
with *auribus arrectis* to the throbbing
noise of my sighs, in great bewilderment
will perhaps accuse me of *intemperantia*.   4
If you saw the high *eximia* beauty
of the cruel arouser of my passion,
not only you would forgive my error, but,
ut aequum est, you would commiserate me.   8
Alas, poor me! I now clearly see
that it is not fitting to my dignity
to be madly in love, and for it I *erubesco*;
however, the foresaid beauty holds me   12
with such *violentia* that unceasingly
opto to escape my prison, but never succeed.

In line 1, *auribus* (in Latin, *auris*) means "ear." *Arrectis*, from *arrectus*, means "straightened," "raised," or "pricked up." In line 2, *hetrusca* is Latin for *Etruscan*—that is, Italian. In line 4, *intemperantia* means "recklessness." In line 5, *eximia* means "excellent" or "exceptional." In line 6, *lanista* means "trainer of gladiators," "exciter," "instigator," or "one who excites to the fight." In line 11, *erubesco* means "I blush" or "I am ashamed." In line 12, *antedicta* means "mentioned above." In line 14, *opto* means "I wish."

Scroffa's sonnet is a good parody of "Voi ch'ascoltate in rime sparse il suono," the first poem of Petrarch's *Canzoniere*. In that sonnet, Petrarch gave a retrospective description of his life, which he considered vainly and regretfully spent in loving a woman—a behavior that had earned the disapproval of his readers but also perchance their pity. Passionate Fidenzio, however, does not have Petrarch's recriminations, as doggedly attracted as he is to young Camillo. Scroffa's mocking levity is also reminiscent of the Latin comedies that university students wrote, of which a number are extant. While making sophomoric fun of everyghing around them, the students made their professors' supposed homosexual passions their main staple of satire.

Paolo Foglietta (1520–90) was born in an outstanding family of Genova, and he lived and died there, except for a short residence in Rome, where he acted as the consul of the Republic of Ragusa. His collection of poetry in Genoese dialect—which is practically incomprehensible to other Italians—had several printings in his own century and made him famous. In its nostalgic recollection of times past, the upcoming poem gives us a quick insight into family life and the intimacy, somewhat exaggerated, of familial relationships.

Za i omi de trent'agni eran figiuoe,
so mamma ghe toccava ancon ro bin,
sì ghe dixeiva "Vuoete fa pishin?"
Ni braghette portavan com' ancuoe. 4
Si creivan che re donne ri figgiuoe
feisan da l'ombrizallo ri meschin,
e a sò moere toccavan ro tetin
e in letto ancon dormivan co sò suoe. 8
Ma tutti aora fan tutto a ro reverso
che à mare sperme son dra scorza fuoera,
che re mate parole cascun dixe.
Si van trovà re donne peccarixe 12
si fan de pezo e per zò ven gragniuoera
e s'impenze ro mondo a ro reverso.

Once, thirty-year-old men were children:
their mothers still touched their wee-wee
and said to them, "Do you want to do pee-pee?"
They did not wear trousers, as they do today. 4
They believed, the dear ones, that women
had children come out of their belly buttons;
they touched their mothers' teats
and slept in bed together with their sisters. 8
Nowadays they do just the opposite,
for they are hardly out of their egg
that they make use of all swear words.
They go about looking for sinful women; 12
they do worse and great disasters result,
and the entire world is hanging downside up.

In line 1, *figiuoe*, or *figli*, means "children." In line 2, *ro bin*, or *il pube*, refers to the pubis. In line 3, *ghe dixeiva*, or *diceva loro*, means "would tell them." *Fa pishin*, or *far pipì*, means "to pee." In line 4, the *braghette*, or *calzoni*, are pants. *Ancuoe*, or *ancor oggi*, means "still today." In line 6, *feisan da l'ombrizallo*, or *facevano dall'ombellico*, means "they made [chidren] from the belly button." In line 7, *moere*, or *madri*, means "mothers." In line 8, the *tetin*, or *tette*, are teats. In line 8, *suoe*, or *sorelle*, means "sisters." In line 10, *à mare sperme son dra scorza fuera*, or *a mala pena sono fuori della scorza*, means "they are hardly out of the bark." In line 11, *mate parole* means "crazy words," or four-letter words. In line 13, *zò*, or *giù*, means "down." *Gragniuoera*, or *gragnuola*, means "hail." The expression literally means "down comes a hailstorm." In line 14, *s'impenze*, or *si dipinge*, is painted. Literally, the line translates into "the world is painted the wrong way."

In the following sonnet, Foglietta's nostalgia for the old days extends to fashions and citizens' rights.

Presto ra toga se metteiva e trava
e come indosso ro çitten l'aveiva
un scambietto fà vogiando o poeiva
perchè ara braga lasca o se n'andava.   4
E poche stringhe ogn' un se destrincava,
quando ri suoe besogni fà vorreiva
e ognun dri membri suoe ben se varreiva
perchè scciavo dre robe o no se fava.   8
Ma per fà ri bisogni dra natura
destrincà tente strinche ne conven,
che spesso a l'homo fan desaventura
perché chi vo insì fuora dentro ten   12
ni un peto pò ciù tia ra criatura;
te pà che staghe fresco ro çitten?

Once a gown was easy to put on and take off,
and when a man was wearing it, he could kick
a leg about, if he wanted, for the pantaloons
were ample, and afterward he could walk on.   4
When he had to go for an urgent need,
he had to untie only a few laces
and could make good use of all his limbs
without actually being a slave to his outfit. 8
Today, if he must answer a call of nature,
he has to get out of so many strings
that it is a real nuisance to the fellow,
because what wants out, he must keep in   12
and, poor devil, he cannot even get out a fart.
Don't you think we, citizens, are in a fix?

In line 1, *metteiva e trava* (in Italian, *metteva e toglieva*) means "put on and took off." The word *çitten* in line 2 and line 14 literally means *cittadino* (citizen), but it indicates "man" in the general sense, a fellow. In line 3, *vogiando*, or *volendo*, means "wanting to." In line 4, *braga lasca*, or *pantolone largo*, means "large pants." In line 7, *varreiva*, or *valeva*, means "would use." In line 8, *scciavo dre robe*, or *schiavo dei vestiti*, means "slave to his clothes." In line 14, *te pà*, or *ti pare*, means "does it seem to you?"

Giulio Cesare Cortese (1575–1624) was born in Naples to a middle-class family, received a degree in law at the local university, and went to work at the king's court. Later, he moved to Florence, where he made a living serving Grand Duke Ferdinando de' Medici. Toward the end of his career, he became governor of Basilicata. Cortese is the author of several burlesque writings in Neapolitan dialect. *Micco Passaro 'nnamorato* narrates the fortunes and misfortunes of a Neapolitan *guappo* (blustering hooligan)

in love. *Viaggio di Parnaso* (Journey to Parnassus) is a parody of literary people. The *Vaiasseide* is a mock-heroic poem about the *vaiasse*, the Neapolitan women in service.

"Aggio paura ca ste dammecelle" is the *Vaiasseide*'s sonnet of dedication. Cortese dedicated his long poem to the women of Florence, who, according to a rather fanciful story told by Bartolomeo Zito, actor-writer and Cortese's contemporary, inspired him to write it. The sonnet, which is in Neapolitan, depicts the encounter of the poet with some Florentine women and shows how strange and laughable they found his deferential greeting to them.

Aggio paura ca ste dammecelle
se penzano ca so' quarche pacchiano,
o ca so' nato fuorze ad Antegnano,
cà me fanno onne iuorno guattarelle.   4
Ca songo segnorazze e ca so' belle,
non sanno ca io so' napoletano?
Quanno le dico: "Vàsove le mano"
a che serve sonà le ciaramelle?   8
Aggio strutto na còppola pe lloro,
e faccio lleverenzie co la pala,
ed esse sempre co lo risariello.   12
Stongo co no golio, che mme ne moro,
de veder una che pe mme se cala,
ma cchiù priesto avarraggio lo scartiello.

I am afraid that these damsels might
think I am some kind of a country hick,
that I may have been born at Antegnano,
for they go on pulling my leg every time.   4
They are great ladies, I know, and beautiful,
but don't they know that I am a Neapolitano?
Whenever I say, "I kiss your hand,"
do they have to start snickering like that?   8
I have worn out a hat to bow to them;
in front of them, I make curtsies by the shovel;
still, they go on giggling at me like mad.
I have a wish—I am dying for it—to see   12
just one of them to bend down as low for me:
before I see it, I will surely grow a hunchback.

Regarding line 3, Antegnano was a hill near Naples—now in the city itself—whose inhabitants were chided for their simple ways. Regarding line 8, the *ciaramella* is a noisy musical wind instrument similar to the oboe, once popular in the Italian countryside; metaphorically, it stands for babble or babbling. The expression could therefore be translated "what is the sense of babbling so?" or "why do you make such a fuss?" In line 9, the poet says, "I have worn out a hat by pulling it off so often in greeting these Florentine damsels." In line 12, *golio* means "desire."

The following sonnet, also in Neapolitan, is the propitiatory introduction to a semiserious collection of lyrics by the title of *La tiorba a taccone*. Cortese may have published the book in 1646 under the pseudonym of Felippo Sgruttendio de Scafato. Some scholars strongly contest the attribution of the collection to Cortese. The sonnet is addressed to the Muses and is a parody of the high-flown literariness of much contemporary verse. It is self-ridiculing, but it contains a less obvious and serious profession of intent.

O vuie che tutte 'n chietta ve ne state
a chisso monte tanto vertoluso,
non pe conta' de Cicco lo zelluso
né de Chiecchia Spechiecchia le baiate,   4
ma a dicere conciette 'mprofecate
de le settenzie che so' lloco suso,
che 'n sentirele po' resta confuso
sto munno, chino d'asene 'mmardate,   8
aggiate mo de me protezione
e dateme lo canto accossì doce
comme è lo suono de sto calascione.
Sprogate vuie pe me ssa bella voce,   12
azzocché senza vuoie cantanno io pone
comme a na vessa non morese 'n foce.

You who are flocking up there together
on that mountain chock-full of virtues,
not in order to write about scabby Cicco
or Chiecchia Spechiechia's absurdities,   4
but to write grand, fruitful ideas, to make
pronouncements worthy of that high place of yours,
which, were they heard, would stop the world
in its tracks, so full of harnessed donkeys it is!   8
Please, extend your protection to me,
and bestow on me a voice as honeyed
as are the sounds of this *calascione*.
Clear up its beautiful voice for me so that,   12
if by accident I were singing without you, I would not
from the beginning peter out in flatulence.

In line 1, the mountain is the Helicon in Greece, where the Muses reside. *In chietta* means "in a group," with a suggestion that the Muses flock together as some chattering women might do. In line 2, *vertoluso* means "virtuous," or full of worthwhile people. In line 3, *selluso*, or *tignoso*, refers to being covered with scabies. Regarding lines 3–4, Cicco and Chiechia Spechiechia are imaginary men of modest extraction and worth, as their ridiculous names suggest. In line 8, *'mmardate*, or *imbardate*, means "harnessed" (Melato). Regarding line 11, the *calascione*, a stringed instrument with two or three strings, was popular with the Neapolitan poorer classes; it did not appear in orchestras or reputed ensembles of any kind. The poet is modest about his own verse, unworthy of being sponsored by the Muses. Even so, unquestionable is his determination to write about small people in a way that can be useful to the world, an intention that even the old, dignified Muses might appreciate.

5.4 The Consolation of Poetry

By the middle of the sixteenth century, a long period of political and cultural transformation arrived at its conclusion. The 1559 Peace of Cateau Cambrésis closed the Italian Wars and formalized the absorption of the peninsula into the sphere of the Spanish empire. By then, Spain's sway over the church had helped to establish a severe form of Catholicism in the entire peninsula. There was an economic retrenchment as well. Italy's slow but steady decline started when the Ottoman domains closed the trade roads to the Middle East and Asia, and it worsened when, after the discovery of America, the commercial hub of Europe moved to the north of the continent. Correspondingly, the majority of Italians became economically cautious, intellectually uncertain, and timorously religious. In the insecurity of the age, many poets suffered from a dislocation in time, and their verse seems to be suspended between the Bembian ideal of classical serenity and the lugubrious self-doubt of post-Tridentine religiosity.

The early lyrics of Giovanni della Casa (1503–56), who was active in midcentury as a high-ranking member of the ecclesiastical bureaucracy, were the expression of a strong need for evasion into a world of classical fantasy and of an all-too-secular longing for a harmony of mind and a balance of spirit that neither religion nor his ecclesiastical career seemed able to provide. The sonnet "La bella greca" is an example of his mythologizing procedure.

> La bella greca, onde 'l pastor ideo
> in chiaro foco e memorabil arse,
> per cui l'Europa armossi, e guerra feo,
> e alto imperio antico a terra sparse;   4
> e le bellezze incenerite e arse
> di quella che sua morte in don chiedeo;
> e i begli occhi e le chiome a l'aura sparse
> di lei che stanca in riva di Peneo   8
> novo arboscello a i verdi boschi accrebbe;
> e qual altra, fra quante il mondo onora,
> in maggior pregio di bellezza crebbe,
> da voi, giudice lui, vinta sarebbe,   12
> che le tre dive (o sì beato allora!)
> tra' suoi bei colli ignude a mirar ebbe.

> The beautiful Greek, for whom the Idean
> shepherd burned in bright and memorable fire,
> for whom Europe took up arms, went to war,
> and tore down an ancient high empire,   4

and the beauty burned to cinders of the woman
who asked to be granted the gift of death,
the lovely eyes and the hair scattered in the breeze
of one who, exhausted, on the bank of the Peneus   8
added new green growth to the nearby woodland,
and add any woman of many the world admires,
any who rose to the highest praise of beauty,
all would be surpassed by you, if Paris were the judge,   12
who, (how fortunate he was!) in his hilly country,
was able to admire three goddesses in the nude.

Replete with images and phrases lifted from Ovid's *Heroides* and *Metamorphoses*, the sonnet pays homage to Elisabetta Quirini, wife of Lorenzo Quirini, a Venetian nobleman and friend of Della Casa. The poet gallantly claims that the most beautiful women of history and legend are not as alluring as Elisabetta. Regarding line 1, Helen, wife of Menelaus, king of Sparta, is the first woman to whom the poet compares Elisabetta. The Idean shepherd is Paris of Troy, King Priam's son, who was brought up by a shepherd on the slopes of Mount Ida. Paris eventually kidnapped Helen and brought her to Troy, hence the Trojan War organized by the Greeks, who wanted to get her back. In line 4, *alto imperio antico* refers to the city of Troy, which was an upcoming Asian power encroaching on Greek supremacy. Regarding lines 5–6, the second woman mentioned is Semele, daughter of the king of Cadmus. Zeus made love to her after entering her room in disguise in the dark of night. She asked to be able to see him the way he appeared to his wife, Hera. When her wish was granted, the god's unbearable splendor burned her to cinders. In line 8, the third woman is Daphne. Apollo pursued her on the bank of the river Peneus, in Thessaly. While running away from him, she asked the gods for help, and they changed her into a laurel tree. Regarding lines 12–13, each of three goddesses—Hera, Aphrodite, and Athena—claimed to be the fairest. Zeus ordered Paris to evaluate their beauty, and Paris decided in favor of Aphrodite, who had promised him Helen, the fairest of all mortal women. One single syntactical period, profusely fantasizing the beauties of several mythical women in relative dependent clauses, embraces the poem, coming to the point of the comparison only in the last tercet. The long suspension seems to emphasize a suppressed tendency to evasion, further stressed by the harsh rhymes of *accrebbe*, *crebbe*, and *sarebbe*, which, at the same time, keep the delaying lines rhythmically and securely in place.

At the time of the Council of Trent (1545–63), the church condemned the poetic use of classical myths as suggestions ideologically misleading. It is not surprising, therefore, that Della Casa's songbook, rich in classical concepts and images, was published after his death. Here is another example of his use of mythology.

O Sonno, o de la queta, umida, ombrosa
notte placido figlio; o de' mortali
egri conforto, oblio dolce de' mali
sì gravi ond'è la vita aspra e noiosa;   4
soccorri al core omai, che langue e posa
non ave, e queste membra stanche e frali
solleva: a me ten vola, o Sonno, e l'ali
tue brune sovra me distendi e posa.   8

Ov'è 'l silenzio che 'l dì fugge e 'l lume?
e i lievi sogni, che con non secure
vestigia di seguirti han per costume?
Lasso, che 'nvan te chiamo, e queste oscure   12
e gelide ombre invan lusingo! O piume
d'asprezza colme! O notti acerbe e dure!

O Sleep, of the quiet, humid, and shadowy
Night placid son, comfort to us weary
mortals, sweet oblivion of the dismal
evils that make life so painful and so harsh,   4
bring solace to my anguishing heart,
which finds no peace; these frail and tired limbs
do soothe, fly to me, o Sleep, unfold and bring
your shadowy wings to rest over me.   8
Where is the silence that shuns the light of day?
Where are the fleeting dreams that, stepping
so lightly, are wont to come in your company?
Alas! I call for you in vain, and in vain   12
I try to lure your dark and gelid shadows!
O pillows of restlessness! Bitter and weary nights!

Regarding line 1, in Greek and Roman mythology, Sleep is the son of Night. In line 9, *dì* (day) and *lume* (light) are hendiadys for "the light of day." The silence of the night dislikes the clamor of the day and its indiscreet light. In lines 10–11, *non secure vestigia* are the insecure, hesitant steps of dreams, because they bring about indistinct visions that are quickly forgotten. In line 13, *piume* (feathers) stands for a bed pillow. *Lusingo* carries the contextual meaning of "I implore, trying to make them friendly."

Sleep, as a restorative pause after a weary day, or as a purveyor of pleasant erotic dreams, was a popular theme in Renaissance poetry.[101] On Della Casa's invocation to Sleep weighs a sad weariness of life. The almost continuous use of enjambment—six in the octave and three in the sestet—stresses the intensity of feeling. The tying together of words that the metrical line would separate slows down the syntactical flow and gives it a protracted, tired rhythm. Della Casa uses the sonnet as a private, secret diary. Poetry, with its stepped-up powers of expression, has become a consolation.

Born to a privileged Florentine family, Della Casa had studied at the universities of Bologna and Padua, and as was customary for young men of his class, he had moved to Rome in order to launch his ecclesiastical career. When he was a young prelate, he penned some poems provocatively licentious. That was the time when the church authorities and public morality had not yet drawn the line between what was and was not allowed. That misjudged act of youthful defiance became later incompatible with the strictures of the Counter-Reformation. In some scholars' estimation, it was one of the reasons Della Casa was not made a cardinal. Whatever the case, in his mature age, Della Casa's lyrics turned to bitterness and regret. He often interwove classical reminiscences with personal references in doleful questionings about the meaning of life and old age. Representative of this mood is "Già lessi, e or conosco in me," a beautiful and perhaps the best known of Della Casa's sonnets.

Già lessi, e or conosco in me, sì come
Glauco nel mar si pose uom puro e chiaro,
e come sue sembianze si mischiaro
di spume e conche, e fersi alga sue chiome;   4
però che 'n questo Egeo che vita ha nome
puro anch'io scesi, e 'n queste de l'amaro
mondo tempeste, ed elle mi gravaro
i sensi e l'alma ahi di che indegne some!   8
Lasso: e soviemmi d'Esaco, che l'ali
d'amoroso pallor segnate ancora
digiuno per lo cielo apre e distende,
e poi satollo indarno a volar prende,   12
sì 'l core anch'io, che per sé leve fora,
gravato ho di terrene esche mortali.

Once I read, and now I recognize in me, how
Glaucus descended into the sea a clean and pure
man, how his features mingled with sponges
and with shells, and how his hair turned into weeds,   4
because in this Aegean Sea that has the name of life
and in the storms of this bitter world I too embarked
as a pure man, and they encumbered my senses
and soul—ah!—with what unworthy weights!   8
Alas! I remember Aesacus, who, while empty
of food, opened and into the sky unfolded
his wings, still marked with white signs of love,
but when he was satiated, in vain he tried to fly: 12
I too have burdened my heart, which in itself
would be so light, with worldly and fatal lures.

A sea monster scuttling about at the bottom of the sea and a bird that can no longer fly are symbols of Della Casa's spiritual condition, of his regrets and weariness of life. "What happened to Glaucus," says the poet in line 1, "happened to me: by entering this world, which is a stormy sea of ambitions and desires, I was contaminated by much filth, and I changed my very being." Regarding line 2, Glauco's original nature could no longer be seen, because incrustations and deformities disfigured his limbs. In Greek mythology, Glaucus was an angler living in Beotia. One day, as told in Ovid's *Metamorphoses*, he heard a mysterious voice inviting him to dive into the sea. He obeyed and quickly metamorphosed into a sea monster. The moral symbolism with which Della Casa endows the legend might have been suggested by Plato's *Republic* 61, Ic. Regarding line 9, the mythical Aesacus, driven mad by the death of Hesperia, his lover, was changed into an aquatic bird, the goosander or the merganser, both of which cannot fly when full of food. The white patches of feathers on the bird's wings were considered a badge of love. In line 10, the word *ancora* can be attributed to either *segnate* or to *digiuno*, but perhaps its attribution is intentionally ambiguous. In line 13, *per sé leve fora* means "in itself, it would be light." The poet's soul, which once was pure and light, cannot rise any longer, as it's held to the ground by the weight of many sins. Biography and spiritual and moral states are resolved into myth. Special emphasis on the poet's state of mind, on his anguish for a wasted life, is created by word transpositions (notice the strong hyperbaton of lines 6–7), the frequent use of enjambment (five in the octave and three in the first tercet), syntactical breaks in the middle of lines, and the slow and uninterrupted flow of ideas and images that create a long, sustained suspension.

Tragically at odds with the world around him was Torquato Tasso (1544–95), author of the historical epic *Jerusalem Delivered*. In his lyric poetry—more than two thousand lyrics are extant—images and musical verbal effects create an impression of fleeting sensations and a languid, brooding mood that transports the reader into a world of fantasy and dream. After a childhood spent with his mother between Sorrento and Naples—in Naples, young Torquato attended a Jesuit school—his father took him on a leisurely journey that touched several courts of northern Italy. In 1561, he was studying at the University of Padua, when he made the acquaintance of fifteen-year-old Lucrezia Bendidio, who'd just arrived in the city in Leonora d'Este's train. He wrote "I' veggio in cielo scintillar le stelle" probably with Lucrezia in mind.

> Io veggio in cielo scintillar le stelle
> oltre l'usato e lampeggiar tremanti
> come negli occhi de' cortesi amanti
> noi miriam talor vive facelle.   4
> Aman forse là suso, o pur son elle
> pietose a' nostri affanni, a' nostri pianti?
> e scorgon le insidie e' passi erranti
> là dove altri d'amor goda e favelle?   8
> Cortesi luci, se Leandro in mare
> o traviato peregrin fossi'io,
> non mi sareste di soccorso avare:
> così vi faccia il sol più belle e chiare, 12
> siate nel dubbio corso al desir mio
> fide mie luci e scorte amate e care.

> I see the stars sparkle in the sky
> more than usual, and tremulously
> flash like the vivid lights that we often
> see in the eyes of gracious lovers.   4
> Do they love up there? Do they perhaps
> take pity on our woes, on our weeping?
> Do they see the snares and the perilous steps
> of men who joyfully love and think of love? 8
> O courteous lights, if I were like Leander
> in the sea, or like a pilgrim straying on land,
> you would not niggardly withdraw your help:

may then the sun make you brighter and lovelier,   12
and in my risky journey, may you be, as I desire,
my trusted and dear, beloved escorts and lights.

In "Quaeris, quot mihi basationes," Catullus asked Lesbia to give him as many kisses as in the silent night there are stars looking down at the furtive passions of humankind (*aut quam sidera multa cum tacet nox, / furtivos hominum vident amores*). Regarding line 9, young Leander of Abidos swam across the Hellespont every night in order to visit his beloved Hero, who lived in Sextus, a town on the opposite side of the sound. The sonnet quickly progresses from the image of the starry sky to the suggestion that the stars might sympathize with human predicaments: nature is transfigured, and the nocturnal vision becomes pervaded by a wave of tender emotion.

In 1565, Tasso entered the service of Cardinal Luigi d'Este, and in 1572, he joined the household of the cardinal's brother, Duke Alfonso II. Lucrezia Bendidio, of a noble Ferrara family whose male members were secretaries and diplomats of the Este court, was still in the duchess's entourage, but now she was married to a Paolo Machiavelli. At court, there were other ladies-in-waiting, such as Laura Peperara and Eleonora Sanvitale. Tasso, who lived in a world of his own imagining, fell in love with each of them in turn and then resentfully felt wounded and mortified.

Non più crespo d'oro o d'ambra tersa e pura
stimo le chiome che 'l mio laccio ordiro,
e nel volto e nel seno altro non miro
ch'ombra de la beltà che poco dura.   4
Fredda la fiamma è già, sua luce oscura,
senza grazia de gli occhi il vago giro:
deh come i miei pensier tanto invaghiro,
lasso, e chi la ragione o sforza o fura?   8
Fero inganno d'Amor, l'inganno ormai
tessendo in rime sì leggiadri fregi
a la crudel ch' indi più bella apparve.
Ecco, i' rimovo le mentite larve: 12
or ne le proprie tue sembianze omai
ti veggia il mondo e ti contempli e pregi!

No longer shiny curls of gold and pure amber
do I believe to be the hair that entwined my chain;
in that face, in that bosom I see nothing now
but the shadow of a beauty that will fade.   4
Cold is the flame by now, its light has darkened,
and those fair glancing eyes are now devoid of grace.
Ah, how was my mind so hopelessly ensnared!
What did compel, alas, what purloined my reason?   8
A brutal deception of Love it was, a deceit that,
weaving in rhymes embellishments so great,
made the cruel woman seem far more enticing.

> Look! I now remove the appearances I faked:
> with the features that are truly yours may the world
> see you now, contemplate you, and evaluate!

12

In line 1, Bembo's line "Crin d'oro crespo e d'ambra tersa e pura" is intentionally overturned. For Bembo's sonnet, see 4.4. In line 4, *ombra della beltà* means "shadow of beauty," or an insubstantial beauty that quickly disappears. Per line 5, when the man's desire is extinguished, the woman does not seem to be as attractive as when he was in love with her and described her in verse. In line 12, *le mentite larve* signifies both the illusions of love and those created by poetic fiction, for there is a double deception here: one is perpetrated by Love, who made him fond of what was not so great, and the other is perpetrated by the lover-poet himself, who praised the woman in verse and made her seem more lovely than she really was. The quatrains contemplate love's deception and arrive at a question: What made him lose his reasons? This question, by diffusing the deceit, dissipates any clear explanation of it. The sestet considers the deception perpetrated by the lover-poet, concluding with a threat: once the poetic embellishment is erased, she will appear to everybody as she really is.

The Este court, with its spectacular celebrations, sumptuous banquets, and spirited love games, was for Tasso a mesmerizing stage. Ferrara had become the theatrical capital of Renaissance Italy. Repertory and amateur companies presented Latin and Italian plays. Tasso's *Aminta*, which dramatizes the loves of shepherds and nymphs, was played by members of the court and was staged on the island of Belvedere, in the middle of the Po River. A character in Tasso's *Dialoghi* 2, 736 explains, "The whole city seemed to me a marvelous and unprecedented luminous and colored spectacle, and the happenings of those days not unlike the actions staged in theaters, in various languages, and by a variety of speakers; and, as I found it insufficient to be a spectator, I wanted to be one of the people that were part of the comedy and to mingle with them." The following sonnet re-creates one of those luminous and colorful spectacles, in this case an open-air ball, the so-called *ballo della fiaccola* (ball of the flaming torch).

> Mentre ne' cari balli in loco adorno
> si traean le notturne e placide ore,
> face, che nel suo foco accese Amore,
> lieto n'apriva a mezza notte il giorno; 4
> e da candida man vibrata intorno
> spargea faville di sì puro ardore,
> che parea apportar gioia ed onore
> a' pochi eletti, a gli altri invidia e scorno. 8
> Quando a te data fu, man cruda e bella,
> e da te presa e spenta, e ciechi e mesti
> restar mill'occhi a lo sparir d'un lume
> ahi, come allor cangiasti arte e costume: 12
> tu, ch' accender solei l'aurea facella,
> tu, ministra d'Amor, tu l'estinguesti!

> While serene nocturnal hours were spent
> in cherished dances, in wide adorned spaces,
> a torch—which Love had lit at his fire—

> brought the cheery day into the dark of night; 4
> and, every time a white hand shook it,
> it scattered sparks of such pure brightness
> that seemed to bring joy and distinction
> to the elected few, envy and scorn to others. 8
> When it passed to your pretty and cruel hand,
> and you took and blew it, and a thousand eyes
> were saddened and blinded as the light went out,
> then—ah!—how you changed ways and custom! 12
> You who were used to light the golden flame,
> now you, minister of Love, you snuffed it out!

In the edition of lyrics published in Padua in 1569, Tasso gave the following explanation for the sonnet: "The dance of the torch, popular in many parts of Italy, is the last dance of the ball, and it is up to the person who at that point receives the torch to put it out and bring the dance and the festivities to an end. I wrote this sonnet on one of these occasions, when a lady ended a pleasant entertainment by extinguishing the flame with uncalled-for hurry" (Tasso, 1965, 68). Regarding line 8, the *eletti* (the chosen) were the men invited by the woman to dance; those who were not invited felt envy and scorn. In line 12, *arte e costume* means "ways and custom," supposedly in having and encouraging others to have a good time. The octave show the festivities taking place in an open-air space, in the dark of a summer night. A torch is being passed from hand to hand. In the sestet, the long shot changes into a close-up. A thousand eyes are expectantly looking at the woman holding the torch—to see who is going to get it next. Instead of handing it over to someone else, she extinguishes it, thus announcing the end of the ball. After a melancholy exclamation in the second tercet, the festive scene ends in a vague feeling of regret.

The court was, for Tasso, a garden of pleasures and also a source of security and prestige. In time, however, his dreamy and tormented disposition transformed that environment into a fount of disappointments, a milieu to which he wanted to belong but felt he could not, and a bitter resentment began to smolder in his heart. Furthermore, the severe criticism encountered by *Jerusalem Delivered*—for having an alleged inconsistency of style and not being heroic enough—helped to tip his mind toward paranoia. He accused a member of the court of trying to kill him, knifed a courtier, publicly accused the duke and the court of heretical leanings, and even denounced himself before the Inquisition. In 1579, back in town after one of his many flights from Ferrara, he attacked the courtly cortege during the duke's nuptials. Restrained by force, he was relegated in the insane section of the Santa'Anna Hospital. Here is a sonnet penned in the hospital when the carnival season of 1580 was approaching.

> Sposa regal, già la stagion ne viene
> che gli accorti amatori a' balli invita
> e ch'essi a' rai di luce alma e gradita
> vegghian le notti gelide e serene. 4
> Del suo fedel già le secrete pene
> ne' casti orecchi è di raccorre ardita
> la verginella, e lui tra morte e vita
> soave inforsa e 'n dolce guerra il tiene. 8
> Suonano i gran palagi e i tetti adorni

di canto: io sol di pianto il carcer tetro
fo risonar. Questa è la data fede?
Son questi i mei bramati ritorni?   12
Lasso! Dunque pregion, dunque ferètro
chiamate voi pietà, Donna, e mercede?

Royal Bride, at hand is now the season
that invites the cunning lovers to the dance,
to spend the silent and frigid nights
in the balmy glow of agreeable lights.   4
The maiden daringly welcomes the secret
pangs of her suitor into her chaste ears
and holds him in suspense between life
and death, keeping him in sweet warfare.   8
The great palaces and the ornate roofs
resound with music; I alone make this dismal jail
echo with crying. Is this the promise made to me?
Is this my long-hoped-for homecoming?   12
Alas! So you, my lady, you call this imprisonment
a "consideration"? This tomb a "recompense"?

Regarding line 1, the royal spouse is Margherita Gonzaga, third wife of Duke Alfonso II and the bride of the above-mentioned nuptuals. Per line 8, during the dance, the maiden (*la verginella*) listens to her lover's confession but leaves him in a painful condition of doubt (*inforsa*), between hope and despair. That state of uncertainty is the "sweet warfare" of love. Lines 11–14 might be a reference to the consideration avowed and to the promises the duke's emissaries made to Tasso when they found him in Turin, where he had escaped in 1579. The sonnet imbues the night with nostalgia for the gay life of the court, its splendors, its entertainment, and its promise of love. Nature has become the registration of an emotional state. At the end, the wistful reminiscence dissolves into an anguished question and a cry for help.

The imaginations of Goethe and Byron turned Tasso into a romantic figure of lore. Some modern Italian analysts saw the poet's disturbed mind as the symbol of a general national crisis, a condition of alienation common to the majority of sixteenth-century Italian intellectuals. Whatever the interpretation, the Estes had good reason to be weary of Tasso's disturbed and disturbing behavior. Ferrara was a fief of the church, to be reabsorbed into papal territory if the Estes could not provide an heir. At the beginning of the Italian Wars, Julius II had declared the fief forfeited and had excommunicated Alfonso I for having allied himself with Louis XII of France. From that time on, the court was under the church's vigilant scrutiny. Furthermore, the present duke's mother, Renée, daughter of King Louis of France, was a devout Calvinist. By her initiative, Ferrara had become the refuge of many reform-minded humanists fleeing from France. In 1536, Calvin himself was in Ferrara as a guest of Renée. In 1554, Ercole II, her husband, worried about the papal disapproval, found it necessary to confine her in the ducal palace and forbade her to propagandize reformist ideas. The present duke, Renée's son, had no male heirs, and in 1598, the pope reabsorbed the duchy into the Papal States.

Celio Magno (1536–1602) was born into a family of Venetian aristocrats. After residing for a while in southern Italy—in Naples, he became a follower of the Catholic reformist Juan de Valdès—and after traveling on diplomatic missions to Syria, Croatia, and Spain, he settled in his native city and served in the administration of the republic, rising to become first secretary to the Senate and later a member of the Council of Ten.

> Di notte in braccio al mio tesor godea
> felice furto; e per accorto farmi
> de l'ora del partir, desto a chiamarmi
> meco un picciol del tempo indice avea.   4
> Guastollo Amor che presso a noi giacea,
> quasi del suo nemico insegna et armi:
> onde il tempo tradimmi, e fe' trovarmi
> dal dì veloce in grembo a la mia dea.   8
> Ma disse Amor: "Sia lieto e dolce inganno
> questo, e segno a voi dia con quanta fretta
> per mai più non tornar l'ore sen vanno,
> e che sol col seguir quel che diletta   12
> in questa vita, d'ogni oltraggio e danno
> contra 'l tempo crudel si fa vendetta."

> Throughout the night, I enjoyed my furtive
> pleasure in the arms of my treasure, and to be
> aware of the moment of departure, I had with me
> a small gauge of time, ready to caution me.   4
> Love, who was lying next to us, broke it,
> being that an ensign and symbol of his enemy:
> so time betrayed me, and the fast-oncoming
> day surprised me in the arms of my goddess.   8
> Then Love said, "May this be a sweet, happy
> deception and a reminder to you of how
> hurriedly the hours go by, never to return,
> and that, in this life, only by following what   12
> most delights, one may take revenge of all
> the offense and damage done by cruel time."

In line 5, the clock is a heraldic device (*insegna et armi*) representing time, which, in the case of furtive amorous encounters, proves to be the enemy of love. What at first sounds like the recollection of a night of pleasure turns out to be a meditation on the transitory nature of all pleasures. The only way we have of revenging ourselves against the passing of time is to grasp the enjoyments that come our way.

Ecco di rose a questa tomba intorno
aprir, quasi in su' onor, pomposa schiera,
che 'l seno aprendo sembran dir: "Tal era
di colei che qui giace il volto adorno;   4
e tal ne sentian l'altre invidia e scorno,
qual di noi gli altri fior a primavera.
Cresceale il vanto odor d'onestà vera
ch'in lei fea con Amor dolce soggiorno.   8
S'oltra ogni stil fiorisce in noi beltate,
è perché nel terren, ch'in sé converse
le belle membra, siam concette e nate.
Ma qui tosto ancor noi cadrem disperse   12
da l'aspra pioggia in che l'altrui pietate
ne tien piangendo eternamente immerse."

Here, around this tomb, a pompous display
of roses is blooming as if in her honor,
and, opening, the petals seem to say, "Such was
the comely face of the woman who lies here,   4
for whom others felt the same shameful envy
that in the spring other flowers feel for us.
Her fame grew with the merit of true goodness,
which found, with Love, a lovely home in her.   8
If beauty blooms in us beyond all poetic praise,
it is because in this earth, into which her beautiful
limbs have changed, we were conceived and born.
Soon here we too shall fall, scattered   12
by the relentless rain in which people's pity,
by their crying, keeps us eternally drowned."

In line 3, *'l sen* refers to the bosom, here the flower's bud. In line 7, *odor* is translated as "fame," but literally, it is "scent," or "inkling." The expression might come from *odor di santità* (a scent of sanctity), used in reference to saints and relics who were thought to emanate a special scent. *Odor* is the subject, and *vanto* (boast, honor, or merit) is the object. In line 9, *oltra ogni stil* means "beyond any possibility of expressing it in words." In line 13, *altrui* means "others," or people, here those who loved the woman and now grieve.

The traditional conceit of the woman whose presence beautifies nature receives here an opulent funereal twist: her remains have lushly fertilized the ground where she is buried, turning it into a luxuriant bed of roses. Magno's meditation on the unavoidable demise of everything beautiful comes to life thanks to sumptuous imagery, asyntactical strophes, and expressive and elaborate structure, which I translated into separate sentences.

The somber thoughts Magno confided to his lyrics do not appear simply to be, as some critics suggest, the effect of a maladjustment to personal circumstances; they also seem the effect of a malaise felt by people at large, signs of the perturbed religiosity of the age.

    Trovo ovunque io giro 'l guardo intento,
trista immagin di morte. Ecc' ora il giorno
da l'Oriente uscir di luce adorno,
eccol tosto a l'occaso oscuro e spento.   4
Così le frondi e i fior, vago ornamento
di primavera a questo colle intorno,
farà languidi e secchi al suo ritorno
de la fredda stagion la neve e 'l vento.   8
Quanto nasce qua giù, quanto con l'ore
crescendo vive, al fin sotto una sorte,
senza riparo aver, mancando more.
E, s'al mesto pensier chiuder le porte   12
col chiuder gli occhi io cerco, il cieco orrore
contemplo allor de la mia propria morte.

    Wherever I turn my eyes and look intently,
I see a sad image of death. Here comes the day
out of the east, resplendent in its light;
soon, in the west, it will be dark and spent.   4
The leafy fronds and the flowers, graceful
adornment of spring around this hill,
with the return of winter, will be made
parched and listless by snow and wind.   8
What is born down here, all that in time
lives and grows, finally, by the same destiny,
having no remedy, wastes away and dies.
And, if I close my eyes, trying to shut the gate   12
to my wistful thinking, then the unseeing
fearful image of my own death I contemplate.

Regarding line 3, "*Ubique pavor et plurima mortis imago*" (everywhere I see a frightening image of death), writes Virgil in *Aeneid* 10, 456 (quoted by Marco Ariani in Segre 2,721). In line 4, *occaso* is the west. To illustrate the end of all things, the poet has chosen poignant images among what is familiar and has distributed them at a regular, rhetorically controlled pace. The measured striding forward of such emblematic sights gives his memento mori the tone of a haunting symphony, until, in the ending, the meditation on the passing of things becomes horror of the eternal darkness and of one's total physical annulment. For Magno, as for Della Casa, poetry became the repository of a constant meditation on life and perhaps the only consolation.

5.5 In the Realm of the Divine

Signs of a renewed religious interest were already evident at the beginning of the sixteenth century. Most religious movements of earlier times had started among the poor and had carried evident economic and political connotations. Of late, many participants and, most significantly, the leaders of the new movement were outstanding members of the prosperous classes and were also to be found in the Roman bureaucracy, all men who felt a strong need to regulate and renovate the church. In the view of many well-wishing reformers, reconciliation with the Protestants was desirable and appeared possible in 1534, when Alessandro Farnese was elected pope as Paul III. The Council of Trent convened in 1545 with the purpose of reconciling Rome with its opponents; in 1563, however, when it closed, the fragmentation of Christianity was sealed forever.

By and by, lyric poets discarded the existential model set by Bembo in favor of religious themes. More common became the meditations about life and death and the theme of one's relation to the divinity. In this section, I chose sonneteers who represent such religious concerns. In chronological order, they are Vittoria Colonna, a promoter of church reforms; Giovanni della Casa and Gabriel Fiamma, two high-ranking members of the church; Giordano Bruno and Tommaso Campanella, persecuted visionaries; and Giacomo Lubrano, the most flamboyant preacher of the post–Counter-Reformation age. The time covered by their sonnets extends from the first stirring of religious revival in the early decades of the century to the firm reestablishment of Catholic orthodoxy by the middle of the next.

In the 1530s, Vittoria Colonna's poetry turned from a spiritual union with her husband to an intense meditation on Christ (for the sonnets celebrating her husband, see 4.5). The progression from a Neoplatonic to a religious stance was not difficult to make. The possibility for humankind to return to its original condition—in Neoplatonic theory, the soul is an emanation of the universal mind—easily blended with the Christian view of the fall from grace, redemption through Christ, and return to God. The meditation on Christ's passion had long dominated Italian devotion, and in Vittoria's time, it had become the fulcrum of the spiritual message preached by such religious leaders as the Spanish Juan de Valdès in Naples and Bernardino Ochino in Rome. Colonna attended the reunions and sermons of both.

> Tira su l'alma al ciel col suo d'amore
> laccio attorto il gran Padre e stringe il nodo
> per man del caro Figlio, e sì bel modo
> non men che l'opra stessa appaga il core, 4
> tal ch'io sento sottil vivace ardore
> penetrar dentro, sì ch'ardendo godo,
> e chiaro ed alto grido ascolto ed odo
> che mi richiama a più vivace onore. 8
> Gradi di fede e caritate e speme
> e di quella umiltà che l'uom sublima
> ne fanno scale infino al Ciel superno,
> ove l'alme beate unite insieme 12
> di mano in man da l'ultima a la prima
> si miran tutte nel gran specchio eterno.

The great Father pulls my soul toward
heaven with his noose of love, which the hand
of his dear Son makes tighter; his fine manner,
no less than his action, so delights my heart   4
that a subtle, lively warmth I can feel
penetrating inside me; then, as I relish the ardor,
I hear a loud, clear thunder, and I listen
as it calls me to a higher state of honor.   8
Degrees of faith, of hope, and of charity,
and of that humility that uplifts humanity,
become steps that guide us to high heaven,
where the blessed souls, coming all together   12
one by one, from the first to the last, all look
at themselves in the infinite mirror of eternity.

In line 2, *attorto* means "twisted." Christ has strengthened the possibility of the human salvation granted by God. The sonnet opens with a cosmic view: God has all his creatures tied to one another with a string of love and pulls them heavenward. He penetrates Vittoria's soul and draws it toward him. A long syntactical period carries the movement of the ascent from section to section in a rhythm that remains constant throughout and with images that move again from heaven to the earth and back to God's eternal, endless splendor.

Colonna penned the sonnet "Vanno i pensier talor" after 1541, the year she took up residence in Viterbo. The pontifical legate governor of the town was the English Reginald Pole.[102] Paul III had summoned Pole to head a commission that had been organized to reform the pontifical administration. In Viterbo, the English prelate became the leader of the so-called Spirituali. This group of Catholic theologians debated on articles of faith and tried to persuade the more conservative members of the church to an agreement with the Protestants. Colonna sought Pole's company and attended his meetings. The Spirituali's main point of debate was the notion of justification by faith, which, for the Church of Rome, meant justification by both faith and works and, for the Protestants, meant justification by faith alone. Here is a sonnet showing the extent to which the Spirituali's discussions influenced Colonna.

Vanno i pensier talor carghi di vera
fede al gran Figlio in croce e indi quella
luce, ch'Ei porge lor serena e bella,
li guida al Padre in gloriosa schiera;   4
né questo almo favor rende più altera
l'alma fedel, poi che fatta è rubella
del mondo e di se stessa, anzi rende ella
a Dio de l'onor Suo la gloria intera.   8
Non giungon l'umane ali a l'alto segno
senza il vento divin, né l'occhio scopre
il bel destro sentier senza 'l gran lume.
Cieco è 'l nostro voler, vane son l'opre,   12

cadono al primo vol le mortal piume
senza quel di Gesù fermo sostegno.

At times our thoughts, imbued with true faith,
go to the great Son on the cross, and from there
the serene and beautiful light he offers
guides them to the Father in glorious throng: 4
but for this life-giving gift, the faithful's
soul, which is rebellious to itself and the world,
does not feel proud; on the contrary, the soul
claims for God alone the glory of that honor.   8
Human wings cannot attain that high goal
without the divine wind, nor can our eye discern
the fine, straight path without his powerful light.
Our will is blind, vain are our actions,   12
at the outset our mortal wings will fail,
if they are not held high by Jesus's stable hand.

Vittoria strives toward an understanding of the theological meaning of the Passion and of salvation. The effort to express the ineffable and explain the inexplicable results in repeated statements of belief and interconnected declarations of doctrine bolstering her faith, a faith renewed in the light provided now by the Spirituali. In line 5, *almo* means "life-giving," from Latin *alere*, meaning "to nourish." For the life-giving gift (*almo favor*) of salvation, humankind cannot claim credit. In lines 6–7, *poi che … stessa* means "the rightful soul acts against the mundane world and the fragile human nature." Per lines 8–9, the credit for salvation goes to God: his alone are the honor (*onor suo*) and the whole glory (*intera gloria*) of it. Colonna insists on the gratuitous character of devine grace. She explicitly states in line 12 that salvation is granted by faith alone: salvation has no need of works, human actions do not count (*vane son l'opre*), and it occurs without the participation of the human will (*cieco è il nostro voler*). Cardinal Pole advised Vittoria not to go beyond the limits (of understanding?) allowed to women and to refrain from dogmatic curiosity. When reconciliation between Catholics and the Protestants no longer seemed possible, Vittoria retired in a convent of secluded nuns. Hers was a deliberate act of humility, as well as a renunciation of her poetic vocation (Russell 2000, 165–66). Even so, her past statements, in writings and in conversations, about justification by faith alone brought about a posthumous condemnation for heresy.

The following sonnet by Giovanni della Casa expresses feelings of repentance and contrition, and for that reason, it is usually assigned to the last period of his life.

Questa vita mortal, che 'n una o 'n due
brevi e notturne ore trapassa, oscura
e fredda, involto avea fin qui la pura

parte di me ne l'atre nubi sue.   4
Ora a mirar le grazie tante tue
prendo, che frutti e fior, gielo e arsura,
e sì dolce del ciel legge e misura,
eterno Dio, tuo magistero fue.   8
Anzi 'l dolce aer puro e questa luce
chiara, che 'l mondo a gli occhi nostri scopre,
traesti tu d'abissi oscuri e misti:
e tutto quel che 'n terra o 'n ciel riluce   12
di tenebre era chiuso, e tu l'apristi;
e 'l giorno e 'l sol de le tue man son opre.

This mortal life, which, dark and cold,
in one or two short nocturnal hours goes
swiftly by, has up to now enveloped
the pure part of me in its murky clouds.   4
Now I turn to contemplate your many graces,
for fruit and flowers, frost and scorching heat,
and the pleasing, measured evolutions of the sky
were brought forth, eternal God, by your mastery.   8
Indeed, the pure and balmy air and this clear
light that reveals the world to our eyes
you drew from dark and commingled chasms:
and anything that shines, on earth or in the sky,   12
was sealed in darkness, and you brought it out;
and works of your hands are the day and the sun.

The octave is structured on a parallel between, on one side, the passage from the primeval chaotic darkness to the light of divine creation and, on the other side, the passage from the gloom of the poet's sinful life to the glowing joy of his reconciliation with God. The sestet is a hymn to the regulated harmony of heavens and earth, in total surrender to God's greatness and the beauty and goodness of creation. In line 11, *abissi oscuri e misti* refers to the dark and commingled matter of the original chaos, per Genesis. In line 12, *l'apristi* means "you opened," or drew them out of the darkness into the light.

Gabriel Fiamma (1530–85) was a Venetian man of the church—and the bishop of Chioggia at the end of his life—who acquired fame as a skillful orator. He penned a collection of sermons and some volumes of lives of saints. His lyric poems, which follow a biographical line of spiritual development from sin to redemption, were published in 1570 with the title of *Rime spirituali*.

Questo mar, questi scogli e queste arene
hanno gran somiglianza col mio male:
ch' un numero d'affanni e pene eguale

a quel di questa sabbia il cor sostiene;   4
e tal durezza di pensieri tiene
la mente in sé, che non l'ha un scoglio tale;
e, come fosse un mar, sempre m'assale
or vento di paura, or di spene.   8
Come l'arena sterile è l'ingegno;
arida l'alma come un duro scoglio;
torbido il cor come turbato mare.
Sempre di lagrimoso umor son pregno,   12
né mi move del mondo ire od orgoglio,
e le dolcezze mie son tutte amare.

This sea, these rocks, and these beaches
do bear a great resemblance to my ills:
for my heart holds as many woes and cares
as is the number of these grains of sand;   4
such is the harshness of thoughts my mind
holds within, that no rock contains the equal;
and down on me, as if on a sea, always blows
a wind at times of fear and at times of hope.   8
My mind is as sterile as the sand,
my soul is as barren as a rocky reef,
and my heart is as troubled as a stormy sea.
Forever I soak in a bath of tears, neither   12
the world's wrath nor its pride can move me,
and my sweet moments are so very bitter.

Many poems of the time were meditations on the passing of time and on the vanity of life. In Fiamma's sonnet, the penitential theme takes on a suggestive personal turn. The landscape is recognizable, being possibly what Fiamma was able to see when he approached the Tremiti Islands by sea as he traveled southward by boat—as we know he did—along the Adriatic coast of the peninsula.

"Quest'ora breve" is Fiamma's self-examination in the manner made popular by the *Meditations* of St. Ignatius of Loyola.

Quest'ora breve e d'ogni gioia cassa,
ch'ha nome vita, ed è polve, ombra e vento,
lieve fugace e vil, ch'in un momento
vola, sparisce, si disperde e passa,   4
rapisce e ritien l'alma afflitta e lassa,
e di vaghezza tal l'empie, ch'io sento
che 'l perfetto del ciel vero contento,
gonfia misera e cieca, a dietro lassa.   8
Ben la chiama e la desta del ciel alto consiglio
del suo fattore, perché volga il pensiero

a la sua vera stanza alma e natia:
ma sorda a le sue voci, il duro esiglio 12
sol ama, e cerca—oh desir vano e fiero!—
che de l'eterno ben chiuda la via.

This brief hour, bereft of every joy,
that we call life—which is sand, shadow, and wind,
which is light, fleeting, and vile and in a moment
flies, is lost, passes away, and disappears— 4
steals and holds my afflicted and tired soul
and muddies it with such lures that I feel
it leaves heaven's true happiness behind,
for it grows pretentious, miserable, and blind. 8
The Creator's high wisdom stirs it and calls
after it, so it may turn its thoughts
toward its original, life-giving, and true abode:
but deaf to his voice, only its harsh exile 12
the soul loves, trying—oh, vain and proud desire!—
to obstruct the path that leads to the eternal good.

Per lines 11–12, as heaven is the soul's proper home (*la sua vera stanza*), the heart is now in exile (*esiglio*). In line 13, the subject of *ama* and *cerca* is *anima* of line 9.

In order to prevent any possible theological misinterpretation on the part of the authorities, Fiamma thought it wise to add a commentary to all his poems. Even so, his collection eventually found its way into the Index of Forbidden Books.

Born to a noble family of Nola, Giordano Bruno (1548–1600) went to study in nearby Naples and, when still young, became a Dominican friar. Accused of heresy four years later, he left the order and embarked on a life of peregrinations, first in northern Italy and then abroad. Everywhere he went, he made himself known as an opponent of the local religion and school of thought.

Bruno believed in an infinite, uncentered universe containing innumerable worlds inhabited by an infinite number of species and forms of life. His philosophy displaced the Aristotelian theory of a geocentric world and reversed the Copernican view of a finite, heliocentric universe. He also maintained that our perception of the world is relative to our position in space and time and that as there are infinite positions, so there are infinite possible ways of viewing the universe. It is therefore impossible to postulate a limit to the progress of human knowledge. For him, the divinity was the intelligence of that infinite universe, and the individual natural beings, who live briefly and die, represent diverse ways of being, all forms of existence possible in the one infinite divine substance that is nature. In his view, only the poet-philosopher could claim knowledge of reality. His moral task consisted, therefore, of pursuing the infinite being and, from a first loving intuition of the ideal beauty, initiating the soul's progress toward the absolute and the eternal.

The sonnet "Amor, per cui tant'alto il ver discerno" is both an exhortation to listen to his unfailing word (*dir non fallace*) and a contemptuous attack on the unbelievers and the cowards who do not understand and who are shifty and blind.

    Amor, per cui tant'alto il ver discerno,
ch'apre le porte di diamante e nere,
per gli occhi entra il mio nume; e per vedere
nasce, vive, si nutre, e ha regno eterno.   4
Fa scorger quanto ha il ciel, terra ed inferno,
fa presenti d'assenti effigie vere,
repiglia forze e, trando dritto, fere
e impiaga sempre il cor, scopre ogni interno.   8
O dunque, volgo vile, al vero attendi,
porgi l'orecchio al mio dir non fallace;
apri, apri, se puoi, gli occhi, insano e bieco.
Fanciullo il credi, perché poco intendi;   12
perché ratto ti cangi, ei par fugace;
per esser orbo tu, lo chiami cieco.

    Love, which lets me see a truth so high
and opens up the black adamantine doors,
enters my soul through my eyes and, in order to see,
is born, lives on, is nourished, and reigns forever.   4
It lets me perceive all the things of heaven, of earth,
and of hell, as truthful effigies of what is not shown;
it gains strength and, launching head-on, always strikes
and wounds the heart and opens up all closed spaces.   8
So, worthless crowd, pay attention to the truth;
turn your ears to my unfailing words; open, open,
if you can, your eyes, you insane, squint-eyed people.
You think it puerile, for you understand little;   12
because you are devious, you believe it shifty;
because you fail to see, you call it blind.

    Regarding lines 1 and 3, for Bruno, love was the means to discover the truth and the divine. The doors in line 2 are the dark doors of ignorance. Per lines 5–6, love allows us to see what is on earth and in heaven, even that which cannot easily be seen. Bruno's truth was not the truth of the Neoplatonists, who eschewed what is human in order to attain the divine. For him, divinity was everywhere, and the truth rested in the willingness to understand the world and everything in it. In line 12, *fanciullo il credi* means "you think it (the truth) childish." The sonnet, metrically irregular—the ninth and thirteenth lines are heptasyllabic, or *settenari*—is one of many in Bruno's *De gl'heroici furori* (The Heroic Frenzies), published in 1585. The title of the book refers to that special madness of love that fuels an all-consuming pursuit of the infinite, a strong yearning to participate in the nature of the divine and the divine in nature.

    For Bruno, the supreme human achievement, the highest degree of philosophical research, was becoming one with nature. This was the aim of his heroic madness. In the following sonnet, the human intellect reaching for the utmost wisdom is represented by Actaeon. After seeing the goddess, who represents knowledge, Actaeon is devoured by his own dogs—that is, he is absorbed and becomes part of nature, just as the intellect that knows is absorbed by what it comprehends, thus becoming part of the cosmic whole into which everything merges and disappears.

> Alle selve i mastini e i veltri slaccia
> il giovan Atteon, quand' il destino
> gli drizz' il dubio ed incauto camino,
> di boscareccie fiere appo la traccia.   4
> Ecco tra l'acque il più bel busto e faccia,
> che veder poss' il mortal e divino,
> in ostro et alabastro et oro fino
> vidde; e 'l gran cacciator divenne caccia.   8
> Il cervio ch'a' più folti
> luoghi drizzav' i passi più leggieri,
> ratto voraro i suoi gran cani e molti.
> I' allargo i miei pensieri   12
> ad alta preda, ed essi a me rivolti
> morte mi dan con morsi crudi e fieri.

> Toward the woods young Actaeon unleashed
> his mastiffs and his greyhounds, and then destiny
> steered him toward a dangerous and risky path
> after the traces left by wild forest beasts.   4
> There, in the water, he caught sight of a breast
> and face of alabaster, of purple, and of gold refined,
> the finest a mortal or a divine being might ever see:
> and there the great hunter became the hunted.   8
> The stag, which to the most
> remote places was moving its nimblest steps,
> by the many big hounds was quickly devoured.
> I extend my thoughts   12
> to a sublime catch, and they, turning back on me,
> give me death with sharp and relentless biting.

According to the myth, one day, as he was hunting, the mythical Actaeon caught sight of the goddess Artemis while she was bathing naked in the river. To punish his effrontery, the goddess changed the young man into a stag, and his own hounds ate him. Regarding line 5, purple, alabaster, and refined gold (*ostro ed alabastro ed oro fino*) are the colors of flesh and hair. In line 9, the stag (*cervio*) is Actaeon, now a stag. In line 13, *sublime catch* (*alta preda*) is divine wisdom, of which the goddess Artemis is the symbol.

Bruno gives a detailed explanation of this sonnet in the fourth dialogue of *De gl'heroici furori*. Actaeon is the human intellect taking off in pursuit of divine wisdom. The fast greyhounds (*veltri*) represent the swift operation of the intellect; the strong mastiffs (*mastini*) stand for the vigorous operation of the will. Love urges the will to seek the divine and, like a lantern shedding light, spurs the intellect forward. The woods (*selve*) are the solitary place where wisdom resides, visited by a few. The risky path (*dubio camino*) is the journey of reason toward divinity, a journey full of doubts and uncertainty. The forest beasts (*boscherecce fiere*) are the intelligible intuitions of ideal concepts, which are concealed and intractable for the human mind. The waters (*l'acque*) are a similitude of all that is above and below the firmament, a watery mirror where the splendor of the divine and the efficacy of its goodness shine. The breast and face (*busto e faccia*) signify the external appearance and the power that a superior mind can apprehend in the act of contemplation. The colors (*ostro ed alabastro ed oro fino*) signify divine power, divine beauty, and divine wisdom. The great hunter became the quarry (*il gran cacciator ... dovenne caccia*). In the same way, the human intellect, once it comprehends the operation of the Intellect, is converted and merges into it, thus becoming the prey from the hunter that it was (Bruno 1928, 75–76).

Se la farfalla al suo splendor ameno
vola, non sa che fiamma al fin discara;
se, quand' il cervio per sete vien meno,
al rio va, non sa de la freccia amara;   4
se il liocorno corre al casto seno,
non vede il laccio, che se gli prepara:
i' al lume, al fonte, al grembo del mio bene
veggio le fiamme, i strali e le catene.   8
S' è dolce il mio languire,
perché quell'alta face sì m'appaga,
perché l'arco divin sì dolce impiaga,
perché in quel nodo é avvolto il mio desire,   12
mi fien eterni impacci
fiamme al cor, strali al petto, a l'alma lacci.

If the butterfly flies to the light that lures it,
it does not know that in the end the flame will
consume it; if, succumbing to thirst, the stag runs
to the brook, he does not know of any cruel arrow;   4
if the unicorn runs to the virgin's bosom,
he does not see the noose that is prepared for him:
in the light, at the spring, in the bosom of my love
I can see the flames, the chains, and the arrows.   8
If my languishing is sweet,
because that high light so fulfills me,
because the divine bow so sweetly wounds me,
because my desire in that noose is so entangled,   12
then the flames in my heart, the darts in my breast,
the knots in my soul shall be my eternal shackles.

Regarding line 5, the men who went hunting for the unicorn always took a young girl with them because the legendary animal was thought to feel a strong attraction for the bosom of virgins. Bruno is aware of the sacrifice required of those looking for the truth. The philosopher who is absorbed into the light of eternal wisdom is like the butterfly drawn to the fire, the stag wounded by the hunter's arrow, and the unicorn drawn to the virgin's breast. The difference is that the butterfly, stag, and unicorn do not know the danger they face; they only know their pleasure and follow their instincts blindly. The poet-philosopher is fully aware of the risks involved. He knows that the fire is the ardent wish to strive after the infinite, the arrow is the impression left by a ray of the supreme light, and the shackles are the truths that tie his mind to the supreme goodness and keep drawing him toward it (Bruno, 1928, 61–62).

Annosa quercia, che i rami spandi
a l'aria e fermi le radici 'n terra,
né terra smossa, né gli spiriti grandi
che da l'astro Aquilon il ciel disserra,   4
né quanto fia ch'il vern' orrido mandi,
dal luogo ove stai salda mai ti sferra,
mostri della mia fè ritratto vero,
qual smossa mai strani accidenti fero.   8
Tu medesmo terreno
mai sempre abbracci, fai colto e comprendi,
e di lui per le viscere distendi
radici grate al generoso seno: 12
i' ad un solo oggetto
ho fisso il spirto, il senso e l'intelletto.

Ancient oak, you spread your branches
in the air and set your roots firmly in the ground;
neither the quaking earth nor the great forces
that strong winds let loose from the northern sky,   4
nor whatever horror the winter sends,
ever dislodges you from where you firmly stand:
you are a truthful image of my faith,
which terrifying events shall never shake.   8
The very same earth
you always embrace, make fertile, and bind,
and, in the earth's bowels, you extend your roots,
which are welcome to its generous breast: 12
to one single object
I direct my spirit, my senses, and my intellect.

Per line 12, the ample breast of mother earth welcomes the roots of the oak tree, a tree that, with its roots and branches, symbolizes the embrace that nature reserves for the philosopher who loves it and wants to know it.

Everywhere he went, Bruno was first welcomed and then rejected because of his unorthodox ideas. At Oxford, he argued against the university theologians. At the Sorbonne, the students objected strongly to his theories and forced him out of France. Bruno moved on to Germany and taught in Wittenberg and Helmstadt.[103] From there, he went on to teach in Prague. In 1591, Giovanni Mocenigo invited him to Venice to teach him his theory of mnemonics. Two years later, the Venetian patrician became suspicious of Bruno's heretical ideas and denounced him to the Holy Office.

He was extradited to Rome. To his judges, he declared,

> I posit an infinite universe, creation of the infinite divine power, because I believe it undignified for the divine goodness to produce one finite world, being able as it is to create this world and other worlds. I, therefore, maintain that there exist an infinite number of diverse worlds, similar to this earth, to the moon and the stars … that these bodies are worlds without number, constituting a universal infinity in infinite space, and that this is called the infinite universe … So, there are two kinds of infinity: the infinity of the universe and the infinity of the worlds within it. This repudiates the truth according the [Christian] faith. (Spampinato 91–93, quoted in Italian)

After a long and torturous trial before the Inquisition, during which he refused to abjure, in 1600, Bruno was condemned to death for heresy and soon after was burned alive in the square Campo dei Fiori in Rome.

𝔗ommaso 𝔈ampanella (1568–1639) was born in a poor family of Stilo, Calabria; entered the Dominican order when young; and soon became known for his philosophical studies. In 1492, he was arrested on suspicion of heresy, put on trial in Naples, and brought to the prison of the Holy Office in Rome. From there, he was released and sent back to his native land. In 1597, as the living conditions of the poor of Calabria had turned him into a political activist, Campanella became the ideological leader of a conspiracy that the local people organized against the regional government and the Spanish viceroy. The plotters' aim was to establish a communistic state with the friar as supreme legislator.[104] Campanella was arrested, brought to Naples, and tortured. Having avoided the death sentence by feigning madness, he was condemned to life imprisonment. He penned the following two sonnets in 1604, when he lived in solitary confinement in the underground prison of Castel Sant'Elmo.

𝔗emo che per morir non si migliora
lo stato uman; per questo io non m'uccido,
ché tanto è ampio di miserie il nido,
che, per lungo mutar, non si va fuora.   4
I guai cangiando, spesso si peggiora,
perch'ogni spiaggia è come il nostro lido;

per tutto è senso, ed io il presente grido
potrei obbliar, com'ho mill'anni ancora.   8
Ma chi sa quel che di me fia, se tace
l'Onnipotente? E s'io non so se guerra
ebbi quand'era altro ente, overo pace?
Filippo in peggior carcere mi serra   12
or che l'altrieri; e senza Dio nol face.
Stiamci come Dio vuol, poiché non erra.

I fear that, in dying, the human condition
does not improve; that is why I do not kill myself:
because so immense is the nest of our miseries
that no matter how we change, we will not escape.   4
By shifting troubles, we often make them worse,
for, afterward, every beach turns out to be a landing.
Sensibility is everywhere, and the present suffering
I could forget, as I forgot a thousand others.   8
But who knows what will become of me, if silent
is the Omnipotent? And if I do not know myself
whether I had war when I was another being, or peace?
Phillip imprisons me today in a jail that is worse   12
than yesterday's: against God's will, he cannot do it.
Then let be what God wants, for he makes no errors.

Per line 6, what seems to be the ending of our troubles (a beach—that is, a final destination) often turns out to be the beginning of new difficulties (a landing—that is, the beginning of a new venture). Regarding line 7, in the book *Del senso e della magia*, Campanella expresses the belief that all nature—plants, stones, metals, the heavens, and the stars—is endowed with sensibility, and he states that with such capacity, God directs all the operations taking place in the universe. In line 12, this is Philip II of Spain, who was also king of Naples and Sicily.

In prison, where he remained for twenty-seven years, Campanella continued to write unrelentingly in order to give theoretical foundation to a program meant to establish a system of communistic governance. His theory posited a Supreme Wisdom who created the universe and then guided it, holding it together in a mesh of correspondences and affinities according to three finalistic principles: power, wisdom, and love. A belief in the communion of all natural creatures sustained the friar throughout life as he went on campaigning for a political-spiritual reform that would unite Catholics and Protestants, take back the church to its basic natural principles, and reestablish its universal ascendency.

*I*l mondo è il libro dove il Senno Eterno
scrisse i proprii concetti, e 'l vivo tempio
dove, pingendo i gesti e 'l proprio esempio,
di statue vive ornò l'imo e 'l superno;   4
perch'ogni spirto qui l'arte e 'l governo
leggere e contemplar, per non farsi empio,

debbe, e dir possa: "Io l'universo adempio,
Dio contemplando a tutte cose intorno."   8
Ma noi, strette alme a' libri e tempii morti,
copiati dal vivo con più errori,
gli anteponghiamo a magistero tale.
O pene, del fallir fatene accorti,   12
liti, ignoranze, fatiche e dolori:
deh, torniamo, per Dio, all'originale.

The world is the book where the Eternal Wisdom
wrote his principles; it is the living temple
where, depicting his likeness and his actions,
he adorned heaven and earth with living statues;   4
so every soul, to evade ungodliness, must read
and contemplate the governance and the art
thereof, so it may say, "By contemplating God
in all the things around me, I fulfill the universe."   8
But we, souls bound to dead books and temples
that are very inaccurate copies of what is living,
value them more than that first superior teaching.
Ah, Cares, make us aware of our failing;   12
ah, Quarrels, Ignorance, Labors, and Pains,
in God's name, let us return to the originals!

Regarding lines 1–4, the universe is the book of God. In it, he has inscribed the principles, ideas, and actions conceived in his mind, with examples that palpitate with life and are not dead like the temples and books set up and written by men. Per line 7, only those who read the book of nature and obey God, thus developing their own potentialities, will be able to say, "*l'universo adempio*"—that is, "I actualize the universe. I bring it, with my awareness of it, to its full completion." Campanella explains this concept in *Il senso delle cose*. Our potentiality is part of nature; by getting to know nature, we develop our full potential, become an integral part of nature, and bring it to its full actualization (Campanella 1925, 331).

The sonnet is a hymn to the beauty and wisdom of nature, of which humanity is an essential part. The theme unfolds in a cascade of metaphors—*book, living temple, living statues, art, dead temples, dead books,* "they copy," *the original*—all figures with cognitive function, balanced in the opposition between the universe as image of God (lines 1–4) and the erroneous copies of it to which humans remain chained (9–11). As Campanella says,

> The Universe is the book and the church of God. We must contemplate the divine art and learn how to live in private and in public. We must not study the dead books and the churches of men, and place them above those of God, thus vilifying our souls and falling in error and grief. Our ills ought to lead us back to the original book of nature and make us abandon the useless sects, as well as all fights, may they be real or on paper. (1954, 18)

In "Io nacqui a debellar tre mali estremi," composed around 1602–4, Campanella states the political aim of his philosophy.

    Io nacqui a debellar tre mali estremi:
tirannide, sofismi, ipocrisia;
ond'io m'accorgo con quanta armonia
Possenza, Senno, Amor m'insegnò Temi.   4
Questi principi son veri e supremi
della scoverta gran filosofia,
rimedio contro la tria bugia,
sotto cui tu piangendo, o mondo, fremi.   8
Carestie, guerre, pesti, invidia, inganno,
ingiustizia, lussuria, accidia, sdegno,
tutti a que' tre gran mali sottostanno,
che nel cieco amor proprio, figlio degno   12
d'ignoranza, radice e foment' hanno.
Dunque a diveller l'ignoranza io vegno.

    I was born to vanquish three great evils:
tyranny, sophistry, and hypocrisy;
hence I realize with what sense of harmony
Themis taught me power, wisdom, and love.   4
These are the true and supreme principles
of the great revealed philosophy,
remedies against the tripartite deception
under which you, o world, tremble and weep.   8
Famines, wars, plagues, envy, treachery,
injustice, lechery, sloth, and wrath
are all subject to those three evils,
which find incentive and root in blind   12
self-love, necessary child of lack of knowledge.
Therefore, I come to uproot all ignorance.

Knowledge is the power that can destroy the evils of the world and bring justice and peace to all, and he, Campanella, will defend and fight for that knowledge. Regarding line 4, in Greek mythology, Themis, wife of Zeus, represented the order of the world. Campanella makes her the personification of justice. In his commentary, he specifies that Themis has taught him the three metaphysical and theological principles of the universe: power, wisdom, and love. Regarding lines 7–8, these principles are opposed by Tyranny (false and imposed power), Sophistry (false and misleading knowledge), and Hypocrisy (feigned love). Per lines 12–13, such evils are born of ignorance, and ignorance in turn gives rise to self-love and to the vices that are plaguing the world. His plan to fight ignorance, he further writes, is in accord with what Solomon said: "In multitudine sapientium sanitas orbis terrarum" (In the multitude of wise men is the salvation of the world) (*Wisdom of Solomon* 6, 24–26).

The sonnet "Nel teatro del mondo" describes human life on the planet as a theatrical performance carried out before the consistory of God and the angels.

> Nel teatro del mondo ammascherate
> l'alme da' corpi e dagli affetti loro,
> spettacolo al supremo concistoro
> da natura, divina arte, apprestate,   4
> fan gli atti e detti tutte a chi son nate;
> di scena in scena van, di coro in coro;
> si veston di letizia e di martoro,
> dal comico fatal libro ordinate.   8
> Né san, né ponno, né vogliono fare,
> né patir altro che 'l gran Senno scrisse,
> di tutte lieto, per tutte allegrare,
> quando, rendendo, al fin di giuochi e risse,   12
> le maschere alla terra, al ciel, al mare,
> in Dio vedrem chi meglio fece e disse.

> On the stage of the world, dressed up
> in their bodies and in their dispositions, directed
> by nature, which is God's art, to perform before
> the high consistory, the souls say the words   4
> and carry out the actions to which they were born.
> From scene to scene, from interlude to interlude,
> they clothe themselves in joy and in suffering,
> as ordained in the comedic, fatal script of life. 8
> They neither know nor may, nor do they wish
> to do or suffer but what the Great Wisdom wrote,
> who, pleased with all, wants to make all glad;
> and when, at the end of every game and quarrel, 12
> all masks are returned to the sea, earth, and sky,
> in God we shall see who best performed and spoke.

Per lines 1–2, all human beings live their lives in the bodies (*corpi*) that were assigned to them and with the feelings (*affetti*) produced by those bodies. Per line 5, each soul receives a task to perform within a specific set of circumstances. Per line 9, the souls must accept the role that God has chosen for them. How well they have performed in their given state and situation will be judged at the end.

The topos of the world as theater was common in classical and contemporary authors. In *Augustus* 99, Suetonius wrote that in point of death, the Roman emperor compared his own life to the performance of an actor in a mime. The same comparison is in Bruno's *The Heroic Frenzies* and Marc'Antonio Epicuro's *Caecaria*. Campanella's sonnet is closely reminiscent of John Chrysostom's second homily on Lazarus:

> In the theatre, when evening comes and the spectators leave, those who remain, stripped of their theatrical ornaments, who before looked like kings and generals, now

clearly appear to be whatever they are in reality. The same is with this life of ours: when death comes and the theatre is empty, when we, having discarded our masks of wealth or of poverty, depart and are judged only by our works, then we do appear as we really are, some rich, some poor, some honorable, some dishonorable.[105]

For early writers, the image of the theater was only an explicatory and decorative analogy. For Campanella, the metaphor had a greater meaning and offered a greater benefit. Poetry, like philosophy and the sciences, was, for him, a road to the knowledge of divinity, and the metaphor was humankind's means of penetrating directly the secrets of reality. Figurative rhetoric is almost magic (*rhetorica, quaedam figurata, quasi magica*), he asserts in *Poeticorum liber unus*. For him, the theater constituted the essential nature of the universe in its ongoing mutation of events and declarations. Life is a theatrical performance, a spectacle of ephemeral actions and feelings, in which all human beings play a part and then disappear. The temporality of being, the fleeting character of human existence, however, did not disquiet the friar; the justice of his mission and his strong sense of responsibility inspired a strong faith in the positive final judgment of God.

In 1626, Campanella was transferred from the Neapolitan prison, which was under Spanish jurisdiction, to Rome. Not long after, Pope Urban VIII released him from jail and allowed him to roam freely in the palace of the Holy Office. In that building, in 1594, he had met Giordano Bruno and other Italian heretics who were afterward executed. In 1634, a conspiracy organized by a pupil of his was discovered in Naples. In the circumstances, Campanella left Rome and took refuge in Paris. There he lived for the rest of his life and, protected by Louis XIII, kept busy with the publication of his writings.

Giacomo Lubrano (1619–92) was a Neapolitan Jesuit and the most famous preacher of his time. When the Council of Trent declared the teaching of the gospel to be an important duty of the church, many religious men became preachers. Towns near and far sought preachers with eager anticipation. Stendhal has famously fictionalized their popularity in *The Charterhouse of Parma*. Lubrano's religious fervor, grandiloquence, and phantasmagorical display of metaphors made his sermons especially spellbinding.

Lubrano's book of verse, with the title of *Scintille poetiche* (Poetic Sparks) and containing 140 sonnets, saw the light in 1674 and 1690 under the pseudonym of Paolo Brinacio. The upcoming sonnet gives several definitions of God, all in harmony with Catholic orthodoxy—and with Christian belief in general—making use of the Aristotelian concepts of potentiality and actuality. It is one of a group of sonnets that develops the same subject and has the collective title of "Ego sum qui sum" (I am who I am), as per the definition that God gives of himself in Exodus 3:1.

Un poter sempre in atto, un centro immenso,
che fuor de l'Esser mio linee non stendo;
luminoso oceàn, che da me uscendo
in me ringorgo, ove tempesta il senso.   4
Formo idee di più mondi, e non ripenso,
del proprio Bel contemplator godendo:
ingenito splendor, che pur nascendo
paradisi di gloria a' miei dispenso.   8

Fulmino i rei senza scoccare un dardo;
di nulla mi ricordo, e nulla oblio;
son geloso e sicuro; amo e non ardo.
La terra, il fato, il cielo, il tempo è mio: 12
pienissimo di me, vivo d'un guardo:
Fattor non fatto, Unico in Tre, son Io.

Potentiality in constant actualization, an immense
center, a luminous ocean I am, because outside
my being I extend no lines, for I flow out of me,
where the senses rage, and flow back into myself.   4
I conceive ideas of many worlds, I don't think
twice, I relish in contemplating my own beauty;
an innate splendor I am and, even as being born,
I dispense celestial glories to my creatures.   8
I strike down the wicked but strike no arrow;
I remember nothing and nothing I forget;
I am jealous and secure; I love and I do not burn.
Earth, fate, the heavens, time are mine: 12
I am totally fulfilled; my life is like a flash;
Creator uncreated, I am One in Three, I am I.

Realizing, after the recitation of many tentative definitions of God, that, God being all things and their opposites, no conceivable definition of him is possible, the poet concludes with the tautology *Ego sum, qui sum* (I am I). Regarding lines 1–2, In God, all qualities are actualized; there is no potentiality in him, as there is in all ordinary substances. Being boundless and infinite, God is both center and periphery. In Dante's *Paradiso* 30, 11–12, God is described as a "point … that seems embraced by what it embraces" (*punto … parendo inchiuso da quell ch'elli include*). Regarding lines 3–4, God is an ocean of light flowing into the universe and going back into itself. Again, in *Paradiso* 30, 61–62, God is "a light that blazingly flows like a river" (*lume in forma di rivera / fulvido di fulgore*). Regarding line 5, being pure act—that is, being absolute without time restrictions and limitations—God can neither remember nor forget. In other words, God, who is outside time, cannot go back to any of his own thoughts, because this would imply a temporal dimension. Only those immersed in the variety of what is declined in time can think twice on the same matter (Pieri, in Lubrano 1982, 212; Alfano and Frasca, in Lubrano, 2002, 101). Regarding lines 7–8, God is not created; he became human in order to save all humankind. The expression "paradisiacal glories" (*paradisi di gloria*) carries a suggestion of the Stabat Mater: "When the body dies, allow my soul to receive the glory of Paradise" (*quando corpus morietur, / fac ut animae donetur Paradisi gloria*). Regarding lines 9–11, God has all the opposites in himself, including jealousy—as God declares in the Bible (Alfano and Frasca 101)—and its opposite: this is due to his sense of security. In line 13, *vivo d'un guardo* tells us that God is eternal, and eternity cannot be measured by the human notion of time. He exists in an eternal moment, in what does not have time duration; hence, he is a flash. In line 14, *fatto non fatto* means that God is not created, because he is eternal, but he creates. He is one and the Trinity.

Each presumed description of God's essence (lines 1–6) is an oxymoron, a *coincidentia oppositorum*, for, in God, potentiality is actuality, the center is the periphery, the flowing out is a flowing in, and what is not a creation creates. In the center of the poem (lines 7–10), the pace of the paratactic litany slows down, and the would-be definitions find expression in less abstract, more extended phrases, until a beating rhythm takes over (lines 11–14), and the sonnet closes with the only possible description of God: "I am I; I am what I am; I am the Ineffable."

5.6 The Lure of Evanescent Things

The medieval view of the universe had posited a fixed universal hierarchy that was reassuring for humankind: on high were the celestial bodies, perfect, incorruptible, eternal, and unalterable; down below was the earth, corruptible and imperfect, place of mutation and human error. The men of the Renaissance, on the other hand, had believed in the centrality and importance of humanity. Pico della Mirandola went as far as to state that man is unique in the great chain of being, the only creature capable of changing his destiny and place at will.

By the beginning of the seventeenth century, the certainty of the Middle Ages and the enthusiasm of the Renaissance had vanished. The geographic discoveries revealed new lands, thus changing the distribution of humankind on Earth. New astronomic studies were about to move the frontiers of the universe to infinity. The earth no longer was at the center of the universe; human beings were demoted to a position of no importance, where the possibility of dominating nature, or even the idea of self-control, was illusory.

The sonnets of this period show divergent reactions to the new view of the world. Some poets seem to have been inspired by a great enthusiasm for the infinite possibilities to come.[106] They were eager to experience the brilliant and infinite variety of things to the fullest. Other sonneteers tended to stress the unstable and deceptive appearance of reality. Giordano Bruno had dared to envision an eternal metamorphosis of nature, a cosmic wholeness in continuous expansion, being one with the limitless and immeasurable greatness of God. All tried to capture and interpret the connections between things, whatever seemed to be the appearance of reality, no matter how illusory.

Giambattista Marino (1569–1625), the most celebrated Italian poet of the seventeenth century, was an irreligious man but outwardly conformist; he bowed to authorities but was enthusiastic about Galileo's revolutionary discoveries.[107] Endowed with a strong hedonistic sense of life, in poetry, he created sumptuous scenes of natural beauty, exploring old and new areas of imagination and metaphorical depiction. Overcoming all anxiety of ontological displacement, he pleasurably surrendered to the forces of nature and represented the world in a transfiguration of images and sensory perceptions. His poetics and style were widely admired, and his followers rose to an undisputed status of avant-garde.[108]

> Pon mente al mar, Cratone, or che 'n ciascuna
> riva sua dorme l'onda e tace il vento,
> e Notte in ciel di cento gemme e cento
> ricca spiega la vesta azzurra e bruna. 4
> Rimira ignuda e senza nube alcuna
> nuotando per lo mobile elemento,

misto e confuso l'un con l'altro argento,
tra le ninfe del ciel danzar la Luna.   8
Ve' come van per queste piagge e quelle
con scintille scherzando ardenti e chiare,
volte in pesci le stelle, i pesci in stelle.
Sì puro il vago fondo a noi traspare   12
che fra tanti dirai lampi e facelle:
"Ecco in ciel cristallin cangiato è il mare."

Pay attention to the sea, Cratone: now in every
bay the waves are sleeping, silent is the wind,
and in the sky, studded with hundreds and hundreds
of gems, the Night is unfolding her dark bluish garb.   4
Look how, naked, without a cloud, the Moon
dances among the nymphs of the sky,
swimming in the great fluid element
where silver mingles and blends with silver.   8
Look how, in this and in that vastness,
luminous and playfully sparkling, the stars
are turning into fish and the fish into stars.
So lovely and pure the deep to us appears   12
that, in so many sparks and lights, you can say,
"The sea has changed into a crystal paradise!"

Here is the main conceit: the star-studded sky reflects itself in the sea and turns the sea into a second sky. From this idea, several images follow, all flowing into the same continuous sequence without distinction of octave and sestet. Regarding lines 1–4, Cratone is an imaginary friend to whom Marino intentionally gave a suggestive pagan name. It is night, the sea is calm, and the sky is full of stars. The landscape is no longer the backdrop in the description of the woman or of the lover in anguish. Here it has become an all-absorbing description of nature. Per lines 5–8, the full moon is reflected in the water (*lo mobile elemento*) and seems to move in a rhythm of dance; the stars too mirror themselves in the sea, creating in it many sparkles of silvery light. In lines 9–11, *queste piagge e quelle* are the expanses of sea and sky, respectively. The metaphors have acquired a metamorphic power: in the sky, now capsized into the sea, the stars swim in the water as if they were fish, and the fish, bathing among the reflected lights of heaven, have turned into stars. In this mesmerizing vision, Cratone and his friend have become part of nature, thanks to some magic enchantment.

Or che l'aria e la terra arde e fiammeggia,
né s'ode euro che soffi, aura che spiri,
ed emulo del ciel, dovunque io miri,
saettato dal sole, il mar lampeggia,   4
qui dove alta in sul lido elce verdeggia,

le braccia aprendo in spaziosi giri,
e del suo crin ne' liquidi zaffiri
gli smeraldi vaghissimi vagheggia, 8
qui, qui, Lilla, ricovra, ove l'arena
fresca in ogni stagion copre e circonda
folta di verdi rami ombrosa scena.
Godrai qui meco in un l'acque e la sponda: 12
vedrai scherzar su per la riva amena
il pesce con l'augel, l'ombra con l'onda.

Now that earth and air burn and flare,
there is no breeze, and no wind is blowing,
and everywhere I look, the sea, pierced
by the sun, sparkles in emulation of the sky, 4
here, where on the beach a tall green oak
opens its arms in spacious rounds and
lovingly admires the lovely emerald
of its mane reflected in the liquid sapphires, 8
Lilla, take shelter here, here where shady
big boughs of leafy branches hang over
and embrace the sand, cool in all seasons.
Here with me, you shall enjoy both shore 12
and water: on this delightful strand, you will
see wave play with shade, fish with bird.

One dimension pervades lines 1–11, where sea and sky silently merge in a union of blazing light. It is the torpid hour of a summer afternoon, when nobody is about, no breath of wind is anywhere, and nature keeps perfectly still. Per line 3, the sun sends its rays to the sea, and the sea, competing with the sun (*emulo del cielo*), flushes them back. Per lines 6–8, on shore, there is an oak tree. It is a southern European oak, with its characteristic large shape (*spaziosi giri*). Its branches (the *crin*, meaning "hair," or the mane of the tree) are emeralds (*smeraldi*). Reflected in the water, they intermingle with the blues of the sea (*liquidi zaffiri*), creating kaleidoscopic effects. From the open blaze of the sun, when everything is quiet and motionless, the description moves to a secluded, verdant alcove: here, man and woman will be taken by the enchantment of summer, when shades play with waves, and the fish play with birds.

Oggi, là dove il destro fianco a Ischia
rode il Tirren col suo continuo picchio,
vidi conca con conca e nicchio con nicchio
baciarsi, e come a l'un l'altro si mischia; 4
e la biscia del mar, che pur s'arrischia
venirne infin colà presso il crocicchio,

ove del sole al luminoso spicchio
la chiama l'angue inamorato e fischia. 8
E vidi ancor d'amor l'algente anguilla
arder fra l'acque, e gir di grotta in grotta
e lor maschi seguendo, occhiate e salpe.
Né però vidi mai, perfida Lilla, 12
te fatta a me cortese, e, se non rotta,
men dura del tuo cor la rigid'alpe.

Today, where with its persistent beating
the Tyrrhenian Sea gnaws at the right flank of Ischia,
I saw how one shell another shell, one conch another conch
embrace and kiss, how with one another they mingle, 4
and how the sea serpent daringly ventures
and comes far out into the cross current, where,
in the gleaming beam of the sun, the snake
in love calls to her pleadingly and hisses. 8
And in the waters I saw the frigid eels
burn for love, and skates and salpas swim
from cave to cave in pursuit of their mates.
But I never saw you, perfidious Lilla, to be 12
kind to me, never saw, if not broken, at least
not as hard that unyielding rock of your heart.

In line 2, *continuo picchio* is the beating of waves breaking against and wearing away the rocky coast of the island of Ischia, off the Gulf of Naples. Per lines 7–8, the sea serpent is luring the female in an area where the rays of the sun hit the water. Regarding lines 5–11, Marino chose the names of the fish with the fitting grammatical gender: the *biscia*, which is feminine, is being enticed by her *angue*, which is masculine—a name preferred to *anguilla*, which is another name for the same fish but is of the wrong grammatical gender. *Occhiate* and *salpe* (skates and salpas, the latter being a small, barrel-shaped fish found in warm waters), words in the feminine plural, are the ones who follow their *maschi* (males). A strong structure from line 1 to line 11 holds together the variegated scene of fish and shellfish in riotous love. The submerged seascape is held together also by the sequence of words, such as *nicchio* (*ch* is pronounced like a hard *k*), *picchio*, *mischia*, *arrischia*, *crocicchio*, *spicchio*, *fischia*, *grotta*, and *rotta*, words as sharp as the shells and rocks they describe. These phonic correspondences—the difficult rhymes and the rhythmic effects of alliteration—and the enjambments suggest a collective erotic abandonment among creatures that customarily are cold, stonelike, and slimy. The closing *terzina* is a plea to the woman, who is colder than the supposedly cold fish.

Onde dorate, e l'onde eran capelli,
navicella d'avorio un dì fendea;
una man pur d'avorio la reggea

per questi errori preziosi e quelli;
e, mentre i flutti tremolanti e belli
con drittissimo solco dividea,
l'or de le rotte fila Amor cogliea,
per formarne catene ai suoi rubelli.
Per l'aureo mar, che rincrespando apria
il procelloso suo biondo tesoro,
agitato il mio core a morte gia.
Ricco naufragio, in cui sommerso io moro,
poich'almen fur, ne la tempesta mia,
di diamante lo scoglio e 'l golfo d'oro.

Over golden waves—the waves were tresses—
sailed, one day, an ivory vessel;
one hand, also of ivory, steered it
through this and that precious turning,
and, while it divided the shimmering,
trembling billows with a straight channel,
Love gathered the gold of the broken
threads and forged chains for his rebels.
In that sea of gold, which with its eddying
revealed a blonde tempestuous treasure,
my heart began to die in agitation.
Rich is the shipwreck where I sink and drown,
because at least, in this storm of mine,
the gulf is made of gold, the rock a diamond.

Marino's virtuosity has produced a cascade of metaphors, all originated by the initial one: the woman's blonde hair is a sea of gold. As the hair is combed, its strands become waves in a stormy sea, the comb is a ship (*navicella*) ploughing the waves, and the golden waves are tossing about the poet's heart. With the hairs loosened by the comb, Love fashions the chains with which he enslaves the hearts of men reluctant to submit to his will. In that tempestuous sea, the poet dies in a shipwreck of passion made precious by gold (her hair), ivory (the comb), and diamond (a ring on her finger perhaps). In line 6, *solco* (furrow, or channel) is the parting of the line. In line 14, *scoglio* refers to a sea rock. Everything moves and shines. In such a rich, beauteous sea, where the poet's heart crashes against a rock of diamond and sinks in a gulf of gold, it is worth drowning. No spiritual or conflicted yearning of love exist there. Erotic feelings extend to all products of nature, including the pleasurable technique of poetry, and the poet's gallantry has produced a most baroque conceit.

In striving for new rhetorical effects, Marino and his followers opened wide the thematic range of the high-style sonnet. The blonde woman of an undefined physical aspect and moral perfection, who had dominated so much sonnet space, is now replaced by women of all types and all social classes—beautiful and ugly, alluring and repulsive—all caught in a variety of activities and moods, all worthy of appreciative consideration. Poets developed an obsessive attention to details and a great interest for what, in a woman, is unusual, bizarre, or even grotesque. Much verse described the old, the lame, those with hunched backs, and the blind. Alessandro Adimari dedicates a whole section of his book to these "irregular" beauties, including "a beauty totally ugly" (*bella totalmente brutta*).[109]

Most courts and stately homes retained black people in their service, and their images appear occasionally in the paintings of the period.[110] A fascinating object of adoration and poetry, for the metaphorical potential, was a beautiful black woman. The topic was already fashionable and is the subject of the following sonnet by Marino.

> Nera sì, ma sei bella, o di Natura
> fra le belle d'Amor leggiadro mostro;
> fosca è l'alba appo te; perde e s'oscura
> presso l'ebano tuo l'avorio e l'ostro.   4
> Or quando, or dove il mondo antico o il nostro
> vide sì viva mai, sentì sì pura
> o luce uscir di tenebroso inchiostro,
> o di spento carbon nascere arsura?   8
> Servo di chi m'è serva, ecco ch'avvolto
> porto di bruno laccio il core intorto,
> che per candida man non fia mai sciolto.
> Là 've più ardi, o Sol, sol per tuo scorno   12
> un sole è nato; un sol, che nel bel volto
> porta la notte ed ha negli occhi il giorno.

> Black, yes, but you are beautiful; among Love's
> beauties, you are a delightful prodigy of nature;
> dawn is dark next to you; compared to your ebony,
> the ivory and the purple fade and lose their luster.   4
> When and where did this ancient world of ours
> ever saw so lively and so pure a light come
> out of dark ink, or when did it ever feel such
> a wave of heat spring out of burned-out coals?   8
> A slave to her, who is a slave to me, here I am
> carrying my heart about tied up with a darkish knot,
> which no white hand will ever be able to undo.
> Where you burn the brightest, o Sun, a sun was born   12
> to put you to shame, a sun that in her beautiful face
> carries the night and, in her eyes, has the light of day.

With the choice of subject, Marino's intention to surprise is obvious. At the time, an unblemished white complexion was especially valued, not only because aesthetic bias reigned—blonde women with flawless skin were considered the most beautiful of all—but also because of widespread diseases, such as smallpox, which left the face spotted and full of blemishes. Here, a continued pleasing surprise are the many oxymorons that substantiate the claim of the woman's beauty. Regarding line 2, the word *mostro* did not have the limited meaning of "monster" it has today. *Mostro di natura* meant something out of the ordinary—a prodigy of nature, in fact—for society in general praised any woman with capacities not expected in a member of her sex to be some extraordinary effect of nature, a *mostro di natura*. Regarding lines 12–13, the land where the sun shines the brightest is Africa, where this woman supposedly was born. The contrast is between the natural sun and her, whom he calls a sun because she is as splendid as the sun and surpasses the real sun in splendor (puts the sun to shame). Regarding line 14, the white of the eyes is the cornea. The sonnet proceeds on a succession of explicit and implied contrasts: black and white, light and dark, warm and cold. The antithetical crescendo is interrupted in the first tercet by a promise of everlasting love and concludes in the second tercet with the paradox of the woman-sun, who has night in her dark face and day in the splendor of her eyes.

Rather gallantly, Scipione Errico (Messina, 1592–1670) viewed stuttering as an added attraction in the woman he admired. Poets now used anything perceived as rare, strange and abnormal as a means to reach for new conceits, in order to surprise and amuse.

Del tuo mozzo parlare ai mozzi detti
mozzar mi sento, alta fanciulla, il core.
Lasso, con qual dolcezza e qual valore
quella annodata lingua annoda i petti! 4
Tu tronco, io tronco il suon mando pur fuore,
ma fan varie cagioni eguali effetti,
ché gli accenti a formar tronchi e imperfetti
te insegnò la natura e me l'amore. 8
Or la beltà de la leggiadra imago,
oimè, qual fia, se delle tue parole
il difetto gentil pur è sì vago?
Eco sei di bellezza? O la favella 12
tra' labri appunta e abbandonar non vuole
di coralli d'Amor porta sì bella?

At the faltering sounds of your stutter
I feel, sublime girl, my heart aflutter.
Alas! With what sweetness and power
that tied tongue of yours does tie all hearts! 4
Both you and I send out truncated sounds,
but such like effects are due to unlike causes,
because, to pronounce imperfect and broken
words, you were taught by nature, I by love. 8
How seductive can the beauty of your
delightful image be, if even that slight
flaw of your speech is so very appealing? 12
Are you Beauty's echo? Or does your speech
stall between your lips because it refuses
to leave so fetching a coral portal of love?

In line 12 of the Italian text, Errico equates the beautiful girl's stuttering with the repetitions produced by echo. In the attempt to distract Hera from what her unfaithful husband, Zeus, was doing, the nymph Echo talked to her incessantly. When Hera became aware of the trick, she changed the nymph into the echo. Per lines 12–14, her voice stopped at her lips, in contemplation of their beauty.

In the next sonnet, Giovan Leone Sempronio (Urbino, 1603–46) describes a girl who walks with a limp. Sempronio's great liking for unusual subjects to gaze at and admire—a visualization here poised between chivalrous gentleness and analytical curiosity—gained his verse the description of "poetry of the gaze" (*poesia dello sguardo*).

Move zoppa gentil piede ineguale,
cui ciascuna ineguale è in esser bella;
e così zoppa ancor, del dio ch'ha l'ale
può l'alate fuggir dure quadrella.   4
Tal forse era Euridice, o forse tale
era Ciprigna, allor ch'a questa e a quella
morse il candido piè serpe mortale,
punse il candido piè spina rubella.   8
Consolisi Vulcan; ché se talora
mosse il suo zoppicar Venere a riso,
oggi sa zoppicar Venere ancora.
E certo questa dea, se il ver m'avviso,   12
solo il tenero piè si torse a l'ora
ch'ella precipitò dal paradiso.

The cripple moves her uneven foot fetchingly
—each woman is beautiful in a different way—
and, although she limps, she is able to escape
the sharp flying arrows of the god with wings.   4
Eurydice was perhaps like her, or such was
perhaps the Cyprian goddess, when a deadly
snake did bite the snow-white foot of one
and an unruly thorn stung the foot of the other.   8
Vulcan may well take heart because, if at times
his limping made Venus break out in laughter,
it is Venus herself who now goes hobbling about.
But no doubt, this goddess, if I see it right,   12
did twist her tender foot at the time when
she happened to tumble down from paradise.

In lines 3-4 of the Italian text, the winged god is Love, or Cupid. A poisonous snake bit Eurydice, wife of Orpheus, while she was running away from the pursuing Aristaeus. In line 6, the Cyprian goddess is

Aphrodite, Venus to the Romans, whose great center of veneration was on the island of Cyprus. Regarding line 9, Vulcan, god of fire and Aphrodite's husband, was born lame. For Sempronio, see also section 5.7.

Girolamo Preti (Bologna, 1582–1626) was a courtier of the Este at Ferrara and the Gonzaga at Mantua and gentleman to Cardinal Francesco Barberini in Rome. In "Mentre in cristallo rilucente e schietto," he exploits the rhetorical possibilities offered by a woman looking at herself in a mirror.

Mentre in cristallo rilucente e schietto
il bel volto costei vagheggia e mira,
armando il cor d'orgoglio, il ciglio d'ira,
del suo bel, del mio mal prende diletto.   4
Vaga del vago e lusinghiero aspetto
dice: "Ben con ragion colui sospira!"
Sembrano a lei, che sue bellezze ammira,
oro il crin, rose il labro, e gigli il petto.   8
Ah, quel cristallo è mentitor fallace,
che scopre un raggio sol del bel eterno,
anzi un'ombra d'error vana e fugace!
Vedrai, se miri il tuo sembiante interno,   12
cui ritragge il mio cor, specchio verace,
angue il crin, tosco il labro, il petto inferno.

When into the clear, shining crystal of a mirror
she gazes admiringly at her handsome face
arming her heart with pride, her brow with anger,
she delights in her own beauty and in my anguish.   4
Besotted with her striking, fascinating sight,
she says, "With good reason my lover sighs!"
To her, as she contemplates her many charms,
the hair seems gold, the lips roses, the heart lily white.   8
Ah! That crystal of yours is a deceitful liar,
for it reflects a mere image of the eternal beauty,
rather than the swiftly vanishing shadow of an error.
You will see—if you consider what you are inside   12
and is reflected in my heart, which is a truthful mirror—
your curls are snakes, your lips poison, your heart one hell.

Per line 10, the beauty that the woman sees in the mirror is only a reflection of the ideal of beauty, which, in Platonic theory, is the lasting reality. If she looked at the inner self, the woman would see what she is really made of—something that his wounded heart sees well enough.

In this sonnet, Bernardo Morando finds pleasure in looking at a woman through eyeglasses. Unusual objects can turn into surprising conceits, and mechanical devices are especially amenable to ingenious antitheses and comparisons.

> Per vagheggiarti, Ermilla, a mio diletto,
> di sferici cristalli i lumi armai;
> chè se per te mancò già spirto al petto,
> or luce agli occhi, ecco, mi manca omai.   4
> Fui lince pria, ma poi che gli occhi alzai
> de' tuoi begli occhi al troppo chiaro oggetto,
> quasi gufo dal sol vinto restai:
> nacque da la tua copia il mio difetto.   8
> Indi per tua fierezza io piansi tanto,
> che questi umori incristalliti in giro
> da le vene del cor trassi col pianto.
> Ma che pro, s'a me l'alma onde t'adoro   12
> manca, non che la luce onde ti miro?
> Se miro, abbaglio, e se non miro, i' moro.

> In order to look at you, Ermilla, to my pleasure,
> with spherical crystals I equipped my eyes:
> because if, thanks to you, my heart is soulless,
> by now my eyes, you see, have lost their sight.   4
> I was a lynx before, but since I raised my eyes
> to far-too-radiant an object as your eyes,
> vanquished by your sun, I became an owl:
> from your abundance my lack has derived.   8
> Then, thanks to your pride, I cried so much
> that these humors, now become round crystals,
> I drew, by weeping, from the veins of my heart.
> But to what purpose, if the soul that worships you   12
> and the sight that could gaze at you are missing?
> If I look at you, I am stunned; if I don't, I am done.

Morando (1589–1656) was a Genovese merchant who frequented the Farnese court of Parma and Piacenza[111] and later in life became a priest.

5.7 Time and Death

The discovery of hitherto-unknown lands and the new astronomic studies produced a disquieting sense of insecurity and loss. The self-assurance of humankind was shaken. The hope in a life after death seemed to disappear. Even the hope for immortality as posthumous fame, as the Renaissance humanists had conceived it, failed. In the baroque age, the world appeared unstable, disturbingly deceptive in its unpredictable and changing appearances. What remained were the perception of a plurality of connections between things and the certainty that the reality beneath them escaped the human capacity of understanding. In poetry, writers communicated this sense of instability with images that suggest constant movement and transformation, such as fountains, waterworks, clocks, and fireworks.

In "Quella che va con tante fiamme e tante," Antonio Bruni (1593–1635) expresses a great sense of disquiet by means of a sustained pyrotechnic metaphor.

Quella che va con tante fiamme e tante
stracciando l'ombre e sibilando intorno
mole di stelle intesta, emola al giorno,
che rassembra nell'aria Etna volante,   4
or par ch'erga le faci al ciel stellante,
de le stelle e del ciel con onta e scorno,
or ruina dal nobile soggiorno
in un lucido turbine ondeggiante.   8
Così svanisce il tutto, e le ruine
si veggon sol de le fiammelle d'oro,
né resta altro che fumo ed ombra al fine.
Quanti cinser di porpora e d'alloro   12
già qui sul Tebro il glorioso crine,
ch'or son ombra e son fumo i fasti loro!

That tower that, studded with a myriad sparks,
goes up and up with many and sundry lights,
ripping the darkness and whizzing around,
and looks like an Etna soaring in the air,   4
now throws its flares up to the starry sky
in contempt and shame of stars and heaven,
and now it crashes down from its lofty home
in a scintillating tumultuous cascade.   8
Thus the whole of it vanishes, only small
remnants of the golden flames can now be seen;
then nothing remains but smoke and shadow.
How many, who once, here on the Tiber, girded   12
their glorious heads with purple and laurel, now
are nothing but shades, and their deeds are smoke!

In line 3, *mole di stelle intesta* means "mass studded with stars." It is the colorful design that fireworks create and leave hovering for a short while in the sky. In line 8, *lucido turbine ondeggiante* is a glittering and rolling whirlwind, or a figure that fireworks might design in the sky only to collapse soon into a rain of sparks. With its brief effects of color and light, a pyrotechnic display has become the emblem of an existential disquiet, whereby the world appears a continuous, dizzying metamorphosis of forms. In line 13, the river is the Tiber, and the reflections are those of the colorful lights in the sky. Bruni, born near Taranto, in the Puglie region, studied law and philosophy in Naples and spent most of his professional life at the service of Cardinal Berlingerio Cessi in Rome and Duke Francesco Maria della Rovere in Urbino.

In "Ahi mondo! Ahi senso!" by Gianfrancesco Maia Materdona—a man of the church from Brindisi who was active at the beginning of the seventeenth century—the edifying intent of the priest takes a turn toward a sumptuous and lugubrious religiosity. Its inspiration was the Hospital for the Incurables in Naples.

> Ahi mondo! Ahi senso! Or ve' qui tanti e tanti
> in tende anguste, ancorché auguste, accolti!
> di profana beltà fur tutti amanti,
> tanto or tristi e meschini quanto pria stolti.   4
> Per picciol riso hann' or continui pianti,
> portan l'inferno ai cor, la morte ai volti,
> vita speranti no, vita spiranti,
> morti vivi e cadaveri insepolti.   8
> Questi è in preda al martir, quegli al furore,
> un suda, un gela, un stride, un grida, un freme,
> un piange, un langue, un spasma, un cade, un more.
> Quinci impara o mortal: dolce è l'errore,   12
> breve è 'l gioir, ma pene amare estreme
> dà spesso al corpo, eterno sempre al core.

> Ah, world! Ah, senses! Here are many and many
> gathered in constricting tents, though so regally ample!
> All were lovers of profane beauty and now are
> as sad and dejected as they were once so foolish.   4
> For a short-lived smile, they are forever weeping,
> they hold hell in their hearts, death on their faces;
> not life inhaling, their life they are exhaling,
> they are living dead and unburied corpses.   8
> One is in thrall to pain, the other to furor,
> one sweats, one freezes, one shouts, one shrieks, one throbs,

one cries, one languishes, one agonizes, one swoons, one dies.
Learn from this, o mortal: going astray is sweet,   12
pleasure is brief, but it often gives horrible pains
to the body, to the heart it gives always eternal suffering.

Per line 2, the tents are large but seem small for the great number of sick people amassed in them. The sickness mentioned in lines 3–4 might have been a virulent from of syphilis, which was spreading out of control at the time.

About Ciro di Pers (1599–1663), a nobleman and a friar, we know that he studied at the University of Bologna; traveled to Malta, which was at the time under Venetian jurisdiction; and participated in an expedition against the Turks. After retiring from active life, he lived in the family castle of S. Daniele, in an isolated area of Friuli, north of Venice. The theme prevailing in his lyrics is the meditation on the fugacity of human life and on time and death. In the following sonnet, the object that gave rise to his melancholy rumination is rather unusual.

Son ne le reni mie, adunque, formati
i duri sassi a la mia vita infesti,
che fansi ognor più gravi e più molesti,
c'han de' miei giorni i termini segnati?   4
S'altri con bianche pietre i dì beati
nota, io noto con esse i dì funesti;
servono i sassi a fabricar, ma questi
a distrugger la fabrica son nati.   8
Io ben posso chiamar mia sorte dura
s'ella è di pietra! Ha preso a lapidarmi
da la parte di dentro la natura.
So che su queste pietre arrota l'armi   12
la morte, e che a formar la sepoltura
ne le viscere mie nascono i marmi.

Are then in my kidneys being shaped
the solid stones so injurious to my existence,
which, having marked the limits of my life,
every day grow heavier and more excruciating?   4
If with white stones others score their joyful
days, with them I mark the days that are disastrous;
stones are used to put up buildings, but these
were made to demolish the fabric of my being.   8
I may well describe my destiny as hard,
if it is made of boulders! Nature has begun
pelting me with stones from my very insides.

Death is sharpening its weapons, I know,
on these very stones, and in my intestines
is carved the marble that will build my tomb. 12

In this sonnet by Giovanni Canale—who was born at Cava dei Tirreni at the beginning of the century—is a skeleton that imparts a lesson on the transience of time.

Tu che dal riguardarmi orror apprendi,
timido parti e la mia vista abborri,
arresta il piede e la mia voce intendi:
se movi il piede, in grave error già incorri. 4
Come a fragil beltà perduto attendi,
che sarà qual son io, pensa e discorri;
un punto mi mutò, da un punto pendi,
e col tempo che vola a morte corri. 8
Begli occhi, vago crin, guance rosate
amabil mi rendeano, e in un momento
divenni schifa polve, ossa spolpate.
A macchinar disegni io vissi intento; 12
ma i disegni, i pensieri e la beltade
al mio estremo spirar spariro in vento.

You who look at me and are horrified,
who abhor my sight and run away in fright,
stand still one moment, hear what I have to say:
if you move one step, you'll make a great mistake. 4
You are spellbound, captivated by fragile beauty,
but you will be what I am now, so stop and think:
one moment changed me, on one you depend;
you shall run to your demise in flying time. 8
Appealing eyes, beautiful hair, rosy cheeks
made me loveable, but in one single moment
I changed into fleshed-out bones and hideous dust.
I lived devising eager plans, but all plans, 12
all thoughts, and all beauty in the wind vanished
the moment my breathing reached its end.

Here, on the other hand, is how Giambattista Marino meditated over the tomb of a beautiful man cut down by death in the prime of life.

Questi è PERIN, qui fera morte il mise,
PERINO il caro, oimè, PERINO il bello,
Narciso, Hila, Giacinto, Adon novello:
barbara mano il suo bel fior recise.   4
Chi nol sospira è vie più crudo e fello
del ferro che 'l trafisse e che l'ancise,
e più rigido e duro anco di quello
che qui del suo morir l'istoria incise.   8
Quanti diè lo sculptor colpi e percosse
su questo marmo, allor che per dolore
molle divenne, e per pietà si mosse,
tanti sentinne in cielo dio nel core,   12
che perché noto il suo martir poi fosse,
vi scrisse col suo stral: "Qui giace Amore."

Here is PERIN, here cruel death has placed him;
PERIN the dear, alas! PERIN the handsome,
a Narcissus, a Hylas, a Hyacintus, a new Adonis:
a barbaric hand cut off his handsome thread.   4
Those who do not sigh for him are meaner
and crueler than the steel that pierced and killed
him, more callous and harder than the man
who has sculpted here the story of his death.   8
As many were the knocks and blows
the sculptor struck on this marble, when,
taken by grief, he kept working out of pity,
so many were the pangs that the god in heaven   12
felt in his heart, and, to make his grief known,
with his arrow he wrote on it, "Here lies Love."

Marino's flippant epitaph to a murdered handsome and narcissistic young man is among a group of sonnets he called lugubrious rhymes (*rime lugubri*) because they commemorated people recently deceased, mostly individuals well known either for their literary and artistic fame or on account of their social stations. In line 1, the name Perino is in capital letters, the way it appeared on the tombstone. Regarding line 3, the beautiful Narcissus was in love with himself. One day, while admiring his own image reflected in a pool of water, he moved closer and closer to kiss it, until he fell into the pool and drowned. Nemesis—goddess of human happiness and misery—changed him into the flower of the same name. Hylas too was handsome, and because of his beauty, Heracles adopted him as his page. When one day he went to fetch water at a fountain, the Naiads—nymphs of rivers, lakes, and brooks—kidnapped him and carried him away. Adonis was a young shepherd dearly loved by Aphrodite. He was so handsome that his name became the eponym of male beauty. In line 4, *il suo bel fior recise* is a mocking reminder of *purpureus veluti cum floss succisus aratro* (like a purple flower cut down by the plow) in *Aeneid* 9, 435–36, where the premature death of Euryalus, the young Trojan hero slain by Turnus on the battlefield, is pityingly lamented by his friends at arms. In line 4, *barbara mano* is the barbarous hand of the man who murdered beautiful Perino. In line 12, the god in heaven is the god of love. For other sonnets by Marino, see the previous section.

In "Quei che le vite altrui tradisce e fura," Giovan Leone Sempronio (1603–46) meditates on the clock. Sundials, sandglasses, and water clocks invaded the space of the sonnet thanks to their symbolic implications and paradoxical potentials. Especially fascinating for a poet was the mechanical clock—invented in the sixteenth century—which, by scanning the seconds, seemed best to represent the volatility of time and convey the sense of impending death. In the following sonnet, Sempronio visualizes no fewer than three different kinds of clocks.

Quei che le vite altrui tradisce e fura,
qual reo su cento rote ecco si volve,
e lui, che scioglier suol gli uomini in polve,
con poca polve or l'uom lega e misura.   4
E se con l'ombre i nostri giorni oscura,
se stesso in ombra ai rai del sol risolve;
quanci apprendi, o mortal, come dissolve
ogni cosa qua giù tempo e natura.   8
Su quelle rote egli trionfa e regna;
con quella polve ad acciecarti aspira;
e tra quell'ombra uccidderti disegna.
Su quelle rote i tuoi persier martira;   12
in quella polve i tuoi diletti ei segna;
e tra quell'ombra ombre di morte aggira.

That betrayer and stealer of people's lives,
now like a criminal turns on a hundred wheels,
and, accustomed as he is to reduce people to dust,
with a little sand ties and measures humankind;   4
and, if with shadows he darkens our days,
under the sun's rays he turns himself into shade:
So learn, o mortal, how down here all things
are dissolved by Nature and by Time.   8
On those wheels, he triumphs and reigns;
with that sand, he wants to blind you,
in that shade, he plans to kill you.
On those wheels, your thoughts he tortures,   12
in that dust, your delights he registers,
and that shade with shades of death he agitates.

In line 1, *Quei* (the betrayer) is Time, represented by all types of clock. In line 2, *qual reo* means "like a criminal." The reference is to the medieval torture of the breaking wheel. The condemned men were tied spread-eagle on the wheel, and their bones were broken up with a cudgel. The allusion in lines 3–4 is to the sandglass. In lines 5–6, Time turns into shade, because on a sundial, time is measured by the size of the shade. A play on words is possible in Italian, where *ombra* has the meaning of both "shade" and "shadow."

In the first eight lines, the references are to the mechanical clock, the sandglass, and the sundial. They are repeated in the same order in lines 9–11 (wheels, sand, shade) and again in lines 12–14 (wheels, dust, shade).

In the sonnet below, Giacomo Lubrano, a Jesuit and a preacher, takes up the water clock as the springboard to a reflection on the fugacity of human existence and the necessity to mend one's sinful ways.

> A che sognar con temerarii vanti
> secoli ne l'età mezzo sparita,
> se bastan sole ad annegar la vita
> minutissime gocciole d'istanti? 4
> Voi talpe di ragion delusi amanti,
> a ravvedervi in picciole urne invita
> meccanico cristal; e in sé vi addita,
> quasi stille del tempo, i giorni erranti. 8
> Quanto è, quanto sarà s'imprime in acque,
> cifra di fughe; e in fluido feretro
> naufraga sepellito il 'fu' che piacque.
> Se no 'l credi, o mortal, vòlgiti a dietro 12
> e mira l'esser tuo, che al pianto nacque,
> struggersi a stille in agonie di vetro.

> Why to dream and boast so foolishly
> about centuries in the age almost gone,
> when a few minuscule drops of time
> are sufficient to drown an entire life? 4
> You moles, deluded lovers of reason,
> this automatized crystal invites you to mend
> your ways, as in itself, it points out how
> fleeting are our days, mere dribs of time. 8
> What is and what will be is written in water,
> a cipher of fugues; and in a fluid coffin drowns
> and disappears what was and gave us pleasure.
> If you do not believe it, o mortal, turn around 12
> and look at your being, which, born to sorrow,
> is wasting away drop by drop, in agonies of glass.

St. Ignatius de Loyola's spiritual exercises had taught Jesuits to begin meditation with the mental visualization of an object, usually one connected with Christ's crucifixion. In this sonnet, it is the water clock—a device that measures time by regulating the flow of a fluid from one glass vial into another—that starts the meditation and provides structure and symbolic imagery to the sonnet. The principle metaphor is water. The life we live turns out to be, in line 4, "tiny drops of moments" (*minutissime gocciole d'istanti*) whose constant dripping drains out our existence (*annegar la vita*), per line 3; the days are, per line 8, "dribs of time" (*stille del tempo*), and what happens in the dimension of time is "written in water" (*s'imprime in acque*), says line 9. Life disappears in a "fluid coffin" (*fluido feretro*), according to line 10, and in that fluid, it "drowns" (*naufraga*), per line 11. "Then why," the poet asks, "do you mortals fantasize so, measuring the past by centuries, when only tiny drips of time are sufficient to separate the present from the past and from the future?" In line 5, the poet says, "You do so because your reason has made you as blind as moles and because your sensual perceptions keep you in thrall." Per lines 6–8, this clepsydra—or water clock—is therefore a "cipher of fugues," a symbol of how rapidly hours fly. The closing is brought about by tying the last warning—"you waste away, drop by drop, in agonies of glass"—to the opening pronouncement of "a few tiny drops of moments are big enough to drain out all life."

Lubrano dedicated thirty sonnets to the moralities inspired by the silkworm. Each poem meditates on a quality of the worm or on a moment in its evolution and then goes on to develop a narrative symbolic of human destiny. In "O glorioso enimma!" the paradoxical transformations of the silkworm are symbols of the resurrection.

> O glorioso enimma! Un morto seme
> schiude a tiepido ciel alma che sente;
> e serpeggiando in atomo vivente,
> a' belgici telai nutre la speme;   4
> trasforma il cibo in stame, e torce e spreme
> da le viscere sue globo lucente;
> fatto subbio del sen, spola del dente,
> ordisce in trame le salive estreme.   8
> Sepolto al fine in funeral volume
> rifà la vita, e Dedalo novello
> su per l'aeree vie batte le piume.
> Nega or, se puoi, che sorgerà più bello   12
> del fango umano incenerito il lume,
> se a' vermin ancor è fosforo l'avello.

> O glorious enigma! A lifeless seed opens
> and into a tepid sky lets out a feeling creature;
> it is a living atom that, whirling itself about,
> gives new confidence to the Belgian looms.   4
> It changes food into thread, from its bowels
> it twists and spews a luminous globe; it makes
> a beam of its breast, a shuttle of its tooth,
> and weaves its last saliva into a silky filament.   8
> At the end, buried in a funereal roll,
> it comes back to life, and, like a new Daedalus,

proceeds to flap its wings on the airy ways.
Can you then deny that out of the human mud, 12
once reduced to dust, a more splendid light will rise,
if the grave of worms can turn into such luminous stuff?

Per line 1, the silkworm is a paradoxical enigma because it seems to appear from nothing: from a lifeless seed (*un morto seme*) out comes a living creature, the hatched worm, the larva. The worm grows and, when fully grown, begins to spin its silky cocoon. Regarding line 4, the silk produced in Italy was exported to the Flanders. In line 6, *globo lucente* (luminous globe) is the cocoon. In line 7, *subbio* is the weaver's beam. In line 9, the cocoon is describes as funereal *volume* because after spewing all its silk thread and creating the cocoon, the worm dies inside it. Per line 10, the worm dies, but a moth is born. The moth bores a hole in the cocoon and flies away. The mythical Daedalus escaped from the labyrinth by constructing wings for himself and his son Icarus and then flew high over the sea. Regarding line 14, *fosforo* is a phosphorescent substance.

The following sonnet was found among the last things Lubrano wrote when, old and paralyzed, he lived in a retirement home for old Jesuits. The man who had delivered terrifying sermons to the crowds, reminding them of their upcoming demise, could consider the future destruction of himself and his work with serenity and in good humor.

Arpiuccia de' libri, empia tignuola,
rodendo il sen di pagine erudite,
ruba con sordo ardir d'avida gola
a saggi estinti postume le vie. 4
Del suo minuto dente a noi s'invola
lo spirto degl'ingegni, e ponsi in lite
ciò che in eredità lascia la scola
confuso e guasto a lettere sparite. 8
Morde chi la produsse e la nutrisce;
nata aborre la luce, e sempre ascosa
appesta i fogli in atomi di bisce.
Del fallo original ombra odiosa; 12
strugge il censo de l'alme, e le sue strisce
son supplici di polve ove si posa.

This little harpy of books, this wicked little bug,
can steal bygone sages of their posthumous life
by gnawing at the core of erudite pages
with the muffled boldness of its avid throat. 4
By its miniscule tooth are thus stolen to us
the souls of geniuses, and what is inherited
from the schools becomes contentious,
ruined and confused by letters that are gone. 8
It bites the matter that made and feeds it;
it abhors the light from birth, and, always hiding,

it infests our pages with atomic wrigglings.
A hideous image of the original failing,
it destroys the wealth of souls and, wherever
it comes to rest, its streaks are agonies of dust.   12

Regarding line 1, the mythical harpies, part women and part birds, made things unusable by dropping their feces on them. What Lubrano calls here a harpy of books is the paper-eating silverfish. In line 2, the erudite pages are the books written by learned people of past ages. Regarding line 4, thanks to the writings they left behind, the learned go on living after death. Per lines 1–4, when in a book, moths eat away some letters, a passage becomes obscure, and scholars argue contentiously about its possible meaning. In line 9, the insect bites the paper on which it feeds. In line 11, as it moves on the page and eats it, the silversmith leaves behind miniscule wiggling traces, literally "atoms of snakes" (*atomi di bisce*). Regarding line 12, the original sin involved eating the fruit of knowledge, and the insect that eats away the knowledge imparted by books is a reminder of it. In line 13, the wealth of souls (*censo de l'alme*) is the knowledge that feeds and enriches the mind. Per line 14, turning the pages into powder, the silversmith condemns a book to agonies of dust (*supplici di polve*). For Lubrano, see also 5.5.

With his stylistic restraint, Antonio Basso showed that baroque poetry was not all rhetorical acrobatics. Basso was a Neapolitan doctor and a member of the literary Accademia degli Oziosi. He published two volumes of poetry in 1645.

Spunta la rosa, e grato il suo vermiglio
aspra contende altrui siepe di spine;
sorge in sembiante altier candido giglio
ma d'alte spade è chiuso entro il confine;   4
vaga la fiamma appar, ma o qual periglio
cela in suo lume, o quai morti ha vicine;
piacer crinita stella infonde al ciglio,
ma letal fato all'uom piove dal crine;   8
piuma all'augel di Giuno aurea fiorisce,
cui laido è il piè; sirena ai divi uguale
aspetto ottien, ch'in pesce indi finisce.
Apprendi alfin da ciò, pensier mortale,   12
qual sia tuo stato, ov' il ciel sempre unisce
con infausto ligame il bene e 'l male.

The rose blooms, but a harsh, thorny hedge
denies its pleasing vermillion to everyone;
the snow-white lily grows to a lofty height,
but a circle of high swords confines it;   4
the flame looks appealing, but what dangers
its light conceals, and what deaths it hides!

The tailed star gives pleasure to the eye,
but from its mane a lethal fate rains on humankind; 8
golden feathers grow on the bird to Juno sacred,
but its foot is loathsome; a divine appearance
has the siren, but at the end, her body turns fishlike.
You, humans who can think, from this learn at last 12
what your condition is, a state in which the heavens,
with an ill-fated tie, the good and the bad always unite.

In line 4, the unyielding swords (*rigide spade*) are the sturdy leaves enfolding the flower of the lily. Regarding lines 7–8, ancient people believed the comets to be warnings of upcoming disasters. Regarding line 10, according to widespread folklore, the peacock screams when it looks at its feet, believing they do not become the rest of the body (White 159).

The warning in Basso's sonnet sounds prophetic. In 1647, when the people of Naples turned against the fiscal policy of the regime, he participated in restructuring the city administration. After a time, however, when the old order was reestablished, the doctor-poet was arrested and executed.

To close this florilegium of sonnets, I have chosen one by Federico Meninni (1636–1712). Meninni, a Neapolitan doctor like Basso, was the author of a substantial collection of poetry and of *Ritratto del sonetto e della canzone*, a well-received treatise on the sonnet and the song (1677).

Questi libri da cui più cose imparo,
e che divoro anco di Lete a scorno,
altri, per innalzar forte riparo
contra l'oblio, divoreranno un giorno. 4
In questo albergo, in cui ricovro ho caro,
mentre le cure a riposar qui torno,
se 'l ciel non fia di sue vicende avaro,
altri faranno in altra età soggiorno. 8
In questo letto, ove fra l'ombre assonno,
perché rechi a' miei sensi alcun ristoro,
altri ancor chiuderà le luci al sonno.
Quindi rodemi il cor più d'un martoro, 12
solo in pensar che qui durar ben ponno
cose che non han vita, ed io mi moro!

These books, from which many things I learn,
which I too devour to spite forgetful Lethe,
other people as well one day will use,
to build a strong defense against oblivion. 4
In this very house, where I return to find
an agreeable refuge and assuage my worries,

if the heavens will not fail in their revolutions,
others will also seek a home in times to come.   8
In this very bed, where in the dark I sleep
to restore new energy to my senses,
still others will close their eyes in slumber.
Thus, more than one sorrow gnaws at my heart   12
just to think that objects that have no life
will go on existing, while I am slowly dying!

Regarding line 2, by drinking the water from this mythical river, people forgot the past. Books, on the other hand, rescue from oblivion people and events that otherwise would be forgotten. In line 7, the poet says, "If the heavens will continue their revolutions"—that is, if time does not come to an end. In everyday objects, in the things that belonged to him and that he used—his books, his house, his bed—the poet reads the transient nature of human existence, for those objects will still be there, in the same house, most likely used by others, but he will no longer exist. In this deeply secular sonnet, do we find a sadness for the seeming inanity of our everyday actions, or is there a serene, if not joyful, realization that life will go on, if not for us, for those we leave behind?

Sections, Authors and Sonnets
in order of appearance

I

1.1 Philosophizing at the Imperial Court — 1

Giacomo da Lentini	Io m'aggio posto in core a Dio servire
	Or come pote sì gran donna entrare
	Lo basilisco a lo speclo lucente
	A l'aire claro ho vista ploggia dare
	Sì alta amanza ha preso lo me' core
Jacopo Mostacci	Sollicitando un poco meo savere
Pier della Vigna	Però ch'amore no si pò vedere
Giacomo da Lentini	Amor è uno desio che ven da core

1.2 Church and Empire — 10

Orlanduccio Orafo	Oi tu, che se' errante cavaliero
Palamidesse	Poi il nome c'hai ti fa il coraggio altero
Rustico Filippi	A voi che ve ne andaste per paura
	D'una diversa cosa ch'è aparita
Guido Guinizzelli	Sì sono angostioso e pien di doglia

1.3 Bourgeois Moralities of Love — 16

Guittone d'Arezzo	Ben saccio de vertà che 'l meo trovare
	Sì como ciascun omo, enfingitore
	Poi non vi piace che v'ami, e ameraggio
	S'eo tale fosse ch'io potesse stare
Chiaro Davanzati	Madonna, or provedete ad una cosa
	Io non dico, messer, che voi pechiate
	Come il castor, quando egli è cacciato
From *Il Fiore*	E quando tu sarai co llei soletto
	Per più volte falli' a lui ficcare
Guido Guinizzelli	Ch'eo cor avesse mi potea laudare
	Chi vedesse a Lucia un var capuzzo
	Io voglio del ver la mia donna laudare
Bonagiunta Orbicciani	Voi, ch'avete mutata la mainera
Guido Guinizzelli	Omo ch'è saggio non corre leggero
Anonymous	Tapina ahimè, ch'amava uno sparvero

1.4 An Accomplished Young Woman — 31

Compiuta Donzella	A la stagion che 'l mondo foglia e fiora

	Lasciar vorria lo mondo e Dio servire
Mastro Torrigiano	Esser donzella di trovare dotta
Chiaro Davanzati	Gentil donzella somma ed insegnata
Compiuta Donzella	Ornato di gran pregio e di valenza
Chiaro Davanzati	Perch'ogni gioia ch'è rara è graziosa

1.5 An Elite of Men and Women — 37

Lapo Gianni	Amor, eo chero mia donna in domino
Guido Cavalcanti	Dante, un Sospiro messagger del core
Dante	Guido, i' vorrei che tu e Lapo ed io
Guido Cavalcanti	S'io fosse quelli che d'amor fu degno
Cino da Pistoia	Come non è con voi a questa festa
	Se conceduto mi fosse da Giove

1.6 Philosophy of Love — 43

Guido Cavalcanti	Chi e' questa che vien ch'ogn'om la mira
	Voi che per li occhi mi passaste 'l core
	Tu m'hai sì piena di dolor la mente
	Noi siam le triste penne isbigottite
	Pegli occhi fere un spirito sottile
Onesto da Bologna	„Mente" ed „umìle" e più di mille sporte
Cino da Pistoia	Amor che vien per le più dolci porte
Immanuel Romano	Amor non lesse mai l'Avemaria
Dante	Tanto gentile e tanto onesta pare
	Un dì si venne a me Malinconia
	Deh pellegrini che pensosi andate
	Oltre la spera che più larga gira
Cecco Angiolieri	Dante Allaghier, Cecco, 'i tu' servo e amico

1.7 In a Satirical Vein — 58

Cecco Angiolieri	La mia malinconia è tanta e tale
	"Becchin' amor!" "Che vuo' falso tradito?"
	I' sono inamorato, ma non tanto
	Tre cose solamente m'ènno in grado
	Per sì gran somma ho 'mpegnato le risa
	S'i' fosse fuoco, arderei 'l mondo
	Li bon parenti, dica chi dir vole
Rustico Filippi	Quando Dio messer Messerino fece
	Oi dolce mio marito Aldobrandino
	Da che guerra m'avete incominciata
	Quando ser Pepo vede alcuna potta
	El Muscia sì fa dicere e bandire

2

2.1 In Celebration of the Good Life — 71

Folgòre	I' doto voi, nel mese di gennaio
	E di febbraio vi dono bella caccia
	Di marzo sì vi do una peschiera
	Di maggio sì vi do molti cavagli
	Di giugno dovvi una montagnetta

Cenne della Chitarra	Io vi doto, nel mese di gennaio	
	Di giugno siate in tale campagnetta	

2.2 Friends and Enemies   78
Dante	Ben ti faranno il nodo Salamone
	Chi udisse tossir la malfatata
Forese Donati	L'altra notte mi venne una gran tosse
Guido Cavalcanti	I' vegno 'l giorno a te 'nfinite volte
Dante	Io sono stato con Amore insieme
	Io mi credea del tutto esser partito
Cino da Pistoia	Poi ch'i' fu', Dante, dal mio natal sito

2.3 Politics and War   86
Dante	Se vedi gli occhi miei di pianger vaghi
Folgòre	Eo non ti lodo, Dio, e non ti adoro
Pietro dei Faitinelli	Voi gite molto arditi a far la mostra
	S'eo veggio en Lucca bella mio ritorno
Immanuel Romano	Io stesso non mi conosco, ogn'om oda
	Se san Pietro e san Paul da l'una parte
Bonuccio Salimbeni	Quando si può, si dee, senza disnore
Franco Sacchetti	Là dov'è pace, il ben sempre germoglia
Petrarch	Fiamma dal ciel su le tue treccie piova
Braccio Bracci	Deh non guastare il popolo cristiano

2.4 Society Changes   97
From *Il Fiore*	Vedete che danari hanno usorieri
Bindo Bonichi	El calzolai' fa 'l suo figliol barbiere
	Fra l'altre cose non lievi a portare
Pieraccio Tedaldi	Il mondo vile è oggi a tal condotto

2.5 Deaths of Dante and Immanuel Romano   101
Giovanni Quirini	Segnor, ch'avete di pregio corona
Bosone da Gubbio	Due lumi son di novo spenti al mondo
Immanuel Romano	Io, che trassi le lacrime dal fondo
Cino da Pistoia	Messer, lo vostro Manoello
Bosone da Gubbio	Manoel, che mettete 'n quell'avello

2.6 Town and Country   107
Pieraccio Tedaldi	Se colla vita io esco de la buca
	I' truovo molti amici di starnuto
	Oggi abbian lunedì, come tu sai
	Corretto son del tutto e castigato
Antonio Pucci	Dante Alighier ne la sua Comedia
	"Deh fammi una canzon, fammi un sonetto"
	I' fui iersera, Adrian, sì chiaretto
	Amico mio barbier, quando tu meni
	Po' che no' fummo ne la zambra entrati
Giovanni Boccaccio	Discinta e scalza, con le trezze avvolte
	Se io temo di Baia e il cielo e il mare
Cecco Nuccoli	El mi rincresce sì lo star di fuore

2.7 The Other Face of Love — 119

Cecco Nuccoli — Ramo fiorito, el di ch'io non te veggio
Ogni pensier, ch'i' ho in te, se dispera

Marino Ceccoli — A la dolce stason ch'ei torde arvegnono
Poi che senza pietà da te m'escacce
Come per' giaccio, fòre andando, sdruce

2.8 The Divided Self: Petrarch — 124

Petrarch — Quanto più m'avvicino al giorno estremo
Benedetto sia 'l giorno, e 'l mese, e l'anno
Padre del ciel, dopo i perduti giorni
Ponmi ove 'l sole occide i fior e l'erba
Questa fenice de l'aurata piuma
Erano i capei d'oro a l'aura sparsi
Se lamentar augelli, o verdi fronde
Cantai or piango, e non men di dolcezza

3

3.1 Literati and Scientists — 135

Antonio Beccari — Se Dante pon che Giustizia Divina
E' me recorda, cara mia valise

Francesco di Vannozzo — Quand'io mi volgo atorno e pongo mente
El poder basso col voler altiero
Italia, figlia mia, prendi dilecto

Giovanni Dondi — Ogni cosa mortal convien che manchi
Hora prov'io che l'è ben vero el detto
Io temo che tu non doventi cervo

3.2 Wisdom and Desires — 144

Niccolò Soldanieri — Pover al mondo over chi è mal vestito
Simone Prudenzani — Le tue parol mi paion cosa vana
Anonymous — Se io 'l potessi far, fanciulla bella
Un abate avea un suo bel catellino
Nel tempo che 'l leone era infermato
Prima ch'io voglia rompere o spezzarmi

3.3 The Sonnet as a Political Weapon — 150

Coluccio Salutati — O scacciato dal ciel da Micael
Burchiello — Oh umil popol mio, tu non t'avvedi
Antonio di Meglio — O puro e santo padre Eugenio quarto

3.4 Literate Citizenry — 156

Giovanni Gherardi — O fonte fonda e nissa d'ignoranza
Filippo Brunelleschi — Quando dall'alto ci è dato speranza
Burchiello — Questi ch'andaron già a studiare a Atene
Nominativi fritti e mappamondi
Un topo e una topa e un topetto
Son diventato in questa malattia
Io ho il mio cul sì forte rinturato

3.5 The Medici and Their Circle		165
Giambattista Alberti	Io già vidi seder nell'arme irato	
Ciriaco of Ancona	Quel Sir, che sotto l'ideale stampa	
Lorenzo de' Medici	O veramente felice e beata	
	Belle e fresche e purpuree viole	
	Più che mai bella e men che già mai fera	
	Cerchi chi vuol le pompe e gli alti onori	
Luigi Pulci	Costor, che fan sì gran disputazione	
3.6 Noblemen		175
Leonello d'Este	Lo Amor me ha fatto cieco e non ha tanto	
Matteo Maria Boiardo	Dàtime a piena mano e rose e zigli	
	Già vidi uscir de l'onde una matina	
	La smisurata et incredibil voglia	
	Se passati a quel ponte, alme gentile	
Gasparo Visconti	Io vidi belle adorne e zentil dame	
	Chi se dilecta udir gran meraviglie	
	Un dì il leon, tra bruti il gran signore	
Niccolò da Correggio	Sì como el verde importa speme e amore	
	L'ordito che Natura a prova cresce	
3.7 Courtiers		185
Giannantonio Petrucci	De sucto al Fato sta ciò che è creato	
	Fu alcuna volta loco da pescare	
	Quel che de' capitani fo lo fiore	
	O tempo, come presto si' volubile	
Benedetto Gareth	Costei che mia benigna e ria fortuna	
	Ecco la notte: el ciel scintilla e splende	
	Voi, Donna, et io per segni manifesti	
3.8 Commoners		193
Gian Francesco Suardi	Io son pur quel predicto e onorevole	
Giorgio Sommariva	Duò, messer me, mo que volì vu fare	
	Se tu te trovi in galia o in bordel	
Antonio Cammelli	Belle donne a Milan, ma grasse troppe	
	"A Roma che si vende?" "Le parole"	
	Più de cent'anni imaginò Natura	
	Danza già in cielo ogni immortal farfalla	

4

4.1 A Raging Fashion		203
Antonio Tebaldi	Del foco che per voi m'arde et incende	
	Io vidi la mia ninfa anci mia dea	
	Se avien che 'l ciel mi dia viver tant'anni	
Serafino Aquilano	Chi el crederia? Fra noi l'idra dimora	
	Io iurerei che non te offesi mai	
	O felice animal, felice dico	
	Se l'opra tua di me non ha già molto	
	Non ti doler di quel che dato m'hai	

4.2 Invasions and Reversals		211
Gasparo Visconti	"A Milan che si fà?" "Chi il ferro lima	
Antonio Cammelli	Il Duca Valentin, veduti i danni	
	Ecco il re dei Romani e 'l re dei Galli	
Niccolò Machiavelli	Io vi mando Giuliano alquanti tordi	
Giovanni Guidiccioni	Da questi acuti e dispietati strali	
Luigi Alamanni	Quanta invidia ti porto, amica Sena	
4.3 At the Curia		220
Pasquino	Belzebù mughia, et nel mughiar si dole	
	Padre dell'universo, almo pastore	
	Io fui Julio Rover, de Savona	
	O musici con vostre barzellette	
Pietro Aretino	Non ti meravigliar, Roma, se tanto	
Francesco Berni	Un papato composto di rispetti	
4.4 A Pundit for All Courts		228
Pietro Bembo	Sì come suol, poi che 'l verno aspro e rio	
	Giaceami stanco, e 'l fin de la mia vita	
	Arsi, Bernardo, in foco chiaro e lento	
	Io ardo, dissi, e la risposta invano	
	Crin d'oro crespo e d'ambra tersa e pura	
4.5 In a Platonic Frame of Mind		234
Vittoria Colonna	Quando io dal caro scoglio guardo intorno	
	Sopra del mio mortale, leggera e sola	
Michelangelo	Non ha l'ottimo artista alcun concetto	
	Tu sai ch'i' so, Signor mio, che tu sai	
	Colui che fece, e non di cosa alcuna	
	I' mi son caro assai più ch'i' non soglio	
	Vorrei voler, Signor, quel ch'io non voglio	
4.6 Love Is an Onion		242
Galeazzo di Tarsia	Te lacrimosa pianta sembro a Amore	
	Amor è una virtù che né per onda	
	Come in limpido vetro o in onda pura	
	Vinto da grave mal uom che non posi	
	Già corsi l'Alpi gelide e canute	
4.7 A Confessed Sensualist		247
Gaspara Stampa	Vieni, Amor, a veder la gloria mia	
	Io non v'invidio punto, angeli santi	
	Per le saette tue, Amor, ti giuro	
	O notte, a me più chiara e più beata	
	Amor n'ha fatto tal ch'io vivo in foco	
4.8 Women's Perspectives		252
Veronica Gàmbara	A l'ardente desio che ognor m'accende	
	Sciogli le trecce d'oro, e d'ogni intorno	
	Là dove più con le sue lucid'onde	

Tullia d'Aragona	Se gli antichi pastor di rose e fiori	
	Qual vaga Philomela, che fuggita	
	Poi che mi diè natura a voi simile	
Barbara Torelli	Spenta è d'Amor la face, il dardo è rotto	
Isabella di Morra	D'un alto monte ove si scorge il mare	
Chiara Matraini	Fera son di questo ombroso loco	
	Alti son questi monti et alti sono	

5

5.1 Ironists and Subversives		265
Francesco Berni	Chiome d'argento fine, irte e attorte	
	Questo è un voto che papa Clemente	
	Fate a modo d'un vostro servitore	
	Non vadan più pellegrini o romei	
Pietro Aretino	Sett'anni traditori ho via gettati	
	Se 'l chiaro Apelle con la man de l'arte	
Niccolò Franco	Tizian, ritratto avendo l'Aretino	
	Donne, m'è di bisogno ch'i no 'l taccia	
	Priapo, io qui compaio ambasciatore	
Benvenuto Cellini	Porca fortuna s' tu scoprivi prima	
5.2 The Benevolence of Critics		277
Benvenuto Cellini	Già molti si son messi a far sonetti	
Benedetto Varchi	Ben mi credea gran tempo, armato	
A. F. Grazzini	Con meraviglia e con gran divozione	
Michelangelo	I' ho già fatto un gozzo in questo stento	
Pasquino	O voi che riprendete 'l fiorentino	
5.3 An Alternative World		283
Maffio Venier	Fia mia, viseto belo inzucherao	
	L'esser ti, co' ti xe, senza cervelo	
	Signora mia, vu manizé per tutto	
	Eccetto l'omo, ogni altra bestia ha ben	
Camillo Scroffa	Cento fanciulli d'indole prestante	
	Le tumidule genule, i nigerrimi	
	Voi, ch'auribus arrectis auscultate	
Paolo Foglietta	Za i omi de trent'agni eran figiuoe	
	Presto ra toga se mettieva e trava	
G. C. Cortese	Aggio paura ca ste dammecelle	
	O vuie che tutte 'n chietta ve ne state	
5.4 The Consolation of Poetry		295
Giovanni della Casa	La bella greca, onde 'l pastor ideo	
	O Sonno, o della queta, umida, ombrosa	
	Già lessi, e or conosco in me, sì come	
Torquato Tasso	Io veggio in cielo scintillar le stelle	
	Non più crespo d'oro o d'ambra tersa e pura	
	Mentre ne' cari balli in loco ameno	
	Sposa regal, già la stagion ne viene	
Celio Magno	Di notte in braccio al mio tesor godea	

	Ecco di rose a questa tomba intorno	
	Trovo ovunque io giro 'l guardo intento	

5.5 In the Realm of the Divine — 307

Vittoria Colonna	Tira su l'alma al ciel col suo d'amore
	Vanno i pensier talor carghi di vera
Giovanni della Casa	Questa vita mortal, che 'n una o 'n due
Gabriel Fiamma	Questo mar, questi scogli e queste arene
	Quest'ora breve e d'ogni gioia cassa
Giordano Bruno	Amore per cui tant'alto il ver discerno
	Alle selve i mastini e i veltri slaccia
	Se la farfalla al suo splendor ameno
	Annosa quercia, che i rami spandi
Tommaso Campanella	Temo che per morir non si migliora
	Il mondo è il libro dove il Senno Eterno
	Io nacqui a debellar tre mali estremi
	Nel teatro del mondo ammascherate
Giacomo Lubrano	Un poter sempre in atto, un centro immenso

5.6 The Lure of Evanescent Things — 324

G. B. Marino	Pon mente al mar, Cratone, or che 'n ciascuna
	Or che l'aria e la terra arde e fiammeggia
	Oggi là dove 'l destro fianco a Ischia
	Onde dorate, e l'onde eran capelli
	Nera sì, ma sei bella, o di Natura
Scipione Errico	Del tuo mozzo parlar ai mozzi detti
G. L. Sempronio	Move zoppa gentil piede ineguale
Girolamo Preti	Mentre in cristallo rilucente e schietto
Bernardo Morando	Per vagheggiarti, Ermilla, a mio diletto

5.7 Time and Death — 334

Antonio Bruni	Quella che va con tante fiamme e tante
Maia Materdona	Ahi mondo! Ahi senso! Or ve' qui tanti e tanti
Ciro di Pers	Son ne le reni mie, adunque, formati
Giovanni Canale	Tu che dal riguardarmi orror apprendi
G. B. Marino	Questi è PERIN, qui fera morte il mise
G. L. Sempronio	Quei che le vite altrui tradisce e fura
Giacomo Lubrano	A che sognar con temerari vanti
	O glorioso enimma! Un morto seme
	Arpiuccia de' libri, empia tignola
Antonio Basso	Spunta la rosa, e grato il suo vermiglio
Federico Mennini	Questi libri, da cui più cose imparo

Bibliography

Original Texts and Translations

Alighieri, Dante. *Divina Commedia*. Critical edition of Società Dantesca Italiana. With commentary by G. A. Scartazzini and G. Vandelli. Milan: U. Hoepli, 1929.

Alighieri, Dante. *Fiore; Detto d'amore*. Critical edition by Paola Allegretti. Florence: Le Lettere, ca. 2011.

Allen, Beverly, Muriel Kittel, and Keala Jane Jewell, eds. and trans. *The Defiant Muse. Italian Feminist Poems from the Middle Ages to the Present*. New York: Feminist Press, 1986.

André le Chapelain, see Andrea Capellano.

Angiolieri, Cecco. *Le rime*. Edited by Antonio Lanza. Rome: Archivio Guido Izzi, 1990.

Antonelli, Roberto, Costanzo di Girolamo, and Rosario Coluccia, eds. *I poeti della scuola siciliana*. Milan: Mondadori, 2008.

Antonio da Ferrara. *Rime*. Critical edition by Laura Bellucci. Bologna: Commissione per i testi di lingua, 1967.

Antonio da Tempo. *Summa artis rytmici vulgaris dictaminis*. Padova, 1332. Published by Giusto Grion with the title of *Delle rime volgari. Trattato di Antonio da Tempo*. Bologna: Romagnoli, 1869.

Aragona, Tullia d'. *Dialogue on the Infinity of Love*. Edited by Rinaldina Russell and Bruce Merry. Chicago: University of Chicago Press, 1997.

Aragona, Tullia d'. *Rime della Signora Tullia di Aragona et di diversi a lei*. Venice: Gabriel Giolito de' Ferrari et fratelli, 1547.

Aragona, Tullia d'. *Sweet Fire: Tullia d'Aragona's Poetry of Dialogue and Selected Prose*. Edited by Elizabeth A. Pallito. New York: Brazilier, 2006.

Aretino, Pietro. *Operette politiche e satiriche*. Rome: Salerno Editrice, 1012–2013.

Aretino, Pietro. *Sonetti sopra i XVI modi*. Edited by Giovanni Aquilecchia. Rome: Salerno Editrice, 1992.

Asor Rosa, Alberto, ed. *Antologia della letteratura italiana*. 5 vols. Milan: Rizzoli, 1965.

Baldacci, Luigi, ed. *Lirici del Cinquecento*. Milan: Longanesi, 1975.

Balduino, Armando, ed. *Rimatori veneti del quattrocento*. Padova: Clesp, 1980.

Beccari, Antonio. *Le rime di Maestro Antonio da Ferrara (Antonio Beccari)*. Edited by Laura Bellucci. Bologna: Patron, 1972.

Bembo, Pietro. *Le rime*. Edited by Andrea Donnini. Rome: Salerno, 2008.

Bembo, Pietro. *Prose e Rime*. Edited by Carlo Dionisotti. Turin: UTET, 1966.

Berisso, Marco, ed. *Poesie dello Stilnovo*. Milan: Rizzoli, 2006.

Fischer, B. and R. Weber, eds. *Biblia sacra iuxta vulgata versionem*. Stutgard: Deutsche Babelgesellschaft, ca. 2007. The Vulgate Bible can also be read online: www.biblestudytools.com/vulgate.

Boiardo, Matteo Maria. *Amorum libri tres*. Edited by Tiziano Zanato. Turin: Einaudi, 1998.

Branyon, Richard A., ed. and trans. *A Treasury of Italian Love: Poems, Quotations, and Proverbs*. New York: Hippocrene Books, 1995.

Brevini, Francesco. *La poesia in dialetto dalle origini al Novecento*. Milan: Mondadori, 1999.

Brunelleschi, Filippo. *The Complete Works*. Edited by Eugenio Battisti. New York: Rizzoli, 1981.

Bruno, Giordano. *De gl'heroici furori*. Edited by Francesco Flora. Turin: UTET, 1928.

Bruno, Giordano. *The Heroic Frenzies*. A translation with introductions and notes. Edited by Paul Eugene Memmo Jr., University of North Carolina Studies in the Romance Languages and Literatures. Chapel Hill: University of North Carolina Press, 1964.

Bruno, Giordano. *The Infinite in Giordano Bruno, with a Translation of His Dialogue "Concerning the Cause, Principle, and One."* Translated by Sidney T. Greenberg. New York: Octagon Press, 1950.

Buonarroti, Michelangelo. *Complete Poems of Michelangelo.* Translated by John Frederick Nims. Chicago: University of Chicago Press, 1998.

Buonarroti, Michelangelo. *Complete Poems and Selected Letters of Michelangelo.* Translated by Creighton Gilbert. Edited by Robert N. Linscott. New York: Modern Library, 1965.

Burchiello e burleschi. Edited by Raffaele Nigro. Rome: Istituto Poligrafico e Zecca dello Stato, 2002.

Burchiello. *Le poesie autentiche.* Edited by Antonio Lanza. Rome: Aracne, 2010.

Burchiello. *Sonetti del Burchiello del Bellincioni e d'altri poeti fiorentini alla burchiellesca.* London, Lucca, and Pisa, 1757.

Cammelli, Antonio. *I sonetti faceti di Antonio Cammelli secondo l'autografo Ambrosiano.* Edited by Erasmo Pèrcopo. Naples: N. Jovine, 1908.

Campanella, Tommaso. *Il senso delle cose e della magia.* Edited by A. Bruers. Bari: Laterza, 1925.

Campanella, Tommaso. "Scelta di poesie filosofiche." In vol. 1 of *Tutte le opere.* Edited by Luigi Firpo. Milan: Mondadori, 1954.

Capellano, Andrea. *Trattato d'amore, Andreae Capellani regi francorum De Amore libri tres.* Edited by Salvatore Battaglia. Rome: Perrella, 1947.

Carmina Burana: die Gedichte des Codex Buranus. Translated by Carl Fischer and Hugo Kuhn. Notes and concluding remarks by Günter Bernt. Zürich-München: Artemis Verlag, 1974.

Casciani, Santa, and Christopher Kleinhenz, trans. and eds. *The Fiore and the Detto d'Amore.* Notre Dame, Indiana: University of Notre Dame Press, 2000.

Caselli, Mariano. *Il Cinquecento.* Rome: Bibliografica, 2007.

Cavalcanti, Guido. *Complete Poems.* Translated by M. A. Cirigliano. New York: Italica Press, 1992.

Cavalcanti, Guido. *The Metabolisms of Desire: The Poetry of Guido Cavalcanti.* Translated by David R. Slavitt. Edmonton: AU Press, 2012.

Cavalcanti, Guido. *The Poetry.* Edited and translated by Lowry Nelson Jr. New York, London, 1986.

Cavalcanti, Guido. *Rime.* Edited by Giulio Cattaneo. Turin: Einaudi, 1967.

Celani, Enrico, ed. *Rime della Signora Tullia d'Aragona, cortigiana del secolo XVI.* Bologna: Forni, 1891.

Ciminelli dall'Aquila, Serafino. *Le Rime.* Edited by M. Menghini. Bologna: Romagnoli dall'Acqua, 1894.

Cino da Pistoia. *Le rime.* Genève: L. S. Olschi, 1925.

Cirigliano, Marc A. *Melancholia Poetica: A Dual Language Anthology of Italian Poetry, 1160–1550.* Leister, UK: Troubadour Publishing, 2007.

Colonna, Vittoria. *Rime.* Edited by Alan Bullock. Bari: Laterza, 1982.

Colonna, Vittoria. *Selections from the Rime Spirituali, with Photographs of Josep Maria Subirach's Passion Facade.* Translated by Jan Zwicky. Illustrated by Robert Moody. Erin, Ontario: Porcupine's Quill, 2014.

Compagni, Dino. *Chronicle of Florence.* Edited by Daniel E. Bornstein. Philadelphia: University of Pennsylvania Press, 1986.

Compagni, Dino. *Cronica delle cose occorrenti ai tempi suoi.* Edited by Davide Cappi. Rome: Carrocci, 2013.

Contini, Gianfranco, ed. *Letteratura italiana delle origini.* Florence: Sansoni, 1970.

Contini, Gianfranco. *Poeti del Duecento.* 2 vols. Milan-Naples: Ricciardi, 1960.

Correggio, Niccolò da. *Opere.* Edited by Antonia Tissoni Benvenuti. Bari: Laterza, 1969.

Corsi, Giuseppe, ed. *Rimatori del Trecento.* Turin: UTET, 1972.

Cortese, Giulio Cesare. *Opere poetiche.* Edited by Enrico Malato. Rome: Edizioni dell'Ateneo, 1967.

Croce, Benedetto. *Lirici marinisti.* Bari: Laterza, 1910.

Cudini, Piero, ed. *Poesia italiana del Trecento.* Milan: Garzanti, 1978.

Cudini, Piero, ed. *Poesia Italiana. Il Duecento.* Milan: Garzanti, 1978.

Dante. *Fiore; Detto d'amore.* Critical edition by Paola Allegretti. Florence: Le Lettere, ca. 2011.

Dante. *La Vita Nuova.* Edited by De Robertis. Milan-Naples: Ricciardi, 1980.

Dante. *Rime.* Edited by Gianfranco Contini. Turin: Einaudi, 1946.

Dante. *Rime della maturità e dell'esilio.* Edited by M. Barbi and V. Pernicone. Florence: Le Monnier, 1969.

Davanzati, Chiaro. *Canzoni e sonetti.* Edited by Aldo Menichetti. Turin: Einaudi. 2004.

Della Casa, Giovanni. *Rime.* Edited by G. Tanturli. Parma: Guanda, 2001.

Della Casa, Giovanni. *Rime.* Edited by Roberto Fredi. Milan: Rizzoli, 1993.

Della Casa, Giovanni. *Rime.* Edited by Stefano Carrai. Turin: Einaudi, 2003.

Dell'Arco, Mario, ed. *Pasquino e le pasquinate*. Milan: Aldo Martello, 1957.
De Robertis, Domenico. *Il libro della "Vita Nuova."* Firenze: Sansoni, 1961.
Dondi dall'Orologio, Giovanni. *Rime*. Edited by Antonio Daniele. Vicenza: Neri Pozza, 1990.
Dondi dall'Orologio, Giovanni. *Tractatus Astrarii*. Edited by A. Barzon, E. Morpurgo, A. Petrucci, and G. Francescano. Città del Vaticano: Biblioteca Apostolica Vaticana, 1960.
Ferroni, Giulio, ed. *Poesia italiana. Il Cinquecento*. Milan: Garzanti, 1978.
Fiamma, Gabriele. *Rime spirituali*. Venice: Franceschi, 1570.
Filippi, Rustico. *Sonetti*. Edited by Pier Vincenzo Mengaldo. Turin: Einaudi, 1971.
Folgore da San Gimignao. *Il gioco della bella vita*. Edited by Michelangelo Picone. San Gimignano: Tipografia Editrice Arti Grafiche Nencini, 1988.
Foster, K., and P. Boyde. *Dante's Lyric Poetry*. 2 vols. Oxford: Clarendon Press, 1967.
Foster, Kenelm. *Petrarch: Poet and Humanist*. Edinburgh: Edinburgh University Press, 1984.
Gambara, Veronica. *Complete Poems*. Edited and translated by Molly M. Martin and Paola Ugolini. Toronto, Canada: Iter Inc. Centre for Reformation and Renaissance Studies, 2014.
Gambara, Veronica. *Le rime*. Edited by Allan Bullock. Florence: Olschki, 1995.
Gareth, Benedetto. *Le rime*. Edited by Erasmo Pèrcopo. 2 vols. Naples: Tipografia dell'Accademia delle Scienze, 1892.
Getto, Giovanni. *Opere scelte di Giovan Battista Marino e dei marinisti*. 2 vols. Turin: UTET, 1962.
Getto, Giovanni, and Edoardo Sanguineti. *Il Sonetto. Cinquecento sonetti dal Duecento al Novecento*. Milan: Mursia, 1957.
Giacomo da Lentini. *Poesie*. Critical edition by Roberto Antonelli. Rome: Bulzoni, 1979.
Gianni, Lapo. *Rime*. Edited by Francesco Jovine. Rome: Bagatto, 1989.
Gigliucci, Roberto, ed. *La lirica rinascimentale*. Rome: Istituto poligrafico e Zecca dello stato, 2001.
Giuliani, Alfredo, ed. *Antologia della poesia italiana. Dalle origini al Trecento*. 2 vols. Milan: Feltrinelli, 1975.
Gorni, G., M. Danzi, and S. Longhi, eds. *Poeti del Cinquecento*. Milan: Ricciardi, 2001.
Guidiccioni, Giovanni, and F. Coppetta Beccuti. *Rime*. Edited by Ezio Chiorboli. Bari: Laterza, 1912.
Guillaume de Lorris, and Jean de Meun. *Le Roman de la Rose*. Edited by Felix Lecoy. Paris: Champion, 1965.
Guinizzelli, Guido. *Rime*. Edited by Luciano Rossi. Turin: Einaudi, 2002.
Guinizzelli, Guido. *Rime*. Edited by Pietro Pelosi. Naples: Liguori, 2003.
Guittone d'Arezzo. *Canzoniere. I sonetti d'amore del codice Laurenziano*. Edited by Lino Leonardi. Turin: Einaudi, 1994.
Guittone d'Arezzo. *Le rime*. Edited by Francesco Egidi. Bari: Laterza, 1940.
Guittone d'Arezzo. *Rime di Fra Guittone d'Arezzo*. Edited by Luciano Valeriani. Florence: G. Morandi e Figlio, 1828.
Hilka, A., O. Schumann, and B. Bischoff, eds. *Carmina Burana*. Heidelberg, 1930–1970.
Jensen, F., ed and trans. *The Poetry of the Sicilian School*. New York and London: Garland, 1986.
Kay, George R., ed. *The Penguin Book of Italian Verse*. Baltimore, Maryland: Penguin Books, 1958.
Lind, L. R., ed. *Lyric Poetry of the Italian Renaissance*. New Haven and London: Yale University Press, 1954.
Lubrano, Giacomo. *In tante trasparenze: il verme setaiuolo e altre scintille poetiche*. Edited by Giancarlo Alfano and Gabriele Frasca. Naples: Cronopio, ca. 2002.
Lubrano, Giacomo. *Scintille poetiche*. Edited by Marzio Pieri. Ravenna: Longo Editore, 1982.
Mancini, Franco, ed. *Poeti perugini del Trecento*. Vol. 1, *Marino Ceccoli, Cecco Nuccoli e altri rimatori in tenzone*. Vol. 2, *Nerio Muscoli*. Perugia: Guerra, 1996.
Marti, Mario, ed. *Poeti del Dolce Stil Novo*. Florence: Le Monnier, 1969.
Marti, Mario, ed. *Poeti giocosi del tempo di Dante*. Milan: Rizzoli, 1956.
Marucci, Valerio, ed. *Pasquinate romane del Cinque e Seicento*. Rome: Salerno Editrice, 1988.
Marucci, Valerio, Antonio Marzo, and Angelo Romano, eds. *Pasquinate romane del Cinquecento*. 2 vols. Rome: Salerno Editrice, 1983.
Matraini, Chiara. *Rime e lettere*. Edited by Giovanna Rabitti. Bologna: Commissione per i testi di lingua, 1989.
Medici, Lorenzo de'. *Canzoniere*. Edited by Tiziano Zanato. Florence: Olschki, 1991.
Medici, Lorenzo de'. *Comento de' miei sonetti*. Edited by Tiziano Zanato. Florence: Olschki, 1991.
Monaci, Ernesto. *Crestomazia italiana dei primi secoli*. Città di Castello: Casa Editrice S. Lapi, 1912.
Monte Andrea da Firenze. *Le rime*. Edited by Francesco Filippo Minetti. Florence: Presso l'Accademia della Crusca, 1979.
Morra, Isabella di. *Canzoniere*. Edited and translated by Irene Musiello Mitchell. West Lafayette, Indiana: Bordighera, 1998.
Morra, Isabella di. *Rime*. Edited by Maria Antonietta Grignani. Rome: Salerno, 2000.
Morra, Isabella di. *Selected Poetry and Prose*. Edited by Elaine Maclanchlan. Chicago: University of Chicago Press, 2008.

Muscetta, Carlo, and Daniele Ponchiroli. *Poesia del Duecento e Trecento*. Turin: Einaudi, 1956.

Muscetta, Carlo, and Daniele Ponchiroli. *Poesia del Quattrocento e del Cinquecento*. Turin: Einaudi, 1963.

Muscetta, Carlo, and Pier Paolo Ferrante. *Poesia del Seicento*. 2 vols. Turin: Einaudi, 1964.

Panvini, Bruno, ed. *I poeti della scuola siciliana*. 2 vols. Florence: Olschki, 1964.

Perito, Enrico. *La congiura dei baroni e il conte di Policastro*. Bari: Laterza, 1926. The texts of Giannantonio Petrucci are in the appendix.

Petrarca, Francesco. *Canzoniere*. Edited by Gianfranco Contini. Turin: Einaudi, 1964.

Petrarca, Francesco. *Le rime sparse*. Edited by Enzo Chiorboli. Milan: Trevisini, 1924.

Petrarch. *Petrarch's Song Book Rerum Vulgarium Fragmenta: A Verse Translation*. Translated by James Wyatt Cook. Binghamton, New York, 1995.

Petrarch. *The Rime Sparse and Other Lyrics*. Edited and translated by Robert M. Durling. Cambridge, Massachusetts, 1976.

Petrarch. *Selected Sonnets, Odes, and Letters*. Edited by Thomas G. Bergin. New York: Appleton-Century-Croft, 1966.

Petrucci, Giovanni Antonio. *Canzoniere*. Edited by Jean Jules Le Coultre. Bologna: Romagnoli, 1879.

Ponte, Giovanni. *Il Quattrocento*. Bologna: Zanichelli, 1966.

Pulci, Luigi. *Opere minori*. Edited by Paolo Orvieto. Milan: Mursia, 1986.

Quaglio, Antonio Enzo. "Gli stilnovisti." In *Lo stilnovo e la poesia religiosa*, 7–148. Bari: Laterza, 1971.

Rustico di Filippo. *Sonetti satirici e gioiosi*. Edited by Silvia Buzzetti Gallarati. Rome: Carocci, 2005.

Sapegno, Natalino, ed. *Poeti minori del Trecento*. Milan-Naples: Ricciardi, 1962.

Sapegno, Natalino, ed. *Rimatori del tardo Trecento*. Rome: Edizioni dell'Ateneo, 1967.

Scroffa, Camillo. *I cantici di Fidenzio*. Edited by Pietro Trifone. Rome: Salerno, 1981.

Segre, Cesare, and Carlo Ossola, eds. *Antologia della poesia italiana*. 3 vols. Turin: Einaudi-Gallimard, 1997–99.

Sommariva, Giorgio. *Sonetti villaneschi*. Udine: G. de Fabris, 1907.

Spagnoletti, Giacinto, and Cesare Vivaldi. *Poesia dialettale dal Rinascimento a oggi*. Milan: Garzanti, 1991.

Spampinato, V. *Documenti della vita di Giordano Bruno*. Florence: Olschki, 1933.

Stampa, Gaspara. *Selected Poems*. Edited and translated by Laura Anna Stortoni and Mary Prentice Lillie. New York: Italica Press, 1994.

Stortoni, Laura. *Women Poets of the Italian Renaissance: Courtly Ladies and Courtesans*. Translated by Anna Stortoni and Mary Prentice Lillie. New York: Italica Press, 1997.

Tarsia, Giangaleazzo. *Rime*. Edited by Cesare Bozzetti. Milan: Fondazione Arnoldo e Alberto Mondadori, 1980.

Tarsia, Giangaleazzo. *Rime*. Edited by Gabriele Turchi. Cosenza: Casa del Libro, 1971.

Tasso, Torquato. *Dialoghi*. Edited by Giovanni Baffetti. Milan: Rizzoli, 1998.

Tasso, Torquato. *Rime per Lucrezia Bendidio*. Edited by Luigi De Vendittis. Turin: Einaudi, 1965.

Tebaldi, Antonio (Tebaldeo). *Rime*. Edited by Tania Basile and Jean Jacques Marchand. 5 vols. Ferrara: Panini, 1989–92.

Tesauro, Emanuele. *Il Canocchiale Aristotelico*. Turin: Bartolomeo Zavatta, 1670. Anastatic reprint by Editrice artistica piemontese Savigliano (Cuneo), 2000.

Tusiani, Joseph, ed. *Italian Poets of the Renaissance*. Long Island City, New York: Baroque Press, 1971.

Vannozzo, Francesco di. *Rime*. Edited by Medin. Bologna: Commissione per i testi di lingua, 1928.

Venier, Maffio. *Poesie diverse*. Edited by Attilio Carminati. Venice: Corbo e Fiore, 2001.

Villani, Giovanni. *Cronica: con le continuazioni di Matteo e Filippo. Scelta*. Edited by Giovanni Aquilecchia. Turin: Einaudi, 1979.

Villani, Giovanni, Matteo, and Filippo. *Croniche*. Trieste: Sezione letterario-artistica del Lloyd Triestino, 1857.

Visconti, Gasparo. *I canzonieri per Beatrice d'Este e per Bianca Maria Sforza*. Edited by Paolo Bongrani. Milan: Mondadori, 1979.

Vitale, Maurizio, ed. *Antologia della letteratura italiana*. Vol. 1, 200–300. Vol. 2, 400–500. Milan: Rizzoli, 1965.

Vitale, Maurizio, ed. *Rimatori comico-realistici del Due e Trecento*. Turin: Einaudi, 1976.

Vivante, Arturo, ed. and trans. *Italian Poetry: An Anthology*. Wellfleet, Massachusetts: Delphinium Press, 1996.

Studies

Amaturo, Raffaele. *Petrarca*. Bari: Laterza, 1971.
Ardizzone, Maria Luisa. *Guido Cavalcanti. L'altro Medioevo*. Florence: Cadmo, 2006.
Avalle, D'arco Silvio. *Ai luoghi di delizia pieni. Saggio sulla lirica italiana del XIII^{mo} secolo*. Milan-Naples: Ricciardi, 1977.
Aurigemma, Marcello. *Lirica, poemi e trattati civili del Cinquecento*. Bari: Laterza, 1973.
Badaloni, Nicola, Renato Barilli, and Walter Moretti. *Cultura e vita civile tra Riforma e Controriforma*. Bari: Laterza, 1973.
Baldacci, Luigi. "Introduzione." In *Lirici del Cinquecento*. Milan: Longanesi, 1975.
Barański, Zygmunt G. "Dolce stil novo." In *The Dante Encyclopedia*, 308–11. Edited by Richard Lancing. New York and London: Garland Publishing, 2000.
Barański, Zygmunt G., and Patrick Boyde. *The Fiore in Context. Dante, France, Tuscany*. Notre Dame, Indiana: University of Notre Dame Press, 1996.
Barbiellini Amidei, Beatrice. *Alla luna. Saggio sulla poesia del Cariteo*. Florence: La Nuova Italia Editrice, 1999.
Barolini, Teodolinda. "Dante and the Lyric Past." In *The Cambridge Companion to Dante*, 14–34. Edited by Rachel Jacoff. Cambridge, New York: Cambridge University Press, 2007.
Barolini, Teodolinda. *Dante's Poets: Textuality and Truth in the "Comedy."* Princeton, New Jersey: Princeton University Press, 1984.
Barolini, Teodolinda. "Lyric Poetry, Dante's." In *The Dante Encyclopedia*, 576–82. Edited by Richard Lancing. New York-London: Garland Publishing, 2000.
Bassanese, Fiora A. *Gaspara Stampa*. Boston: Twayne Publishers, 1982.
Bassanese, Fiora A. "Gaspara Stampa." In *Italian Women Writers. A Bio-Bibliographical Source Book*, 404–13. Edited by R. Russell. Westport, Connecticut, and London: Greenwood Press, 1994.
Battaglia, Salvatore. *Grande dizionario della lingua italiana*. 21 vols. Turin: UTET, 1961.
Battisti, Eugenio. *Filippo Brunelleschi: The Complete Work*. New York: Rizzoli, 1981.
Battistoni, Giorgio. *Dante, Verona, e la cultura ebraica*. Rome: Giuntina, 2004.
Bertelli, Sergio, Franco Cardini, Elvira Garbero Zorzi. *The Courts of the Italian Renaissance*. New York, New York: Facts on File, 1986.
Bertoni, Giulio. *Il Duecento*. 3rd edition. Milan: Vallardi, 1964.
Biadene, Leandro. "Morfologia del sonetto nei secoli XII e XIV." *Studi di filologia romanza* 4 (1889): 1–234.
Bondanella, Peter, and Julia Conway Bondanella, eds. *Dictionary of Italian Literature*. Westport, Connecticut: Greenwood Press, 1996.
Borsa, Paolo. *La nuova poesia di Guido Guinizzelli*. Florence: Cadmo, 2007.
Borsellino, Nino. *Gli anticlassicisti del Cinquecento*. Bari: Laterza, 1973.
Botterill, Steven. "Autobiography and Artifice in the Medieval Lyric: The Case of Cecco Nuccoli." *Italian Studies* 46 (1991): 37–57.
Botterill, Steven. "Cecco Nuccoli: An Introduction." *The Italianist* 8 (1988): 16–32.
Botterill, Steven. "The Trecento. Minor Writers." In *The Cambridge History of Italian Literature*, 108–18. Edited by Peter Brand and Lino Pertile. Cambridge: Cambridge University Press, 1996.
Boyde, Patrick. *Dante's Style in his Lyric Poetry*. Cambridge: At the University Press, 1971.
Brand, Peter, and Lino Pertile, eds. *The Cambridge History of Italian Literature*. Cambridge: Cambridge University Press, 1996.
Brugnolo, Furio. "Parabola di un sonetto del Guinizzelli." In *Per Guido Guinizzelli, Il Comune di Monselice (1275–1976)*, 53–105. Padova: Antenore, 1980.

Brugnolo, Furio, and Gianfelice Peron, eds. *Da Guido Guinizzelli a Dante: nuove prospettive sulla lirica del Duecento. Atti del Convegno di Studi, Padova-Monselice, 10–12 maggio 2002.* Padova: Il Poligrafo, 2004.

Buck, August. *Italienische Sonette.* Tübingen: M. Neimyer, 1954.

Calcaterra, Carlo. "Il poeta dei cinque sensi." In *Il Paraso in rivolta,* 11–82. Bologna: Il Mulino, 1961.

Calenda, Corrado. *Per altezza d'ingegno. Saggio su Guido Cavalcanti.* Naples: Liguori, 1976.

Carrai, Stefano. *La lirica toscana del Duecento. Cortesi, guittoniani, stilnovisti.* Rome: Laterza, 1997.

Carrai, Stefano. *Lirici del Quattrocento nell'Italia centrale.* Pisa: Libreria del Lungarno, 1994.

Carrai, Stefano, and Giuseppe Marrani, eds. *Cecco Angiolieri e la poesia satirica medievale. Atti del Convegno Internazionale. Siena, 26–27 ottobre 2002.* Florence: Edizioni del Galluzzo, 2005.

Carrai, Stefano. *L'usignolo del Bembo.* Rome: Carocci, 2006.

Catalano, Michele. *La tragica morte di Ercole Strozzi e il sonetto di Barbara Torelli.* Genève: Olschki, 1926.

Cerchi, Paolo. "The Baroque: Lyric Poetry." In *The Cambridge History of Italian Literature,* 301–8. Edited by Peter Brand and Lino Pertile. Cambridge: Cambridge University Press, 1996.

Ceruti, Antonio. *I principi del duomo di Milano fino alla morte di Giangaleazzo Visconnti.* Milan: G. Agnelli, 1870. See pp. 223–24 for Salutati's sonnet.

Cervigni, Dino S., ed. *Petrarch and the European Lyric Tradition.* Vol. 22, *Annali d'Italianistica.* 2004.

Ceserani, Remo, and Lidia De Federicis. *Il materiale e l'immaginario.* Vol. 1, *Dall'alto medioevo alla società urbana.* Vol. 2, *La società dell'antico regime.* Turin: Loescher, 1990.

Ciavolella, M. *La "malattia" d'amore dall'antichità al Medioevo.* Rome: 1976.

Clements, Robert J. *The Poetry of Michelangelo.* New York: New York University Press, 1965.

Contini, Gianfranco. "Esercizio di interpretazione sopra un sonetto di Dante." In *Varianti e altra linguistica. Una raccolta di saggi (1938–1968),* 161–68. Turin: Einaudi, 1970.

Croce, B. "I versi di un reo di stato." In vol. 1 of *Uomini e cose della vecchia Italia,* 1–13. Bari: Laterza, 1927.

Cucchi, Maurizio, ed. *Dizionario della poesia Italiana.* Milan: Mondadori, 1983.

Dall'Orto, Giovanni. "L'omosessualità nella poesia volgare italiana fino al tempo di Dante. Appunti." *Sodoma* 3, no. 3 (1986): 13–37.

De Caprio, Vincenzo. "La poesia profana umbra del Trecento." In vol. 1 of *Storia e Geografia, Letteratura italiana,* 507–11. Edited by Alberto Asor Rosa. Turin: Einaudi, 1987.

Dionisotti, Carlo. *Geografia e storia della letteratura italiana.* Turin: Einaudi, 1967.

Dossena, Giampaolo. *Storia confidenziale della letteratura italiana.* 4 vols. Milan: Rizzoli, 1987.

Ducros, François. *Tommaso Campanella, poète.* Paris: PUF, 1969.

Elwert, W. Theodor. *Italienische Metrik.* Munich: Max Hueber, 1968. Translated into Italian as *Versificazione italiana dalle origini ai giorni nostri.* Florence: Le Monnier, 1973.

Elwert, W. Theodor. *La poesia lirica italiana del Seicento.* Florence: Olschki, 1967.

Ferroni, Giulio, and Amedeo Quondam. *Petrarchismo mediato. Teoria ed esperienza della lirica a Napoli nell'età del manierismo.* Rome: Bulzoni, 1973.

Flamini, Francesco. *La lirica toscana del Rinascimento anteriore al tempo del Magnifico.* Bologna: La Fotocromo Emiliana, 1977.

Flamini, Francesco. *Notizia storica dei versi e metri italiani dal medioevo ai tempi nostri.* Livorno: Raffaello Giusti, 1936.

Foà, Simona. "Immanuel da Roma." In *Dizionario Biografico degli Italiani.* Rome: Istituto della Enciclopedia Italiana, 2004.

Foscolo, Ugo. *Vestigi della storia del sonetto italiano dal MCC al MDCCC.* Zurich: Orell und Füssli, 1816.

Frare, Pierantonio. *Per istraforo di prospettiva. Il Cannocchiale aristotelico e la poesia del Seicento.* Pisa: Istituti editoriali e poligrafici internazionali, ca. 2001.

Friedrich, Hugo. *Epoche della lirica italiana.* Vol. 1, *Dalle Origini al Quattrocento.* Vol. 2, *Il Cinquecento.* Vol. 3, *Il Seicento.* Milan: Mursia, 1964–76.

Friedrich, Hugo. *Epochen der Italienischen Lyric.* Frankfurt am Mein: V. Klostermann, 1964.

Fubini, Mario. "Il sonetto." In *Metrica e poesia. Lezioni sulle forme metriche italiane,* 146–167. Milan: Feltrinelli, 1970.

Galdi, Ladislao. *Introduzione alla stilistica italiana.* Bologna: Patron, 1971.

Getto, Giovanni. *Interpretazioni del Tasso.* Naples: Edizioni scientifiche italiane, 1951.

Getto, Giovanni. "Il barocco in Italia." In *Manierismo, Barocco, Rococò: concetti e termini. Convegno internazionale Roma 21–24 April 1960,* 81–106. Rome: Accademia Nazionale dei Lincei, 1962.

Getto, Giovanni. "Sulla poesia del Cariteo." In *Immagini e problemi di letteratura italiana,* 9–47. Milan: Mursia, 1966.

Getto, Giovanni. "Immagini del sonetto." In *Immagini e problemi di letteratura italiana*, 9–48. Milan: Mursia, 1966. First published as the introduction to Getto, G., and E. Sanguineti. *Il sonetto. Cinquecento sonetti dal Duecento al Novecento*. Milan: Edizioni Corticelli, 1957.

Getto, Giovanni. "Introduzione al Marino." In *Barocco in prosa e poesia*, 11–58. Milan: Rizzoli, 1969.

Getto, Giovanni. "Introduzione." In *I Marinisti*. Vol. 2, *Opere scelte di Giovan Battista Marino e dei marinisti*, 9–89. Turin: UTET, 1962.

Gigliucci, Roberto. *Oximoron Amoris, retorica dell'amore irrazionale nella lirica italiana antica*. Rome: De Rubis, 1990.

Gigliucci, Roberto. *Il Petrarchismo: un modello di poesia per l'Europa*. Rome: Bulzoni, 2006.

Girardi, E. N. *Studi sulle rime di Michelangelo*. Firenze: Olschki, 1974.

Giunta, Claudio. *La poesia italiana nell'età di Dante: la linea Bonagiunta-Guinizzelli*. Bologna: Il Mulino, 1998.

Goldberg, Jonathan. *Queering the Renaissance*. Durham, North Carolina, and London, 1993.

Gorni, Guglielmo. *Dante prima della Commedia*. Florence: Cadmo, 2001.

Gorni, Guglielmo. *Guido Cavalcanti, Dante e il suo primo amico*. Rome-Florence: Aracne, 2009.

Granada, Miguel A. "New visions of the cosmos." In *The Cambridge Companion to Renaissance Philosophy*, 270–86. Edited James Hankins. Cambridge: Cambridge University Press, 2007.

Jaffe, Irma B., and Gernando Colombardo. *Shining Eyes and Cruel Fortune: The Lives and Loves of Italian Renaissance Women Poets*. New York: Fordham University Press, 2002.

Kennedy, William J. "European Beginnings and Transmissions: Dante, Petrarch, and the Sonnet Sequence." *Cambridge Companion to the Sonnet*. Edited by A. D. Cousins and Peter Howarth. Cambridge: Cambridge University Press, 2011.

Kleinhenz, Christopher. *The Early Sonnet. The First Century (1220–1321)*. Lecce: Milella, 1986.

Kristeller, Paul Oscar. *Renaissance Thought II: Papers on Humanism and the Arts*. New York: Harper, 1965.

Larivalle, Paul. *Pietro Aretino*. Rome: Salerno, 1997.

Malato, Enrico. "La scoperta di un poeta: Giulio Cesare Cortese." *Filologia e critica* 2 (1977): 37–117.

Marti, Mario. *Cultura e stile nei poeti giocosi del tempo di Dante*. Pisa: Nitri-Lischi, 1953.

Marucci, Valerio. *L'età della Controriforma e del barocco*. Palermo: Palumbo, 1978.

Marucci, Valerio, ed. *Pasquinate del Cinque e Seicento*. Rome: Salerno Editrice, 1988.

Marucci, Valerio, Antonio Marzo, and Angelo Romano, eds. "Presentazione di Giovanni Aquilecchia." *Pasquinate romane del Cinquecento*. Rome: Salerno Editrice, 1983.

Mazzacurati, Giuseppe. "Bosone da Gubbio e la sua opera." In vol. 1 of *Studi di filologia romanza*, 277–336. Livorno: Vigo, 1884.

Meninni, Federico. *Ritratto del sonetto e della canzone (1677)*. Edited by Lizia Carminati. Lecce: Argo, 2002.

Mineo, Nicolò. *Dante*. Bari: Laterza, 1971.

Mirollo, James V. *Mannerism and Renaissance Poetry*. New Haven, Connecticut: Yale University Press, 1984.

Mirollo, James. *The Poet of the Marvelous*. New York: Columbia University Press, 1963.

Moleta, Vincent. *The Early Poetry of Guittone d'Arezzo*. London: Modern Humanities Research Association, 1976.

Montanelli, Indro. *L'Italia della Controriforma*. Milan: Rizzoli, 1969.

Moretti, Walter. *Torquato Tasso*. Bari: Laterza, 1973.

Nardi, Bruno. "Filosofia dell'amore nei rimatori italiani del Duecento e in Dante." In *Dante e la cultura medievale*, 1–88. Bari: Laterza, 1942.

Nigro, Salvatore S. *Pulci e la cultura medicea*. Bari: Laterza, 1972.

Noferi, Adelia. *L'esperienza poetica del Petrarca*. Florence, 1962.

Oldcorn, Anthony. "The Cinquecento Lyric Poetry." In *The Cambridge History of Italian Literature*, 251–68. Edited by Peter Brand and Lino Pertile. Cambridge: Cambridge University Press, 1996.

Orvieto, Paolo. *La poesia comico-realistica dalle origini al Cinquecento*. Rome: Carocci, 2000.

Orvieto, Paolo. *Studio sulla poesia volgare fiorentina del Quattrocento*. Rome: Salerno, 1978.

Orwen, Gifford P. "Cecco Angiolieri: A Study." Chapel Hill, North Carolina: North Carolina Studies in the Renaissance Languages and Literatures, 1979.

Pagani, Walter. *Repertorio tematico della scuola poetica siciliana*. Bari: Adriatica Editrice, 1968.

Parenti, Giovanni. *Benet Garret detto il Cariteo. Profilo di un poeta*. Florence: Olschki, 1993.

Pasquini, Emilio, and Antonio Enzo Quaglio. *Le origini e la scuola siciliana*. Bari: Laterza, 1971.

Pasquini, Emilio, and Antonio Enzo Quaglio. *Lo Stilnovo e la poesia religiosa*. Bari: Laterza, 1971.

Pastor, Ludvig. *The History of the Popes from the Close of the Middle Ages*. Translated by Annabel Kerr. Edited by Ralph Francis Kerr. St. Louis, Missouri: B. Herder, 1923.

Pazzaglia, Mario. *Letteratura italiana*. Bologna: Zanichelli, 1979.

Pellizzari, A. "Filippo Brunelleschi scrittore." *Rassegna bibliografica della letteratura italiana* 27 (1919): 292–315.

Pelosi, Pietro. *Guido Guinizzelli: stilnovo inquieto*. Naples: Liguori, 2000.

Pertile, Lino. "Dante." In *The Cambridge History of Italian Literature*, 39–69. Edited by Peter Brand and Lino Pertile. Cambridge: Cambridge University Press, 1996.

Pertile, Lino. "Il nodo di Bonagiunta, le penne di Dante e il dolce stil novo." *Lettere italiane* 46 (194): 44–75.

Piemontese, Filippo. *La formazione del canzoniere boiardesco*. Milan: Marzorati, 1953.

Pizzagalli, Daniela. *La signora della poesia: vita e passioni di Veronica Gambara, artista del Rinascimento*. Milan: Rizzoli, 2004.

Ponte, Giovanni. *Introduzione a Il Quattrocento*. Bologna: Zanichelli, 1966.

Pozzi, Giovanni. *La rosa in mano al professore*. Friburgo: Edizioni Universitarie, 1974.

Pozzi, Giovanni. *Poesia per gioco. Prontuario di figure artificiose*. Bologna: Il Mulino, 1984.

Quaglio, Antonio Enzo. *La poesia realistica e la prosa del Duecento*. Bari: Laterza, 1971.

Rabitti, Giovanna. "Chiara Matraini." In *Italian Women Writers. A Bio-Bibliographical Source Book*, 243–52. Edited by R. Russell. Westport, Connecticut, and London: Greenwood Press, 1994.

Rendina, Claudio. *Pasquino, statua parlante*. Roma: Newton Compton, 1991.

Rendina, Claudio. *The Popes, Histories and Secrets*. Translated by Paul D. McCusker, JD. Santa Anna, California: Seven Locks Press, 2002.

Reynolds, Anne. "Francesco Berni: Satire and Criticism in the Italian Sixteenth Century." In *Comic Relations: Studies in the Comic, Satire and Parody*, 129–38. Edited by Pavel Petr, David Roberts, and Philip Thomson. Frankfurt am Main and New York: P. Lang, 1985.

Rossi, Antonio. *Serafino Aquilano e la poesia cortigiana*. Brescia: Moricelliana, 1980.

Rossi, Luca Carlo. "Una ricomposta tenzone (autentica?) fra Cino da Pistoia e Bosone da Gubbio." *Italia medioevale e umanistica* 31 (1988): 45–79.

Rossi, Luciano, and Sara Alloatti Boller, eds. *Intorno a Guido Guinizzelli. Atti della giornata di studi, Università di Zurigo, 16 giugno, 2000*. Alessandria: Edizioni dell'Orso, 2002.

Rossi Bellotto, Carla. *Il Pistoia: spirito bizzarro del Quattrocento*. Alessandria: Edizioni dell'Orso, 2008.

Roth, C. "Lo sfondo storico della poesia di I. Romano." *La Rassegna mensile di Israel* 17 (1951): 424–46.

Ruschioni, Ada. *Morfologia e Antologia del sonetto*. 2 vols. Milan: Celuc Libri, 1975.

Russell, Rinaldina. "Chiara Matarini nella tradizione lirica femminile." *Forum Italicum* 34, no. 2 (2000): 415–27.

Russell, Rinaldina. "Introduction to Tullia d'Aragona." *Dialogue on the Infinity of Love*. Edited and translated by R. Russell and B. Merry. Chicago: University of Chicago Press, 1997.

Russell, Rinaldina. "L'ultima meditazione di Vittoria Colonna e l' Ecclesia Viterbiensis." *La parola del testo* 4, no. 1 (2000): 151–66.

Russell, Rinaldina. "The Mind's Pursuit of the Divine: A Survey of Secular and Religious Themes in Vittoria Colonna's Sonnets." *Forum Italicum* 26, no. 1 (1992): 14–27.

Russell, Rinaldina. *Tre versanti della poesia stilnovistica*. Bari: Adriatica Editrice, 1973.

Russell, Rinaldina. "Veronica Gàmbara." In *Italian Women Writers: A Bio-Bibliographical Source Book*, 145–53. Edited by R. Russell. Westport, Connecticut, and London: Greenwood Press, 1994.

Santagata, Marco. *Amate e amanti. Figure della lirica amorosa fra Dante e Petrarca*. Bologna: Il Mulino, 1999.

Santagata, Marco. *La lirica aragonese. Studi sulla poesia napoletana del secondo Quattrocento*. Padova: Antenore, 1979.

Santagata, Marco, and Stefano Carrai. *La lirica di corte nell'Italia del Quattrocento*. Milan: Franco Angeli, 1993.

Santangelo, Salvatore. *Le tenzoni poetiche nella netteratura italiana delle origini*. Genève: Olschki, 1928.

Sapegno, Natalino. "Antonio Pucci." In *Pagine di storia letteraria*. Florence: La Nuova Italia, 1986.

Sapegno, Natalino. *Il Trecento*. Milan: Vallardi, 1966.

Saslow, James M. *The Poetry of Michelangelo*. New Haven: Yale University Press, 1991.

Savona, Eugenio. *Repertorio tematico del dolce stil nuovo*. Bari: Adriatica Editrice, 1973.

Schevill, Ferdinand. *Medieval and Renaissance Florence: The Coming of Humanism and the Age of the Medici*. New York: Harper, 1961.

Schiesari, Juliana. "Isabella di Morra." In *Italian Women Writers: A Bio-Bibliographical Source Book*, 279–85. Edited by R. Russell. Westport, Connecticut, and London: Greenwood Press, 1994.

Sensi, Claudio. *L'arcimondo della parola. Saggi su Giacomo Lubrano*. Padova: Liviana, 1983.

Spiller, R. G. *The Development of the Sonnet: An Introduction*. London and New York: Rutledge, 1992.

Spongano, Raffaele. *Nozioni ed esempi di metrica italiana*. Bologna: Riccardo Patron, 1966.
Sturm, Sara. *Lorenzo de' Medici*. New York: Twayne, 1974.
Sturm-Maddox, Sara. *Petrarch's Laurels*. University Park, Pennsylvania: Pennsylvania State University Press, 1992.
Symond, John Addington. *Italian Literature: From Ariosto to the Late Renaissance*. New York: Capricorn Books, 1964
Tartaro, Achille. *Forme poetiche del Trecento*. Bari: Laterza, 1971.
Tartaro, Achille. *Il primo Quattrocento toscano*. Bari: Laterza, 1971.
Tartaro, Achille. *La letteratura civile e religiosa del Trecento*. Bari: Laterza, 1972.
Tateo, Francesco. *Alberti, Leonardo e la crisi dell'Umanesimo*. Bari: Laterza, 1971.
Tateo, Francesco. *I centri culturali dell'umanesimo*. Bari: Laterza, 1971.
Tateo, Francesco. *Lorenzo de' Medici e Angelo Poliziano*. Bari: Laterza, 1972.
Tateo, Francesco. *L'Umanesimo meridionale*. Bari: Laterza, 1972.
Tieghi, Laura. "È tutto ciò in sì alto stile dettando: Giovanni Della Casa e Galeazzo di Tarsia." In *Giovanni Della Casa Ecclesiastico e Scrittore. Atti del Convegno (Firenze-Borgo San Lorenzo, 20–22, 2003)*. Rome: Edizioni di Storia e Letteratura, 2007.
Tissoni Benvenuti, Antonia. *Il Quattrocento settentrionale*. Bari: Laterza, 1972.
Took, John. "Petrarch." In *The Cambridge History of Italian Literature*, 89–107. Edited by Peter Brand and Lino Pertile. Cambridge: Cambridge University Press, 1996.
Toscano, Tobia. R. *L'enigma di Galeazzo di Tarsia*. Naples: Loffredo, ca. 2004.
Usher, Jonathan. "Origins and Duecento: Poetry." In *The Cambridge History of Italian Literature*, 5–27. Edited by Peter Brand and Lino Pertile. Cambridge: Cambridge University Press, 1996.
Vaganay, Hughes. *Le sonnet en Italie et en France au XVIe siècle*. New York: B. Franklin, 1960. Originally published in Lyon, France, in 1903.
Valency, Laurice. *In Praise of Love*. New York: MacMillan, 1958.
Vitale, Maurizio. *La lingua dei poeti realistico-giocosi del '200 e del '300*. Milan: La Goliardica, 1955.
Walker, Paul Robert. *The Feud That Sparked the Renaissance: How Brunelleschi and Ghiberti Changed the Art World*. New York: William Morrow, 2002.
Warnke, Frank J. "Aphrodite's Pristess, Love's Martyr." In *Writers of the Renaissance and Reformation*. Edited by Katherina M. Wilson. Athens: University of Georgia Press, 1987.
Warnke, Frank J. *Three Women Poets: Renaissance and Baroque*. Louisburg: Bucknell University Press, 1986.
Watkins, Reneé. "Il Burchiello 1404–1448: Poverty, Politics, and Poetry." *Italian Quarterly* 14 (1970): 21–57.
Wilkins, Ernest Hatch. *A History of Italian Literature*. Cambridge: Cambridge University Press, 1974.
White, T. H., ed. and trans. *The Bestiary: A Book of Beasts*. New York: Putnam, 1960.
Wilson, Katharina M., ed. *Women Writers of the Renaissance and Reformation*. Athens and London: Univestity of Georgia Press, 1987.

Notes

1. The hendecasyllable—eleven-syllable line—is the most common meter of Italian poetry. It is to Italian what the iambic pentameter is to English. The words are arranged in the verse line so that the dominant accent always falls on the sixth position and another accent on the penultimate. The most accredited theory is that Lentini derived the sonetto from the stanza of a song. The Italian name *sonetto* is supposed to have derived from the Provençal *sonet*, which indicated a melody, a text with a melody, and also—as in the Italian *sonetto*—an isolated stanza without music (Elwert 26).
2. Examples of the degraded, popularized use of this distinguished literary tradition were the many sonnets written to celebrate family occasions even for and by people of no noticeable literary bent. Many years ago, for instance, in a small Italian town, a friend of my grandfather penned some celebratory sonnets on the occasion of my parents' wedding.
3. The notaries were professional men who drew up various forms of contracts and public instruments and gave them official validity. They would perform the duties that contract lawyers of today do in the USA. In Sicily, men such as Lentini might have worked for families and businesses and in the imperial chancery of Palermo. In the bureaucracies of the northern communes, the notaries were matriculated in powerful professional associations called *arti* (guilds). The preparation of notaries started at an early age and required specialized training. The University of Bologna offered a much-attended notarial program of study. Frederick II founded the University of Salerno—which later became the University of Naples—as an alternative to the type of training offered by the University of Bologna, which he suspected of anti-imperial bias.
4. Born in Italy and brought up in Sicily, Frederick became king of Sicily and southern Italy in 1198, king of Germany and northern Italy in 1212, and emperor of the Holy Roman Empire in 1220. Frederick chose to make his residence in Italy, and as soon as it became possible, he relinquished the German part of his domain to Conrad, the son he had from his wife, Costanza of Aragon. The Hohenstaufen were descendants of Conrad III of Swabia (1138–52), the first of his family to become emperor of the Holy Roman Empire. They took their name from Hohenstaufen Castle at Weiblingen, or Wybling, in Württemberg. From Wybling came *ghibellino*, the word Italians used to indicate those who championed the emperor's cause.
5. Frederick entertained a variety of intellectual interests and was a poet himself. According to some sources, he spoke several languages: Italian, German, Provençal, French, Greek, and Arabic. Poetry was a tradition in the imperial family. His father, Henry VI, had written verse in the manner of the German minnesingers, and two of Frederick's sons wrote verse in Italian. Frederick was an outstanding legislator and administrator. His Italian kingdom has been defined as both a tyranny and the first modern state. Both definitions might claim legitimacy. Upon nomination, he eliminated all feudal and ecclesiastic entitlements and organized an administration evenly distributed throughout the realm. By extending his influence to the north of Italy, which was jurisdictionally subject to imperial authority, Frederick encountered the hostility of the popes, who objected first to his delaying the crusade he had promised for the conquest of the holy land and afterward to his having arrived at a political solution with the Arabs who occupied Jerusalem. Frederick required absolute obedience from his subjects, and his orders could be questioned at a peril. Indicative of Frederick's authority, and of the fame his interest in matters of science enjoyed, is a fanciful anecdote found in a *crònica* written at Parma in the 1280s by a Franciscan friar named Salimbene de Adam. One day at court, the discussion was about whether better digestion would take place in a man who went to bed immediately after dinner or in one who went out hunting after eating. In order to conclude the debate, the emperor selected two faithful courtiers and gave them the same meal to eat. He then put one man to bed, telling him to go to sleep quietly; he sent the other out for a vigorous riding bout. Later, he had both men killed and had a postmortem performed to see which one had better digested his dinner. Salimbene's story is reported by Dossena (81).

6   University teaching was based on the professor's lecture (*lectura*) and on the following discussion, which was called *disputatio*, during which the students could exercise their argumentative skills. The *disputatio* presented opposing theses, proofs, and counterproofs, all proceeing in syllogistic fashion.

7   Besides being the emperor's master falconer, Mostacci was a nobleman and a trusted diplomat. Extant documents show that around 1260–62, Manfred, the emperor's son, sent him on ambassadorial missions to Aragon and the Middle East.

8   No original manuscript of Sicilian poetry has survived. We have only copies made by scribes of northern Italy. In the process of transcription, the original language—which was probably a high-style Sicilian—was adapted to the Tuscan idiom. Many rhymes were thus altered.

9   During Frederick's last bitter struggle against papal authority and the rebellious cities of northern Italy, Pier della Vigna fell from grace. Accused of treason, he was divested of all duties, blinded by order of the emperor, and incarcerated. He died in prison by suicide. Dante made him a character of *Inferno* (canto 13, 22–78).

10   The name Ghibelline derived from Weiblingen, the location of Hohenstaufen Castle in Württemberg. It was also the battle cry of the imperial army. The Guelfs derived their name from the German Welf dynasty, one of the rivals for the imperial title at the end of the twelfth century. The separating line between Guelfs and Ghibellines, however, did not exclusively indicate a difference between programs and political ideologies. Often, the names simply indicated opposing forces vying for political power in the city or the region.

11   At the time, the captain of the people was a judicial and security officer representing the interests of the business community, exclusive of the elite families who ran the commune.

12   *Il Fiore* consists of 3,248 hendecasyllables, and *Le Roman de la Rose* consists of 21,781.

13   In *Purgatorio* 26, 112–14, Dante greets Guinizzelli as his mentor and father of the new generation of poets: "my father and of others (poets), my betters, who ever used sweet and graceful rhymes of love" (*il padre / mio e degli altri miei miglior, che mai / rime d'amor usar dolci e leggiadre*). In his treatise on poetics—the *De vulgari eloquentia* 1.10.4—Dante presents him as the forerunner of all the poets who wrote perceptive and delicate rhymes of love (*dulcius subtiliusque poetati vulgariter sunt*).

14   See previous note.

15   The name of Cino's family was also written as Sigisbuldi and Sinibuldi.

16   In his theory of love, Cavalcanti followed the theories of Ibn Rushd (1126–38), the Arabian Spanish philosopher better known to Europeans as Averroes (Bruno Nardi 22–33). According to Averroes, the sensitive soul, which contains the faculties of perception, imagination, cogitation, and memory, is separate from the intellect. The power of abstraction and intellection pertains to the universal intellect, which is one and eternal. The human intellect participates in it in life; in death, it separates from the body and is reabsorbed into the universal intelligence from whence it came. It is not surprising, therefore, that the religious authorities condemned Averroes's theories, namely that the world and the changes in it are eternal, that there is only one universal intellect, and that the souls of men are mortal—all theories, however, that prevailed in Italian universities for centuries to come. For more recent considerations on Cavalcanti's philosophy of love and its derivations, see Ardizzone's study in the bibliography.

17   Aristotle's *De anima* was the basis of the medieval natural philosophy of mind. Galen, or Claudius Galenus, was a Greek doctor and a prolific writer on medicine; he had a large practice in imperial Rome and was personal physician to Emperor Marcus Aurelius and Emperor Commodus. His authority remained undisputed until the sixteenth century.

18   According to Contini (2, 530), in this sonnet, Cavalcanti ridicules both himself and the rhetorical expertise of Guittone, who made great use of the rhetorical figure of repetition.

19   In his commentary, Dante writes, "My thought rises into the essence of her in such a way that my intellect cannot understand it ... but at least I understand that this is the thought of my woman, for I often feel her name in my mind" (*Vita Nuova* 41, 7).

20   Cecco's grandfather, named Angioliero, had been the banker of Pope Gregory IX. Both father and grandfather occupied positions in the city government and became members of *Milites Beatae Virginis Mariae* (Knights of the Blessed Virgin Mary), the same lay Franciscan order to which Guittone d'Arezzo belonged (see 2.3).

21   This reading of the sonnet is by Ceserani-De Federicis 1, 820. The stilnovo women, I may add, are not always silent. During any festive gathering, they carry on normal conversations with men; see Cino's sonnet in 1.5. On occasion, they even make fun of them, as in the *gabbo* (mockery) episode of *Vita Nuova* 14, in which Beatrice and her friends laugh about Dante's emotional reaction to her presence.

22   The themes, poetic personae, and satirical stances of these satirical poets were in keeping with those of the Latin tradition of poetry that the goliards cultivated. These were European students in the habit of moving from university

to university, and thus, they acquired the epithet of *clerici vagantes*. Famous are the goliard songs preserved in a manuscript found in Benedictbeuern, a Bavarian Benedictine monastery. In the 1930s, Carl Orf set to music twenty-four of these Latin songs in his *Carmina Burana* (Songs from Beuern).

23   The *plazer* was a Provençal lyric genre that listed a number of pleasurable things.

24   There were quite a few *brigate* throughout Tuscany. In *Inferno* 29 118–23, Dante denounces one of them with vehemence because of the lavishness and profligacy of its entertainments.

25   The *enueg* was a Provençal poem that listed a number of unpleasant things.

26   Forese was a first cousin of Gemma Donati, Dante's wife, and the brother of Corso Donati, the head of the Black faction. Corso was a brilliant, handsome, and arrogant man, according to the contemporary historian Giovanni Villani. Forese died in 1296. *The Divine Comedy* features him purging his sin of gluttony on the sixth cornice of purgatory (*Purgatorio*, cantos 23 and 24).

27   After the demise of the Ghibellines, the Florentine Guelf party split into two factions: the Whites and the Blacks. The Whites, led by Vieri de' Cerchi, a man of low origin and recently acquired wealth, were interested in asserting the power of the upcoming classes, the *popolo grasso*. The Blacks, whose leader was Corso Donati, championed the cause of the aristocracy and enjoyed the backing of the less powerful guilds.

28   Dante enrolled in the guild of doctors, apothecaries, and dry-goods retailers, supposedly because books were sold in drugstores.

29   In *De vulgari eloquentia* (2.2.8), a treatise on the history of language and poetry that Dante began writing around 1306, Dante ranks Cino as the most important Italian love poet of the age, and he ranks himself as the poet of morality. Similar political views kept the friendship of these two men alive. When, in 1312, Henry VII of Luxemburg entered Italy to be crowned in Rome, they both hoped the emperor would establish political unity and restore peace in the country. For related sonnets, see the next section.

30   At first, Clement V tried his best to defend the interests of the church against the interference of the French king, but he was eventually forced to make significant concessions. One was moving the papal seat from Rome to Avignon, a town situated in Angevin lands—that is, in territory belonging to the royal family. Another concession was the suppression of the order of the Knights Templar. The Templars were a military crusading order who, in time, became banking agents in the trade between Western Europe and the Levant. Forced to confess to heresy under torture, they were put on trial and executed; their property was confiscated and versed into the king's coffers.

31   Writing to Henry of Luxemburg, Dante defines himself as "a man preaching justice." By 1314, the concept of justice, in all its facets and applications, had become the focal point of his thoughts. In the song "Tre donne intorno al cor mi son venute," written around 1304, he had featured three female figures symbolizing justice in the absolute, human justice, and the law. In the *De vulgari eloquentia* (1306), he had declared himself the moral poet par excellence. In *Convivio*, probably written by the spring of 1307, justice had appeared as the virtue that chooses rectitude and applies it in all areas of human endeavor. In *De Monarchia*, a treatise on political theory written at the time of the emperor's arrival, Dante upheld the moral and spiritual function of the empire in guaranteeing justice and order on earth. Finally, in *The Divine Comedy*, he posited justice as a universal power that rules human affairs and governs the relationship between God and the created order.

32   Romano wrote commentaries to sacred texts in Hebrew and works of poetry in both Hebrew and Italian. Of his Italian poems, only five remain. Four sonnets are included in this volume. Best known is a type of songlike poem called *bisbidis*, presumably written around 1312. It celebrates the court of Cangrande della Scala in Verona. In the last years of his life, Romano gathered his Hebrew poems into a collection under the title of *Mehaberot* in the manner of the Arab *maqamot*.

33   While she was campaigning for peace in Florence, St. Catherine was attacked by a mob of angry protesters and was almost lynched. Barely rescued, and with no one willing to offer her shelter, she left the city.

34   There were about forty banks in Florence. The richest was the Bardi bank, which was also a trading company with twenty-five branches throughout Europe. Other Florentine banks of the time were those of the Peruzzi, Acciaioli, Antellesi, Bonaccorsi, Cerchi, Cocchi, Frescobaldi, and Strozzi. From the historian Giovanni Villani (1280–1348), we learn that in Florence, besides banks, there were two hundred business concerns, thirty hospitals, and between eight thousand and ten thousand children who, in preparation of their work, were learning to write and read in public schools. Of them, fifteen hundred were learning double-entry accountancy, and more than six hundred attended higher public schools.

35   In his *Del pregio*, Dino Compagni (1255–1324), who is best known as a historian, wrote that a prince, if he wants to be held in good esteem, must be fair to all subjects, capable of acquiring and holding new territory, and generous in

36 Bosone was appointed *podestà* by several cities of central Italy: Arezzo in 1316, Viterbo in 1317, Lucca in 1319, and Todi in 1324. The position of podestà was created to guarantee impartiality toward the local factions; for that reason, only an outsider could be chosen for the office.

37 Both Romano and Bosone produced works that had something to do with Dante. Bosone explained allusions and symbols of *The Divine Comedy* in a *capitolo* in *terza rima*. Romano described a journey through hell and paradise in the "Ha-Tofet ve-ha Eden," the last poem in the *Mehaberot*. In his journey, Immanuel travels through hell and paradise under the guidance of Daniel, just as Dante, the pilgrim of *The Divine Comedy*, is guided through hell, purgatory, and paradise by Virgil. Some interpreters saw in Immanuel's guide his friend Dante; others thought the guide to be the man in whose home the author spent the last years of his life.

38 For the attribution of the first sonnet to Cino da Pistoia, see Simona Fuà's entry in *Dizionario Biografico degli Italiani*. Whatever the attribution, the interest in the exchange of the two sonnets, which are unquestionably related, remains.

39 The word *satire* has here the original meaning of the Roman *satura*, a multilingual, realistic, ironic, or parodic composition of varied content—much, in fact, in the manner of Romano's *bisbidis*.

40 The citizens of Florence enjoyed a high level of literacy, and poetry was not the exclusive pursuit of the privileged classes. Writing and reading were necessities for all those in trade—that is to say, for a high percentage of the population. For the citizens who could not engage private tutors, the commune provided primary and secondary schools.

41 The Bardi bank made heavy loans to the king of Naples and the king of England. Edward III, thus financed, started the Hunded Years' War. When, in 1342, he let it be known that he was not going to honor his debts, the Bardi bank, and other Florentine firms connected with it, collapsed.

42 In Naples, there were also some ill-famed and far less glamorous quarters than those inhabited by the aristocracy and bankers. Young Boccaccio must have known these parts of town well, judging by a famous story of *Decameron* that describes them and their inhabitants with some gusto and in convincing detail.

43 Male-to-male love poetry was not a rarity in those times, which were freer and more diversified in mentality and habits than is generally thought. For the love sonnets of Cecco Nuccoli and Marino Ceccoli, see the next section. Two other poets who produced homoerotic verse were Meo de' Tolomei and Nicola Muscia (or Musa) da Siena. Mario Marti mentions them both in *Poeti giocosi del tempo di Dante* (1959, 272 and 292–93). See also Anna Bruni Bettarini, "Le rime di Meo dei Tolomei e di Muscia da Siena," in *Studi di Filologia Italiana* 32, 1974.

44 There was one exception to Petrarch's political aloofness: he showed enthusiasm for Cola di Rienzi (1313–54), the populist leader who, for a while, established a democratic government in Rome and attempted to arouse Italy's national conscience.

45 Giovanni Visconti was archbishop of Milan. He shared the lordship of the city with his nephew Bernabò, who was married to Regina of the Della Scala family of Verona. Petrarch was their guest from 1353 to 1361.

46 Giovanni Andrea Gesualdo, *Il Petrarcha colla sposizione di misser Giovanni Andrea Gesualdo* (Venice: Giovann' Antonio di Nicolini e fratelli da Sabbio, 1531). Ludovico Castelvetro, *Le rime del Petrarca brevemente sposte per Lodovico Castelvetro* (Basel: Pietro de Sedabonis, 1582). See Chiorboli 143–44.

47 Giovanni Dondi's most famous creation was the astronomical clock planetarium that he made for Giangaleazzo Visconti. It was both a measurement of time and a representation of planetary motions. He called it Astrario (clock of the planets). The clock is lost, but an accurate description of it and several illustrations are in his treatise *Tractatus Astrarii*. Giovanni's father, Jacopo, was an engineer. He had studied the possible industrial application of the water springs in the Euganean area, near Venice. He too made clocks: an astrological clock of his was for a long while on the tower of the Da Carrara residence at Padua. Now it is kept in the Palazzo del Capitano.

48 It was the so-called *Tumulto dei Ciompi* of 1378. The *ciompi* were the salaried workers of the wool industry, who, at the time, represented one-third of the male population of Florence. The workers who organized the rebellion were the carders.

49 Giangaleazzo was the nephew of Bernabò Visconti, who, with his uncle Giovanni, had been the host of Petrarch from 1353 to 1361. See section 2.8.

50 Alexander Wesselovsky, a Russian philologist and literary theorist who was doing research in Italy in the 1860s, attributed to Gherardi a work he called *Paradiso degli Alberti*. This is a collection of short stories, mythological excursions, landscape descriptions, imaginary journeys, and conversations held around 1389 by a group of Florentine humanists—among them Coluccio Salutati—in the gardens of a villa that Antonio degli Alberti owned at Badia

a Ripoli, on the outskirts of the city. It is interesting to note that the word *paradiso* comes from the Persian word *pairidaeza*, which means "garden" (*Enciclopedia Garzanti di filosofia*, 1998, 833).

51 There was a humorous, jocular side to young Brunelleschi's character, if we go by a celebrated short story attributed to Antonio di Tuccio Manetti, mathematician, astronomer, architect, literary man, and supposedly the author of a life of Brunelleschi. The story in question makes Filippo the protagonist of an amazingly clever prank played on a credulous but not totally stupid member of his group of friends, a carpenter called Grasso (Fatty)—hence the title *Novella del Grasso legnaiuolo* (The Tale of the Fat Carpenter). By the concerted participation of friends—among them the sculptor Donatello—and other amused pranksters, Grasso is induced to believe he has become someone else. The cleverness of the prank is in the way the tricksters eliminate all external elements of the carpenter's personality, all points of reference to his identity, so that the bewildered man is induced to believe, disbelieve, doubt, be almost convinced, be resigned to, be persuaded of the switch, and, in the end, remain undecided on whether he has been dreaming and at what point exactly. An added topical touch is the part a professor plays in the story. This man—not surprisingly, identified by tradition with Giovanni Gherardi—is called in to give his expert opinion on Matteo's change of identity. As proof of its likelihood, the professor develops the erudite argument—backed by Ovid's authority—of how frequently metamorphoses occurred in classical times. For this presentation of the story and for the parallel between the illusion created by the prank and the one created by Brunelleschi's perspective, see Battisti in Brunelleschi's *The Complete Works* (326–28).

52 Brunelleschi was also the creator of inventive new *ingegni*. These were machinery for the theater that made mountains and heaven move and actors fly through the air. The machines that Brunelleschi created for the *sacre rappresentazioni* (miracle plays) staged during the Ecumenical Council held in Florence in 1439 were described by an amazed spectator, the Russian cardinal Abraham of Suzdal (Elvira Garbero Zorzi, in E. Bertelli, 130).

53 The street called Calimala took its name from a powerful guild of entrepreneurs, whose businesses and investments were diversified, a great part of which consisted of importing raw wool from England and turning it into luxury cloth. As the Calimala shop owners were Burchiello's neighbors, it is no wonder that the barber sided with the party of the rich guilds.

54 There were branches of the Alberti firm in London, Barcelona, Paris, Bruges, Gand, Brussels, Greece, and Syria.

55 In *Libri della Famiglia* (Books on the Family), Alberti examined the relationship between family and society with the happiness of the individual and the family's prosperity in mind. In *De re edificatoria* (On the Art of Building), he considers architecture capable of bringing about the harmony of all the rational activities of humanity. The city is like a house, he writes, and the house is like a small city, because both of them posit and can satisfy individual and social necessities. Alberti wrote also on painting and sculpting. In Florence, he designed and saw to the construction of Palazzo Rucellai. In Mantova, he planned the churches of St. Sebastian and St. Andrew. At Rimini, he designed the Church of Saint Francis, which is known as the Tempio Malatestiano because it was built in classical style and commissioned by the local lord, Sigismondo Malatesta. Among other artists working in Florence at this time were Donatello, Masaccio, and Brunelleschi.

56 Ciriaco dei Pizzicolli (1391–1452), born to a well-to-do merchant family of Ancona, was, at the time, best known for his study in city planning and archeology—he is considered a precursor of modern archeology. He traveled in search of archeological sites in the eastern coastal regions of the Adriatic and in the Middle East. He reported his extensive findings in *Commentari*. In Constantinople, where he resided during the siege of 1422, he was employed by the Ottomans as surveyor. Both the Visconti of Milan and the Medici of Florence befriended him. Later in life, he became bishop of Ancona, and after death, he was declared a saint. He is now venerated in the Ancona cathedral as the city patron saint, a promotion that let all his other achievements fall into oblivion.

57 Cosimo de' Medici was the primary sponsor of Ficino's studies. To him and the members of his group, he gave the use of the Medici villa at Careggi. Lorenzo, Cosimo's grandson, was often present at those meetings, and after taking over the reins of government, he contributed to changing those informal gatherings into the more regular organization of the Platonic Academy.

58 Niccolò III died in 1441. He had three children, who, in turn, succeeded him: Leonello, who died in 1450; Borso, who died in 1471; and Ercole I, who died in 1493. Ercole's children were Cardinal Ippolito; Isabella, wife to Francesco II Gonzaga of Mantua; Beatrice, who married Ludovico Sforza, duke of Milan; and Alfonso I, who became duke and the third husband of Lucrezia Borgia.

59 Leonello was also handsome, as his portraits, one by Pisanello and the other by Jacopo Bellini, attest.

60 At the time of Boiardo, the University of Ferrara was a center of medical and scientific studies. After leaving Rome in 1500, the renowned philosopher Pomponazzi taught at that university, and there, in 1505, Nicholas Copernicus graduated in jurisprudence.

61 In 1441, Francesco Maria Sforza, considered the best condottiere of his time, married Bianca Maria Visconti—daughter of Filippo Maria, the last in the direct Visconti line—and, in 1450, succeeded her father at the head of the Milanese state.

62 Isabella d'Este's description of Correggio was "*Il più attilato e de rime e cortesie erudito cavagliere e barone che ne li tempi suoi se ritrovasse in Italia*" (quoted by Tissoni Benvenuti, 138). Niccolò da Correggio was related to the Este family. His mother was the natural daughter of Niccolò III, the duke of Ferrara and grandfather of Ippolito, Beatrice, Isabella, and Alfonso. He was also a cousin of Matteo Maria Boiardo, because a Boiardo had married a Correggio. Isabella d'Este distinguished herself for the variety of interests and for her patronage of the arts. Daughter of Ercole d'Este, duke of Ferrara, and sister of Beatrice, wife of Ludovico il Moro, lord of Milan, Isabella was married to Gianfrancesco Gonzaga, marquis of Mantua. At Mantua, Vittorino da Feltre had launched his progressive humanistic school, the *Casa Gioiosa* (the House of Joy). The school was mainly for the education of princely male offspring, but girls, and some children of commoners, were also admitted. These courts spawned other female promoters of the arts and literature. One was Elisabetta Gonzaga, Gianfrancesco Gonzaga's sister. She married Guidobaldo, son of Federico of Montefeltro, duke of Urbino. She appears as the mistress presiding over the conversations and games of that court in Baldassar Castiglione's *The Book of the Courtier*. When circumstances required, these women proved to be skilled rulers of their states. So did, in absence of their husbands, both Isabella d'Este and Veronica Gàmbara (for Gàmbara, see 4.8).

63 Both Democritus (ca. 400–ca. 370 BCE) and Lucretius (ca. 98–ca. 54 BCE) held that all things are made of indestructible atoms and that their constant motion explains the alternating creation and destruction of everything in the universe.

64 Both the Roman epigrams of Martial and those of the Greek anthology were popular, but modern Italians were penning new epigrams as well. Among them were the Greek epigrams of Politian and Giano Lascaris and the Latin epigrams of Michele Marullo Tarcaniota and Jacopo Sannazaro. Their subjects ranged from the biographical to the historical and sometimes included racy subject matter. Politian's epigrams are now in a new edition: *Epigrammi greci*, edited by Antos Ardizzoni and published in Florence in 1951. The *Epigrammata* by Michel Marullo Tarcaniota, who died in 1500, was published in *Hymni et epigrammata Marulli* (Bononiae: Impressum per Benedictum Hectoris, 1504). They can be read in the translation of Charles Fantazzi in Tarcaniota's *Poems* (Cambridge, Massachusetts: Harvard University Press, 2012). The *Epigrammata* by Sannazaro, mostly written in the 1480s, can now be read in *Gli epigrammi di Jacopo Sannazaro nell'edizione aldina del 1535*, which was edited by Chiara Frison and includes a presentation by Angela Caracciolo Aricò (Padua: Il Poligrafo, 2011). The Greek epigrams by Lascaris are in *Epigrammi greci*, edited by Anna Meschini (Padua: Liviana, 1976). Pages 75–88 of Antonio Rossi's *Serafino Aquilano e la poesia cortigiana* are instructive on the epigrammatic ending in courtly poetry (Brescia: Moricelliana, 1980).

65 In *Anthologia Latina*, a successful publication in those years, we find the following passage: "*Me nive cadenti petit modo Iulia … Iula sola potes nostras extinguere flammas: non nive, non glacie, sed potes igne pari*" (Julia pursues me as alluringly as falling snow … Only you, Julia, can extinguish my flames: not with snow, not with ice, but with an equal amount of fire). *Poetae latini minores. Recensuit et emendavit Aemilius Baehrens* (Lipsiae: B. G. Teuber, 1879), epigram 107.

66 Elisabetta Gonzaga is celebrated in Baldesar Castiglione's *The Book of the Courtier* as the duchess chair of the conversations and games taking place at the court of Urbino in 1502.

67 In December 1494, Charles VIII of France, easily persuaded by Ludovico Sforza, entered Italy at the head of a large army with modern artillery and well-trained soldiers. Finding no resistance, he moved through the peninsula unimpeded and, in February 1495, took possession of Naples. Adverse circumstances, however, soon forced Charles to withdraw. In March, Pope Alexander Borgia organized a league of Italian states and attacked the retreating army at Fornovo. Charles managed to pass through and escaped to France. He died shortly after, when he struck his head against the lintel of a door as he was coming back from the hunt.

68 The territories occupied by Cesare—Romagna in 1500–1501 and Camerino and Urbino in the Marche in 1502—were nominally part of the Papal States but in fact constituted a refractory region of semiautonomous city-states and feudal principalities. Cesare's ruthless repression of the baronial families had the effect of freeing the papacy from its dependency on the noble families of Rome and the petty despots of the countryside. In virtue of these events, Machiavelli placed on Cesare Borgia his hopes for an Italian state strong enough to confront all foreign invaders, and temporarily setting aside his republican principles, he wrote *The Prince*.

69 This Giuliano de' Medici was the son of the Piero who succeeded his father, the Magnificent, in 1492 and whom the Florentines kicked out of the city in 1494. Giuliano took up the reins of the government in 1513, when his uncle, Giovanni de' Medici, was elected pope with the name of Leo X. He died in 1516 and was succeeded by his nephew

Lorenzo, duke of Urbino, who died in 1519. Michelangelo made the statues of these younger Giuliano and Lorenzo, duke of Nemours and duke of Urbino, respectively; they adorn their tombs in the Medici Chapel of the Church of San Lorenzo.

70 The friar Girolamo Savonarola became the head of the Florentine government in 1494. Before him, Piero de' Medici, son of Lorenzo the Magnificent, was in charge of the city. When, during the invasion of Charles VIII of France, Piero proved incapable of negotiating the safety of the city, the republicans revolted, deprived him of his property, and exiled him. In this juncture, Savonarola rose to power and, backed by the poorest strata of society, established a rigorous form of government in contraposition to the Medici regime, a regime he had been accusing of political and moral corruption for years. The friar's radical ways, however, antagonized both the Florentine upper classes and the church. In 1498, Pope Alexander VI accused him of heresy and had him arrested, and the Florentines hanged him and burned his body in Piazza della Signoria.

71 In *Discorsi*, the ancient Roman Republic is viewed as the ideal form of society. Even in *The Prince*, which has the specific aim of indicating to a forceful leader how to establish and maintain a new state, Machiavelli considers the democratic form of government the one most likely to last the longest, because more citizens have an interest in supporting it.

72 The sack of Rome marked the debacle of the pope's policy and encouraged the Florentines to turn against the house of Medici, of whom Pope Clement VII was the head. The new republican administration did not consider rehiring Machiavelli, probably because in the end, he had made a partial reconciliation with the Medici regime, sacrificing forever the possibility of returning to political life.

73 In Paris, Alamanni wrote lyric verse, a comedy, a tragedy, and *La coltivazione*. The last is a short and graceful poem on agriculture in the manner of Virgil's *Georgics*. He dedicated it to Francis I of France.

74 After the sack of Rome, Clement VII made peace with Charles V, and in 1531, the emperor agreed to reinstall the Medici at the head of Florence.

75 Pasquino was not the only Roman statue to produce verse. There were other statues of literary bent situated in different streets of the city. Their poetic parturitions were not always hostile to the church, for at times, they expressed the views and desires of the men in charge of events. In fact, it became customary to collect Pasquino's more acceptable literary output and print it in the editorial offices of the Vatican.

76 Rodrigo Borja—Italianized as Borgia—was born in Valencia, Spain. He moved to Italy when Pope Callistus III, his uncle, made him a cardinal. Elected pope with the name of Alexander VI in 1492, he became known for his nepotism and scandalous private life. When a cardinal, he fathered several children. The most famous were Cesare and Lucrezia, whom he had from a Roman beauty by the name of Vannozza Cattanei. When pope, he had living with him a beautiful young mistress, Giulia Farnese, whose brother he made a cardinal. This brother was a man with an excellent humanistic education who'd already launched an ecclesiastic career, and in time, he became an outstanding reformist pope with the name of Paul III. The maneuvers that Alexander initiated in order to promote the interests of his children inspired rumors of intrigue and even of murder. The Roman press, so to speak, was ferociously hostile to him and to all the members of his family. Alexander had some good qualities: he was an unsurpassed diplomat and proved to be an expert, if irreligious, administrator of the church.

77 This sonnet was not the only pasquinade excoriating Pope Alexander. A Latin composition began by saying, "*Octo pueros genuit totidem puellas: hunc merito poterit dicere Roma Patrem*" (He fathered eight illegitimate boys and as many girls: Rome can rightly call him father). Another Latin pasquinade maintained, with allusion to the pope's past and ongoing practice of simony, "*Vendit Alexander claves, altaria, Christum, / emerat ille prius, vendere iure potest*" (Alexander sells the keys, the alters, and Christ; he first bought them, now he has the right to sell them).

78 Much had happened to the house of the Medici after Lorenzo the Magnificent's death in 1494. The leadership of the family and of Florence passed on to Lorenzo's elder son, Piero. In 1494, however, when Charles VIII, marching through Italy, imposed humiliating demands on the Florentines, the populace, headed by the influential friar Girolamo Savonarola, revolted. Piero and all the Medici, who had favored the French, left the city. In 1503, Piero died, and his younger brother, Giovanni, the future pope Leo X, became, in absentia—that is, from the Vatican—the head of the Florentine Medici party.

79 Leo X engaged such outstanding painters and architects as Raphael and Bramante and literati as authoritative as Bembo, Bibbiena, and Giovio. Leo X reorganized the local university of Rome, founded a college of Greek studies, and greatly increased the holdings of the Vatican Library.

80 When he traveled through Europe, Giovanni entertained Erasmus in his quarters, and Erasmus, knowing that his host was a pious youth, dedicated to him his translation of the Gospels.

81 One of Leo's minor but commendable initiatives was to establish credit associations that allowed the poor to borrow money at low interest rates. He also initiated the ordination of native clergy in newly explored lands (the son of the king of Congo was the first African to be consecrated as bishop). Leo condemned the Averroistic theory on the mortality of the soul, which still prevailed in Italian universities, and ordered, with scant effect, the reform of morals and some established church practices. He gave Henry VIII of England—who was not yet rebellious—the title of *defensor pacis* for writing against the Protestants (Rendina, *The Popes* 441–46).

82 After that long and much maligned assembly, the seclusion of the cardinals appointed to choose a new pope became the rule. Their isolation in the Sistine Chapel was henceforth indicated by the word *conclave* (from *cum clavis*, meaning "with key").

83 The figure of Pietro Aretino loomed large in the bohemian milieus of the city. In Rome, he wrote the *Cortigiana*, the first of his scandalous dialogues of Roman whores, which turned the vogue of Platonic treatises into an obscene vituperation of politicians and high society. Aretino provoked an even greater scandal in 1524 by publishing sixteen pornographic sonnets with illustrations by Marcantonio Raimondi (none of which, in reverent respect for prudishness, I've included in this book). Raimondi's artwork was a reproduction of the corresponding coital positions originally drawn by Giulio Romano. Aretino's literary obscenities; his virulent and vituperative attacks on Giovanni Matteo Giberti, the powerful pontifical datary; and an attempted assassination on his person finally persuaded him to leave Rome for good in 1525.

84 It is not surprising to read that Clement, coming from a banking family, was a sort of financial expert. He is credited with the establishment of a bank called Monte della Fede, which—as Mario Caravale tells us—was the first public debt institution and placed the church in the avant-garde of exceptional financing (Rendina, *The Popes* 453).

85 The Spanish empire of Charles V comprised Austria, Hungary, and Bohemia, territories he inherited from his paternal grandfather, Emperor Maximilian; the Netherlands, which had been the dowry of his grandmother, Mary of Burgundy; and Spain and the Americas, which he inherited from his maternal grandparents, Ferdinand the Catholic and Isabella of Castile. To these territories Charles added the duchy of Milan and the kingdom of Naples. Charles's son, Philip II, tried to extend his imperial domain farther by marrying Mary Tudor, the Catholic queen of England.

86 It is my belief that although lamented for its limitations, Bembo's model and prescriptions for a common literary language created the basis of a cultural unity that in time became political and revolutionary. Due to their cultural and administrative fragmentation, Italians did not have a national language. Bembo shrewdly understood that no matter how geographically far flung and linguistically separated Italian literati were, they shared a patrimony of vernacular texts, a literary tradition that could be encouraged and regulated. For the writers of poetry, the *Canzoniere* was the best known of these texts, and for its linguistic homogeneity and distillation, it was approachable by all. Bembo's edition of the *Canzoniere* became a best seller. Sixty-four editions appeared between 1537 and 1565 in Italy alone; one hundred forty editions came out in the rest of Europe.

87 The seating arrangement offered an easy opportunity for the players to communicate without being heard by anyone else. During a similar game described in *Orlando Furioso* 7, 12, Ruggero and Alcina whisper in each other's ear and agree to meet after dinner in his bedroom. Popular at the time, the game is described in two sixteenth-century texts: *Dialogo de' giuochi che nelle vegghie Sanesi si usano di fare del Materiale Intronato* (Siena, per Luca Bonetti, 1572) and an end-of-the-century commentary, *Le Rime del Bembo commentate dall'Amaidemo* (Codice Vaticano, 8825). Vittorio Cian quotes and discusses both texts in "Il Bembo e i giuochi alla Corte d'Urbino," which is the second appendix in *Motti inediti e sconosciuti di M. Pietro Bembo* (Venezia: Tipografia dell'Ancora, 1888), issued in Milan by Sylvestre Bonnard in 2007. At some point in time, the game became a children's game. I played a simplified version of it at the age of ten in the countryside south of Urbino. For us children, the fun of playing it was in discovering how altered the original message had become, when it was finally retrieved at the end of the circle, after being murmered all along by each child in the ear of the next one.

88 Michelangelo completed the *The Last Judgment* in 1541 (see 5.2).

89 Cavalieri was not the only man with whom Michelangelo fell in love. We know the names of others: Gherardo Perini, Francesco Bracci, and Febo del Poggio.

90 For the history of women's literary activity in the Renaissance, see R. Russell's introduction to *Italian Women Writers: A Bio-biographical Source Book* (Westpoint, Connecticut, and London: Greenwood Press, 1994). See also *Publishing Women: Salons, the Press, and the Counter-Reformation in Italy*, edited by Diana Robin (Chicago: University of Chicago Press, 2007).

91 Cosimo de' Medici became the legitimate successor of the house of the Medici in 1537 and, eventually, grand duke of Tuscany. He was the son of Giovanni delle Bande Nere and Maria Salviati. His father descended from Lorenzo de'

92   Medici, brother of Cosimo the Elder, while his mother was the daughter of Jacopo Salviati and Lucrezia de' Medici, a daughter of Lorenzo the Magnificent.

92   On Tullia d'Aragona's life and writing, see the introduction to her *Dialogue on the Infinity of Love*, with translation by R. Russell and B. Merry and an introduction and notes by R. Russell (Chicago: University of Chicago Press, 1997).

93   Barbara Torelli's postmortem misadventures are little known. The scholar who first contested the authorship of her sonnet was Michele Catalano, when he investigated the web of intrigues and gossip that developed around her in his *Lucrezia Borgia duchessa di Ferrara* (Ferrara: Taddei, 1920). However, in a second lengthy study, *La tragica morte di Ercole Strozzi e il sonetto di Barbara Torelli* (Genève: Olschki, 1926), he presented documentation clearly indicating that Torelli was after all the author of the contested poem. In that work, besides confirming the poetic activity of said Barbara Torelli, he proved the existence of another female poet by the name of Barbara Torelli. This second Barbara Torelli was born at Parma in 1546, was known by several literati of her time, and kept a correspondence with, among others, Giambattista Guarini, the celebrated author of *Pastor Fido*. Catalano's second publication apparently never came to the knowledge of modern scholars, for they still contest the authorship of the famous sonnet.

94   Favale, the Morra estate, no longer figures on the map. The name that remains is that of Valsinni, from Sinni or Siri, the small river Isabella often mentioned. The area is now in the province of Matera.

95   *Jet*—the jet of a foundry—is *getto* in Italian and *ghet* in Venetian. With the word *ghet*, the Venetians indicated the foundry, the district where the foundry was, and the Jewish quarter, also located in that district, hence *ghetto* in Italian and in other languages.

96   Publications of correspondence in Latin had been popular since antiquity.

97   The accusation was of sodomy, which stood for homosexuality. In 1557, the imputation to Cellini was specifically for "having kept in his bed Fernando di Giovanni di Montepulciano as his wife" (Dossena 4.145). The previous year, while working on the statue of Perseus, Cellini had been accused of seducing his young assistant—"a very pretty lad," in his words—and threatened with jail by the boy's mother. A colorful scene in which the boy's mother, who happens to be prostitute, attempts to extort from the sculptor some money can be found in pages 355–62 of *The Life of Benvenuto Cellini*, translated by John Addington Symons (New York: Scribner's, 1924).

98   Mario Sansone, "Relazione fra la letteratura Italiana e letterature dialettali," in *Problem e orientamenti di lingua e letteratura italiana, IV, Letterature comparate* (Milan: Marzorati, 1948).

99   What linguists call Venetian dialect was at the time the official language of Venice, used by common people, the aristocracy, and members of the government in official documents and assemblies.

100   Maffio Venier's ferociously injurious attacks on Veronica Franco were clearly motivated by his unyielding unwillingness to acknowledge her literary talents and show respect for her dignified demeanor. Maffio is also known for a burlesque, a notoriously explicit and now irretrievable pamphlet by the title of *Il libro chiuso di Maffio Venier* (Maffio Venier's Closed Book). The obscene burlesque manner was an old Venetian tradition to which Aretino had recently given new flair. Lorenzo Venier, Maffio's father, was the author of *Puttana errante* (Wandering Whore), a directory—with descriptions of services provided and commentaries—of Venetian prostitutes. It became a European best seller.

101   Some of the scholarly studies on the topos of sleep are the following: A. Seroni, "Sulle fonti del sonetto al sonno," in *Da Dante a Verga*, 15–21 (Roma: Editori Riuniti, 1972); F. Gandolfo, *Il "dolce tempo," mistica, ermetismo, sogno nel Cinquecento*, 168–69 (Roma: Bulzoni, 1978); and Stefano Carrai, *AD SOMNUM. L'invocazione al sonno nella lirica italiana* (Padova: Antenore, 1990).

102   Reginald Pole, an English Catholic cardinal, became archbishop of Canterbury in 1556, during the reign of Queen Mary.

103   In England, Bruno published his Italian writings, most subversive of which was *La cena delle cereri* (the Ash Wednesday Supper), a work that asserts the plurality of worlds and the infinity of the universe. In Germany, Bruno published his Latin writings.

104   Campanella described the organization of his utopic republic in his 1602 *La città del sole* (City of the Sun). This work posits a rigid communistic state in which there is no private property, marriages are decided by a commission on health, and children are brought up and educated together by state instructors.

105   *Four Discourses of Chrysostom* can be read, in a different translation, online at *www.tertullian.org /fathers/ Chrysostom-four-discouses*.

106   Galileo believed that science could give man extraordinary powers. In his *Dialogue Concerning the Two Chief World Systems* (1632), the Francesco Sagredo character, the author's mouthpiece, is joyfully enthusiastic about the infinite, ever-changing universe that new science has revealed. The Filippo Salviati character, scientist and astronomer, clearly

107 articulates the idea that when human beings have deciphered the mathematical characters describing the phenomena of nature, they will have attained certain knowledge of the world.

108 In his long poem *Adone*, Marino celebrated Galileo and gave a short dissertation on the stains of the moon.

109 Giambattista Marino's stylistic manner falls into the general category of baroque, a term used to designate the style of the architecture, art, and literature of Europe from the end of the Renaissance to the dawn of modernity. The fashion began in Italy and Spain, where the Church of Rome encouraged a richly ornamented art that would enhance the religious fervor of the faithful. In literature, the baroque style is known for its great use of rhetorical figures and tropes, especially metaphors and conceits.

Regarding the metaphor and the conceit, important were Matteo Peregrini's *Delle acutezze che altrimenti spiriti, vivezze, e concetti volgarmente si appellano* (1639) and Matteo Caravita's *In lode del concetto*, written at the end of the century. The great theoretician of the metaphor in all its aspects and declinations was Emanuele Tesauro (1592–1675), author of *Il Cannocchiale aristotelico*, a work published in 1654. For Tesauro, the ingenious metaphor was an instrument that enhanced the power of perception and understanding.

110 The frescoes by Andrea Mantegna that cover the walls of the Camera degli Sposi in the Ducal Palace of Mantua and Paolo Veronese's *Feast in the House of Levi*, a painting now at the Accademia of Venice, attest to the presence of black servants in sixteenth-century courts.

111 The court of Parma and Piacenza came into existence in 1545, when Pope Paul III made Pier Luigi Farnese, his son, duke of Parma and Piacenza. The history of the Farnese family shows the connection that existed among Italy, the papacy, and Spain. Ottavio, Pier Luigi's son, married Margherite of Austria, daughter of Emperor Charles V of Spain. Elizabetta Farnese (1672–1766), the last in the Farnese line, married Philip V and became queen of Spain.

Made in the USA
Middletown, DE
02 August 2021